Pedro Moya de Contreras

PEDRO MOYA DE CONTRERAS

Catholic Reform and Royal Power in New Spain

1571–1591

STAFFORD POOLE, C.M.

UNIVERSITY OF CALIFORNIA PRESS / *Berkeley, Los Angeles, London*

University of California Press
Berkeley and Los Angeles, California

University of California Press, Ltd.
London, England

© 1987 by
The Regents of the University of California

Library of Congress Cataloging-in-Publication Data
Poole, Stafford.
    Pedro Moya de Contreras: Catholic reform and royal
power in New Spain, 1571–1591.
    Bibliography: p.
    1. Moya de Contreras, Pedro, ca. 1530–1591.
2. Catholic Church—Mexico—Bishops—Biography.
3. Catholic Church—Mexico—History—16th century.
4. Mexico—Church history—16th century. I. Title.
BX4705.M738P66   1987   282′.092′4 [B]   86–1410
ISBN 0–520–05551–9 (alk. paper)

Printed in the United States of America
1   2   3   4   5   6   7   8   9

TO JON STAFFORD ORBIN

The men of that century were capable at one and the same time of heroic and shining virtues and of blind and terrible prejudices. . . . This is to be seen in a man like Doctor Moya de Contreras, as repugnant and odious in diligently carrying out the tortures of the Inquisition as he is illustrious and great in presiding over and inspiring the Third Mexican Council—a strange and mysterious duality that causes him, at the one and same point of his life, to go from the somber and ferocious execution of the ordinances of Torquemada to the sweet and holy practices of the gospel.

Vicente Riva Palacio, *México a través de los siglos*

Contents

Acknowledgments

I would like to express my gratitude to all those who have in any way contributed to this book. First of all, this means Father John Francis Bannon, S.J., and Father Ernest J. Burrus, S.J., both of whom guided me through my doctoral dissertation. Others who have made valuable suggestions, supplied information, or otherwise helped include Professor Lewis Hanke; Professor Philip Wayne Powell; Bishop José Llaguno, S.J., of Sisoguchi, Mexico; Professor Ismael Sánchez Bella; Dr. José de la Peña Cámara; Professor Victoria Hennessy Cummins; Professor John Frederick Schwaller; Helen Rand Parish; Professor Robert Ryal Miller; the administration and staff of the Archivo General de Indias, Seville; and the director and staff of the Bancroft Library, Berkeley, to whom appreciation is also extended for permission to quote from the Mexican council documents in that library. The Dominican Communities of Saint Albert's College, Oakland, and of the Berkeley Priory gave me hospitality during my researches at the Bancroft Library, and the Padres Paúles of the church of San Vicente de Paúl, Triana, Sevilla, accorded me similar hospitality in Spain. All quotations from the Hans P. Kraus Collection have been made with the permission of the director of the Hispanic Division of the Library of Congress.

Research into the European sources of this book was made possible by grants from the American Philosophical Society and the Vincentian Fathers' Scholarship Fund. The manuscript was typed by the author *qui portavit pondus diei et aestus,* who must therefore accept responsibility for errors.

Introduction

> I believe that no less honor and praise are due to [Moya de
> Conteras's] name than to that of the inestimable Hernán Cor-
> tés, conqueror of New Spain. . . . For however great may be
> the deeds of Cortés, if his achievement is compared with the
> celebration of this council, we can justly and properly say: the
> latter is not to be judged as less illustrious than the former.
> The first benefited the province only once, the second does so
> forever.
>
> *Juan Pérez de la Serna,* archbishop of Mexico, in his intro-
> duction to the first printing of the acts of the Third Mexican
> Provincial Council, 9 September 1622

Despite Archbishop Pérez de la Serna's assertion about his illustrious
predecessor in the see of Mexico, Pedro Moya de Contreras has not
achieved a celebrity comparable to that of Fernando Cortés. Rather, he
has become one of the lost men of Mexican history. The enigma of
Moya de Contreras, to which Vicente Riva Palacio addressed himself in
México a través de los siglos (1888–1889), not only remains unresolved; it
has not been studied. Though Moya may not have merited the glory
that Pérez de la Serna imputed to him, neither has he deserved the
obscurity into which his name has fallen.

My own interest in Moya began many years ago in graduate
school. Since then, for almost a quarter of a century, I have been
involved—sometimes intensely, sometimes casually—with the Third
Mexican Provincial Council and its increasingly fascinating archbishop.
During those years my opinion of Moya has fluctuated notably. My
first acquaintance came from the pages of Mariano Cuevas and Fortino
Hipólito Vera. From there I advanced to Cristóbal Gutiérrez de Luna,
Moya's first biographer, whom I failed to appreciate properly because
his work seemed better suited to canon lawyers seeking evidence for
canonization processes than to the historian. From my studies of the
council—especially those concerned with the opposition to it—there

1

emerged a picture of the archbishop as a regalist, diplomat, and career-ist of the type that still disfigures too many chanceries. The outlines showed a typical ecclesiastical bureaucrat, an apparatchik so deeply entwined with the Spanish crown that he seemed to be a servant of Caesar rather than of Christ, an organizer rather than an inspirer, a consolidator rather than an innovator. This view of a rather cool, per-haps detached and calculating, personality did not help to resolve the paradox first noted by Riva Palacio: how could the first inquisitor of New Spain have been the moving force behind something as humani-tarian as the Third Mexican Provincial Council, so worthy of the spirit of Bartolomé de las Casas? How could the bigot who presided over the first *auto de fe* in New Spain be the same man at whose departure the Indians and blacks wept and who died so poor that Philip II had to pay his funeral expenses?

Since those earlier days, the research done by Richard Greenleaf has destroyed the image of the bloodthirsty inquisitor depicted by Di-ego Rivera in his famous murals in the Palacio Nacional in Mexico City. Rather, Moya's tenure as inquisitor (and it was rather brief) has come to be seen more in terms of a man of law acting in accord with the law—and acting with discretion and comparative restraint. Although Moya was an intensely private person who revealed little of himself in his letters and papers, new insights about the man and his intriguing, complex, and reserved personality have begun to emerge from studies of his actions, his letters, and his policies, as well as from a renewed appreciation of his first biographer.

These new insights include his concern for the criollos and his farsighted attempts to integrate them into the life and government of New Spain. Like all peninsular Spaniards, he believed that life in the New World had a debilitating effect on character and that the land was beset by idleness and excessive liberty. He refused, however, to regard the criollos as second-class citizens. Moreover, late in life his pastoral concern for the Indians led him to undertake the study of Nahuatl so that he could minister to them in their own language. One can only speculate about how different the subsequent history of Mexico would have been if his outlook had prevailed.

His constant policy was to accomplish his ends not only without compromise but also without undue abrasiveness. Despite a certain natural combativeness, and even arrogance, that asserted itself on oc-casion, he preferred the ways of reason and persuasion. His loyalty to the king was unquestioned and unshakable. He was a regalist, but his relations with lesser civil authorities varied from deferential to provoca-tive. He lived in an archbishop's palace but kept a simple table. He lived like a monk and died in poverty. He was an educator and humanist who supported the work of the university and especially of the Jesuits. He had a deep and abiding concern for improving the quality of the clergy in his archdiocese and was solicitous of the poor, the orphaned, and girls without dowries. And most of all he was a reformer in the mold of the Council of Trent.

A highly respected priest of my acquaintance was once described as "a most appealing example of a post-Tridentine priest." The phrase conjures up a set of characteristics and values that can better be experienced than described. The best type of priest to emerge from the aftermath of the Council of Trent (1545–1563) and from the seminaries of the Catholic (or Counter-) Reformation was very much an organization man: something of a legalist, he was proud of his calling and status and was possibly a little triumphalistic and formal in his ways. But he was also dedicated, giving of himself and his time, and devoted to the correct fulfillment of the liturgy. He was narrow perhaps, but educated and even scholarly within limits: a man who read his breviary and had a deep, if somewhat structured and formal, spiritual life. Such a priest gave great service to God and man and if he seems anachronistic in a more turbulent age, his passing may yet prove a matter of regret.

The best description of Moya de Contreras can be summarized in similar terms: as Jiménez Rueda and Greenleaf have noted, Moya was above all a bishop of Trent and the Catholic Reformation of which Trent was the most important part. The first Counter-Reformation bishop of Mexico and the first diocesan priest to hold the post, he governed at a time when, though most bishops in the New World were drawn from the orders, the status of the diocesan clergy was about to rise because of the reforms enacted at Trent. He hated heresy and upheld orthodoxy, was capable of both bigotry and tolerance, and was dedicated to the reform of the diocesan clergy and their advancement over the mendicants. He was concerned for the correct and punctilious celebration of the liturgy and supported ecclesiastical and lay education. In many ways he brings to mind his contemporary Saint Charles Borromeo, that other paragon of the Catholic Reformation. In his personal life and education, his ideas on reform, his devotion to law and correct procedure, his visitations of his archdiocese, his pastoral concern for the Indians, even in undertaking the study of theology after his appointment as archbishop, Moya de Contreras personified the spirit of the Catholic Reformation. Both the pages of the third council and Moya's letters are full of references to, and citations of, Trent. It was to the clergy of that age what Vatican II has been to the clergy of a later one.

The Catholic Reformation—a varied and complex movement—emerged as the church's response to the religious reforms and divisions of the sixteenth century. Although it originated with individuals, religious orders, and reforming popes, its definitive blueprint was drawn up by the Council of Trent, which clearly and emphatically defined the Catholic doctrinal position, especially in opposition to the teachings of Luther, and formulated a detailed program for the reform of discipline. In so doing it also helped to introduce a greater degree of polarization and intolerance. The sixteenth century was not an ecumenical age.

In a century that saw the permanent sundering of Europe into warring religious factions, purity of doctrine was the paramount concern of reformers and Catholics alike. Orthodoxy was often the primary standard by which all things were judged. The humanistic and rationalistic outlook of the Renaissance gave way to religious crusading, and education was subordinated to the needs of religious controversy. Within this context the Catholic church became more defensive and self-contained. The Index was devised, and the Roman Inquisition revitalized.

The Catholic Reformation was not, however, a movement of total uniformity. The age-old antagonisms between the religious orders and the bishops continued in full fury. Within the church the differing schools of theology, represented principally, but not exclusively, by the Dominicans and the Jesuits, struggled with one another as bitterly as they did with the Protestant reformers. Some Catholic reformers were puritanical and intolerant, whereas others sought a rapprochement with the Protestants.

Although in one sense the church may have passed from the age of Erasmus to that of Galileo, the Catholic Reformation was more than just reaction. The Council of Trent had approached its theological definition from a scriptural and pastoral point of view. The church sought to rediscover itself by returning to the sources in scripture, theology, and liturgy. The scandals of the Renaissance church were for the most part a thing of the past. Seminaries prepared an educated and zealous clergy. In Spain a revitalized scholasticism flourished at Salamanca, Alcalá de Henares, and other major universities. Foreign missions, stimulated by the geographical discoveries of the Renaissance, again became the focus of the church's activities. The Far East and the New World were the poles of a vast missionary enterprise. Charitable and humanitarian activities multiplied: schools, hospitals, orphanages, relief for the poor. Liturgy was reformed and great emphasis was placed on splendid and well-executed ceremonies, enhanced by the exuberant and vigorous output of the baroque. It was the age of John of the Cross, Teresa of Avila, Charles Borromeo, Reginald Pole, Ignatius of Loyola, and Pius V. The church again displayed that inner dynamism that eternally confounds the "prophets of gloom," as they were called by John XXIII.

In general, it was an age that was difficult to categorize—rather like our own.

The spirit of reform had touched Spain before most other countries of Europe. Isabel of Castile had been dedicated to church reform, often of an intolerant kind, and had entrusted much of this work to her confessor, Cardinal Ximenes de Cisneros (1436–1517), a Franciscan who was twice regent of the kingdom. Their reform efforts, which admittedly included the more repressive activities of the Inquisition, helped remove the abuses and causes that gave rise to heterodox movements elsewhere. Indeed, the Spain into which Moya was born had never experienced the Reformation or the onslaught of Protestantism. It has often been asserted that Spain imprinted its own characteristics on the entire Catholic Reformation movement: orthodoxy (often carried to extremes), a crusading and militaristic spirit, intransigence, and intolerance, combined with a puritanical self-righteousness. Although this may be true, sixteenth-century Spain also gave birth to the exalted and common-sense mysticism of Teresa of Avila and John of the Cross; the revitalized Thomism of Francisco de Vitoria, Melchor Cano, and Domingo de Soto; and the crusading humanitarianism of Las Casas.

In New Spain the spirit of the new age left its imprint on the approach to the humanitarian movement—that is, the attempt to obtain just treatment for the Indians. By Moya's time the Erasmian influence was gone and the age of the great defenders of the Indians had passed. Las Casas and Motolinía (Toribio de Benavente) were dead, Gerónimo de Mendieta and Bernardino de Sahagún were approaching the end. The crusade on behalf of the Indians was now less prophetic, less charismatic, and hence less personal. Just as the process of reform was now less individual and more institutional throughout the universal church, so, too, the humanitarian agitation of individuals and "schools" of reform gave way in Moya's time to the more organizational approach of the Third Mexican Provincial Council. The question of whether the latter tactics were more successful than the former will no doubt be debated by historians for years to come. Facing a situation that had altered drastically since the early days of the missionary enterprise, Moya and his fellow bishops pursued substantially the same ends as Las Casas—but through organizational structures and councils rather than through books, lobbying, or crusades. It was only natural that the bishops should rely on the conciliar method of seeking reform and change, for they had seen the successful results in Trent.

This approach was not confined to New Spain. It was paralleled in

Lima by Saint Toribio de Mogrovejo, who as archbishop of that city used methods similar to Moya's. Among these was the holding of a provincial council that had widespread influence outside the immediate jurisdiction for which it was intended. An interesting comparison could be made of the backgrounds, methods, and approaches of the two men.

Churchmen such as Moya de Contreras and Mogrovejo represented the Tridentine reform movement at its best, before it became encrusted with excessive baroque ornamentation and burdened with the worst excesses of seventeenth-century regalism, extravagance, and complacence. Although there seems to have been a decline in the quality of bishops and in the general level of the church in New Spain after 1600, current research makes generalizations suspect. The archdiocese of Mexico suffered greatly from not having a resident bishop for almost twenty years after Moya's departure in 1586. That aside, however, is it not possible that the very process of institutionalization was self-defeating? Structure and consolidation can bring system, order, and permanence to a movement, but they can also stifle its spirit; this kind of success may breed ultimate failure. Still, whatever the outcome, Moya de Contreras does stand out as one of the great bishops of the Spanish empire in the second half of the sixteenth century.

From the modern point of view, Moya's regalism—his excessive deference to royal control of the church—is a serious shortcoming. Despite many statements by the Council of Trent in favor of ecclesiastical liberty, the church that had so strongly resisted Protestantism seemed unable to resist the encroaching power of the state. The church needed the state for the Catholic Reformation, and it paid the price in loss of freedom. Moya worked very closely with, and within, the governmental system. He accepted the leadership of the king in religious matters without question, and despite his differences with lesser officials, he always viewed the king as the dominant and directive force in the church. His failure to fight the erosion of the church's freedom of action is disappointing to the modern observer, just as it was to some of his fellow bishops.

Although one might think that the age of Moya de Contreras, or more generally the last third of the sixteenth century in New Spain, would have been studied exhaustively, that is not the case. Both Moya and the age in which he lived have received short shrift. There are few adequate biographies of the principal figures, lay or ecclesiastical, of the period. A key peninsular personality such as Juan de Ovando is almost unknown—he did not merit even a note in the famous Espasa-Calpe encyclopedia. The marqués de Villamanrique warrants study, especially in his relations to the church and their impact on his infamous *residencia*. None of the bishops who attended the Third Mexican Provincial Council has ever been the subject of a scholarly biography. The personnel of the *audiencias,* and in particular their relations by blood, marriage, and business to the local colonial elite, are only now coming under investigation.

Like the colonial church, the society of New Spain was nearing the end of its formative stage in 1570. It was settling down to a way of life that was assuming a distinctive character. It was reaching maturity. Moya's life gives us tantalizingly incomplete glimpses of this process. His insistence on rewarding and helping those he called "the children of this land" reflects his reaction to a nascent criollo consciousness. He faced it in his own archdiocese, for half of the diocesan priests who served under him were criollos. The fascinating recurrence of the same family names in positions of power and influence, overlapping both church and state, may well reflect the growing network of relationships that was building up a colonial power structure. These relationships may account for the apparent reluctance of the crown to reform or take drastic measures against that structure. The long conflict between the religious orders and the diocesan clergy, as well as within the religious orders themselves, reflected a peninsular-criollo tension, as Moya himself was well aware.

Generally, then, this is a period that is still open to the zealous researcher. The following pages attempt to lay some groundwork and offer some data. It is hoped that scholars and ambitious graduate students (not that there is necessarily a distinction between the two) may find much in these pages to inspire and help them to a deeper study and consideration of the man and his work. Moya de Contreras and his age both deserve it.

I. The Preparation of a Letrado

A look at a relief map of Spain shows a land divided by numerous mountain ranges into a series of plateaus and valleys. One of the more flat and arid of these valleys, that of Castile in the area of La Mancha, rises in the south into the Sierra Morena, which separates New Castile from Andalucía. As the sierra slopes down into the province of Córdoba, the soil takes on a reddish color, and the slanting hills, blanketed with olive orchards, and more recently with fields of sunflowers, reach almost to the walls of the city of Córdoba, once the heart of Arab Spain. In the northwest corner of the province, off the road to Pozoblanco and perched on a promontory that exposes it to all the winds, is the tiny village of Pedroche. Deriving its name from the rocky terrain on which it lies, Pedroche looks very much like any other provincial village in the backwater of southern Spain. Brief notes in obscure histories say little more than that it was once more important than it is today.

Pedroche is an ancient village, conquered by Spanish Christians in 1130. In the sixteenth century it was larger and more populous than it is now, and some of its sons made significant contributions to church and state. Its greatest claim to fame, however, is that it was the birthplace of Pedro Moya de Contreras, first inquisitor of New Spain, third archbishop of Mexico, *visitador*, captain-general and viceroy of New Spain, and president of the Council of the Indies.[1]

He was probably born around the year 1530, although the precise date is uncertain. His father, Rodrigo de Moya Moscoso, and his mother, Catalina de Contreras, both belonged to the lower nobility— the group variously styled *caballeros* or *hijosdalgo*. They came from the class that had been the backbone of the Reconquista, the centuries-long struggle to reclaim Spain from Arab domination. It was an old family on both sides, dating back to the Middle Ages and the early years of the reconquest. The Moyas were Galician in origin and derived their name from Alvaro Marino, who had participated in the conquest of the town of Moya in Cuenca in 830 and had received its name as a reward. The Moscoso branch of the family, of which the future archbishop seems to have been proud, claimed descent from the Visigoths.[2] He habitually used its coat of arms, though never the name. As archbishop of Mexico he used a quartering of the Moya, Contreras, and Moscoso arms.[3]

How or why the family came to be situated in a comparatively obscure village is not known. They may, like many of the lower nobility after the reconquest, have fallen on difficult times. The hidalgos were numerous, often landless, and not infrequently poor.[4] Moya sometimes mentioned kinship with the Mohedanos of Pedroche and Córdoba, a family that included a viceroy of Naples, Juan de Mohedano, and Antonio Mohedano, a famous local painter, but the only other relatives known with any certainty were a sister and an uncle.

The uncle was Don Asisclo Moya de Contreras.[5] A native of Pedroche like his nephew, he was a graduate in law from the university of Salamanca and had a distinguished career as a deputy in the Aragonese *cortés* (parliament) and bishop of Vich in Catalonia. In 1561 he attended the final session of the Council of Trent and in 1563 was named archbishop of Valencia, but he died in 1565 before taking possession of his see. In an age when blood relationships counted for so much, it scarcely seems possible that an uncle of such importance and position did not have some influence on the early career of his nephew; yet there is no evidence that such was the case. In all of his known correspondence, Pedro Moya de Contreras makes only one passing reference to his uncle. The young Pedro would find his patron elsewhere.

Quien quiere saber que vaya a Salamanca. For a young man of the lower nobility, there was only one educational magnet in all of Spain: Salamanca. Already three centuries old, the university was enjoying an unprecedented growth and prestige in the sixteenth century, with more than six thousand students and eleven chairs of theology by the time that Moya arrived there. Whereas scholasticism had declined into formalism and logic chopping in the rest of Europe, Salamanca resounded with the names of great Dominicans such as Vitoria, Soto, and Cano. The Dominican theological renaissance was centered in the convent and college of San Esteban, where the traditional Thomism of the order was revitalized and brought to bear on the pressing problems of the age: human rights, international law, just war, freedom of the seas, and the right of conquest.[6]

If, in accordance with the medieval aphorism, theology was the queen of the sciences, then at Salamanca it was a reign without rule, for it was the study of law that held sway. Law—whether canon, civil, or a combination of the two—offered a young man in sixteenth-century Spain entry into well paying and prestigious jobs in church and state. The growth of the Spanish empire and its governmental machinery created a demand for *letrados:* men from the middle ranks of society, skilled and trained in law, who occupied the key positions in the burgeoning bureaucracy and who formed a governing elite. Doctors and *licenciados* from Salamanca and other major universities could be found all over the New World, where they held positions as *oidores, alcaldes,* bishops, canons, university professors, and town councilmen.[7] The golden age of Salamanca faded in the following century, but in Moya's time it was a bastion of regalistic and Counter-Reformation thought and a gateway into the letrado world of law, administration, and status—a veritable *plaza de armas de letras.*

It was probably at Salamanca that Pedro Moya de Contreras met the decisive influence in his life, Juan de Ovando. Although Ovando was one of the most important figures in sixteenth-century Spanish civil and ecclesiastical administration, relatively little is known about him. For the most part he has received even less attention from historians than has his illustrious protégé, and he still awaits a worthy biographer. For a brief period he stood at the summit of the colonial government of Philip II and was renowned for his legal skills, administrative ability, and forward-looking ideas. He came and went quickly compared with other royal favorites, but in less than ten years he left a deep imprint on Spanish colonial policies.

Juan de Ovando was born at Cáceres, Extremadura, in 1514.[8] The Ovandos were one of the first families of the province and were closely interrelated and intermarried—Juan had two grandfathers who were named Ovando. The famed Nicolás de Ovando, first governor of Española, was his great-uncle. His father was illegitimate but had been acknowledged by one of the family and raised among them. Young Juan was a fellow of the Colegio Mayor de San Bartolomé at Salamanca, where he received the degree of licenciado in law—perhaps both canon and civil, since he was well acquainted with both. He was a cleric, though how far advanced in orders is unclear.

Ovando taught at Salamanca until 1554, when he left for Seville. Within two years he had become the *provisor* of the archdiocese and the virtual ruler of the see in the absence of its archbishop, Fernando de Valdés, who was deeply involved at court, in the Inquisition, and in conflicts with his cathedral chapter. Ovando had his own problems with the chapter. In 1556 a certain Doctor Constantino applied for a vacant canonry and was supported by a majority of the chapter. Ovando opposed the appointment on the grounds that Constantino was Jewish, unorthodox in doctrine, and married. In the dispute that ensued, Ovando excommunicated the entire chapter. Constantino was given the appointment, but Ovando was vindicated when the Inquisition later arrested and imprisoned Constantino for holding Lutheran teachings.[9] The affair made Ovando enemies, and when an attempt was made to have him named inquisitor of Seville, the appointment was thwarted on the grounds that the offices of inquisitor and provisor were incompatible. In about 1564 Ovando came under the patronage of Diego de Espinosa, who in that year became the president of the supreme council of the Inquisition. Espinosa was responsible for Ovando's rise, just as Ovando would be for Moya's.[10]

It is not clear how Moya first met Ovando. Some biographers give the impression that Moya became Ovando's page when the latter was president of the Council of the Indies—an impossibility, as Moya was already embarked on his own career by the time Ovando was appointed to that post. One source says that Ovando met Moya on a visit to Pedroche.[11] Although this is possible, it is more likely that Moya met Ovando at the Colegio Mayor de San Bartolomé when Ovando was still teaching at Salamanca and that he entered his service there. The men seem to have had a close relationship, though their correspondence is so businesslike that for the most part it is impossible to detect any true warmth. Even as archbishop of Mexico, Moya always showed his patron the greatest deference and respect and at times displayed an unrestrained admiration. Whatever their personal relationship, Ovando thought enough of the young man to be deeply involved in his education, if not to pay for it, as the biographers claim.

Both Ovando and Asisclo Moya de Contreras had been *colegiales*, or fellows, of San Bartolomé. Founded in 1401 by Diego de Anaya, the archbishop of Seville, this was one of four such *colegios*, or residential colleges, at Salamanca.[12] A *colegio mayor* was not a college in the modern American sense, but a combination of residence, fraternity, and private tutorial service, all within the framework of the university and sometimes having special privileges within it. The colegiales tended to be clannish and mutually supportive, even after graduation. They produced a long line of civil servants, lawyers, and churchmen, who maintained a kind of "old boy" network that promoted their careers.

"The whole world is full of *bartolomicos*" was a saying of the time. As the oldest of the colegios mayores of Salamanca and one of the most closely knit, San Bartolomé had great prestige. If the graduates of Salamanca were regalists, the bartolomicos were the most regalist of all. Ovando, the prince of letrados, was part of this network, and he formed his own core of protégés, not all of them fellow bartolomicos. He was an early patron (1562) of Mateo Vásquez—who later was secretary to both Cardinal Espinosa and Philip II—and of Benito Arias Montano, a well-known writer and librarian of the Escorial. The latter case is all the more interesting because Arias Montano was a *converso*, a "new Christian" of Jewish descent.[13] Ovando, his protégés, and the colegiales, especially those of San Bartolomé, represented a new breed of Spanish civil servant: peninsular, divorced from the Flemish orientation of the early years of Charles V, concerned primarily with Spain and its empire, and devoted to reform, efficiency, and organization.

Although there is no documentary evidence that Moya was a bartolomico, it is difficult to see how he could have been otherwise, given the histories of his uncle and Ovando.[14] The rosters of the university include his name as a student in canon law for the years 1551–1554, although he may have arrived earlier. He studied no theology at Salamanca but specialized in law. According to his biographers, he graduated with a doctorate in both canon and civil law, but there is no contemporary documentation of his receiving such a degree. Because the doctorate usually required about seven or eight years of residence, the evidence seems to be against his having taken that degree at Salamanca and to favor his completing the doctoral degree at another university—in all likelihood Seville. His earliest signatures, dating from 1569, use the title of doctor, and it is hardly credible that he should have done so if his degree had not been valid. A false use of the title would have opened him to accusations by the many enemies he made later in life. One of Moya's biographers states that he was originally intended for a literary career.[15] This would have been unusual for his class and for that age; he did, however, have marked literary tastes and interests throughout his life.

Ovando left Salamanca for Seville in 1554, and significantly, this is the last year in which Moya's name is included in the university rosters. Quite probably, he left with his patron and acted as Ovando's secretary during the subsequent years, perhaps at the same time completing his education. His letters indicate a thoroughgoing acquaintance with Seville, and especially with the workings of the archdiocesan administration, which could have come only from prolonged personal contact.[16] At an unknown date, but probably in the middle or late 1560s, he was appointed to the post of *maestrescuelas* of the cathedral of the Canary Islands. It was the first step of an ecclesiastical career, although it seems certain that he was not yet a priest.[17] A maestrescuelas was a member of the cathedral chapter, but the nature of the office and the customs of those times allow for the possibility that he was only in minor orders, or was perhaps a deacon.

Although it is not known exactly how long he spent in this post, it is certain that during the years 1567–1569 he was both maestrescuelas and provisor of the diocese, at first under Bishop Bartolomé de Torres, who arrived in the Canaries in 1567 but died within a year (on 1 February 1568). The bishop had brought with him a well-known Jesuit, Diego López, who immediately became a good friend of Moya's. Under López's direction, Moya made the famous spiritual exercises of Saint Ignatius of Loyola. This was his first known contact with the Jesuits, and his esteem for that order, together with his liking and respect for its members, continued throughout his life.[18]

It is tempting to speculate on the influence this stay in the Canaries had on the young cleric's attitudes. The islands were Spain's first experience with conquest and colonization, and its first dealings with a more primitive, non-Christian population. The situation was similar to that later encountered in the Indies, and many of the disputes that raged across the Atlantic, such as those over the *encomienda* and the treatment of the natives, were first fought in the Canaries. Memories of these disputes and of the Spanish conquest of the Canaries were still fresh when Moya arrived there and may have influenced his later attitudes toward the Indians of New Spain, though there are no explicit references to the islands in his correspondence.

While Moya was in the Canaries, Ovando was serving as a member of the supreme council of the Inquisition. In 1566, through the influence of Cardinal Espinosa, he was asked to make a *visita*, or general investigation, of the university of Alcalá. Some of his friends tried to persuade him to remain in Seville, but he recognized the offer as a turning point in his career. He discharged the commission successfully and was almost immediately asked to make a similar investigation of the Council of the Indies, the second in that institution's history.[19] A cascade of reports, complaints, and denunciations reaching Spain, especially from Peru, had given such a dismal account of the state of affairs in the Indies and reflected so badly on the knowledge and competence of the council that Philip II had resolved on a thorough investigation. In all probability he was gently prodded into this by Cardinal Espinosa.[20] The investigation began in the last months of 1567 and was concerned more with finding solutions to the problems and remedying deficiencies than with punishing delinquents—most of whom, it seems, died or retired before the final report was submitted to the king in 1571. Although it was unusual for a visitador to participate in the implementation of the reforms he suggested, Ovando apparently did this with the consent of Philip II. He was dedicated to genuine reform in both church and state, and as visitador was responsible for the famous *junta general* of 1568, which helped to draw up an overall plan of reform for the Indies. In August 1571 Philip II appointed him president of the Council of the Indies, a post that had been vacant for a year. He was also president of the Council of Finance, the only man of that century to hold both positions simultaneously.

Even as visitador, Ovando had attempted to begin codification of the laws and ordinances of the Indies, and this attempt continued throughout his term as president of the council. His work of reform and centralization included the establishment of the Inquisition in New Spain and the issuance of the famous *Ordenanza del Patronazgo* of 1574 (to be discussed in the next chapter), which codified the royal right of patronage and gave it a strength it had never had before. Ovando died suddenly on 8 September 1575, shortly after the king had appointed him archbishop of Santiago and president of the Council of Castile. Much of his work on the Council of the Indies was left unfinished, including the *recopilación*, or codification, of the laws of the Indies.[21]

Ovando's zeal to impose law and order on the chaotic and uneasy situation in the New World, particularly in Peru, could not be realized without trusted confidants on the scene. For this reason appointments to higher offices in the colonies from 1567 onward reflected his influence. In this he was supported by Espinosa, who used his immense influence with Philip II to secure the needed approval. Because of this dual influence Francisco de Toledo was named viceroy of Peru and Martín Enríquez de Almansa viceroy of New Spain.[22] There is no doubt whatever that Moya owed his rapid rise to Ovando. He habitually described himself as Ovando's *hechura* (client or protégé) and on several occasions repeated his reference of 24 January 1575 to "this dignity in which Your Very Illustrious Excellency has placed me."[23] Although there is no documentary proof, it is obvious that Moya's precipitous rise from provincial schoolmaster to archbishop of Mexico within the space of five years was part of a deliberate plan on Ovando's part. The choice of Moya as first inquisitor of New Spain in 1570 was doubtless meant to deliver that all-important post to a man Ovando could trust. Nor could Ovando have been ignorant of the fact that Alonso de Montúfar, then archbishop of Mexico, was old and ailing and that a successor would soon be needed. In Ovando's eyes Moya was probably already wearing a miter when he sailed for the New World. Moya was to be an extension of Ovando in reforming, organizing, watching, and reporting.[24] The president of the Council of the Indies could hardly have made a better choice.

So it happened that in 1569, when Ovando was still a member of the supreme council of the Inquisition and was conducting his visita of the Council of the Indies, Moya was appointed one of the inquisitors of Murcia. His career in that post has been somewhat exaggerated by his biographers and by other historians. He was not the sole inquisitor of Murcia, but only one of three, and his name always appears last on the list. Furthermore, he saw only about six months of active service in the post. He took formal possession of the office on 30 October 1569, but returned almost immediately to Córdoba to collect his belongings. His name does not appear on any inquisition documents until 9 January 1570, nor does it appear after 1 July of that same year. The experience, however, must have been a valuable one, because the Inquisition of Murcia was plagued with inefficiency, corruption among its *familiares*, and general unpopularity among the local populace.[25] On 18 August 1570 Moya was named inquisitor of the newly established Inquisition of New Spain. The preparatory phase of his life was over. He now assumed the first of the offices for which he would become famous.

Moya's life prior to 1571 can be studied only in outline. As noted, there are few certain dates for this period. On the supposition that he must have been in his early thirties at Salamanca and that he was about the same age as his fellow bishops of New Spain, his birthdate would fall around the year 1530. Most of his early life, at least after his departure from Salamanca, must thus have been spent either in Ovando's service or in the Canary Islands; and most of these years are unaccounted for.

Moya was described by his first biographer, Gutiérrez de Luna, as being

of well-proportioned body, rather average in height, well formed and graceful in all his members, without any defects of nature. His face was pleasant and handsome, his complexion rosy, his hair of light color mixed with gray, accompanied by a natural gravity and composure, mild of temper and very humble in his manner, so that solely by the authority of his countenance those who looked at him and spoke with him were put at ease and obliged to a decent respect. He was very upright and well-bred. He spoke to all with great civility and with great courtesy, with his biretta [ecclesiastical cap] in his hand. He was very clean and neat both in his clothing and in the furnishings of his house, not too attentive to food and very temperate, because his ordinary table expenses did not include any dainty fare.[26]

There are two basic portraits of Moya, both dating from after his appointment as archbishop (see illustrations following p. 162). One, now in the museum of Chapultepec Castle in Mexico City, is dated 1583 and shows him as viceroy. It also depicts him as more or less clean-shaven. The other is in the chapter hall of the metropolitan cathedral of Mexico City, where he is lightly bearded according to the style of the late sixteenth century. Moya was asthmatic, a fact that may be reflected in the rather thin, drawn look of these portraits, but there are only a few indications that this affliction ever seriously hampered his work.[27] He always regarded the New World as being injurious to his health. Despite Gutiérrez de Luna's claim that he was "without any defects of nature," these portraits also show, in varying degrees, that he suffered from a moderate to severe exotropia of the left eye.

A third portrait is in the Oakland Museum, Oakland, California. Its provenance is uncertain but it may well be a copy drawn at second or third hand or from written or oral descriptions. Only the beard and clothing resemble the other portraits; the facial characteristics are almost entirely different.

Despite the obscurity of his early years, some facts do stand out in Moya's preparation for his later career. He came from a family of hidalgos, heirs to the warrior class that had borne the brunt of the reconquest, and that in the aftermath often found itself without resources. The hidalgos contributed large numbers to the growing bureaucracy and elite of government. Moya's background, education, and formation prepared him for a role among that elite, among the letrados who were gaining a monopoly on positions in the machinery of church and state. As a client of Ovando's, he was associated with a new breed of imperial civil servant: regalist, dedicated to reform—whether ecclesiastical or civil—and to the centralization of authority. Had he not chosen (or been chosen for) the way of the church, Moya might well have lived out his days as a judge, a legal advisor, or even a member of some important royal council. As it was, like many other letrados he found himself in the New World, confronting challenges and experiencing opportunities not to be found in the Old. His special sphere of activity would be the city and archdiocese of Mexico, an area on which he would have a profound and lasting influence.

II. A City Founded on Water

In 1585, fourteen years after Moya de Contreras set foot in Mexico City, two Franciscan friars described it as the most populous and most noble city in all New Spain, and, for that matter, greater than any in Peru. With some qualifications this description was equally true in 1571.[1]

The Mexica (or Aztec) capital of Tenochtitlán had been almost totally destroyed in the course of the Spanish siege (1520–1521). A Spanish Renaissance city had risen on its ruins, with the newer name of Mexico-Tenochtitlán. Later it was simply called Mexico. Like its predecessor, the new city was situated on a marshy island in the midst of a lake—or, to be more exact, a series of lakes—in the central plateau. It was connected with the mainland by a series of causeways (*calzadas*). "For this reason," the two Franciscans reported, "it is said that Mexico is founded on water, and as a matter of fact it is . . . and if the buildings are tall and heavy, they constantly sink little by little," an observation as true today as it was four centuries ago.[2] Drainage of the valley (the famous *desagüe*) was begun in 1608 and not completed until the nineteenth century, at a dreadful cost in Indian life and labor.

In 1571 the principal entrance to the city was a causeway that came from Guadalupe (Tepeyac) in the north. This was the ordinary point of entry, even for carts and travelers from Veracruz, who veered to the north and then approached by way of Guadalupe and Tlaltelolco. By Moya's time it had become customary to meet all important visitors to the city at Guadalupe. In addition two other causeways ran from Xochimilco in the south and Tacuba in the west.[3] The city was also connected with the mainland by two aqueducts, one from Chapultepec, the other from Santa Fe, about two leagues from the city. As in the days of the Aztecs, the general area was a garden spot, and the surrounding valley, the fabled Vale of Anáhuac, was consistently described as fertile and pleasant, at least before it was deforested by the Spaniards.

The colonial city of Mexico was a delight, especially for Spaniards, for whom city life was the apex of civilization. The houses were well built and the streets attractive, clean, and wide—wide enough for three carts or nine horsemen to go abreast—though some contemporaries considered them rather too uniform, unlike the narrow, serpentine thoroughfares so common in Spain.[4] The heart of the city was a spacious central square, the Plaza Mayor, now called the Zócalo, which was abutted by two smaller squares. Facing it was the original cathedral of Mexico, behind which the beginnings of the present cathedral were being built. On the east side of the square stood the *casas reales*, which included the palace of the viceroy and the offices of the audiencia and the treasury officials, the very heart of the colonial government. A good part of the city was still served by canals rather than streets despite the Spaniards' efforts to fill in many of the original waterways. The principal canal passed by the main square where the old cathedral and the casas reales were located.[5]

Mexico was in reality two cities, one Spanish, one Indian, with mixed areas in between. The limit of the Spanish district was called the *traza*, a term that was more or less equivalent to "pale." Surrounding the traza were four L-shaped Indian districts (*barrios*) derived from preconquest tribal divisions: San Juan (Moyotlán) to the southwest, Santa María (Talquechiuhcán) to the northwest, San Sebastián (Atzacualco) to the northeast, and San Pablo (Teopán) to the southeast. The original reason for the division was defensive: in the early years of the conquest the Spanish were still a minority surrounded by a potentially rebellious Indian majority. Fear of native uprisings in the city persisted until the end of the century. As time went on, the division was justified on humanitarian and religious grounds—to make it easier to evangelize the Indians, for example, or to keep them apart from the corrupting influence of the Spaniards. As Mexico came to have more and more inhabitants of mixed blood (*castas*), it was deemed necessary to keep the Indians separate from them also, partly out of fear that the lawlessness of the castas might prove contagious. As a result the boundaries were changed many times during the century, once by Moya himself in an order of 21 August 1585. In time the original well-defined limits became blurred and the boundaries of the various districts more difficult to determine.[6] The Indian districts had their own governors and councils and a certain degree of self-government.

According to the prejudices of the observer, the inhabitants of Mexico City were either praised as courteous, well spoken, and cultured, or condemned as extravagant, drunken, and immoral. Many of them belonged to the lower nobility and were people of quality, while an even larger number pretended to be so. Although with the passage of time and the settlement of the land the initial rudeness of the settlers was steadily being softened by a developing society, the population was still restless, mobile, and somewhat rootless. Perhaps because of this, the people were fond of display and flaunted what wealth they had with all the enthusiasm and vulgarity of nouveaux riches. Despite stringent royal laws, gambling for recklessly high stakes was rampant. The rich were numerous, but, as the two Franciscans noted sadly, the poor became daily still more numerous. The children of the city were a special delight to visitors, and the saying went that Mexico had four things that were worthy of praise: *calles, casas, caballos, y criaturas*—streets, houses, horses, and children.

At the top of local society stood the peninsular Spaniards, who monopolized the highest posts in church and state and were popularly known by the opprobrious nickname of *gachupines.*[7] Below them were the criollos, persons of European blood born in the New World, who were growing increasingly hostile to the peninsulars and resentful of what they considered to be their own second-class citizenship. Already noticeable in the sixteenth century were the stirrings of criollo consciousness and identity, the awakening of those whose feelings of alienation were to play such an important part in the movement for independence.[8]

Below the criollos on the social scale were the Indians, the blacks, and the various groups of mixed blood, the most important of which were the *mestizos*—persons of mixed Spanish and Indian descent. Marginal to both European and Indian societies, and feeling rejected by both, they posed a serious social problem. There were also African slaves, imported for work in the mines when the Indians proved too frail, and those who were a mixture of white and black, called *mulatos.* These racial groups constituted the majority of the slum dwellers and vagabonds of New Spain and were a volatile social mix.[9]

Spaniards of that century could not live without some form of municipal organization or city life. For them such organization was the only way a person could live in a civilized manner (*políticamente,* which is closer to its Greek root *polis,* or city, than is the modern English *political*). They rejoiced that their town, no matter how small or how colonial, had all the structure, authorities, and offices that any city in Spain could boast. This outlook was intensified in the New World, both because of a desire to compensate for any inferiority felt vis-à-vis the peninsula and because of a sense of nostalgia for life as it was lived in the old country. The New Spaniards tried to be more Spanish than Spain.

They could be especially proud of Mexico City. It was first and foremost the seat of the viceroy, the lord and ruler of all New Spain. He was literally the alter ego of the king, for Philip II lived not only in Spain but also vicariously in Mexico City through the viceroy, whose residence was called royal and even, on more formal occasions, "His Majesty's royal residence." The power that went with the title, however, was neither regal nor absolute. The Spanish crown, which trusted none of its civil servants in the New World, was careful to balance one authority against another and deliberately left lines of jurisdiction vague and over-lapping to prevent the accumulation of power.

The person of the king was also represented by a corporate body, the audiencia, which ranked just below the viceroy and in some ways was his equal. Though modeled on peninsular antecedents, the audi-encia in the New World was really an institution distinct from that of Spain. Each audiencia district was regarded as a kingdom in the Span-ish empire. Consisting of four to six judges, called oidores, the audien-cia combined two functions: that of supreme law court and that of administrative council to the viceroy and, through him, to the king. As a council the audiencia was subject to the viceroy, who acted as its president. As a law court it was independent of him and responsible only to the Council of the Indies and the king. The audiencia of Mex-ico, like that of Lima, was distinctive in that it separated civil and criminal jurisdictions into separate tribunals (*salas*). The oidores acted as judges only in civil cases. Criminal cases were tried by the *alcaldes del crimen,* who were also independent of the viceroy: he did not preside at their meetings or see their correspondence with the king. The audien-cia was an appellate court and had original jurisdiction only in speci-fied cases.[10]

As a council or government bureau, the audiencia was supposed to work with the viceroy in matters affecting the treasury, war, and rou-tine governmental operations. It ruled the district in the absence of the viceroy. Judicial and executive functions were not separated, and the audiencia came to exercise something close to legislative power. Like so many institutions imported from Spain, the audiencia was stronger in the New World than in the Old.[11]

Below the audiencia were the lesser functionaries, the most important of whom were the treasury officials (*oficiales reales*) who handled
the revenues and finances of the crown and who lived in the casas
reales, both as a sign of status and as a means of surveillance.

These various civil servants were not gray and faceless bureaucrats
but rather the lineal and spiritual descendants of the conquistadores.
Many were turbulent, aggressive, and ambitious. Like so many other
Spaniards, they had come to the New World to make their fortunes
and to establish a place for themselves in an emerging society. They
were strong, assertive, and often combative personalities, inclined to
bend or violate laws passed by a government thousands of miles away,
determined to seize the opportunities afforded by life in a new land.

Theoretically, all local officials from the viceroy down were subject
to regulations that severely limited their freedom of action. The government of Philip II is popularly regarded as having been absolute
and highly centralized. A Spanish king, however, was viewed more
as a dispenser of justice than as a giver of laws, and in practice
government was a careful balance among distinct, and often opposed,
special interest groups. The result was a surprising vacillation in the
decision-making process and an equally surprising willingness to
change policy or alter decrees under pressure from colonial interests.[12]
The centralization of the government and the exercise of absolute
authority were tempered in a special way by the problem of commu-
nications that were slowed by the vast distance between Spain and
the New World. In addition, the Spanish crown—reacting to foreign
piratical activity—had adopted a convoy (*flota*) system, whereby all
shipping and correspondence were carried by only two convoys a
year. Correspondence was brought on a special ship (*navío de aviso*),
and the distances involved, together with the infrequency of the convoys, meant that dealings between the colony and the metropolis
often extended over a matter of years. This agonizing slowness gave
local officials greater latitude than the letter of the law allowed.

If any profession other than the clergy had a hold on sixteenth-
century Mexico, it was the law. The colony seemed to swarm with
lawyers, judges, notaries, and all the apparatus of the legal system.
Spaniards of that century were a litigious people who went to court with
amazing frequency. Yet the legal profession was neither popular nor
esteemed; on the contrary, as in other societies, lawyers were regarded
as parasites, or, at best, as necessary evils. Justice was neither even-
handed nor cheap: wary colonials knew that it would cost money in
both fees and bribes. The latter not only speeded up the legal process
but also helped to ensure favorable verdicts.

Only one figure in the city equaled the viceroy in power and prestige, and that was the archbishop. As the first churchman of New Spain he presided over an ecclesiastical structure that permeated almost every aspect of colonial life. Associated with him and theoretically under his leadership were nine or ten suffragan bishops, governing dioceses that extended from Guadalajara to Guatemala.

The church had arrived in definitive form in New Spain with "The Twelve," the first Franciscans who in 1524 had begun the systematic evangelization of the newly conquered land. For almost two decades thereafter the church in New Spain was in the hands of the religious orders—Franciscans, Dominicans, and Augustinians—with results that will be detailed in chapter V. Not until 1530 was Mexico made a diocese. Its first bishop, Fray Juan de Zumárraga (1476–1548), a Basque Franciscan, was consecrated in Spain in 1533. Mexico was raised to the rank of a metropolitan see in 1546. Its boundaries, crossing and overlapping civil jurisdictions, extended from the gulf coast to the Pacific. By 1571 the dioceses of Yucatán, Chiapas, Nueva Galicia (including modern Jalisco and Zacatecas), Antequera (modern Oaxaca), Tlaxcala (which had actually preceded Mexico), Michoacán, Guatemala, Vera Paz in Guatemala, and, apparently, Comayagua in Honduras had been added, joined by Manila in 1579.[13]

The church's influence was pervasive. From baptism to funeral, from birth to death, the lives of the Spanish settlers, the converted Indians, the black slaves, and the various castas were touched—however remotely—by its ceremonies and ministrations. Elaborate celebrations and rituals not only elevated the mind and heart to divine worship but also relieved the monotony of colonial life. Numerous holydays of obligation, together with the patronal feasts of schools, religious orders, churches, and confraternities, gave a welcome respite to those who had to work for their living. Sometimes the effect of religion was superficial, its ceremonies becoming externalized observances that sought occasional consolation or favor in the outward devotions of popular cult or in quasi-superstitious practices.[14] At other times colonial religion was deeper and more committed, expressing itself in Iberian mysticism or in charitable and educational endeavors.

The average inhabitants of New Spain do not seem to have been well instructed in their religion. The Christianity of the Indians was heavily mixed with syncretism and superstition, and Inquisition records show that many Spaniards verged on religious illiteracy, with their knowledge of their faith confined to the mechanical recitation of a few prayers. The Jesuit Juan de la Plaza told the bishops of the Third Mexican Council that the religious beliefs of the people of New Spain were often nothing more than inherited opinion, not unlike the religion of the average Moslem, a position supported by the general tenor of the conciliar legislation. In addition, the large numbers of rootless and vagabond peoples—mulattoes, mestizos, and Spaniards, all of whom were invariably described in contemptuous terms by their contemporaries—were not strongly touched by religious influence.

Though the church's influence was extensive, its power was not. Paradoxically, the Spanish government, which was responsible for much of the church's influence, was equally responsible for restricting its freedom. Relations between church and state were governed by a complex series of laws and privileges collectively called the *patronato real*, described by one Spanish writer as "the most precious pearl in the royal diadem."[15] Originating in the Middle Ages as a means of supporting churches by endowment, the patronato had come to embody the concept of a state church, with the state having the predominant role. These rights and privileges had been acquired over a century or more by means of diplomacy, threats, extortion, and a sincere devotion to reform. As with so many institutions transplanted from the mother country to the colonies, the rights of the patronato were stronger and more deeply entrenched in the New World than in the Old.

The papacy was ultimately unsuccessful in resisting these encroachments on ecclesiastical freedom. Pope Saint Pius V (1566–1572) had sought to prevent the extension of the patronato. Gregory XIII (1572–1585) had offered even more resistance. Partly because of this opposition and partly because of Ovando's urge to reform and regularize all aspects of life in the Indies, Philip II issued his famous Ordenanza del Patronazgo on 1 June 1574. A severe and peremptory document, it both codified the rights of royal patronage as they had existed up to that time and extended them.[16]

These rights cut deeply into the jurisdiction of bishops over their own dioceses. No church or monastery could be founded or endowed without royal permission. The king had the right to found all ecclesiastical offices and to draw the boundary lines of dioceses. Archbishops and bishops were nominated by the king, who presented their names to the pope. Although the pope actually bestowed the office, royal nomination was equivalent to outright appointment. Similarly, lower ecclesiastical officers such as canons and chaplains were appointed by the king, though the canonical conferral (*colación*) was by the bishop. The bishops' power to appoint lower ecclesiastical officers was narrow and temporary. Additional provisions affected religious orders (these will be detailed in chapter V).

In practice, the patronato amounted to domination of the church by the state, a domination that increased as time went on. The bishops' freedom of action over their clergy, and hence over the correction of abuses, was frustrated by constant governmental intrusion and by the necessity of referring even trivial matters to the Council of the Indies. When the rights of the patronato were well used, the result was, admittedly, a thriving and apostolic church with bishops of high quality. When they were ill used, the result was suffocation.

Those who accepted the patronato and defended it theoretically were called regalists. They believed that the rights of the patronato were inherent in sovereignty and belonged to it by definition. Moya was himself a regalist; his background, education, and temperament made him so. His position was not always popular with his suffragans and would at times put him in difficult situations in their regard.

The church was entirely supported by the state through a system of tithes (*diezmos*) collected by the crown and redonated according to a complex formula.[17] This system, from which the Indians were supposed to be exempt, increased the church's dependence on the state. Deprivation of income was a favorite way of compelling churchmen to follow civil orders. The church, however, was a growing economic entity in its own right through its accumulation of lands and buildings. This process, enhanced by donations and bequests, was still in its early stages in 1571, but it was already encountering opposition from lay circles, along with demands that it be limited. Full retribution for this enrichment would be exacted after independence.

In most areas of life the distinction between church and state, between the legal and the moral, the religious and the civil, was often blurred. The canon law of the church was also public law. It is not surprising, then, that during the Third Mexican Provincial Council the city council of Mexico City made recommendations about the lives of priests (and cited the Council of Trent in support of its suggestions) or that the bishops passed legislation on the sale of slaves and silver. Civil officials were theoretically obligated to support the censures and other ecclesiastical penalties imposed by bishops, although in practice they more often hampered them. By the universal law of the church, clerics were independent of civil jurisdiction and subject only to ecclesiastical courts. The archbishop's palace in Mexico City even had its own jail for clerics.

There were constant intrusions into this exemption by the civil authorities, however, especially by the viceroys and audiencias, who claimed to represent royal patronage in the Indies. This was a recurrent source of conflict in the sixteenth century, just as it would be in the nineteenth. Such conflicts were inevitable; viceroys and archbishops were natural rivals. The coexistence of two systems with overlapping and opposing jurisdictions (so favored by the Spanish crown as a form of checks and balances), each of which claimed the allegiance of the average citizen, could not possibly be peaceful. The result was the growth of an attitude that in a later context would be called anticlerical. In the national period, anticlericalism sought to keep the church and the clergy out of public life and to restrict both to a ministerial or cultic role. In the sixteenth century the church's place in public life was generally accepted and enshrined in law, but many believed that its role should be decidedly limited in practice. Both attitudes had the same goal: the restriction of the church as a force in society. Viewed in this way the patronato itself was fundamentally anticlerical. In Moya's day this process was still inchoate but was gaining ground. The church had lost much of its independence and was well on the way to losing more. Moya's complaint that the bishops' jurisdiction was held in such contempt that lay brothers in the religious orders were treated with more respect was probably exaggerated, but it was nonetheless firmly rooted in reality.

The church was further weakened by dissension within its own ranks. Bishops not only struggled with the civil authorities but also fought with one another. The enmity between the religious orders and the diocesan clergy, including the bishops (some of whom were former religious), was venomous to the point of violence.[18] Diocesan priests were often at odds with their bishops. Bishops resented the Inquisition and its officials. The stereotype of a monolithic Spanish church must yield to an often unseemly and unedifying spectacle of petty squabbles, jurisdictional quarrels, injured honor, and childish petulance.

The city of Mexico had four parish districts: the cathedral (or *parroquia mayor*), Santa Catalina, Vera Cruz, and San Pablo.[19] In addition the various religious orders had churches attached to their schools and convents, but these were not parish churches in the technical sense of the term. In canon law permission to build a religious house automatically carried with it permission to build a church or chapel to which the faithful could come to fulfill their Sunday obligation (except on Easter Sunday).[20] Most of the parishes also included chapels of ease (*ermitas*), which were located within the parish boundaries and sometimes had regular ministrations, sometimes not. In addition to the ordinary parish priests attached to these churches, there were numerous chaplaincies (*capellanías*), endowments or foundations given for the recitation of a prescribed number of masses by a priest whose salary was paid out of the endowment.[21]

The church was both a source of the Spaniard's identity and the principal educational force in the colony. When Moya arrived, the outstanding educational institution was the Royal and Pontifical University, the city's pride, which held a monopoly on higher degrees.[22] The Franciscans had a college at Tlaltelolco, called Santa Cruz, which had originally been intended as a training school for an Indian elite. Its failure was one of the tragedies of Mexican history.[23] During Moya's episcopate, and over his strong objections, the Augustinians, under Alonso de la Vera Cruz, opened their famous college of San Pablo, located in the parish of the same name.

There were also numerous preparatory schools. To care for the growing problem of orphan boys (usually illegitimate mestizos who were not acknowledged by their fathers), Archbishop Zumárraga and Antonio de Mendoza, the first viceroy of New Spain, had founded a school at San Juan Letrán. Its principal patron was the king, but its administration was rotated annually among the oidores of the audiencia. By the 1570s it had fallen on such hard times that Moya strongly recommended that it be entrusted to the Jesuits, but the latter refused to accept it.[24] A school called Nuestra Señora de la Caridad had been founded for orphan girls and was directed by the Confraternity of Charity, with four or five chaplaincies attached to it. Like the school of San Juan, it had originally been intended for mestizas, but began to accept peninsular and criolla girls when no educational institution for them was forthcoming.[25]

The European population of New Spain in 1570 was an estimated sixty-three thousand, of whom twelve thousand lived in Mexico City. One out of every twenty-five was a cleric, a proportion that would increase with time.[26] This European population was minuscule in comparison with the immense number of Indians who still lived in what had once been their land. Today there seems no good reason to doubt that a catastrophic decline in the native population occurred in the century following the conquest. Although there is an intense debate among historians on this point, the claims of those who hold for a population decline have not been satisfactorily refuted.[27] European diseases such as smallpox, typhus, influenza, and measles devastated the highly vulnerable and immunologically unprepared native population. One of the worst of these epidemics, the dreaded *matlazáhuatl* of 1576, occurred during Moya's episcopate and may have killed as many as two million Indians. He himself witnessed the devastation and depopulation of entire provinces and gave a heroic example in ministering to the stricken natives. In addition to epidemics, the Indians suffered from economic exploitation and the culture shock caused by the jolting transferral from native to European life and the resulting widespread alcoholism.

Loss of so many natives had an economic impact on New Spain, as they were the basis of its economy. The era of cheap and abundant labor came to an end. Despite the irksome mercantilistic legislation of the crown, New Spain had a growing and thriving commerce based on mining and agriculture, and hence on native labor. As Moya wrote to

Ovando, "This whole country is businesses."[28] Silver mining was one backbone of the economy, with cattle raising and agriculture, especially maize growing, playing comparable roles. All of these depended on the labor of the Indian, which by 1570 had taken a compulsory form in the *repartimiento,* a system of conscript labor universally denounced by reformers in both church and state.

Theoretically, the Indians were free subjects, or, more exactly, wards of the Spanish crown, protected by an elaborate network of laws and royal decrees. They were exempt from the jurisdiction of the Spanish, as contrasted with the episcopal, Inquisition, as well as from payment of tithes. In fact, however, they were exploited, oppressed, and downtrodden. Their principal, though not exclusive, defender was the church, or, if one prefers, churchmen, especially the bishops and the mendicants. The Franciscans crusaded for the Indians in a personal, charismatic, and apocalyptic way, whereas the Dominicans preferred the cooler rationalism of theology and law. But throughout the sixteenth century the condition and status of the Indians was a question that agitated and occasionally disrupted the entire colony. It was a question that deeply concerned Pedro Moya de Contreras and the great council he convoked in 1585.

This, then, was the world Moya entered in late 1571, in which he would spend the fifteen most important years of his life. It was a world that had already begun to feel the impact of Ovando's reforms. With Moya's arrival it also began to feel the impact of the Catholic Reformation. The two movements, civil and religious, would work and grow in tandem, and Moya de Contreras would be in the forefront of both.

III. The Inquisitor of New Spain

What exactly was the Inquisition? In the widest sense it was an investigative ecclesiastical court with jurisdiction over cases involving deviation from doctrinal and moral norms. More specifically, the term can refer to any of three different tribunals. Originally, inquisitorial functions had been part of the office of individual bishops, who were often called inquisitors ordinary because the power came with the office. In the thirteenth century the papacy established a new, international tribunal, independent of the bishops and commonly called the Roman Inquisition, whose judges were usually Dominicans. After two centuries this tribunal went into decline, and it was almost extinct until it was revived by the popes of the Counter-Reformation. It never existed in the New World. The Spanish Inquisition, founded at the request of Ferdinand and Isabel in 1480, was distinct from both these tribunals.

Until the arrival of Moya de Contreras the episcopal Inquisition was the only form known in New Spain, although in the earlier years of Spanish rule its functions had sometimes been carried out by the religious orders by reason of privileges granted by Rome. Inevitably, the efficiency of inquisitorial procedures varied from bishop to bishop and according to circumstances. This unevenness tended to make it a generally more benign institution than the more rigid, centralized Holy Office of the mother country. The bishops themselves, always jealous of their powers, looked askance at the new tribunal, of which they were often highly critical. Still, the very reason for the establishment of the Holy Office in the New World was the fact that the episcopal Inquisition had not been effective—at least not effective enough to satisfy Philip II.[1] To this may be added the fact that the influence of the Counter-Reformation was being felt throughout the Catholic world. It had contributed to the revitalization of the previously moribund Roman Inquisition in Europe and had helped to renew the crusading zeal of Catholics everywhere. And, of course, it fitted in with Ovando's plan for reform, centralization, and control of the Spanish dependencies.

On 25 January 1569 Philip II issued a royal *cédula* that established the tribunal of the Holy Office of the Inquisition in New Spain. A subsequent decree of 16 August 1570 elaborated the territorial jurisdiction of the Inquisition, namely, the districts of the audiencias of Mexico, Guatemala, Nueva Galicia, and Manila.[2] Other royal orders instructed the viceroy and the audiencias to cooperate with and favor the new tribunal. A cédula of 16 August 1570 appointed Pedro Moya de Contreras the first inquisitor of New Spain. In a second cédula two days later the appointment was made in the name of Cardinal Espinosa, the grand inquisitor, with the approval of Philip II.[3]

Ovando's influence on the appointment is easily supposed. Despite this, and despite the fact that it was a clear advancement, Moya tried to refuse it. An offer of 3,000 pesos a year in salary and a canonry in the cathedral of Mexico City did not stop his protestations. He pleaded the debilitating effects of his asthma and the fact that he was deeply involved in trying to arrange a suitable marriage for his sister, who was living in a convent in Córdoba. Whether he really did not want to go to the New World or was merely following a set formula of humility, his pleading was in vain. Ovando took over the arrangements for his sister, and Moya had no choice but to accept. The licenciado Alonso de Cervantes, whom Moya had known in the Canary Islands, was appointed as prosecutor, and Pedro de los Ríos as secretary. All three men were diocesan priests or clerics, not Dominicans or religious, for the religious played only a tangential role in the new tribunal.[4] If nothing else, Ovando, who was seeking to curtail the immense powers of the orders, would have seen to that.

On 29 August 1570 Moya was in Seville and went to the Casa de Contratación, where he received his expense money of some 300 ducados.[5] He and his companions were not, however, able to depart from Sanlúcar de Barrameda until 13 November.

In the sixteenth century voyages to the New World were not something to be anticipated with enthusiasm. They were usually long and irksome and always dangerous. Passengers had to supply their own food, though the rough seas often reduced them to such a state of seasickness that little thought could be given to eating. In addition to the dangers of storm and shipwreck, there was constant and imminent peril of attack by English or French pirates. Life on board could be claustrophobic, boring, and seemingly endless.[6]

Moya's voyage was calm at first. The three men made their first stop at Santa Cruz de Tenerife in the Canaries on 20 November. Cervantes was a native of the islands, and Moya, of course, knew them from his tour of duty as maestrescuelas. They were unable to make their planned connections with the convoy commanded by Pedro Menéndez de Avilés (who a few years earlier had founded Saint Augustine, Florida). As a result they were stranded for six months before they could take passage on 2 June 1571 on one of six ships that were leaving for Española and New Spain. The voyage was uneventful until their arrival off Cuba, where Cervantes contracted a fever and died. Later, on 1 August, their ship ran aground, and Moya and Ríos escaped in a small boat with the inquisition records. Shortly thereafter they succeeded in booking passage on a small ship that had also left from Tenerife, and on it they arrived at San Juan de Ulúa on 18 August, doubtless with a great feeling of relief.[7]

The inquisitorial team then headed for Mexico City. The viceroy, Martín Enríquez de Almansa, had sent out orders that they were to be received and treated as their dignities demanded, and so their trip inland was rather like a triumphal procession. Ten leagues from the city three canons of the archdiocesan chapter met them and paid their respects in the name of that body.[8] Shortly afterward, Moya sent Ríos ahead to inform the viceroy of his coming, to present his credentials, and to ask about the proper form for entering the city, as well as about what accommodations had been prepared for them. Four leagues from the city he was met by delegates from the city council. Finally, on Wednesday, 12 September 1571, at one o' clock in the afternoon—nine months after his departure from Spain—Moya de Contreras entered Mexico City. He was met by all the dignitaries of city and church, with the notable exception of the viceroy and the audiencia. He did not view their absence as a good omen. The viceroy's excuse was that he was waiting for the day of the taking of the inquisition oath to pay the customary respects.

Moya and Ríos were lodged in the local Dominican house and there they opened the first inquisition offices. Later, after some altercations with the viceroy, they moved into more permanent headquarters selected by Enríquez, a house rented by the tribunal from Juan Velázquez de Salazar, a *regidor* who at that time was in Spain on city business. There was enough room for all the inquisition activities, including the setting up of jail cells. Moya was pleased with the viceroy's selection, but it was just about the last action of Enríquez that would please him.

Martín Enríquez de Almansa, lord of Valderrábano, was viceroy of New Spain from 1568 to 1580. He was not a firstborn son and hence did not inherit the family title, but he was a descendant of Castilian royalty on both parents' sides and connected with the highest nobility of Spain. Although he epitomized the Spanish concept of honor and service, Enríquez was a reluctant viceroy. He was sixty years old when he reached New Spain and was soon plagued by ill-health. He was an able administrator, a Catholic of strong convictions, and a humanitarian, especially in his concern for the Indians. He applied himself assiduously to the work of his office and rarely left Mexico City. His single-minded devotion to duty had caused him to leave his family in Spain, and in 1574 he was left a widower. Like his king, he personally attended to the smallest details of government. His many excellent qualities, however, were offset by outbursts of temper and a decided brusqueness in dealing with others. His strong sense of honor and position once led him to rebuke Ovando for not having addressed him with sufficient respect. This same attitude determined his attitude toward the viceregal office, and he was universally praised for having raised its prestige to new heights.[9]

If Moya had initially been bothered by the failure of the viceroy to meet him at the outskirts of the city, he was not in the least encouraged by his first interview with him. Like Moya, Martín Enríquez was punctilious about points of ceremony. Nor did he look kindly on the intrusion of a new and alien jurisdiction into his territory. The arrival of the Spanish Inquisition was upsetting a delicate and well-balanced arrangement of local power. Also, like so many of the viceroys, he found himself in frequent conflict with his ecclesiastical counterpart. At their first interview, Moya noted, a large crowd of spectators had gathered to witness the first encounter. Moya complained sharply to Ovando that he was kept standing and not asked to cover his head, as if he were just another of the viceregal retainers. The viceroy, he wrote, spoke to him "with great authority and abruptness," and Moya quickly took his leave, saying that he had come only in order to fulfill his obligation. In a second interview on the following day Enríquez was more polite, but that did not help. Moya smarted under the realization that the viceroy had won the first joust. Relations between the two men had gotten off to a bad start and would remain bad as long as they were in New Spain together.[10]

The sources of friction were many. The civil authorities chafed at the ceremonies and protocol of the Inquisition, which they found annoying and demeaning. They were required to participate in the autos de fe, but their precedence and responsibilities were assigned them by the tribunal. The inquisitors designated where the viceroy and the audiencia would sit and stand during the ceremonies, and the civil officers had to accompany the inquisitors back to their headquarters after the auto de fe was over. A preoccupation with precedence and ceremonies was characteristic of all Spaniards of that age, and the occasions for conflict were thus many and varied. Relations with the audiencia were complicated by the fact that the latter body was also a law court, and there were numerous quarrels over jurisdiction.[11]

The sparring between the viceroy and the new inquisitor was endless and at times descended to pettiness. Moya brought with him a royal cédula of 1571 that gave the Inquisition authority over government officials. Enríquez complained that such a thing had never been done in Spain. The new inquisitor also issued an order that no one could leave New Spain without a license from the Inquisition. Surprisingly, Enríquez did not contest it. He did, however, try to avoid taking the public oath in support of the Inquisition, but eventually had to yield. He also wanted to decree the day for the oath taking personally before assigning a permanent residence to the Inquisition. Moya held his ground and won on this point also. The viceroy in turn adamantly refused to permit the Inquisition's *alguacil* to carry his baton of office when he entered the viceroy's presence, holding that it was incumbent on the Holy Office to recognize him as its equal, if not its superior. Enríquez would not yield on this point, even when Moya pointed to the precedent of Philip II's own court. The viceroy also refused to allow the Inquisition's notaries to bring royal cédulas to him personally, demanding that they go through the regular machinery of government. Because Moya did not want inquisition papers to pass through the hands of lower bureaucrats, he resisted this demand and apparently won his point.[12]

The new inquisitor was equally successful in preventing the viceroy from giving jurisdiction over cases that involved appeals to Spain to the audiencia. In turn, Enríquez refused to agree to Moya's choice of officials for the Inquisition and tried to impose two members of his household as alguaciles. Moya was incensed, both over the intrusion into his jurisdiction and because one of the two lacked the requisite *limpieza de sangre* (proof of the absence of Jewish or Moorish ancestry). Martín Enríquez in turn complained that Moya was appointing only wealthy *encomenderos* as familiares. These men, he said, were convincing the Indians that the Inquisition had jurisdiction over them. The ultimate indignity was that the viceroy would not allow the inquisition officials a place in the cathedral sanctuary but tried to banish them to the choir stalls. Moya managed, however, to secure a royal order (13 March 1572) directing that inquisitors should have good seats in the cathedral on Sundays and feast days "as befits ministers of so holy an office."[13]

In view of the formidable reputation that the Spanish Inquisition has always enjoyed in polemical literature and fiction, it is surprising to find that the civil authorities treated it so arbitrarily. Moya complained vehemently to Ovando that the viceroy, despite all his protestations to the contrary, definitely treated the Inquisition "with contempt."[14] Enríquez would later be rebuked by Ovando for this, but the rebuke seems only to have inflamed his dislike for Moya all the more. The squabbles were petty on the surface, but they were also symptomatic. The inquisitor and the viceroy each knew that the first days of the new tribunal would determine its eventual position in the colonial power structure. Each man was jealous of his own jurisdiction and had strong ideas about the nature of his office. They were jockeying for position. Eventually the crown had to intervene and restrict the authority of both.

The two were finally able to agree on a date for the formal oath taking and the installation of the Holy Office in New Spain. On 2 November 1571 a procession issued from the inquisitorial offices, complete with officials, a herald, and a band of *chirimías*, trumpets, sackbuts, and drums. A proclamation was read seven times, summoning "all persons whatsoever . . . both men and women, of whatever condition and quality they may be, from the age of twelve upward" to be present in the cathedral the following Sunday to hear the oath and swear to it.[15]

On Sunday, 4 November, the ceremony began with a solemn procession from the headquarters of the Inquisition to the cathedral. Moya was accompanied by the viceroy and senior oidor of the audiencia, preceded by standard-bearers, officials of church and state, and the faculty of the university. At the cathedral door they were met by the archdiocesan chapter and by representatives of the three major religious orders, the Franciscans, Dominicans, and Augustinians. The mass was begun with a sermon preached by Fray Bartolomé de Ledesma, a Dominican and the administrator of the archdiocese for the infirm archbishop, Alonso de Montúfar. Prior to the elevation of the host, Pedro de los Ríos went to the pulpit and read an instruction from the king that the Inquisition was under the protection of the "royal arm." Moya's title as inquisitor was read out together with the oath he had sworn on 26 October to carry out his office faithfully and justly and to guard the secrecy required by the tribunal.[16] He then read the edict of the new inquisitor that no one present was to admit or consent to be admitted among them any heretics without denouncing them to the Holy Office. At the conclusion of the edict he read the words of the oath and the assembled throng gave their assent. He then went down to a velvet-covered table set up in the sanctuary, with the book of the gospels and a gold-plated silver cross lying on it. Martín Enríquez put his right hand on the gospels and swore the oath, albeit with ill grace. After this the edict of grace was read whereby everyone was given sixty days (instead of the more customary thirty) in which to decide whether or not they had committed any of the various acts that had been explained in detail and to make them known. Moya later expressed his satisfaction with the entire ceremony and its results.[17]

Although Moya had won the skirmish on the oath taking, he suffered a setback when Enríquez would not permit the reading of the catalogue of forbidden books in the cathedral. As a result, this had to be done in the chapel of a Franciscan convent, probably that of San Francisco. Moya also issued an edict against forbidden books and commanded a visitation and inspection of all bookstores. All were forbidden to read the prohibited works, and no bookseller could have them or sell them under pain of excommunication. The same edict also called for an inspection of all books in monasteries and religious houses, and even went so far as to demand inspection of images and holy pictures that might have writing on them.[18]

In the Counter-Reformation milieu the censoring and prohibition of books was of paramount importance and had come to be one of the major functions of the Inquisition. In 1573 Moya issued an official index of forbidden books for New Spain. The tribunal was also very watchful of printers, especially because so many of these were foreigners. In 1571 Moya prosecuted Pedro Ocharte or Ochart, a Frenchman, for having read and praised a book that contained Protestant ideas. Ocharte was acquitted after torture, but another printer, Juan Ortiz, was reconciled in the auto de fe of 1574, fined 200 pesos, and banished permanently from New Spain.[19]

In addition to all this, Moya arranged that no one should leave the country without having obtained the permission of the Holy Office as well as the usual licenses obtained from the government.

Numerous denunciations and cases now came before the Holy Office. One biographer says that many of the bishops hastened to turn over cases that had been initiated before the episcopal Inquisition, but this statement must be treated with caution.[20] Many bishops were even less enthusiastic about the Holy Office than Enríquez was.

In the first years of its operation the Inquisition conducted over 170 trials and investigations. Inventories were drawn up, research was done into previous cases, documents were reclaimed from private possession, and lists of reconciled and penanced heretics were drawn up and indexed. The tribunal operated with a high degree of dispatch and efficiency. In all of this Moya seems to have been the prime mover and to have shown that same sense of organization and administration that marked him later as archbishop, visitador, and viceroy.

During the first decade of its existence in New Spain, the Inquisition concentrated mostly, though not exclusively, on Protestants, especially French and English corsairs. Many of the latter were survivors of Sir John Hawkins's ill-fated visit to the Mexican coast in 1568, when the English expedition was destroyed by Enríquez. More than a hundred of the survivors had scattered throughout New Spain and were viewed by the Inquisition as a threat to Catholicism and an avant-garde of Lutheranism, the catchall term for Protestantism. Though living over a large area of the colony, most were eventually rounded up and arrested by the inquisition police.

The tribunal also dealt with French corsairs. The most famous of these was Pierre Sanfoy, who with four companions was brought to Mexico City in 1571 to stand trial. The Sanfoy incident is significant because he had been protected for some time by Enríquez, who claimed that his case fell under civil, rather than inquisitorial, jurisdiction. It was necessary for the king to outline legal procedures for the viceroy in order to assure that Sanfoy be turned over to the Inquisition. As the viceroy had already been rebuked by the crown for his disrespect to Moya (on 24 March 1572), he yielded the prisoner to the Inquisition. The king had emphasized the need for the religious and civil authorities to present a united front.

The English and French pirates formed the bulk of the cases at the first auto de fe held in the New World, which took place on 28 February 1574.[21] On 8 February a public proclamation was made of the coming event. Notification was given to the viceroy and the civil and ecclesiastical *cabildos*. Word was sent to places as distant as Oaxaca and Veracruz. The crowd that eventually showed up was the largest ever gathered in one spot in the memory of most colonials, and the resulting auto de fe was one of the largest ever held anywhere. A platform was set up at a corner of the cathedral that commanded two squares so that the maximum number of people could be accommodated. The bishop of Tlaxcala, Gómez de Carvajal, preached the sermon. The procession of penitents came from the offices of the Inquisition, followed in the middle by Moya de Contreras, with the viceroy on his right, and the oidores in order of seniority. The officials took their places on the platform. The viceroy, audiencia, and officials of the Holy Office sat under a canopy. As a sign of his rank, the viceroy had a chair of velvet and two cushions of the same material on the seat at his feet; the inquisitors and the audiencia had seats of leather.

The inquisitors and oidores probably became acutely aware of their leather chairs before the day was out, because the reading of the causes lasted from seven in the morning until six in the evening. The accused wore *sambenitos,* special cloaks that identified them as penitents. They also wore collars around their necks and carried candles in their right hands. At this auto de fe sentences were meted out to Sanfoy, Juan Ortiz, and seven English pirates. Sanfoy was given two hundred lashes and sentenced to six years in the galleys, almost the equivalent of a death sentence. Of the Englishmen, one was burned at the stake, one was garroted, two were sent to the galleys, one was sent to prison (but apparently allowed comparative freedom in later life), and two, including their chronicler, Miles Philips, were sentenced to three years of labor in religious houses. Besides the pirates, numerous others were punished for moral offenses, such as bigamy.[22]

Under Moya's leadership the Holy Office also dealt with moral lapses such as bigamy and blasphemy. The trials of *judaizantes*—that is, of those accused of continuing to practice the Jewish religion—really began after his term. The auto de fe of 1574 was the first and last at which Moya participated personally. Because of his appointment as archbishop of Mexico, he stopped acting as inquisitor from October 1574 on.[23] Hence he did not participate in the auto de fe of 1575 as inquisitor but as archbishop. It is ironic that as archbishop he refused to take part in the auto de fe of 1577 on the grounds that he did not like the place the inquisitors had assigned to him. Actually he was indignant because the tribunal had taken one of the cases from his jurisdiction.

It is not easy to summarize Moya's activities as inquisitor or to evaluate them in historical or even human terms. Certainly he was a man of the law, and his attention to law and proper procedure helped to exonerate persons who had been falsely accused. Under his guidance the Inquisition of New Spain was a legal tribunal, not a witch-hunt. If one accepts that the Inquisition can be justified in some way, Moya emerges as one of the best of the inquisitors. He was a man of his age. As a Spaniard and a Counter-Reformation cleric, he was horrified by heresy, which he regarded as a threat to the very fabric of society. Considerations such as these, however, are offset by a reading of the minutes of the tortures suffered by men such as Ocharte and Ortiz while Moya sat by waiting for their confessions and ordering additional jars of water poured down their throats. There was a certain cold-bloodedness in his character that would reappear during the visita. Perhaps this is a problem that modern historians, like Bravo Ugarte before them, can never resolve.

The detection and pursuit of the unorthodox was not the only reason for the Inquisition's existence in New Spain. Its introduction at a late stage in the development of colonial institutions not only upset the political balance of power but was also a definite shift of ecclesiastical authority toward the crown and the mother country. It meant the removal from the bishops of one of the powers that had traditionally been identified with their office and that they had freely used for half a century. Although the Indians remained under the episcopal Inquisition, the Holy Office was now the chief instrument of doctrinal and moral control. It was one more step, like many others that would follow within the next few years, in the direction of centralization and consolidation of civil and religious authority.

One lasting effect of Moya's three years as inquisitor was his hostility to Martín Enríquez. In one sense the two men were playing out the roles assigned them by the crown: counter-balancing each other in the power structure of the Spanish empire. In another sense they represented two different points of view regarding that power structure. Basically they were two strong personalities of divergent beliefs and stations, squaring off over certain issues and building a lifelong enmity. The issues would change during the eight years of their association, but the personal antagonisms would remain.

Whatever the final verdict may be on Moya de Contreras's term as inquisitor, it was really rather short, for he quickly vaulted to a higher and more responsible position, that of archbishop of Mexico.

IV. The Archbishop of Mexico

Cristóbal Gutiérrez de Luna, Moya de Contreras's first biographer, who was also a personal friend and eyewitness to many of the events in his life, states quite clearly that Moya was not ordained to the priesthood until 1571. Given the conditions of that age, it is possible that he held most of his ecclesiastical positions while still in minor orders, or perhaps in the major orders of subdiaconate or diaconate. It may well be that he was a deacon before coming to New Spain, because Gutiérrez de Luna makes no mention of Moya's receiving any of the major orders in Mexico City. In addition, his ordination to the priesthood so quickly after his arrival would indicate that he had received the major orders and so did not have to observe the *interstitia,* or intervals between the reception of the various orders, required by canon law. (These, however, were not always observed in practice, and dispensations could easily be obtained).[1] Whatever the precise order in which he was ordained, Moya was very quickly made archbishop of Mexico and was the first diocesan priest to hold that position. Within the space of three years he had risen from an obscure provincial position to one of the most important ecclesiastical posts in the New World. His rise was rapid, but it was hardly accidental.

Since 1554 the archbishop of Mexico had been Alonso de Montúfar, a Dominican who had been born near Granada about the year 1489 and had entered his order at the age of fifteen. After holding various teaching and inquisitorial posts, Montúfar was appointed to the Mexican archbishopric and consecrated in 1553, but he did not take possession of his see—which had been vacant since the death of Zumárraga in 1548—until the following year. Montúfar had to work under trying conditions. He convoked and presided over the first two Mexican Provincial Councils (1555 and 1565) and played an important role in the opening of the Royal and Pontifical University. Like many bishops of the time, he found himself in chronic conflict with the priests of his archdiocese, especially the chapter, and with the religious orders, especially the Franciscans. The chapter, under the leadership of its archdeacon, Juan Zurnero, was particularly troublesome and at one time had even tried to have Montúfar declared incompetent. These difficulties, plus his advanced age and many illnesses, tended to make Montúfar's last years very unhappy, and for a large part of his term the real direction of the archdiocese was entrusted to an administrator, Bartolomé de Ledesma, later bishop of Oaxaca. The accusation that Montúfar was a mediocrity, who seemed all the more so in comparison with Zumárraga, is unfair, not only in view of the enormous problems that the second archbishop had to face but also in view of the advanced age at which he received his office.[2]

In 1572 Philip II named Moya coadjutor bishop of Mexico *cum iure successionis* (with right of succession). Shortly thereafter Montúfar died and was buried in the priory of Santo Domingo among the men of the order to which he belonged. On 22 June 1573 the king notified Viceroy Enríquez that he was to direct the chapter to yield the administration of the archdiocese to Moya while they waited for the arrival of the bulls of appointment. It had become customary for a bishop-elect to assume the rule of a diocese before his confirmation or consecration, partly because of the long delay involved in sending to Rome for the bulls of appointment. Enríquez's feelings at the elevation of his adversary can only be imagined. Ovando had already written to Moya on 15 June to ask him to continue as inquisitor, at least until the pending cases had been completed.[3]

Moya made his first appearance before the archdiocesan chapter on 30 October 1573, at which time Zurnero transferred the administration of the archbishopric to him in the name of that body. The papal bulls of appointment were dispatched from Spain in April 1574, but they were delayed in transit. In August Moya received some authorized copies from Havana and on that basis decided to go ahead with his consecration, even though he would have preferred to have the originals.[4] These copies were presented to the chapter on 27 August, and on the following 8 September the archbishop-elect went through the formal ceremony of taking possession of his see. Earlier he had received word from the inquisitor general that since he could no longer assist at the Holy Office he was being replaced by Alonso Ganero de Avalos, the Inquisition's prosecutor. On 28 September he personally presented the originals of the papal bulls (dated 15 June 1573) to the chapter and made the profession of faith required of all bishops-elect. Since the pallium had also arrived from Rome by that time, he set his consecration for 21 November.[5]

For some reason the consecration was delayed and did not take place until 5 December 1574. The consecrating bishop was Antonio de Morales of Puebla, and the bishops of Tlaxcala, Nueva Galicia, Yucatán, and Chiapas were also present. On 8 December, the feast of the Immaculate Conception, another ceremony was held for the formal bestowal of the pallium.[6]

These ceremonies were great public events, celebrated with both religious and civil pomp. One highlight of the occasion was the presentation of one of the first dramas written in New Spain by a criollo, something of a landmark in Mexican literary history. It was called *Desposorio espiritual entre el Pastor Pedro y la Iglesia Mexicana* (Spiritual Betrothal Between the Shepherd Pedro and the Church of Mexico) and was written by Juan Pérez y Ramírez, a descendant of a conquistador. The drama was a pastoral allegory of the type so favored by authors and audiences of that time and so wearying to modern readers. The players were dressed as shepherds and shepherdesses, with names like Faith, Hope, Charity, Grace, Prudent, and Modest. There was also a figure representing Divine Love, and the inevitable clown was included for comic relief. The entire work was highly laudatory of the new archbishop.

> Let the earth rejoice, the sea and the sky
> from which so much good has come to us
> and such glory and consolation to the soul.
>
> Blessed be the earth where he was born
> and blessed be the sea which he has traversed
> to the land that has deserved so much.[7]

Amid the general rejoicing Moya detected one sour note: Enríquez and the entire audiencia arose and left the cathedral before the performance. Furthermore, when Moya had walked by the viceroy in procession and given him a blessing, Enríquez had taken no more notice than if the archbishop had been a "simple cleric."[8] Enríquez was still smart-ing from the rebuke administered by the crown for the disrespect that he had shown Moya at the time of the latter's arrival in New Spain.

There was an additional point of tension. Acting under royal orders, Enríquez had just introduced the *alcabala* (general sales tax) into New Spain, an act that had alienated not only the merchants but also some of his most devoted supporters. Despite what Moya later wrote, the tax was unpopular in the colony. Most merchants feared that the percentage would rise and felt that they were being bled by the various exactions of the crown. The viceroy did not like introducing the tax, but as the king's chief representative he had no choice. Moya was unsympathetic to the alcabala, partly because of his strong sympathy for the criollos, but he was not in the position of having to impose it or publicly defend it. Hence in addition to the animosities inherent in their offices and the bad relations that had existed from the beginning, a situation was developing in which Moya could be viewed as the defender of the criollos against the viceroy. He seems to have been the first archbishop to be cast in this role, though it became quite common in the following century when prelates would use their criollo partisans as support against the viceroys. One of the celebrations for the new archbishop was to provide the material for an explosion.

The celebrations and theatrical presentations continued for some time. Another dramatic highlight was a *coloquio* written by Fernán González de Eslava and dedicated to the archbishop.[9] It was a prose work interspersed with music and again heavily weighted with alle-gory. This time Adulation and Vainglory strove with Diligence, Care, Prudence, Joy, and Courage. Moya, a man of pronounced literary tastes, enjoyed these productions very much and arranged for a whole series of *farsas* and *entremeses* to be given in the cathedral immediately after the mass at which he received the pallium. One of these short comedy interludes provoked a famous clash between the archbishop and the viceroy and poisoned their relationship still further, while keeping the populace keyed up with rumors and gossip.[10]

The skits were presented on a stage set up next to the main altar, with Moya, the bishops of Tlaxcala, Yucatán, Chiapas, and Nueva Galicia, the viceroy, the audiencia, and a very large crowd of people present. One of the pieces was a satire on the alcabala in which a collector went to the house of a poor man and in a series of humorous dialogues tried to explain what the alcabala was. Finally he confiscated the bedclothing, while the poor man's wife and children, left almost naked, made a great commotion. It was a bit of crude and raucous comedy, broadly acted by a mulatto comedian, and it provoked loud and derisive laughter. Enríquez, not noted for his lighthearted sense of humor, was upset over both the subject matter and the locale of the farce and what he considered to be an attack on royal policies. He blamed the new archbishop for the whole thing and seemed quite happy to be able to put his adversary in his place. "I might forgive him all the other short skits, but this I could not stomach," he wrote to Ovando.[11]

Enríquez denounced the skit and the archbishop to the Council of the Indies and took some drastic measures of his own. Two days after the performance, he secured from the audiencia an order that such productions were not to be presented in churches without the prior approval of the audiencia. Although this could have been viewed as a flagrant attack on ecclesiastical freedom, Moya did not contest it. He was content to say that he had not read the script ahead of time but had turned the task of censorship over to Domingo de Salazar, the Inquisition's censor of books. If there had been any scandal, it was either because of improvisation by the actors or because of the prejudices of those who watched. He pointed out that the public had enjoyed the skits, a fact that was already abundantly clear to the viceroy and the oidores.[12] Moya was obviously worried about his position in the whole matter and realized he could be cast in a bad light. He had already begun to distance himself from responsibility for the presentation and to spread the blame. He now began writing long letters of self-justification to the Council of the Indies, claiming that the farce had been brought from Castile by one of the bishops and that it had been popular in the mother country. He considered it harmless amusement.

The whole affair was worsened when a placard was placed on the door of the cathedral denouncing Enríquez as the author of the alcabala and other unpopular taxes. The viceroy sent a notary to remove the offending broadside and tear it to pieces.[13]

The audiencia, as happy as the viceroy to have an opportunity to bolster its authority and keep an adversary in an awkward position, issued an order on 20 December asking the archbishop to command all clerics to give testimony concerning this affair and to order those who failed to do so to be imprisoned in solitary confinement. Behaving as if they had uncovered a gross case of lèse-majesté, the oidores began a hunt among the poets, writers, and clerics of the city, trying to find anyone who might have been involved. Juan de Victoria, the master of the cathedral chapel, was arrested for having presented the comedy, as was the mulatto comedian for having acted in it.

On that same day (20 December) Fernán González de Eslava was arrested at his home by the officials of the audiencia, and despite his protests that he was a cleric (though not yet a priest) he was imprisoned in the archdiocesan jail under heavy guard. The following morning he was taken through the streets to the audiencia's criminal chamber (*sala del crimen*). This was the second time he had been paraded through the streets under guard, and the news of his arrest spread quickly throughout the city. In the *sala* he was met by two oidores, who took him to the room where prisoners were judicially tortured, so that during his interrogation his imagination could conjure up what might lie in store for him. He was repeatedly questioned under oath about his part in the coloquio and what he knew about the libelous placard, but he heatedly denied any knowledge of the latter. After signing a copy of his testimony, he was returned to prison, where he remained for six days without being given any reason for his imprisonment. On 5 January he was released without comment. In the meantime rumors circulated that he had been tortured, sent to the galleys, or burned at the stake. Even after his release he was kept under house arrest. Although Eslava was a cleric under his jurisdiction, Moya seems to have done nothing to secure his release.[14]

Victoria was eventually released on bail. The mulatto comedian, the most visible and defenseless of the various participants, was punished severely. After that the excitement seemed to subside.

In his letters to Spain Moya claimed not to know the reasons for the viceroy's hostility, although he suspected that the religious orders (with whom the archbishop's relations were already bad) were inciting him to it. The archbishop, of course, fully understood the reasons for the viceroy's enmity. Moya was definitely worried, both because he might have gone too far and because he knew that he could be made to look like the villain in the affair. He was correct. Both he and the viceroy were rebuked for their roles in the turmoil, but Moya suffered the more. The Council of the Indies ordered that "the archbishop is to conform in all matters with the viceroy and if he does not, he is to be reprimanded . . . he is not to do a thing without first consulting the viceroy." The king's words to Moya were especially blunt:

> It has displeased us, and your answer that you did not see these presentations and delegated the examination of them does not excuse you. For you should know that negligence is a fault in prelates, and so I charge you to see to it for the future both that you try to give in public the good example that is proper and that the ecclesiastical persons of your diocese do the same.[15]

This slightly ludicrous affair was once again a symptom. It showed not only the tensions between civil and church officials that were all too ready to surface but also the isolated and narrow atmosphere of

Mexico City, in which the smallest details of protocol and privilege took on unwarranted importance—and where excitement of this sort provided welcome entertainment. The king's rebuke was an inauspicious beginning for Moya, and he took it seriously. He was not only more circumspect in his subsequent dealings with the viceroy and audiencia, but he sometimes came close to timidity. It was to be many years before he would again feel secure enough to challenge the local authority more openly. Enríquez did not emerge unscathed either. Having suffered two rebukes from Spain for his dealings with Moya he sought to resign in late 1574. His resignation was not accepted, but he continued his efforts until he succeeded in 1580.

AN ARCHBISHOP'S LIFE

From 1575 until 1583—that is, from Ovando's death until Moya's appointment as visitador—Moya de Contreras concentrated on being archbishop of Mexico. He avoided direct involvement in civil affairs and contented himself with the care of his archdiocese.

Moya was in many ways a new kind of archbishop. Tridentine bishops were men who began the reform of the church with the reform of themselves. Turning their backs on the wealth and ostentation of Renaissance prelates, they tried to live poorly and simply. People expected this of bishops who had formerly belonged to religious orders, but it was still a novelty among diocesan (or secular) priests. Despite their frequent severity and even puritanism, men like Moya stressed service and dedication, though always within an institutional framework. They were guided and governed by the decrees of Trent and pursued reform with lawbook in hand.

Moya's house was more like a monastery than an episcopal palace. His retinue was small, consisting mostly of the sons of nobles in Mexico City itself. During the day he habitually stepped outside to see if there were any poor persons on whom he might bestow alms. He gave away so much of his income that he was short of money throughout his life. His disconcerting habit of giving away household goods to anyone in need was a constant source of frustration to his majordomo. Once, when the archbishop had given away some silver plate, the majordomo blamed the pages for its disappearance. Moya informed him with a smile, "Don't blame them, because they really did not take it, rather a secret thief whom God has placed in this house. Let it be enough to say that it is good that you do not know who it is."[16]

As archbishop he continued to exercise many of the functions of an ordinary parish priest. During Lent he habitually heard confessions in the cathedral and made a special effort to have the Indians and blacks come to him. In 1575 he undertook the study of Nahuatl and was soon proficient enough that he could both converse and hear confessions in it. He often went on sick calls, even at night and in the worst kinds of weather.[17]

Both for his own sake and for that of his clergy he organized regular courses in moral theology, which were conducted in his residence. To teach them he turned neither to the university nor to the many learned religious in the city, but to the Jesuit Pedro Sánchez. (The Jesuits represented both the new reform and the new approach to theology.) The archbishop himself attended these courses as a simple auditor. Because of these conferences he came to realize his own need to learn systematic theology and so again turned to the Jesuits. He undertook private study with the Jesuit Pedro de Ortigosa, a close friend and advisor whom he always revered as his master. The archbishop is supposed to have remarked that after his courses with Ortigosa he regretted the years he had spent in the study of law, because theology had shown him how empty it was.[18]

It is surprising to a modern reader that a man should begin to study theology, which nowadays would be considered a prerequisite, after becoming archbishop. However, in the days when the Tridentine reforms, especially the establishment of seminaries, had not made themselves uniformly felt throughout the Catholic world, it was possible and even common for a man to be ordained to the priesthood with no more than a degree in the liberal arts or canon law, and in many cases without any formal education at all. The paths to the ministry were informal and haphazard at times, and Moya still had a foot in two worlds, the Old and the New.

He also held literary conferences and discussions in his home to which he invited doctors from the university and masters from among the religious orders. They often dined with him, and he would enjoy their literate conversation, which he artfully directed toward scholastic disputation. He had Ortigosa send some of the brighter students from the Jesuit college to hold conferences with him during his free time, and during the autumn vacation he would often visit the students to talk to them and ascertain what they had learned during the school year.[19]

As a Counter-Reformation and Tridentine archbishop, Moya had entered a situation that was still very pre-Trent in character. Aside from the vexed question of the religious orders and their jurisdiction (discussed in the following chapter), there were other questions of reform and organization that demanded his time and attention. The most pressing of these involved his clergy.

THE CLERGY OF MEXICO

One of his first concerns was the archdiocesan chapter. This body acted as a board of advisors and helped the archbishop with the administration of the archdiocese. Inevitably there were points of friction over questions of jurisdiction, the extent and need of consultation, and financial matters. In New Spain most of the chapters were highly independent, claiming the right to transact the full business of the diocese whenever the bishop was absent, whereas the bishops maintained that their presence was necessary for validity and legality. In addition there were struggles over the extent of a chapter's control of money and property.[20] Because the chapter also ruled the diocese *sede vacante* (in the interim when there was no appointed bishop), it was possible for it to accumulate a power that an incoming prelate like Moya would find unacceptable. The resulting disputes were sometimes acrimonious in the extreme, and the bishops did not always emerge victorious. Antonio de Hervías of Vera Paz was exiled from his diocese by the audiencia of Guatemala because of the intrigues of his canons, and Juan de Medina Rincón resigned his see because of his difficulties with his chapter.[21]

The canons were sometimes less than worthy of their offices. They were often appointed directly by the king without any consultation with the bishop. They merely presented their letters of appointment, which the bishop had to accept. Zumárraga had complained of an appointee who had to come to Mexico City with his mistress, whom he called his sister. Another had brought four young Indian girls disguised as boys. The members of the chapter were well paid, but despite this they were often notorious for their greedy ways. In Moya's time the chapter of the archdiocese of Mexico was led by Juan Zurnero, the archdeacon. Because the post of dean had been vacant for many years, he had been able to make himself the veritable ruler of the chapter and even styled himself "the protector of the chapter."[22]

The age and prolonged illnesses of Archbishop Montúfar had created a power vacuum into which Zurnero moved. In 1571 he led a movement to have Montúfar declared incompetent and a candidate of the chapter's choice installed as coadjutor with effective rule of the archdiocese. The cabal was aborted only when the provisor had Zurnero thrown into the ecclesiastical jail.[23]

When Moya took office, he found a chapter that had arrogated to itself many functions and was accustomed to acting as an autonomous unit. It handled all the cathedral accounts and had assumed the right of appointing and controlling the majordomo in charge of all cathedral income. From this it had moved to assuming control of all the temporal goods of the archdiocese. Under Zurnero's leadership it had grown accustomed to making constitutions and to ruling the archdiocese as if the archbishop did not exist. Moya summed up the situation by describing the chapter as *tan enseñoreado*.[24]

Although he complained vehemently to Ovando about this situation, the new archbishop was determined not to provoke the chapter into a confrontation. He preferred the way of diplomacy. He worked to have the best men appointed to the chapter and made a strong and sustained effort to see that the canonries were filled with criollos.[25] His approach was justified: as early as September 1575 he could write to Ovando that his relations with the chapter were good and that he treated it with respect.[26] Though it is not clear whether he was able to reduce the chapter's power to any extent, his letters are refreshingly free of complaints about it and of those unseemly squabbles that disfigured the relations between so many other bishops and their clergy.

A primary concern of the Council of Trent had been the improvement of the condition, status, and education of the diocesan clergy. This same concern is a constant leitmotif in the letters and reports that Moya sent back to Spain. On 1 September 1574 he wrote to Ovando about the need to implement the decrees of Trent in his archdiocese because of the freedom and laxity of the diocesan clergy. He suggested that the king send a cédula commanding the viceroy and audiencia to favor the implementation of Trent.[27] It was this concern for the condition of the clergy that prompted him to be so favorable to the work of the Jesuits, whom he saw as the instruments for priestly formation and education in his archdiocese.

One of the most revealing reports that the archbishop ever sent to the Council of the Indies was a person-by-person evaluation of the clergy of the archdiocese of Mexico, written on 24 March 1575.[28] In it he gave a brief description and summary of each diocesan priest under his administration. These descriptions are succinct, often tantalizingly vague, and very subjective, yet they show not only his concern for the clergy but also some of the problems he encountered with them.

Of the 156 priests listed by the archbishop, sixty-eight were peninsulars and eighty were criollos. The birthplaces of eight were not given, perhaps because they were foreigners. Only one of the priests was specifically designated a mestizo, although it is possible that there were others who passed as Europeans. The higher dignities, such as cathedral canonries, were more or less evenly divided between peninsulars and criollos. Eleven peninsulars and eight criollos occupied the higher dignities, with peninsulars holding the three highest posts below that of archbishop. Throughout the colonial period criollos were only rarely able to obtain the very highest ecclesiastical positions, but they were at this time beginning to fill all the lower or second-echelon positions, a control they would consolidate and retain throughout the colonial epoch.

As to the quality of these priests, there are interesting indications, though the lack of comprehensive information makes generalizations somewhat suspect. The foremost problem was lack of education. No less than fifty of the priests were classified as being educationally deficient in some way, some to the point of illiteracy. In this regard the peninsulars and criollos were almost evenly divided. This is rather surprising, as one would assume that there were more educational opportunities available in Spain. It also raises questions about the quality and motivation of those diocesan priests who migrated to the New World. Well-educated peninsular priests had the least incentive for leaving the country.

A proportionately higher number of criollos (though still small in comparison with the total) were listed as being deficient in Latin, perhaps understandable in a colonial situation. Three criollos, one of whom was the illegitimate son of a former oidor, were described as being illiterate or almost so, whereas none of the peninsulars were described in this way. Two peninsulars were "mass priests," that is, incapable of fulfilling any ministry except that of saying mass. One peninsular priest and one criollo had no other occupations than singing in the cathedral choir and playing in its orchestra. Sixteen peninsulars and forty-four criollos were listed as being able to speak Nahuatl, a proportion that is not surprising for those born and raised in New Spain. Two peninsulars and nine criollos could speak Otomí, two peninsulars could speak Huastec, and one Matlatzinca. One peninsular priest, brought over at an early age and raised in New Spain, could speak nothing but Otomí. About half a dozen of the priests were former members of religious orders.

As for those whose relations with women were or had been suspect, the peninsulars and criollos were again evenly divided. Those who neglected their priestly duties for worldly pursuits, such as owning mines and ranches, or who were accused by the archbishop of being avaricious and greedy, were all, however, peninsular. A picture emerges of peninsular priests of low education and scant prospects in Spain who migrated to the New World more for the sake of gain than of religion, or who were corrupted by the opportunities for good living in New Spain.

Although about a third of the clergy were criticized by the archbishop for some defect of character or education, it is significant and a little surprising that the percentage was not higher. Conditions in the colony were new and strange, even after half a century. Before Trent there was no formal system for educating and training priests, the general level of the diocesan clergy was rather low, and the Catholic Reformation had yet to make its full impact. Moya was fortunate to have had as many good priests as he did. And this was in the "church of friars" in which the preponderance of work had been done by the mendicant orders.

Of the problems that the archbishop discovered among his clergy, that of ignorance troubled him the most. One solution was the educational work of the Jesuits, who had arrived in New Spain in September 1572. He praised them highly and saw them as the source of good priests for the future. In fact, Moya pinned the hopes of his archdiocese on their work, a feature that marks him as very much a man of the Catholic Reformation.

Another solution was to guarantee that the men appointed to the various ecclesiastical livings, called benefices, were the best. For this reason the Ordenanza del Patronazgo of 1574, whatever else can be said about it, was a godsend. It regularized and detailed the process of appointment to benefices, enabling the archbishop to declare benefices open, to appoint examiners for candidates, and, most important, to participate more directly in the choice of candidates. The bestowing of benefices was henceforth to be through a process of competition (*oposición*) and examination rather than by appointment or maneuvers on the part of the viceroy and audiencia.[29]

Despite this, most of the bishops were not pleased by the increased regalism, centralization, and intrusion of civil authority into church life that was codified in the Ordenanza. The reaction of most was to protest, but it was not, as one modern work claims, "an absolutely unanimous reaction."[30] One exception was Moya. He approved of the Ordenanza, although he later came to doubt the practicality of one or two of its articles. On 20 October 1574 he wrote to Ovando to express his happiness with it because it had not only put the religious in their place but also provided for the awarding of benefices, including *doctrinas* (Indian parishes generally staffed by religious), to the diocesan clergy, to whom, in his opinion, they properly belonged. Among the good effects that he cited was that it would reward the criollos and "encourage them to put aside laziness and vice (which they now commonly embrace) and devote themselves to study and to the Mexican and Otomí languages, which are the theology most useful for the natives." It was one of the few times that the archbishop ever expressed the popular stereotype of the criollos.[31]

If Moya was happy over his strengthened position, Viceroy Enríquez was correspondingly irritated. He disliked the idea of losing some of his patronal power. As a partisan of the religious against the bishops, a stand he now began to assume and that became standard for most later viceroys, he was opposed to their losing any of their Indian parishes or churches of ease. So the stage was set for yet another confrontation.

Moya's tactic was to proceed slowly in declaring benefices open for competition. Many were small, remote, and poor. He believed that before any widescale collation could take place, the geographical areas would have to be consolidated so as to equalize not only the areas of responsibility but also the salaries. This inevitably included some of the churches of which the friars had charge or which they visited. The only alternatives would be to demand that the encomenderos provide better salaries for the *beneficados* or to continue allowing the Indians to make donations of food to their priests, a practice Enríquez had recently forbidden on the grounds that it was open to abuse.[32]

At first the viceroy was opposed to these changes, although he vacillated in his opposition. Behind the viceroy Moya claimed to see the baleful specter of the religious who were fighting for their parishes. And so the archbishop quickly lost hope that the Ordenanza would be promptly implemented. He was correct, because Enríquez suspended it and promised the religious that there would be no innovation until he had further word from the king. The viceroy soon changed his mind, however, and in a blatant show of favoritism ordered the immediate application of the Ordenanza in those articles that referred to the bishops and the diocesan clergy, but not those that referred to the religious. This would have involved an immediate opening of all the benefices of the archdiocese. The viceroy knew that Moya did not have the men to fill them and would be compelled to preserve the status quo. Moya complained to Ovando that Enríquez wanted nothing more than to appoint all the men himself, and he was further irked by the viceroy's refusal to give him a clear explanation for this stand.[33]

Nevertheless, Moya continued his slower tactics. In January 1575 he appointed the board of examiners in a decree that read almost like a paraphrase of the Council of Trent. The instructions given the examiners were exacting and the criteria for candidates demanding.[34] At the same time he kept up a flow of letters to Spain to justify his actions and to explain why he was not immediately implementing the Ordenanza.[35] By the middle of 1575 the archbishop had opened no more than eight benefices to competition. He then went to Cuernavaca on his doctor's orders for a rest and to begin his study of Nahuatl. In the meantime Enríquez grew increasingly irritated, and in Moya's absence he had two noisy meetings with the archdiocesan vicar general, during which he accused Moya of disobeying the royal will. Even though he stormed about the room, making sarcastic remarks about the archbishop and threatening to open all the benefices to religious, he seems to have been unwilling to take the matter further.[36]

By February 1576 thirty-seven presentations had been made, after which the number declined. After that time it seems no longer to have been a major issue. Moya was content with the situation and remarked on a visible improvement in the quality and lives of the clergy. By this time even Enríquez had come to agree with his approach. In that same year the king expressed his approval of Moya's procedures, including favoring criollos for benefices.[37]

THE VISITATIONS

One of the principal means enjoined by the Council of Trent for the effective administration of a diocese was visitation by the bishop.[38] The old scandal of absenteeism, by which a bishop might remain outside his see for years or even his entire lifetime, and the general neglect by other bishops in the pre-Reformation period had led to the awareness that a true bishop was a man involved personally in all aspects of his diocese, a shepherd who could truly call his sheep by name. Moya made at least two, and probably more, visitations of his archdiocese before his involvement in the business of government, both civil and ecclesiastical, put an effective stop to them. In this way he was able to learn the needs and conditions of both clergy and people firsthand.

In the course of these visitations the archbishop investigated the administration of the sacraments and the instruction and good example given to the Indians. These visitations were conducted without fanfare and without expense to the places visited. He never took more than six servants and had his baggage carried by cart rather than by Indian porters.[39] Once arrived at a parish, he would inspect the sacristy, often during the siesta hour, to make sure that all vessels, vestments, and implements for divine worship were there and that they were in clean and decent condition. He would do the same in the church and would even check the streets outside to make sure they were clean and cared for. He would talk to the Indians in their own language, give the young ones gifts to quiet their fears, and then try to find out how well they were instructed. Those pastors who had done well were frequently given some gift, usually gloves, by the archbishop. He was very careful in proceeding against any priest who had been denounced for a crime or moral defect, and he was exact in seeing that due legal process was followed. In general, praise was given publicly but admonitions privately.[40]

Moya's first visitation was made during the summer months of

1576. What he found among both religious and diocesan clergy was "little instruction, many people, and a vast land." He found fault in particular with the Franciscans, with whom he was already on bad terms. In the province of Jilotepec there were more than twenty-five thousand people capable of going to confession, yet the Franciscans had only one guardian (superior of a house) who could speak the native language and another friar who was learning it. He saw again the sumptuous monasteries of the Augustinians, whose extravagance he condemned. Monasteries big enough to hold fifty friars actually had only four. In contrast, Moya said that he had been edified by the diocesan clergy, some forty-three in number, who were very dedicated and who were asking for help, even to the extent of offering to share their benefices with others. The religious, he said, had never volunteered to do that.[41]

The most afflicting sight Moya saw during his visitation was the devastating effects of the epidemic that had been raging for months among the Indians of Mexico and Tlaxcala. The natives called it the *cocolistli*, which meant epidemic in general, or by the more specific name of matlazáhuatl, which referred exclusively to the epidemic of 1576. It has variously been identified as typhus, influenza, or some form of smallpox, but because of the vagueness of symptomatic descriptions in that age it is impossible to identify it with certainty.[42] It began in the spring of 1576, was at first confined to the Indians, and lasted about a year and a half.

Its effects were catastrophic and demoralizing. So many were sick that often there was no one strong enough or healthy enough to help the living or bury the dead. The churches could not hold the bodies, which as a result littered the squares, fields, and streets. When entire households died, there was sometimes no one to inform the local priest. The clergy and civil officials were occupied day and night with burying the dead. Early accounts agree that it was necessary to dig large trenches, into which the bodies were dumped indiscriminately by night and then covered over. Priests blessed entire fields as graveyards.[43]

Contemporary accounts also agree that both civil and religious authorities reacted to the catastrophe with heroic efforts. Enríquez, Moya, the audiencia, the diocesan clergy, and the religious all did what they could to help the suffering and prevent the spread of the disease. New hospitals were built. Moya contributed to both the temporal and the spiritual good of the afflicted, personally visiting hospitals and allowing religious to administer the last rites (something they could ordinarily do only when there were no diocesan priests in their area). Many religious died while ministering to the stricken. Enríquez ordered a census of the victims and found that the number of dead by far exceeded those of the epidemic of 1545. One modern author estimates that it halved the number of Indians in New Spain. The Jesuit Father Pedro Sánchez, who was an eyewitness, estimated that two-thirds of the natives died.[44] Moya himself thought that perhaps one hundred thousand Indians had perished by the end of 1576.

The epidemic began to abate in the immediate environs of Mexico City around December 1576 but continued undiminished in the outlying districts. By that time also it had begun to touch mestizos, blacks, and a few Spaniards. By the spring of 1577 it had reached Michoacán and Nueva Galicia and caused immense devastation around the mines of Zacatecas and Guanajuato. In December 1576 Moya informed the king that he intended to go on his second visitation in order to come to the aid of the Indians. He had previously intended to visit Pánuco, which had not seen a bishop in fifteen years. Even the districts near Mexico City itself had not been visited for seven years.[45] With the decline of the pestilence in the capital, Moya went on this second visitation, and the spring of 1577 found him in the areas of the modern states of Mexico and Oaxaca.[46]

By mid 1577 the epidemic had passed its zenith, but its effects on the natives, the economy, and even the religious psychology of the colony would be felt for decades to come. Free labor grew scarcer and more expensive, and the colonials came to rely more and more on the repartimiento, or conscript labor, for workers. Preachers and theologians examined the all-too-obvious sins of the Spaniards to find and denounce those that had triggered this visitation of the divine wrath. And, as always, it was the Indians who suffered and died.

It is not clear how many visitations of his archdiocese Moya made. He did make a visitation in the Pánuco area some time before 1579. He was also on visitation at the time of his appointment as visitador in 1583. Whatever the number may have been, it is abundantly clear that this was one aspect of the Tridentine reform that Moya took very seriously.[47]

PROTECTOR OF THE INDIANS

On 27 May 1582 Philip II wrote to Moya about the incredible reports of Indian suffering that had been reaching him. Most of these were denunciations of the mistreatment of the natives by encomenderos and included stories of excessive work, exposure to the elements, and one particularly horrifying account of a mother who had killed her newborn child rather than allow it to be raised in such misery. The king's letter bristled with indignation, probably not least because the crown was always happy to have an excuse for reducing the powers of the encomenderos.

The king went on to say that he had written to the civil authorities of New Spain to direct them to put an end to these abuses. He now asked Moya to keep a close watch both on the civil government and on the status of the Indians "as your predecessors did" and to report any lapses to him. Though he had no such formal title, Moya, like Zumárraga and Las Casas before him, was now cast in the role of protector of the Indians.[48] It was a duty he viewed seriously, although his approach was quite different from that of his predecessors. By asking the archbishop to monitor the civil government, the crown may also have been laying the groundwork for the forthcoming visita.

Moya believed fervently in a ministry to the natives, and he put this belief into practice in his own life. He apparently acquired enough facility in Nahuatl that he could both preach and hear confessions in it. When the Jesuit Juan de Tovar translated a Spanish catechism into Nahuatl and recast it in the form of simple dialogues, Moya had it published at his own expense and gave away free copies to the Indians.[49]

Nevertheless, his letters lacked the intensely personal, charismatic, and often exaggerated approach favored by many churchmen before him. He was not a Las Casas or Mendieta. His dedication was strongly tinged with paternalism and pious condescension. He believed strongly in the policy of *congregación*, whereby the Indians were removed from their seminomadic ways or from small population centers and redistributed in larger, more manageable, units. Like his contemporaries, he was oblivious to the culture shock that this disruption caused. Like any Spaniard of the sixteenth century, he felt that city life was indispensable for civilization and Christianization. Generally speaking, the bishops and diocesan clergy also supported this policy. The religious, who had earlier supported and encouraged it, had by the 1580s turned against it, sometimes because resettlement might have hurt the monasteries they had in the areas affected. After the epidemic there were only a few scattered settlements that could be relocated. The viceroys and audiencias tended to side with the religious and often frustrated or ignored royal orders in this regard, something for which they were habitually denounced by the bishops.

Moya was convinced that the policy of resettlement would do away with the large and sumptuous monasteries of the religious, many of which were located in sparsely populated areas and, he believed, were exploiting Indian labor. He desired that such reconcentration be carried out with all possible kindness and gentleness, however, and that it should be done through the agency of the native chiefs rather than by a stark order from the viceroy.

And so it is clear that the idolatry and drunkenness and the heinous sins that arise from them and great offenses against God, to all of which isolation lends itself, would be avoided. And they would apply themselves better to work and to mechanical tasks, and in fact it would take care of their instruction, government, and progress because they are so miserable, lazy, and of such limited understanding that it is necessary to reward and compel them to do what they ought in the same way as with children.[50]

It is clear from this quotation, and from many other letters that he wrote to Spain, that Moya had a low opinion of the overall abilities of the Indians. Why? Undoubtedly, after more than half a century of epidemics, exploitation, and cultural disruption, the Indians of his time were in a far more wretched condition than they had been in the earlier days of Spanish rule. Also the bright hopes of the early years that the Indians would be the foundation of a magnificent new Christian commonwealth based on Aristotelian or Erasmian principles had evaporated in the harsh realities of the colonial situation. It should be noted, however, that a jaundiced view of human nature in general was characteristic of most of the great minds of the Catholic Reformation. Orthodox Catholic bishops, priests, and theologians sometimes sounded as Calvinistic as their contemporaries in Geneva. Moya's opinion of the Europeans in the New World, shared by most of his fellow bishops and clearly reflected in the documents of the Third Mexican Provincial Council, was no more flattering than his opinion of the natives. In a land so decayed in virtue, he once observed, bishops would have to work miracles to rebuild such dead temples.

In light of all this, it is most surprising to find Philip II writing to Moya in 1578 to express his concern over reports that the archbishop had been admitting mestizos and others "who are not suitable" to holy orders. This, the king said, was causing the inevitable *inconvenientes* (the catchall Spanish word for any problems, difficulties, or eyebrow raising) among people in Mexico City. Interestingly, he did not direct Moya to stop his practice but merely warned him to proceed with greater caution. It is difficult to judge the reliability of the reports that the king was receiving, but it is most doubtful that Moya would have conferred orders on anyone who was not suitable or adequately prepared, whether Indian, mestizo, or Spaniard. What had reached the royal ears may have been nothing more than another of those numerous denunciations that regularly crossed the Atlantic. Moya had more than enough enemies to account for them.[51]

JESÚS MARÍA

Another area of concern for the archbishop was the number of poor and orphaned girls in Mexico City. Most of these were daughters and granddaughters of conquistadores or early settlers of New Spain who, because they lacked dowries, could neither be married nor enter a suitable convent. (Dowries were necessary to support the nunneries.) This presented a serious social problem in a society that, in accordance with the adage *aut murus aut maritus* (either cloister or husband), saw only two alternatives for women: marriage or the convent. It was for their sake that the archbishop helped with the foundation of a convent called Jesús María in 1580. If some facets of Moya's life are enigmatic and obscure, the story of his involvement with this foundation, with its overtones of hidden scandal and intrigue, must certainly be the most tantalizingly mysterious of all.

Though he has often been credited with being the sole founder of Jesús María, the convent had actually originated with a pious layman named Pedro Tomás de Denia. Appalled by the dishonorable situation of the undowried girls, he had conceived the idea of a convent dedicated solely to their good. He enlisted the help of Gregorio Pesquera, a conquistador and adventurer who had come under the influence of Las Casas and who, at an advanced age, devoted all his time to religious work and to helping the poor. Pesquera made a sizable personal donation, and Denia conducted a fund-raising tour of the northern mines. He also interested both Enríquez and Moya. The archbishop made his own appeal for funds among the principal citizens of the city. Enough money was raised to permit the purchase of a building (through the agency of the oidor Pedro Farfán) next to the parish church of Vera Cruz. Moya arranged for ten nuns from the convent of La Concepción to administer the convent, which opened in January 1580 with some fifteen poor girls as the first postulants.

Although their efforts had secured enough money to buy the house, it was insufficient to endow it. Denia and Moya each tried to solve the problem in his own way.

Some time after 1580 Denia journeyed to Spain in an attempt to secure a donation from Philip II and to obtain through intermediaries some special spiritual privileges from Rome for the convent, which he hoped would attract pilgrims and bring in donations. He was completely unsuccessful on both counts. Fortunately for his endeavors, he carried with him a letter from Moya to be given to the king personally (*en sus reales manos*) as a last resort, should all other efforts fail. Denia secured an audience with Philip II in Lisbon (Portugal had recently been added to the Habsburg domains) and presented the letter. The results were spectacular. The king decreed that tribute from the first free encomienda to revert to royal control as a result of the New Laws of 1542 should be allotted to Jesús María. The total allotment was to be 60,000 ducados over the course of twenty years, a truly munificent sum. Within six days he issued a directive (4 February 1583) in which he declared himself to be the chief patron of the convent, ruled that Moya was to have a voice and vote in all decisions affecting it, and, perhaps at Denia's urging, added that the location of the convent was not to be changed. He also arranged through his ambassador in Rome to have the pope make Jesús María the most heavily indulgenced chapel in all New Spain.[52]

What was in Moya's letter that so radically changed the king's mind? According to the Mexican savant Carlos de Sigüenza y Góngora, who wrote a history of the convent a century later, the reason was the following. When Moya arrived in New Spain he was accompanied by a little girl about two years old, named Micaela de los Angeles, who, he said, was his niece, as in fact she seems to have been. She was treated with far greater deference than her uncle's position warranted. This was attributed, according to Sigüenza y Góngora, to "the importance of her royal blood, of which even her childish actions gave witness and although the reasons for bringing her to these kingdoms would be at a very high level, they were not so hidden that they did not become known later on, at length to the point of an almost certain knowledge of who she was." The story that circulated, though not repeated by Sigüenza y Góngora, was that she was an illegitimate daughter of Philip II by Moya's sister.

The little girl was originally housed in the convent of La Concepción under the care of the abbess, Isabel Bautista, who acted as the girl's governess. Both later went to the new foundation of Jesús María. According to Sigüenza y Góngora, the archbishop wrote to the king about the abbess's care of the child, which prompted the sudden and unexpected royal largesse.[53]

Clearly the story cannot be verified. It is certain that when Moya arrived in Mexico his sister was in a convent in Córdoba and that he was very concerned about arranging a marriage for her, even as his uncle, the archbishop of Vich, had been before his death. Moya had tried to use this as an excuse for refusing the post of inquisitor in New Spain. Part of the problem was raising a dowry, a fact that would account for his concern for women in a similar situation in Mexico City. He was also concerned that his sister was well known in Córdoba, making a marriage vital if she was to retain her respectability. Once in New Spain he was eager to be free of his responsibility. In 1574 he obtained letters of credit for 12,000 pesos from three leading citizens of Mexico City, and this amount, together with a gift from Ovando, was used to arrange a marriage. After Moya's return to Spain in 1586, his sister's husband, Fernández de Figueroa, was made a knight of Santiago.[54]

Aside from the fact that it probably took some daring for Sigüenza y Góngora to hint at what he did, even in 1682, it is also true that his account of the founding of the convent tallies closely with the documentary evidence. He clearly had access to the archdiocesan archives, because he reprinted in full both Philip II's cédula and a decree of Moya's that changed the location of the convent. He also seems to have been careful not to speculate on matters about which he had no evidence. It is safe to say that Moya did bring with him a little girl who may have been his niece, although he never once mentions her in any of his correspondence. It is possible that she was somehow related to the royal family of Spain. Whether she was the daughter of the king or of some Habsburg black sheep will never be known for certain. It is fascinating, however, to speculate on the extent to which Philip II may have been personally indebted to Moya.

Sigüenza y Góngora adds that the little girl grew up in Jesús María, where she died at the age of thirteen after suffering a mental disturbance of some sort. According to him she was still honored by the nuns in 1684 as the source of their special royal patronage.

Moya's own efforts to assure the support of the convent involved him in a long controversy with Denia and Pesquera. When he drew up the constitutions for Jesús María (which, among other things, forbade the admission of mestizas), he included a provision that allowed the admission of dowried nuns and also permitted wealthy citizens to provide dowries. Pesquera opposed this as contrary to his original intention, and in 1581 he secured an order from the audiencia that would have lessened the archbishop's control over the convent and its endowment. Both Moya and the nuns at La Concepción brought suit before the audiencia to have the ruling reversed and also appealed to Philip II to see that the original constitutions were observed.[55]

The situation was complicated further when the nuns of La Concepción became dissatisfied with the house purchased for Jesús María and Moya somewhat reluctantly permitted them to build a new one. As it turned out, the new house was rather expensive. When Denia returned to New Spain in 1585 or 1586 he reacted strongly against the change, which he considered both unnecessary and extravagant. However, it was not until after Moya had returned to Spain in mid 1586 that he made strenuous efforts to regain control. The convent itself began to thrive, and in the succeeding century it became one of the most famous religious sites in all New Spain.

AT WAR WITH THE VICEROYS

As archbishop of Mexico Moya could not possibly avoid being involved in the constant conflicts and bickering between churchmen and civil authorities. Despite his often-professed desire to remain aloof, he engaged in full-scale combat with the viceroys and the audiencia. However, the *regimiento* of Mexico City, which, like Moya, reflected a strong pro-criollo feeling, supported him in his struggles with the civil government and the religious. It was the beginning of a system of alliances that lasted throughout the colonial period.

Moya's own punctiliousness and concern for precedence and ceremonial niceties, common enough in post-Tridentine bishops and exaggerated by the small-town atmosphere of Mexico City, made him suspicious of every lack of respect shown by civil officials and wary that protocol be observed. His arrival in New Spain as inquisitor had set the stage for some of these conflicts with Enríquez. The parody of the alcabala at the reception of the pallium and the struggle over benefices had worsened an already bad situation. The relations between the two men were characterized by a constant, if controlled, hostility, and moments of comparative peace came only when the crown intervened.

Martín Enríquez de Almansa was not the sort of man who allowed his religious beliefs to blind him to the shortcomings of the clergy. The chronicler Torquemada says that he combined a natural seriousness with great severity and that he raised the general prestige of the vice-regal office, which up to that time had been rather undistinguished. Coming to office at a time of civil turmoil following the New Laws (1542) and real or fancied conspiracies (such as that of Martín Cortés), he governed tactfully and well. He also had strong ideas about the relations of church and state and treated ecclesiastics with far greater aloofness and less respect than his predecessors had done. Churchmen were not automatically granted audiences and not infrequently were forced to cool their heels in anterooms.[56] In modern terms he would be called a devout, but somewhat anticlerical, Catholic.

The viceroy seems to have been discouraged over the outcome of the fracas over the alcabala skit, in which he felt himself to be the loser. In 1574 he asked the king for permission to resign and return to Spain, giving his age and health as reasons. The king asked him to stay on but did offer him the option, if the case were urgent, of turning his powers over to Moya and returning immediately on the next flota.[57] This suggestion alone would have been sufficient to keep him in New Spain. He had also requested that instead of a residencia he be given a visita at the end of his term, which he considered more honorable for an outgoing viceroy. This request was approved by the Council of the Indies.

Perhaps because he was disillusioned with Enríquez or because he merely wanted to keep the peace, Ovando seized on the viceroy's offer of resignation with almost indecent haste. He urged the king to accept it and drew up a list of possible replacements—all letrados. Although he gave many reasons for preferring them to nobles, Ovando was advancing his own plan for putting New Spain under a government of letrados. Though initially favorable, the king eventually rejected the suggestion, which was too much at variance with tradition—the vice-king could not be a mere civil servant. Moya de Contreras was high on the list of suggested replacements. This was premature, but it may well have planted a thought for the future in the royal mind. Ovando, who should have known better, bombarded the king with a series of *consultas,* urging speed in the selection of a new viceroy. Haste was not, however, part of Philip II's nature.[58] Enríquez remained in office until 1580, five years after Ovando's death, years filled with conflict with Moya.

Most of the issues over which the two men squabbled will seem impossibly petty to modern readers: the correct form of address for the archbishop (*muy reverendo* or *reverendísimo*), who should preach the Lenten and Advent sermons, who should carry the canopy in processions with the Blessed Sacrament, and whether or not the archbishop could have a kneeler in the sanctuary during the funeral of the brother of the late viceroy Antonio de Mendoza. The situation verged on comedy on the first Ash Wednesday after Moya's consecration. It was understood that the archbishop would place ashes on the viceroy's forehead, but who would come to whom? Moya stood on the top step before the altar and Enríquez knelt in his place. After a long pause the archbishop came down one step but the viceroy did not move. He came down another step, then another, and finally went to the viceroy's kneeler and gave him the ashes. It was a defeat for the archbishop, and he wrote to Ovando to protest that lay brothers in religious orders were given more respect than bishops.[59] To prevent such confrontations Moya took to avoiding the viceroy altogether.

The crowning insult was Enríquez's insistence that his name should precede the archbishop's in the recitation of the mass prayer *Et famulos tuos.* Although Moya could point to ample precedents, including that of the royal court, where the name of the archbishop took precedence over that of the king, he contented himself with further complaints to Ovando. Domingo de Salazar, as bishop of Manila, later claimed that the archbishop's name had been omitted altogether and reproached Moya for showing too much meekness toward the viceroy.

A more serious source of discontent was that Enríquez was very free in interpreting his privileges as vice-patron of religious affairs. He allowed the archbishop to have no say in the construction of the new cathedral. He permitted the Franciscans in Celaya to build a monastery in that town and to administer the sacraments to the exclusion of the resident diocesan priest. He appointed a pastor at the port of San Juan de Ulúa without the consent of the archbishop. Enríquez had become such a partisan of the religious against the diocesans that some of the religious began to make extravagant claims about his power—for example, that he was the supreme authority in both church and state. The celebrated Franciscan ethnographer Alonso de Molina, in the introduction to a Nahuatl dictionary that he had written, spoke of "Your Excellency being head of this new church . . ." Moya was happy to inform Ovando that this had been denounced to the Inquisition.[60] Regalist though he was, he was not prepared to see his chief antagonist given that sort of credit.

Philip II and Ovando constantly urged peace, and Moya as constantly reassured them that he was attempting to have peace, if only because of his own Christian virtue. "It has given no small pleasure to the people to see how I answer the viceroy's haughtiness with humility." In his "humility" he went so far as to remove the canopy from in front of his residence "in order not to leave him a target to shoot at." The viceroy grumbled that the archbishop was merely trying to impress the people. When Enríquez complained about the 4,000 pesos Moya spent in refurbishing the archiepiscopal palace, the archbishop denounced him to Ovando for being as miserly as "a dull-witted Genevan" and passed on this interesting verdict of María de Mendoza, the sister of the first viceroy: "Never have I seen signs of piety and such great pride combined."[61] Moya's own conclusion was that Enríquez had a simple desire to contradict and oppose everything he did, that the viceroy was attempting to turn the whole archdiocese over to the friars, and that he interfered in matters that properly belonged in the ecclesiastical sphere.

Behind the bickering and trivial complaints, the denunciations to Spain, and even the laughable episodes between the two men, there lay the less pleasant reality of a power struggle. They tested each other's strength and searched for weaknesses, while avoiding open confrontation of the kind that would lead to the riots characteristic of the following century. Moya was at a disadvantage because of his deep-seated regalism and his sensitivity to the rebuke the king had given him after the alcabala incident. But no matter what appeared on the surface, the two men were in earnest—and they were enemies.

Eventually, however, the two came to have a grudging respect for each other. As early as 1574 Enríquez wrote that Moya was one of the "men of this century," even though the viceroy recognized that "our blood did not agree, as the Italians say." When Enríquez was named viceroy of Peru in 1580, Moya wrote, with somewhat less grace than his adversary, that Enríquez would "serve His Majesty satisfactorily in Peru, as he has done in this country."[62]

Moya was vastly relieved when Enríquez was named viceroy of Peru. His replacement in New Spain was the amiable Lorenzo Suárez de Mendoza, Conde de Coruña. When Enríquez left Mexico City, he went to the Franciscan house at Otumba, where he stayed for a week with his successor, who was journeying to his new post. The two conferred at length and undoubtedly the viceroy-archbishop situation played some part in the retiring viceroy's advice to his successor. Enríquez's own state of mind can easily be gathered from one of his written comments to Coruña: "It is my habit to say that I consider the government of this land a misfortune for a man of honor." It also emerges in his judgment on his countrymen: "In addition, the Spaniards, after profiting from the Indians, take better care of their dogs than they do of them."[63]

Enríquez went to Lima, where, it is said, he attempted to introduce the alcabala but failed because of local opposition. He governed that viceroyalty until his death in 1583. Torquemada, the eternal gossip, who had a fondness for signs and omens, wrote, "They say that at his death many birds were seen over his house, of the kind they call carnivorous or flesheaters. I don't know what this meant. God knows, for he knows all things. And I do not put any credence in the populace, which was divided into many and varied opinions."[64]

The lackluster Coruña entered Mexico City on the feast of Saint Francis of Assisi (4 October 1580). Like Enríquez, he was a widower but was of a more advanced age and more pliable disposition. He was affable but ineffective as a ruler, and because of this Moya found him easier to deal with and praised him highly in his reports to Spain. According to one story, it was Coruña who came to the conclusion that the government of New Spain needed a visita and who wrote to Philip II to ask for one. A visita would be granted, but the new viceroy would be dead before it came about.

After Coruña's death in 1583, Moya had almost two and a half years of respite from viceroys. From June 1583 until September 1584 the audiencia ruled in its interim capacity, after which time Moya himself was acting viceroy until October 1585. During that time he made repeated requests to Philip II for a permanent viceroy, an appointment he considered essential to the good government and progress of the land. His urgent pleas were finally answered in the summer of 1585, when the king appointed Alvaro Manrique de Zúñiga, Marqués de Villamanrique, as viceroy of New Spain.

The old antagonisms flared up anew. Moya's relationship with the new viceroy was to be as hostile as his relations with Enríquez had been, but with a notable difference. For years Moya had been cautious, and at times almost timid, in his dealings with the viceroy and audiencia. Now he was more sure of himself and more secure in his position. Few men in the Spanish dependencies stood higher in the royal esteem and confidence. His positions as retiring viceroy and still active visitador gave him an advantage with Villamanrique that he had never had with Enríquez. It was not just that he was more belligerent and more obdurate with the new viceroy; he seemed almost to seek occasions to be so, and an unpleasant arrogance and truculence became noticeable in his personality. Possibly, also, he may have been goaded by the rebukes of his fellow bishops, who did not always share his subservience to civil authority.

Matters got off to a bad start even before the new viceroy arrived in Mexico City, for (as will be seen in chapter IX) Villamanrique began to interfere in the affairs of the Third Mexican Provincial Council in a heavy-handed way from the moment of his arrival in New Spain. And almost immediately bad feelings erupted over one of those small matters of protocol so dear to that age and place. Moya bristled from the first over the salutation of the viceroy's first letter to him, which he did not consider honorific enough, and to show his displeasure refused to answer the letter personally or to sign the audiencia's answer.[65] Villamanrique was equally perturbed when he learned of this through hearsay rather than from the archbishop personally. Moya sent a Dominican friar to meet the viceroy and instruct him on the correct manner of addressing a bishop in New Spain. Villamanrique huffily replied that because he came from Old Spain, he would follow the usage of that country. When the Dominican replied that Moya was the viceroy and deserved a more honorific title, Villamanrique retorted that since the day he had set foot in the colony, Moya had been archbishop and visitador, nothing more. At Puebla the new viceroy received a more conciliatory letter from Moya that seemed to put an end to the matter. It was, however, hardly an auspicious beginning. It seems clear that Moya was being deliberately provocative, as if to let the viceroy know from the beginning what their respective positions were.

Matters deteriorated again when Villamanrique arrived at Guadalupe. When Moya came to visit him and his wife, one of the viceroy's servants tried to prevent Moya's trainbearer from entering the viceregal presence. The archbishop made a scene and Villamanrique, by his own account, tried to soothe Moya's ruffled feelings. The incident was apparently forgotten, but when the new viceroy made his formal entrance into Mexico City on 28 October 1585, the archbishop remained at home and did not even come to receive Villamanrique when he visited the cathedral. The snub caused a stir among the populace.

Two days later Moya came to see the viceroy and his wife. To prevent a repetition of the Guadalupe incident, Villamanrique gave instructions that he be allowed to enter as he pleased. Pleasantries and small gifts were exchanged, and the meeting went smoothly. The viceroy even took the archbishop in his own carriage to the country to watch an exhibition of falconry. He also sent his personal carriage to bring Moya to a conference at Chapultepec in December. There the peace was again shattered because of disagreements over their respective jurisdictions in the visita Moya was conducting. Their bad relations were further worsened when, early in 1586, Villamanrique discovered that Moya, in his capacity as visitador, had been investigating some of the viceroy's official actions. Brimming with indignation and self-righteousness, he fervently denounced the archbishop to the Council of the Indies and piously stressed his unselfish desire to serve the king and fulfill the royal will in everything. The confrontations ended only with Moya's departure for Spain in mid 1586.

Moya's years as archbishop of Mexico were a turning point in the history of the church in that archdiocese. With him came the church of the Catholic Reformation, especially as embodied in the reforms of Trent. His whole approach to being archbishop—the concern for the improvement of the clergy, the visitations, the assertions of episcopal power, his personal piety—all show him to have been in the mainstream of the movement that was then spreading throughout the Catholic world. Law and organization played major roles in this movement, and Moya, a man of law, exemplified both the good and bad aspects: concern for justice, efficient administration, and good order, together with a preoccupation with protocol and position, the narrowness of view that sometimes characterizes the legal and administrative mind.

This narrowness is most evident in his attitude toward the Indians. It was paternalistic and condescending, based on a low opinion of Indian capacity. It reflected both the social reality of the 1570s and the Counter-Reformation distrust of human nature. Yet this rather negative attitude existed side by side with a profound pastoral dedication and desire to help. His dedication was not expressed in the sort of fiery defense of the Indians found earlier in such men as Antonio de Montesinos or Bartolomé de las Casas. It was rather like the approach to charity to be found in the later Catholic Reformation—for example, in seventeenth-century France, in which a profound Christian charity and compassion for the poor and suffering coexisted with an unquestioning acceptance of the social and political system in which this suffering took place. As archbishop, Moya would never have criticized royal policies toward the Indians as Mendieta and Las Casas had done. He was very much a part of the governmental system and probably saw no fundamental reason for such criticism. If royal policies resulted in injustice, the fault lay with the officials on the scene, not with the king, and Moya was more than willing to criticize the local scene. In all things, including most church matters, the king's decision was final and the royal will was to be obeyed.

This same attitude is revealed in his relationship with Enríquez and Villamanrique. Although civil and religious officials had inherited conflicts of long standing, the fact was that neither side really went out of its way to be conciliatory. Moya's deep-seated respect for civil government, his own Christian convictions, and the initial rebuke received from Philip II put him at a disadvantage in the earlier phases of these struggles. When he felt secure enough, he showed a truculence that ill became a churchman. In one sense it can be said that his priorities were wrong. He took his stand on petty matters rather than facing the truly important problem, that of the patronato itself. If he was not a bartolomico, he certainly thought like one. As a regalist he was compelled by his own outlook to fight on narrower terrain. And there can be no doubt that the distractions of these disputes hindered his primary mission in New Spain, that of being archbishop.

The viceroys, however, were not his only antagonists. As archbishop he waged another struggle that was even more destructive of the church's mission, that with the mendicant friars.

V. The Parallel Churches

One of the most harmful of the persistent conflicts that rent the church in New Spain in the sixteenth century was that waged between the bishops and the religious orders. The latter were called mendicants, a term that originated in the Middle Ages to describe a new kind of order composed of men who lived according to a religious rule yet were not monks—that is, were not bound to a single autonomous unit known as a monastery. Rather, they were international groups, committed to an active ministry such as preaching and theoretically supported by begging—hence the name. The most important of these groups in sixteenth-century New Spain were the Franciscans, the Dominicans, and the Augustinians. Their members were called friars (*frailes*) and were addressed as *Fray,* a title derived from the Latin word for brother.[1]

From the beginning the mendicants had been a source of controversy with bishops and with the older monastic orders. For the bishops, the mendicants' most galling privilege was exemption—that is, their freedom from control by the bishops in their internal, communitarian life, a freedom that sometimes extended into their ministry. Bolstered by other privileges granted by the papacy, this exemption tended to make the mendicants independent and even arrogant in their dealings with the episcopacy. It is small wonder that bishops often viewed religious in their dioceses with distaste and that the Council of Trent, dominated by bishops, tried to restrict or even abolish these privileges.[2]

The situation was aggravated in New Spain by the fact that the mendicants had arrived first. During the crucial early years of the missionary enterprise the friars not only carried on the evangelization of the new land but did so without accountability to any bishop. Their form of organization became the organization of the new church. To compensate for the lack of bishops they were given extraordinary privileges by the papacy, the most notable being a brief of Pope Leo X (25 April 1521) and the famous bull *Exponi Nobis* of Adrian VI (10 May 1522). In areas where there were no bishops, the former gave the religious the power of administering the sacrament of Confirmation (though only Motolinía seems to have used it, and there were claims that he had a personal privilege to that effect), of conferring minor orders, and of blessing chapels, altars, chalices, and sacred furnishings—all functions ordinarily reserved to bishops—as well as of granting the indulgences that a bishop could grant in his diocese.

The *Exponi Nobis,* more commonly known as the Omnímoda, granted to religious provincials who were two days' journey from a bishop "all manner of our authority in both *fora*" (*omnimodam auctoritatem nostram in utroque foro*). The phrase "both *fora*" was ecclesiastical terminology for universal jurisdiction. On the face of it, this was a delegation of the pope's own authority and could be interpreted to include just about every act of which a bishop was capable, with the exception of ordination to the priesthood. This bull, which the Augustinian chronicler Juan de Grijalva called "the widest bull ever dispatched in the Roman Curia," became the single most powerful weapon in the hands of the religious in their struggles with the bishops. In Robert Padden's trenchant phrase, it was "a very piece of the rock of Saint Peter."[3]

The mendicant orders in New Spain expanded rapidly, almost too rapidly for their own good.[4] Thus it happened that when the first bishops arrived they found a vigorous and functioning ecclesiastical system that left no real place for them. And no matter how well it may have functioned, it nevertheless stood outside the regular administrative machinery of the Catholic church, which envisioned permanent organization in the form of bishops and their dioceses. The Mexican church has aptly been called "a church of friars."[5] The diocesan and episcopal administration was superimposed on a preexisting one. A power struggle was inevitable. The bishops wanted to move from what was essentially improvisation to the accustomed order. The mendicant missionaries resisted and fell back on the various privileges that had been granted them, especially the Omnímoda. Ironically, many of the bishops had themselves been chosen from among the members of the mendicant orders. But whatever their previous opinions of the religious-diocesan question, they usually, though not always, adopted a new stance on becoming bishops.

To the sixteenth-century Spanish mind the religious were in an irregular position as missionaries, one that was deemed incompatible with their vocation. Full-time, permanent missionary work was considered a deviation from the norm, and it was unheard of to find them acting as parish priests. The average Spaniard thought of religious as those who, even though they performed external works such as preaching and teaching, devoted the greater part of their lives to living their community rule, praying, and seeking contemplation, all within the confines of their religious houses. Martín Enríquez warned the Conde de Coruña in 1580 that in New Spain he would see religious in a role that he had never seen them in before and that they had a liberty of action and life that was unknown in the mother country.[6]

The friars also tended to stand outside the regalistic structure that had been erected by the Spanish crown. By their very nature the orders were supranational and were more dependent on Rome than on the Escorial. Their papal privileges made them independent not only of the bishops but also, to a certain extent, of the king. This meant that the struggle between the religious and the bishops would be played out against the background of the crown's attempts to control and centralize the church's life in its dominions, a struggle of papal privilege versus royal patronage.

The crown exploited these antagonisms. In the early days the government had sided with the friars because they were useful for bolstering Habsburg imperial institutions and because as defenders of the Indians they were a potent counterbalance to the encomenderos. With the establishment of the hierarchy and the close control of the patronato, the crown began to side with the bishops against the mendicants. As with everything else in the Spanish empire, this was a delicate balancing act, the pitting of one against the other without siding totally with either. The crown was never entirely successful in subordinating the friars because they were essential to the Christianization of the Indians, and to emasculate that work would have been to void the very raison d'être of the Spanish presence, at least according to the common opinion of the age.

The age of Moya de Contreras was a time of crisis for the mendicants. It was not just that their exclusive claims to the apostolate were being challenged. They were also undergoing a crisis in their ideals and in their approach to the missionary enterprise. The dream of an ideal Christian commonwealth built on the docile and easily converted Indians had not materialized. As the native population declined, there was increased pressure on the Indians for labor. There was also a growing realization that Christianity was still a veneer for the majority of them and that the missionary task would be long, arduous, and frustrating. It was a period of transition from the visionary to the mundane and practical. As a result the religious were subject to new strains.

Fundamentally, however, the dispute between the religious and the bishops was over power and jurisdiction. As so often happened, the struggle was fought on somewhat more superficial issues.

A key point of contention was that of competence in the ministry. In New Spain such competence usually meant knowledge of the native languages. There had been a conscious decision, enunciated by the First Provincial Council of 1555, to use the native languages as the instruments of evangelization. Hence the missionaries who best knew the native tongues would be the best prepared for their task. The bishops and diocesan clergy railed against the *idiotismo* of the mendicants, who in turn scored the ignorance of the diocesans. The latter, they claimed, did not have the best interests of the natives at heart, because they were interested only in making a living. Generally speaking, the religious had a better image as missionaries than did the diocesan clergy.[7]

Contention arose also over the construction of priories and religious houses, which the mendicants, again relying on their papal privileges, built without the permission of the bishops, though often with the approval of viceroys or audiencias. These monasteries—as they were popularly, but inaccurately, called—had chapels that could legally function as churches of ease. Although they were not parishes in the technical sense of the term, the faithful could come to them to fulfill their ordinary religious obligations and even to receive those sacraments that ordinarily could be received only in diocesan parishes. All too often the religious administered the sacraments to the natives without any formal control by the bishop. The bishops accused them of constructing large and lavish buildings without the personnel to fill them. Supposedly there were to be a minimum of four or five friars in each religious house, but this was not always observed in practice.[8]

The bishops also accused the religious of excessive esprit de corps—of being more interested in the advancement of their orders and their dominion (*imperio*) than they were in the good of the Indians. It is undoubtedly true, as Robert Ricard has pointed out, that the friars' rule over docile and compliant natives did give them a taste for authoritarian government.[9] The bishops often accused them of brutality toward the Indians, and there were enough incidents to support the charge. Despite numerous royal commands to the contrary, the religious even maintained prisons for delinquent natives, and Moya accused them of continuing to do so while he was archbishop.[10]

This corporate pride of the mendicants was especially irksome to the diocesan clergy, not only because it was matched by a corresponding disdain for those who were not religious, but also because the diocesans did not have any special founder, habit, or tradition around which they could rally. In reaction some began to speak of themselves as wearing the "habit of Saint Peter," thus emphasizing the fact that their foundation antedated that of any religious order. One of the more curious manifestations of this mutual hostility was a custom whereby some of the mendicant superiors would punish their delinquent subjects by depriving them of their religious habits and forcing them to dress like diocesan priests. The diocesans were infuriated over what they considered an insult to their state and petitioned the Third Mexican Council to put an end to it.[11]

A crucial question of jurisdiction concerned marriage cases. The validity or nonvalidity of a marriage was and is one of the basic areas of a bishop's jurisdiction. Although the question of polygamy was probably academic by midcentury in all but the outlying districts, that of the Indians' capacity for entering into lawful and valid unions still provoked problems. Generally the religious upheld the validity of native marriages and the diocesan clergy did not.[12] Again, it was a question of power. In effect the religious were claiming the same rights of judgment and jurisdiction over marriages that the bishops had, a claim the bishops rejected. The great defender of the mendicants' rights in this regard was the Augustinian Alonso de la Vera Cruz, who dealt with the dispute in his *Speculum Coniugiorum* (1556). Vera Cruz claimed that by reason of their privileges the religious had greater powers than pastors and that, as for judging the validity of marriages, they were the equals of bishops by reason of the Omnímoda.[13]

One of the bitterest conflicts involved the collection and distribution of tithes and the relative means of supporting religious and diocesan clergy. Technically, all tithes in the New World were the property of the crown and were "redonated" according to a complex formula. Ecclesiastical expenses were paid out of the royal treasury, and the king was the patron and benefactor par excellence of ecclesiastical establishments. Both groups were supported by royal donations, by private alms, and by the labor of the Indians, but the greater portion of royal support went to the bishops and the *clérigos,* thus bolstering the diocesan church structure. Both the mendicants and the diocesans depended in large part on the labor and offerings of the natives, but the religious claimed that by reason of their vows of poverty and simple lifestyles they were less burdensome to the Indians. They alleged that the diocesan clergy were more so because, in the phrase of the day, they had to be supported "according to their state."[14] Naturally enough, both bishops and diocesan clergy wanted the Indians to pay tithes, whereas the religious strenuously opposed this. The bishops claimed that the friars were afraid that their exclusive position would be undermined, which was true, whereas the mendicants maintained that the Indians were too poor to pay tithes, which was also true.[15] At heart it was a question of strengthening or limiting the diocesan church structure.

The struggle between the two groups was waged with equal bitterness over the question of the doctrinas—parishes that consisted entirely of recently converted Indians. These churches and their congregations had passed from the purely missionary stage to one in which they were like ordinary, functioning parishes, but with Indian parishioners. They did not, however, have the legal status of parishes. The bishops viewed these doctrinas with their neophyte congregations as intermediate stages on the way toward being parishes in the strict sense of the term. In accordance with the practice of that century, this meant with diocesan priests as pastors. The bishops believed that the mendicants should push on to further missionary activity and lay aside a form of work that was prejudicial to their community life. "Coadjutor" was the word most often used by the bishops to describe the role of the religious. The latter naturally resisted this subordination, invoking their papal privileges and pointing to the insufficiency both in numbers and learning of the diocesan clergy.[16] With equal vigor they resisted the efforts of the bishops to make visitations to the doctrinas.

In the context of sixteenth-century Spanish government, it was inevitable that these clashes and struggles should involve the civil arm. In New Spain this meant the viceroys and audiencias. As both were generally hostile to the bishops, with whom they carried on their own form of warfare, they naturally gravitated to the cause of the mendicants.[17] This outlook was inconsistent with the general policy of the crown, but the attitude of the civil authorities was determined by local conditions. Even the Inquisition was involved. The bishops were resentful that the religious arrogated inquisitorial powers to themselves, especially in areas where they were out of the bishops' reach. The bishops themselves were not above using their own inquisitorial powers as a means of monitoring the orthodoxy of the friars and of controlling them by the threat, real or implied, of investigations and processes.[18]

The First Mexican Provincial Council of 1555, under the presidency of Archbishop Alonso de Montúfar, a Dominican, had attempted to curtail the power of the mendicants. It decreed that only the bishop and his provisor could make decisions in marriage cases and that other judges should not interfere (*no se entremeta*), a wording that the religious considered to be gratuitously offensive. In another decree the bishops attempted to prevent the mendicants from building monasteries and churches without the permission of the local bishop. Some of the bishops interpreted this to mean that the religious should no longer have charge of doctrinas and attempted to have them removed.[19] The friars responded by appealing to their privileges. They also emphasized the impracticality of the decree on marriage cases, as in the New World distance alone would have made it impossible to have recourse to the bishops for all the necessary dispensations and canonical processes. Also it was a burden on the Indians to force them to pay the fees for the various tribunals.

The mendicants appealed to the king, who eventually found in their favor. By two cédulas of 30 March 1557, Philip II decreed that the religious should be left in peaceful possession of their privileges, including that of jurisdiction in marriage cases, and that for the sake of peace diocesan clerics were not to be stationed where the friars were.[20] In an additional directive of 9 April that same year, the king reviewed his previous orders that churches and religious houses were not to be built without the permission of the local bishop and concluded that if these instructions were carried out, nothing would ever be built. Consequently he decreed that henceforth the religious should be free to establish their foundations without the prior consent or approval of the local bishop, but subject to the approval of the viceroy. For the time being, at least, the mendicants had triumphed.[21]

The bishops were not ready to surrender. The major attack on the privileges of the religious came from the Council of Trent, which closed in 1563 after eighteen years of sporadic meetings. Trent attempted to restrict, and even abrogate, what its bishops considered to be the excessive privileges of the mendicants. Diego Basalenque, an Augustinian chronicler, claimed that this was the result of lobbying by the bishops of New Spain, but that is doubtful because their influence at Trent was negligible.[22] The bishops of Europe had no more love for the friars than did their confreres in the New World. In 1564 Pope Pius IV, who did so much to implement the decrees of Trent in other areas, issued the bull *In Principis Apostolorum Sede,* which revoked all the privileges of religious that were not in conformity with the Tridentine decrees. The religious, apparently led by Alonso de la Vera Cruz, immediately appealed against this to Philip II, and through him to the Holy See. Their efforts were rewarded when in 1567 Pope Saint Pius V, himself a Dominican, issued the bull *Exponi Nobis Nuper,* which restored their privileges.

Between these two bulls the Second Mexican Provincial Council of 1565 had been held, but it does not seem to have entered deeply into the dispute. It was called to promulgate and implement the legislation of Trent, but that which concerned the mendicants does not seem to have been considered. This somewhat restricted scope, plus the fact that the council met in a context of hiatus in government and turmoil in civil life, meant that it was destined to have limited effectiveness.[23]

With the accession to power of Juan de Ovando, there was a definite shift in crown policy. Ovando himself was a clérigo, but even beyond that, the entire thrust of his policies militated against the independence and autonomy of the mendicants. A royal order of 25 February 1573 finally revoked the right of the friars to make decisions in marriage cases.[24] The Ordenanza del Patronazgo of 1574 sought to bring them almost totally under crown control and aroused their desperate opposition. This policy continued after Ovando's death, although the shift was never total or final. The crown continued its customary tactic of pitting one power group against another and eroding the positions of those who were too independent.

MOYA DE CONTRERAS AND THE RELIGIOUS

When Moya de Contreras became archbishop of Mexico he inevitably found himself embroiled in conflicts with the mendicants. In part this was because he inherited longstanding disputes from his predecessors. In part it was also because of his own belief in the powers of a bishop and because crown policy now chanced to coincide with Tridentine reforms.

To his credit it must be said that Moya did not initiate these conflicts. For the most part he reacted to the existing situation or to what he considered provocations. It is not surprising to find him voicing the same accusations that bishops had been leveling for decades, but according to his own protestations he always tried to maintain good relations with the religious of New Spain. It was they, he said, who made this impossible. The evidence seems to support his claim, for he was basically conciliatory. "By nature I am not one for carrying out things with rigor, especially when better results can be achieved with gentleness and moderation, so that no one can claim to have been treated badly."[25]

He did have good relations with some of the religious—for example, the Jesuits (although their situation was decidedly different from that of the mendicants) and the Discalced of Saint Francis (barefoot Franciscans). Further, he maintained good relations with individuals among the various orders, such as the Dominican Domingo de Salazar and the Franciscan Alonso Ponce. He was not reluctant to admit the good done by the mendicants and to encourage them. He could praise them for their regularity, devotion, and prayer. Generally, however, his stand was the same as that of all the other bishops of New Spain throughout the sixteenth century.

The first conflict was over the *cruzada:* the various indulgences and spiritual privileges that had originally been granted as a reward for military service against the Moors. Military service was eventually replaced by a donation of money. By Moya's time the cruzada had become a standard means of raising money for religious activities, although occasional voices protested that it should still be used only for its original object of financing crusades. The problem of the cruzada was similar to that of the tithes—that is, should it be asked of the Indians? The same religious who opposed the tithing of the natives opposed the preaching of the cruzada as a burden and an exploitation. Those who favored it, like Moya, saw the opposition of the religious as a further attempt to retain control over the natives and to deprive them of needed spiritual benefits.

When the first preachers of the cruzada arrived in New Spain in 1574 Moya found himself in the irritating position of having to ask the cooperation of the mendicants, because "the orders have taken over the best and most populous part of New Spain and have such a command and domination over the Indians." The Franciscans, who were divided into criollo and peninsular factions, were not in a position to offer effective opposition. The Augustinians were eventually persuaded to accept the preaching, albeit reluctantly. It was the Dominicans who presented the most effective resistance. They were eventually persuaded to yield to the first preaching of the bulls, but they never did give up their hostility to the cruzada and resisted the later publications. To Moya this was further evidence of the folly of putting so much power in the hands of the religious. "May God put an end to it," he observed. He also signaled the danger that had long been apparent to the crown and its councils: even the king was powerless to do anything regarding the Indians because of the control the mendicants had.[26]

The subsequent publications of the cruzada were not successful, but this seems to have been because of the epidemic of 1576 and the drastic decline of the Indian population rather than because of Dominican opposition. The religious did, however, put so many obstacles in Moya's path that he was driven to make the unworthy suggestion that they be given the task of collecting the donations and be paid the salaries of collectors, in the hope that self-interest would triumph over principle.[27]

Moya had a prolonged clash with the Augustinians over their fa-mous college of San Pablo. This was a project initiated by Alonso de la Vera Cruz shortly after his election as vice-provincial of his order. He secured from Philip II a cédula that turned the parish of San Pablo and the care of its Indians over to the Augustinians. The reasons alleged were the good that would come to the Indians from the presence of the friars and the opportunities for the latter to keep abreast of the native languages. The king, however, directed Martín Enríquez to consult with both Moya and Vera Cruz before any action was taken. Naturally the Augustinian enthusiastically espoused the proposal, and the arch-bishop just as vehemently opposed it. Not unexpectedly, too, the vice-roy found in favor of the Augustinians and ordered the dispossession of the diocesan pastor of San Pablo. Moya brought suit before the audiencia, and the litigation dragged on through 1575 and 1576. When the audiencia found in favor of the Augustinians, Moya appealed di-rectly to the king. His appeals failed, and the Augustinians remained at San Pablo.[28]

To finance the proposed college Vera Cruz sought a grant of funds from the royal treasury. The officials in Mexico, including Coruña, sent favorable recommendations to Spain, but the grant was never made, an outcome Moya may have influenced. Vera Cruz then turned to private donors and obtained sufficient funds through contributions to buy property and begin construction. Although the college was offi-cially established in 1578, Moya was still opposing it more than three years later.[29]

He lost his battle. The college was built and the parish remained in the hands of the Augustinians. The college became one of the most famous in New Spain and set very high standards. According to Gri-jalva, students from San Pablo were not subject to examination when they entered the University of Mexico and Bishop Diego Romano of Tlaxcala, who was very exacting when examining the credentials of religious presented for ordination, habitually exempted the graduates of San Pablo.[30] It is not clear whether or not Moya ever reconciled himself to the existence of the college or what his subsequent relations with it were.

If the Franciscans offered Moya little trouble in regard to the cru-zada, they more than made up for it in other areas. In 1574 he sent to Spain a report on their usurpations of ecclesiastical jurisdiction and followed that with another list of complaints.[31] He viewed them as one of the chief sources of disquiet in New Spain. Contrary to royal and papal orders, they were continuing to administer the sacraments to non-Indians and were still making judgments in matrimonial cases. Contrary to the royal order of 1560, they continued to maintain stocks and prisons for the Indians. When the diocesan pastor of San Juan de los Chichimecas came to Mexico on business, the Franciscans moved in and took over the parish by order of their commissary, Miguel Navarro.[32] They also invaded the territory of other orders and had recently seized a doctrina belonging to the Dominicans of Talquiltenango, near Cuernavaca. The Dominicans asked Moya to excommunicate the Franciscans, but he declined in order not to make a bad situation worse.

Some of the archbishop's most exasperating conflicts with the Franciscans involved convents of nuns. Typical was the convent of La Concepción, one of the oldest and most distinguished in the city, whose nuns Moya had employed to administer Jesús María. The nuns were divided into two factions, one wanting the convent to be under the direction of the archbishop, the other wanting the Franciscans. Moya was able to assert his authority over it and later claimed that it was one of the most observant religious houses in New Spain.[33]

Rather more bizarre was the struggle with Navarro over the nuns of Santa Clara. This convent was ruled by a small clique of criolla nuns, who claimed to be exempt from the archbishop's jurisdiction. They based their claim on certain papal privileges, though they refused to show them to him. The Franciscans themselves were split over the question. The criollo faction wanted to accept the direction of the convent, whereas the peninsular group opposed it. Some time in 1573 or 1574 Moya excommunicated both the superior and her administration, whereupon they appealed *por via de fuerza* to the audiencia. To his disgust the audiencia both accepted the case and found in the nuns' favor.[34]

Moya considered much of Navarro's behavior to be totally irrational, and with good reason. The commissary's eccentricities gave evidence of a disturbed personality. Early on an August morning in 1574, for example, Navarro took six or seven nuns from Santa Clara to the old church of San Juan. They took possession of it with the announcement that they intended to found a convent there. This was done without a word to either civil or ecclesiastical authorities. Moya's attempts to oust them resulted in a near riot among the local Indians, but he was finally able, through his provisor, to persuade them to leave. When they departed, they did so in procession, carrying the processional cross covered with black cloth (as on Good Friday) and reciting Psalm 114, "When Israel came forth from Egypt . . ." They certainly did not lack flamboyance. Navarro was so angered by the failure of the local Franciscan provincial to support him in this venture that he exiled him from the city. Moya, in his turn, began to press for the commissary's recall to Spain.[35]

Moya also accused Navarro of allowing the nuns of Santa Clara to be professed (admitted to vows) before they had finished the required year of novitiate. This may have been either a means of acquiring and spending their dowries or an attempt to fill the convent with criollas.[36] The result of this extravagance was that the convent was impoverished. When Navarro was finally relieved of his post, he turned the direction of Santa Clara over to the Franciscan provincial of Michoacán rather than to the provincial of Mexico.

Much to Moya's disappointment, when a new commissary finally arrived he did not bring with him the cédulas that would have turned the direction of the convent over to the archbishop. The commissary general in Spain had given verbal orders that the Franciscans relinquish the convent, however, and he had further directed that these be communicated to Moya. The archbishop accordingly took over the convent and, with the consent of the viceroy, promptly exiled the superior and her clique to the school of La Caridad and replaced them with a temporary administration brought in from La Concepción. He then convoked a junta of theologians and canonists, who validated his jurisdiction over Santa Clara but also declared that most of the professions were invalid. This latter question was eventually forwarded to Rome for settlement.[37]

The exiled nuns refused to accept this verdict and made the inevitable appeal to the audiencia, which ruled in their favor and ordered their return to Santa Clara. The other nuns at Santa Clara in turn made their own appeal to keep the exiles out. The exiles did not return, both because they were fearful of their reception at the hands of the others and because they did not want to be under Moya's authority. They were eventually sent back to Spain in 1577.[38]

The final outcome of the case is not clear. A later letter of Moya's seems to indicate that a royal order returned the convent to the direction of the Franciscans, but that the nuns preferred to be under the authority of the archbishop. There are also indications that the Franciscans later helped the nuns in their poverty and that Moya was desirous that they should continue this service.[39]

The archbishop must certainly have wearied of all this bickering. In 1574 he wrote to Ovando, "With all this I shall have satisfied my conscience, which does not extend itself to claiming more nuns than I presently have charge of."[40]

Not all of Moya's relations with religious were so hostile. In 1577 a group of Discalced Franciscans, who practiced a particularly austere form of life, passed through Mexico on their way to the Philippines. Of the twenty-two who had been sent from Spain, only nine arrived in New Spain, and most of these were exhausted and sick.[41] They stayed for a while to recuperate and attracted so much favorable attention by their piety and preaching that Moya formed the idea of having them found a monastery in the city. In addition to the good they could do, he thought, they might be a good example to the other religious. He was finally able to secure this in 1580, and thereafter had nothing but praise for the good they did. He also arranged to exempt them from the authority of the other Franciscans in the city.[42] It should be noted that, unlike the other religious, they were in no way a threat to his jurisdiction or the established ecclesiastical system.

THE JESUITS

The other order with which Moya had good relations was the Society of Jesus, whose members he had known and respected since his days in the Canary Islands. In that age the Jesuits were not usually grouped with the mendicants under the general designation of religious. Nor had they been in New Spain long enough to establish a power base, make formidable enemies, or threaten the bishops' authority, as they were to do in the seventeenth and eighteenth centuries.

The first Jesuits reached New Spain in September 1572. Moya was overjoyed to hear of their arrival and sent some Inquisition ministers to meet them at San Juan de Ulúa. He even offered to pay for their journey inland, but that matter had already been entrusted by Philip II to the treasury officials of New Spain.[43] From the outset the archbishop not only favored their work but also never missed an opportunity to praise the order in his letters to Spain. He constantly asked for more of them. At Moya's urging Philip II wrote to Everard Mercurian, the Jesuit superior general, in 1574 and 1575 to ask for additional personnel for the Jesuit college in Mexico City. Moya himself wrote several letters to Mercurian to ask for additional men, and on 1 October 1576 he sent an appeal directly to Pope Gregory XIII. His appeals met with success, because from the original fifteen in 1572, the Jesuits had grown to some 155 by the time of Moya's return to Spain in 1586.[44]

The first Jesuit school in Mexico City was the Colegio de San Pedro y San Pablo, which was later succeeded by the Colegio de San Ildefonso. Classes began in 1573 and the results were so good that in 1575–1576, after philosophy had been added to the curriculum, the Jesuits determined to begin granting degrees. The rector and faculty of the Royal and Pontifical University of Mexico opposed this competition and petitioned Philip II to prevent any school from claiming university honors. The king ruled against the Jesuits and refused to change his mind despite Moya's urgings. The Jesuits then appealed to the pope, who issued a bull permitting them to establish faculties even in places where these already existed. The king confirmed this in 1579.[45]

Moya conceived the idea of allowing the Jesuits to attend and graduate from the University of Mexico without paying tuition and of having them teach at the university, arguing that the work they did for the education of youth would be more than ample repayment. The university faculty split over the question, but the Jesuits themselves rejected the idea, saying that it would introduce ambition and competition into their order—but also perhaps because they feared the animosity of the university people.[46]

The archbishop also tried to turn the moribund college of San Juan Letrán over to the Jesuits. Although he felt that it had the potential for being one of the best colleges in New Spain, Moya denounced it to Philip II for producing poor results in spite of the money that had been poured into it. By 1578 it housed some seventy or eighty boys of mestizo or low birth under the direction of a laymen and a cleric, who taught them to read and write. Those who did not remain or who were expelled swelled the ranks of the vagabonds. Accompanying funeral processions was the only occupation of those who remained in the school. In response to the archbishop's urgings, Philip II issued a cédula (Madrid, 29 July 1578) that gave the administration of the college to the Jesuits. This came to naught, however, when the Jesuits refused to accept it on the grounds that girls and hospital inmates were being trained in other parts of the building. The opposition of the viceroy may also have played a part in the refusal.[47]

Moya gave the Jesuits a residence at Tepoztlán so that their men could learn Nahuatl and Otomí among the natives, but the Jesuits turned down his request that they become full-time parish priests there. A Jesuit contemporary called Moya "the true father of the Company [of Jesus] in New Spain."[48] His patronage of the society was probably one of his most important contributions to the Catholic Reformation in the land.

THE STRUGGLE OVER THE DOCTRINAS

In addition to the provisions already mentioned, the famous Ordenanza del Patronazgo of 1 June 1574 contained articles designed to bring the mendicant orders under the control of the government. These decreed that no religious, whether provincial or subject, could journey to Spain without royal permission. No provincial or superior could exercise his office until the viceroy or governor had been fully informed of his election. The religious were required to submit three lists to the viceroy. The first was of all towns in which they served. The second was an annual list of all their members, together with a description of their qualities. The third was a list of all the mendicants employed in the doctrinas, which was to be drawn up and given to the bishops so that they would know how well their doctrinas were being served. A religious functioning as a pastor or parish priest could not be removed from his post until after the viceroy had been informed. Finally, all benefices, including the doctrinas of the religious, were to be opened to candidacy by oposición.[49]

As mentioned in an earlier context, the entire Ordenanza was classic regalism in action, devised by one of the most dedicated regalists in Philip II's government. It was also a body blow to the privileges of the friars and a conscious effort to put an end to the existence of two parallel churches in New Spain. If the mendicants accepted the provisions of the Ordenanza they would soon find themselves reduced to appendages of an ecclesiastical structure centered totally on the Escorial. Martín Enríquez informed the orders of the Ordenanza, and the provincials of the three principal ones (Franciscans, Dominicans, and Augustinians) quickly responded. They offered no objections to most of the provisions, but the requirement that they give a list of their members in the doctrinas to the viceroy for transmission to the bishop they found totally unacceptable, because it would have subjected them in some way, however indirectly, to the jurisdiction of the local ordinaries. They also rejected the viceroy's participation in the appointment or removal of parish priests as an intrusion of the civil government into purely ecclesiastical affairs. They stated jointly that in their ministries they could not be responsible to any authority outside their own orders.[50]

Moya was sure that the religious were going to send representatives to Spain to appeal against the Ordenanza, and in a letter of 20 October 1574 to Ovando he tried to block their personal access to the king. He gave various reasons for this, but it is apparent that his true fear was that their personal appeals, as opposed to more formal legal documents, would be effective. He even claimed to have persuaded some of the principal religious to admit openly that the royal order was a good and holy one, and indeed that it had been far too long in coming. That claim is hardly credible. More realistically, he admitted that he had to deal diplomatically with the religious, because they were still needed for the instruction of the Indians, by whom they were held in affection. Moreover the religious were necessary for "the Christian state."[51]

This last point, of course, was the crucial weakness in the Ovando and regalist position. The king, the Council of the Indies, and the bishops all wanted to control and subordinate the religious, gradually removing them from the more important posts and replacing them with a more pliant diocesan structure. The "American reality," however, was that they still needed the religious and depended on them for the evangelical task, which the government took quite seriously. The friars' threat to withdraw from the field was no idle one, and such a move would have caused irreparable damage to the church's mission in New Spain. It would also have undermined one of the bases for the crown's claim to dominion in the New World. This dilemma on the part of the government explains its many retreats and changes of policy during the following ten years, the publication and revocation of cédulas, and what on the surface could be interpreted as an incredible indecisiveness.

Any success Moya may have had in persuading the friars to admit the good of the Ordenanza was short-lived. As its implications began to sink in, their resistance stiffened and they buried their rivalries to form a common defense. On 11 December 1574 they presented a statement of position to Enríquez in which they threatened to withdraw from the mission field rather than accept the Ordenanza. In their eyes it meant the end of their orders, and if they had to choose between the missionary task and survival, they would choose the latter. On the following day they sent a letter to Philip II in which they repeated their threat.[52]

Moya discounted the threat. In a letter to Ovando (20 December 1574) he said that the religious were reluctant even to leave a town of only twenty Indians (it would, he said, be like asking them to pluck out their eyes) and would be much more hesitant to abandon their monasteries, which for them were houses of leisure and recreation. He did, however, have to admit that there were not enough diocesan priests to prevent the mendicants from carrying out their threat. He went on to give a lengthy description of the lives of the religious and the complaints he had had against them. It was a classic statement of the case the bishops of New Spain had against the friars.[53]

He began by saying that ordinarily there were two religious living in a monastery large enough to support fifty or sixty. In general, they did not know the native languages, with occasional exceptions in the larger cities, such as Tlaxcala and Texcoco, where the religious houses had a larger number of members. The religious made the Indians come to the monasteries from the other towns in order to hear mass on Sundays and feast days and to be instructed. They had their own Indian officers, whose duty it was to denounce the sins of the Indians, and they punished the transgressions of the natives in their own prisons, thus usurping the jurisdiction of the bishops. The outlying towns were visited only sporadically, and when the religious did visit them, they baptized the children, did whatever else was needed, and then returned home. Those who fell ill between the visits were brought by other Indians to the monasteries to receive the last rites. This was often a distance of two, three, or four or more leagues, and often the sick died before they reached the monastery. The same thing happened to babies who were born sickly. The newly delivered mothers had to bring them to the religious houses to be baptized and perhaps to be buried.

If one asked the religious why they did not go out to the people to minister to them, they commonly retorted that because they were not parish priests (*curas*) in the legal sense, they had no strict obligation to administer the sacraments. They did so out of charity, rather than strict justice, because, unlike diocesan pastors, they held no formal office and were not paid for their ministry. Moya claimed to have heard this from one of the prinicipal Dominicans just a few days previously when the two of them had been arguing this point. If the friars were reminded that all the souls in their districts belonged to them, they answered that they belonged to the bishop. As for getting them to act in accordance with an enlightened conscience, they acted deaf and answered with ridicule that they were being asked to do something absurd.

The archbishop claimed that the only motive of the religious was that they wanted neither to be obligated to do anything nor to recognize any superior; they simply wanted to do their own will in everything. Nothing made any difference to them except that they be curas and that they not be visited or have to obey a bishop. They ignored the fact that they themselves said the bishop had charge of everything, and that if this were true, he ought to know what was happening. If the religious lived properly and carried out their duties, the bishops would be the heralds of their virtues.

With regard to the order in the Ordenanza that they were not to transfer members from one monastery to another without notifying the local bishop and civil authority, the religious provincials answered that this would strip them of their authority, their rules, and even their entire order. They claimed that it would prevent their governing and correcting their members as they ought. From what Moya could learn, this order was not an inconvenience for them, and many of the religious prelates, especially those who were newly elected, made such changes more out of emotion than by reason or need (a probable reference to the criollo-peninsular antagonisms).

Moya cited many other arguments put forward by the religious in their defense, but he considered most of these to be aimed more at preserving their dominion and freedom from obligation than for the good of the church. He had also learned that they had presented their case in writing to the viceroy for forwarding to the king. This dismayed him, as it seemed a sure indication that the Ordenanza would not be implemented until the king had been heard from again. He had talked to the viceroy and found him "indifferent and undecided" and unable to arrive at a decision. Moya insisted that he be informed of any and all vacancies in the doctrinas so that he could begin filling them with diocesan clergy. The viceroy disagreed, telling the archbishop that he could do nothing in view of the attempts to have the Ordenanza suspended until the king had answered the various appeals. Moya had also heard from some of the friars whom he considered trustworthy that the viceroy had said he would do nothing until he had further word from the king.

Realistically, Moya had scant hope of seeing the Ordenanza implemented. The viceroy was siding with the religious, although they had not been that friendly before. They had gone to Enríquez to seek permission to administer the sacraments, and he had given it "as if he were a prelate." People were scandalized and were saying that "the viceroy is the only one who administers the sacraments."

In concluding his indictment, Moya insisted again on the consolidation of the outlying districts and the realignment of parish boundaries. He also suggested that the salaries of diocesan priests be increased. For any of this to come to pass, however, an explicit order would have to be sent to the viceroy. To make the religious obey the Ordenanza, it would be necessary to have it confirmed by the pope and to have pressure put on the superiors general of the mendicants.

The mendicants prepared to fight the royal instruction through the representatives, mostly provincials, whom they chose to send to Spain.[54] These representatives probably did not leave New Spain until some time early in 1575. The outcome of the dispute was inevitable. The instructions regarding the religious and their doctrinas were rescinded, and the friars were allowed to resume their former behavior.[55] This victory for the mendicants was undoubtedly aided by Ovando's sudden death in September 1575 and by the long delay in choosing a new president for the Council of the Indies. The government, or at least the council, had retreated, but it would be only a matter of time before it would again attempt to assert control. And it was inconceivable that the bishops could live peacefully with a system that permitted the religious to be so independent.

The controversy was revived with full fury just prior to the Third Mexican Provincial Council. In 1583 Diego Romano, the energetic and sometimes aggressive bishop of Tlaxcala, sent a request to Philip II that emphasized two points. First, he said, the religious were ministering to the natives not by reason of any office they held (that is, not out of justice or because of a formal contract or obligation) but only out of charity and as an act of virtue. They could thus not be held directly accountable for any deficiencies; their bond to their work was looser than was the case with diocesan pastors. Because of this, the bishops could not feel that they were adequately fulfilling their obligations toward the natives. Second, he argued, the bishops now had enough clerics to minister to the natives (a claim that was not true). He suggested that these diocesan clerics now assume the doctrinas being served by the religious.[56]

This reasoning appealed to the Council of the Indies, which still maintained its hostility toward the friars. At its suggestion the king dispatched a cédula to Romano on 6 December 1583 in which he decreed that henceforth diocesan clerics were always to be preferred to religious when parishes or benefices fell vacant. This preference applied not only to those to be established in the future but also to those already in existence. The uneasy truce was thus broken and the war renewed. When this cédula reached Mexico, it was presented to the audiencia, which was governing in the interim between the death of Coruña and Moya's appointment. Because there were simply not enough clerics to replace them, most of the bishops took no steps to remove the religious from their doctrinas, but Bartolomé de Ledesma, now bishop of Oaxaca, did present a few of his priests as candidates for the better Indian parishes.[57]

Before taking any steps, Moya decided to consult with the leaders of the principal religious orders. When he did so, he delivered a rather condescending homily in which he urged them to be grateful for a ruling that would be so helpful to their own religious observance and advancement in virtue. In contrast he described the disorder and scandal that had resulted from their wandering lives, especially because so many of their members were still quite young—in other words, were criollos, who were generally considered to have a deleterious effect on religious observance. Finally, he offered them the best of their houses to retain in perpetuity.[58]

The friars were unimpressed and replied that they would consult with the king and with their own superiors. Moya claimed that some of them later admitted to him privately the justice of the Ordenanza but said that they had to yield to the majority, who, being criollos, had developed a taste for power and relaxed living. On 23 October the provincials of the three orders informed Moya that they intended to appeal to the king. Moya inferred that this meant the sending of delegates rather than an appeal in writing, and as he had done in 1575, he attempted to block their personal access to Philip II. He pointed out that the Franciscans were already under orders from their superiors in Spain to send no more envoys to the mother country, but to transact all business through the commissary general in Spain.[59]

His attempts to forestall the delegation failed. In September 1583 the representatives of the religious left for Spain, but they were delayed by shipwreck off the coast of Bermuda the following January. They were able to depart again in March 1584, by which time the news of the forthcoming provincial council had already been published. In Spain they were well received by all except the Council of the Indies, which continued its resolutely antimendicant stance. At court, which was in residence at Madrid, they encountered a shadowy personage, referred to only as the Abad de Burgundí, who had been both an oidor and a visitador in New Spain, and who now became the champion of the mendicants. He went to the king and explained the situation, and Philip II asked him to remain at court until the matter had been settled. He soon became the most influential spokesman for the cause of the religious because he was not an interested party and enjoyed a high reputation.

The representatives were granted a private audience by the king, the very thing that Moya had tried to forestall. Their case was presented by Diego de Soria, an Augustinian, after which all their reports and documents were turned over to Diego de Chávez, the king's confessor, and to the Council of the Indies, whose new president, Fernando de Vega, later bishop of Córdoba, was trying to be impartial. The councilors remained adamant about the Ordenanza, however, and the religious, through Chávez, petitioned for a change of judges. Philip then appointed Chávez head of an ad hoc committee that included Vega and the Abad de Burgundí. The matter was studied thoroughly, especially as Philip, with his famous deliberateness, demanded three successive verdicts. Despite the strong opposition of the Council of the Indies, the committee found in favor of the religious and suggested that their obligation in the doctrinas be changed to a formal one of justice, just like that of diocesan pastors. The representatives returned to New Spain in 1585 on the same flota that brought the new viceroy, Villamanrique.[60]

On 25 March of that same year (or 1 June, according to Encinas), Philip issued a cédula in which he reviewed the orders he had given in 1583 and the appeals that had been made against it, declared his intention to wait for fuller information, and asked the bishops and the mendicant provincials to hold meetings and to inform him of their opinions. In the meantime the bishops would still have to make any visitations of the doctrinas personally, rather than through vicars; the religious were not to lose their exemption; and the king took it upon himself to change the obligation under which they worked from one of charity to one of justice, thus making his own addition to canon law and theology.[61]

Although the status quo had been retained, the king had left an opening for a future revision of crown policy. As will be seen in detail in chapter X, the bishops used the provincial council as an instrument for renewing the attack on the mendicants' privileges. They ordered the compiling of all the documents dealing with the matter, appointed a committee of bishops to give them careful canonical consideration, and then reached the conclusion they had intended from the beginning, entirely rejecting the canonical basis for those privileges. In their general letter to Philip II (5 December 1585) they leveled a comprehensive attack on the whole system of religious privilege.[62] The religious made a spirited defense. Once again their provincials went to Spain to plead their cause before the king, but unfortunately there is only scattered documentation concerning their efforts. Such evidence as does exist indicates that the defense they followed was very similar to that which the religious had been using for decades.[63]

As so frequently happened in the government of Philip II, the decision seems to have been to make no decision at all. The crown never followed through fully on Ovando's grand design, but in all the years of maneuvering it did succeed in restricting the religious and strengthening the diocesan structure, and in the process it gained more control over both. The attempt to replace the religious with diocesan priests in the doctrinas received still greater emphasis and was carried much further in the following century by Bishop Juan de Palafox y Mendoza, a man whose personality and career offer interesting parallels to those of Moya de Contreras. Palafox's activities not only marked the culmination of royal control but also saw the beginning of that generalized hostility toward the Jesuits that characterized the Spanish government down to the expulsion of the Society in 1767. In the process of governmental exploitation of the controversy over the respective powers of the bishops and the friars and the extension of royal control over the church, the religious society that had been so favorably viewed in 1585 thus became an enemy by 1642.[64]

The whole controversy presents an amazing spectacle to the modern reader. That men whose lives were supposedly committed to a common mission and to a high degree of self-abnegation could have engaged in struggles that at times were so petty, so squalid, and so unseemly can truly cause sad astonishment. The bishops undoubtedly had law and tradition on their sides, as well as other strong arguments. The religious undoubtedly had the reality of the situation on theirs, although they were definitely guilty of excesses. Both sides went too far, and there is more than enough reproach to go around. Ultimately it was a power struggle in which there was no victor except the Spanish crown. The real losers were the church's missionary work and the natives. For the church it meant the obstruction and retardation of an urgent mission. For the Indians it meant being reduced to the status of pawns in a tawdry game of power politics.

There is at least one indication that the difficulties of his office discouraged Moya. In 1582 he wrote a personal letter to Philip II asking, among other things, that he might be relieved "of this exile" and allowed to return to Spain, where he could serve the king more closely as his "chaplain." He complained about the difficulty of reforming the clergy and in general believed that a post back in Spain would suit him better in both body and spirit. Little did he realize that the most important stages of his career lay just ahead—stages that would carry him to the highest levels of power in the New World. His work was just beginning.

VI. The Visita

In an especially apt choice of words, Ernst Schäfer once referred to the "purgatory of the visitas."[1] The concept of a purge by investigation and punishment, in which government was tried like gold in the fire and the impurities removed, well describes the visita. Faced with the wholesale corruption that was epidemic throughout its American possessions, and unable to trust even its highest officials, the Spanish crown fell back on the visitador, an all-powerful inspector general who would descend on the officials of the colonies, supposedly in secret and without notice, and demand a full accounting of their stewardship.

Although Schäfer estimated that in the period from 1524 to 1700 there were some sixty or seventy visitas of the eleven audiencias in the New World (excluding that of Buenos Aires), strangely enough the institution as such has not been studied as closely as it deserves.[2] The sixteenth century in particular was important for the development of the visita. Though it had peninsular antecedents, the visita, like the patronato, emerged as a stronger institution in the New World than in the Old. There was more need of it because of the geographical distance from the mother country, the de facto independence of colonial officials, the tendency of such officials to be absorbed into the colonial elite, and the policies of the Spanish government itself, such as the deferral of salary increases in the hope that future rewards would assure good behavior.

In the sixteenth century there were at least three major visitas of New Spain: those of Tello de Sandoval (1543), Jerónimo de Valderrama (1564), and Moya de Contreras (1583–1589).[3] The last visita was far more exhaustive and complete than either of the other two. Unlike the others, it covered almost every aspect of governmental administration and finances. The only important area that was not covered was the treatment of the Indians, although it was originally intended to deal with that also. Unlike the visita of Sandoval, that of Moya came to full term. Still more, because his appointment as viceroy arrived during the course of the visita, he enjoyed the rare advantage of being the most powerful single individual in the Spanish New World.

Any study of a sixteenth-century visita inevitably becomes involved in the controversy over the respective meanings of the terms visita and residencia. The confusion of the two words can be found not only in some history books but also in the *Recopilación de leyes de las Indias* and the cataloguing of the Archive of the Indies. One authority speaks of an "excess of confusion" among modern historians.[4] There has been a tendency to consider the two institutions as almost indistinguishable throughout the colonial period.[5] Carlos Molina Argüello holds out against this tendency and traces the origin of the confusion to the usage in the 1680 edition of the *Recopilación*, whose text he considers to be deformed in some places and gibberish in others. Although this is not the place to enter deeply into the dispute, it will be seen that Moya's visita argues for a clear distinction between the two mechanisms in the sixteenth century. Reference has already been made to the fact that Martín Enríquez requested a visita rather than a residencia at the conclusion of his viceregal term. He seems to have regarded a visita as reflecting less on him personally.[6] It is true that in the beginning Moya's commission as visitador included the taking of the residencias of Enríquez and Coruña, but it is difficult to argue from this that the terms were synonymous. In fact, he did not take these residencias, and neither does he seem to have made any effort to do so. His visita was clearly distinct in all its aspects from a residencia and seems to offer proof of that distinction on the part of the crown.

Accounts of Moya's visita can be found in histories such as those of Suárez de Peralta, Gutiérrez de Luna, and Torquemada. Later historians, such as Sosa and Bancroft, based their accounts on the earlier ones.[7] Although these early accounts are sketchy and generic in the extreme, they agree on certain points. The first is that Coruña's term of office (1580–1583) was marked by official laxity and the growth of numerous abuses. "This gentleman governed little. They say that he was very pleasant and fond of hunting," wrote Torquemada, yet it was probably Coruña's reports to Spain that prompted the visita.[8] The accounts also agree that Moya suspended numerous royal officials, including oidores, and inflicted capital punishment in at least one case. There was also agreement that his visita dramatically increased the royal revenues from New Spain.

These points, however, only hint at what actually happened. Studied in detail, Moya's visita offers a fascinating glimpse into the mentality and workings of colonial life and government and the problems that plagued the administration of the Spanish empire.

THE BEGINNINGS

Moya was not the crown's first choice as visitador. That honor fell to Francisco de Villafañe, one of the members of the Council of the Indies, who received a series of commissions from Philip II between 3 and 8 June 1582 that gave him authority to investigate almost all facets of life in New Spain, including finances, the actions of royal officials and bishops, and the treatment of the Indians. The visita was to be secret, as was customary, and Villafañe was given power to suspend guilty officials.[9]

For reasons now unknown, Villafañe was unable to accept the commission. Almost a full year elapsed before it was entrusted to Moya. Nothing is known about the deliberations that led to this choice, how it was made, or the reasons for the delay. Even though Moya may not have been under a cloud or suffering official displeasure after his rebuke by Philip II in 1575, he nonetheless acted with discretion, restricting himself to the work of an archbishop. His letters and reports to Spain, which were clear, organized, and comprehensive, were valued by the king, who from 1579 to 1582 began to show increasing appreciation of his work and to praise it highly. In 1582 Philip waxed positively lyrical on the virtues of his archbishop.[10] This growing esteem undoubtedly influenced the choice.

However it may have happened, a series of cédulas in the spring of 1583 not only appointed Moya visitador but also defined his powers and duties in terms far broader and stronger than those given to Villafañe.

The basic decree of the visita was issued by Philip II from Aranjuez on 3 May 1583. This directed the archbishop to make a visita primarily of the audiencia and of all its officials. He was also charged with taking the residencias of Enríquez and Coruña, though in fact he did not do so. He was commissioned to investigate the instruction and good treatment of the Indians, although again there is no evidence that he did so. At the conclusion of the visita he was to bring all the documentation to the Council of the Indies.[11] In order to give him a clear idea of what was required, all the commissions that had been given to Villa-fañe were forwarded to him.

A second flurry of cédulas, dated 22 May 1583, further clarified Moya's duties and added various details. He was given the right to attend the meetings of the audiencia if he chose in order to monitor its functions.[12] The first mention was made of a special visita of the *hacienda*, or financial mechanisms of government. He was also allowed to publish news of the visita in the various provinces in order to encourage denunciations. One directive gave him authority over the *alguaciles mayores* and *menores* of Mexico City and Veracruz in order that he might employ them in his investigations. He was given the right to inspect the treasury officials of Veracruz as well as judicial power over cases involving those who felt themselves aggrieved by the officials being inspected, including even the viceroy (a power Moya did not hesitate to use). Instructions were issued on how the visita was to be financed, and the president and oidores of the audiencia were given explicit orders not to interfere with or hinder it in any way. A highly detailed commission on the visita of the treasury officials of Mexico City directed not only what was to be inspected, but also what was to be done with the findings. For this purpose Moya was also given the power to review the accounts of these officials as they had been taken by the audiencia. Further details were added on the investigation of the treasury officials of Veracruz. He was commissioned to investigate the treasurer (*tesorero*) and officials of the royal mint.[13]

This formidable list of duties was waiting for Moya when he returned to Mexico City from a visitation of his archdiocese in September 1583. By royal order the visita was to be kept secret in accordance with established practice, although leeway was given for publishing it in the provinces. The audiencia especially was to have no part in it or even to know about it.[14] The secret, however, could not be kept. Because of rumors and speculations, and also because he wanted to invite denunciations, the archbishop found it necessary to inform the audiencia on 23 September and to publish the fact formally in Mexico City the following day. Shortly afterward it was published throughout New Spain.[15]

Despite his wide grant of powers, Moya sought more. He considered the audiencia totally unfit for any investigative task because, after the death of Coruña, it had been deeply involved in almost everything that had been going on in New Spain. He told the king that people were afraid to say what they really thought and had been silenced by fear or threats. Others had been bought off by lands, ranches, and shares in mills, all of which the oidores had been very liberal with since the death of the viceroy. Moya noted, however, that the audiencia had begun to act more discreetly after the publication of his appointment. He promised to keep an eye on the audiencia but insisted to the king, as he would for the next year, that the only permanent solution to these problems was the appointment of a new viceroy.[16]

At the beginning of the visita, Moya asked Pedro Gallo de Escalada, the general notary of mines and registers (*escribano mayor de minas y registros*) to turn over to him all the materials that had already been submitted as evidence concerning abuses in the administration of the royal treasury (*real hacienda*). Gallo de Escalada had been complaining about the general situation, especially the treasury officials, since 1570. Because of what he was told by the notary, Moya also sought authority from the king to audit a wide number of accounts, including those of the collector of the alcabala, the *depositario general* of Mexico City, the collector of duties at the forts of San Juan de Ulúa, and the superintendents (*obreros mayores*) of the construction and maintenance of the cathedrals of Mexico City, Tlaxcala, Oaxaca, Yucatán, and Michoacán. He also requested authority to investigate property ownership by the oidores and the other royal officials "because the excess has been great and damaging to many and people are on the watch, waiting for the remedy." He detailed a long list of lesser officials, reaching to the lowest local level, who also required investigation. The problem with these, he reported, was that their term of office in any area was so short that their delinquencies frequently went undetected and unpunished. Like most visitadores, Moya was seeking to extend his powers and the scope of his investigation. These requests were granted by Philip II in 1584.[17]

Moya also suggested that the king appoint a commission to take the residencias of most of the officials—justices, councilmen, peace officers, majordomos, and notaries of every kind—of Mexico City. Such residencias were usually taken by the audiencia, but this, he said, was a formality and "more by way of compliance than reform."[18] He also recommended an examination of the accounts of municipal properties and funds (*propios*) to find out how these were distributed and their revenues spent. The archbishop was looking for a full-scale and thorough investigation of every aspect of government and finance in New Spain.

The visita was a slow process. Moya deliberately took his time, refused to be hurried, and reported all his moves to the king. The active period was to last some two and a half years, until the summer of 1586, and some of the investigations were not finished until 1590.[19]

Despite this, the visita made considerable headway during its first year. Moya made the process of denunciation easier by obtaining an order from the king on 19 February 1584 assuring secrecy, especially from the audiencia, for those who made denunciations.[20] On 1 April 1584 he decreed the establishment of an archive in the viceregal palace in which all the account books, registers, and ledgers of the various officials of New Spain were to be kept. Supervision of the archive was entrusted to Diego Ramírez, the accountant (*contador*) of the royal treasury. It was an unfortunate choice, as Ramírez would soon be one of the prime targets of the investigation. All the officials of New Spain were ordered to bring their books to this archive and turn them over to Ramírez.[21]

Moya's hand was considerably strengthened, and his workload enormously increased, when the flota from Spain arrived on 15 September 1584 with the news that Philip II had appointed him acting viceroy. Because of difficulties caused by some of his investigations, the archbishop delayed the publication of this news until 26 September. Ten days later he moved into the viceregal palace. He forbade the customary public celebrations, both out of a sense of austerity and a sense that such celebrating was inappropriate when the government itself was under investigation. Moya clearly considered himself an interim viceroy and kept up his pleas to Philip II to appoint a permanent one. The new office slowed the progress of the various investigations because of added distractions. In addition the most active period of the visita coincided with the celebration of the provincial council and its attendant worries. For the next thirteen months Moya de Contreras would fill all the supreme offices and be the undisputed ruler of the civil and religious life of New Spain.[22]

Both as visitador and viceroy, Moya inevitably became involved in criminal prosecutions, an area forbidden to churchmen by canon law. Philip II had issued a cédula on 19 February 1584 that permitted him to act as a judge in criminal cases, but Moya was not satisfied. He asked for a more explicit permission, both from the king and the pope.[23] This was eventually granted, but even then he was bothered by his canonist's scruples and, as the visita proceeded, turned the final determination of criminal cases over to Santiago del Riego, the alcalde del crimen of the audiencia.[24]

Moya's dominant position was weakened at the end of 1585. On 13 May of that year, the king appointed the marqués de Villamanrique as viceroy of New Spain. Moya learned of this on 26 September.[25] It was an answer to his repeated requests, but it was also to cause him numerous vexations. He was to have as many difficulties with Villamanrique as he had had with Enríquez.

THE AUDIENCIA

The audiencia, a powerful body in New Spain at any time, was even more so in 1583. The fact that the only authority superior to it was that of the viceroy gave it both power and prestige. The weak rule of the conde de Coruña and the interregnum that followed it for almost two years left the audiencia virtually unchallenged.[26]

If the power was great, so were the opportunities to abuse it. The salaries of officials at all levels in the Indies, although higher than those of their counterparts in Spain, were nonetheless inadequate because of the higher price scale in the New World. The crown's policy of deferring salary increases made it difficult for oidores to live in the style to which they felt entitled. There were strong temptations to make money or establish profitable connections in some illegal fashion. As the visita was to show, the oidores were little better than civilian conquistadores, who had come to the New World to gain status and make their fortunes. They were as venal, ruthless, and unethical as any of the original conquerors of the land.

Moya's visita disclosed an appalling pattern of corruption in the audiencia that can be taken as typical of the problems faced by Spanish colonial administration. Of special concern to the crown was the corruption of justice and the judicial process. This not only included favoritism toward relatives, friends, and the payers of bribes, but also ranged from such minor matters as holding meetings outside the audiencia chambers to the graver ones of abuse of judicial torture and the death penalty. Influence peddling, whether in lawsuits or the bestowal of favors, was a consistent failing of the oidores. In the business-oriented atmosphere of Mexico City, justice had become a commodity like any other.

Illegal business activities, of which the most flagrant was land speculation, were among the commonest delinquencies. Lands were acquired by a variety of means, mostly illegal, with the Indians and their towns the usual victims. The titles were obtained by deceit, by generous grants from viceroys (especially Enríquez and Coruña), or by the force and fear inherent in the office of oidor. Sometimes they were sold immediately for profit. At other times the oidores would buy numerous small parcels of land that they would consolidate into cattle ranches. These acquisitions were often made through third parties and the purchase and ownership would be hidden behind a web of transactions of bewildering complexity. Land purchases from Indians or their towns were sometimes so coercive as to amount to little more than extortion. The oidores would erect buildings or mills and usurp both the agricultural and water rights of the nearby natives. By means of friendly *repartidores* they would obtain Indian conscripts to work for little or nothing at improving these ranches. The oidor or his relatives would then settle down to the comfortable life of the country gentleman or else sell the improved land for sizeable profits.

The oidores also blurred the distinction between public and private funds. Money deposited in the strongbox, such as that of the *bienes de difuntos,* often served for loans without collateral or term. Conflicts of interest were frequent, as oidores went into debt with persons who had suits before the audiencia, loans that they often failed to repay, or perhaps were not expected to. Some were addicted to gambling and amassed debts with those who were interested parties to audiencia suits. Oidores would take excessive salaries and expense money when sent on special commissions such as visitas or residencias. They usurped jurisdictions that did not belong to them and formed close business alliances with the local elite: merchants, ranch owners, encomenderos, and shipmasters. Together they engaged in extensive and complex business deals that ranged from the Philippines to Peru and Seville.

Another source of profit was illegal marriages. The laws of the Indies were very strict on the subject of oidores' marrying in the colonies, because this inevitably involved them with relatives and with problems of favoritism.

When Moya began his investigation, the audiencia of Mexico had five oidores: Pedro Farfán, Francisco de Sande, Diego García de Palacio, Pedro Sánchez de Paredes, and Hernando de Robles. A sixth, Lope de Miranda, was in Spain during the course of the visita, but he figured prominently in its investigations. The president, Doctor Luis de Villanueva Zapata, had died on 25 October 1583. From Coruña's death in that same year until the assumption of the viceroyalty by the archbishop, this controversial and turbulent body ruled the colony.[27] Having no immediate authority higher than themselves, and feeling no accountability, they became the five petty tyrants of New Spain.

The audiencia took immediate steps to protect itself. Two oidores went to see Moya and informed him that they intended to seek royal permission to see all the documentation of the visita. This, of course, would have effectively hampered any denunciations. Moya sharply reminded them of the law of secrecy, which, as letrados, they should have known. The oidores later wrote to Philip II to request access to the documentation, but the archbishop had forestalled them. The king refused the request, but Moya had to show them the cédula personally to convince them that they would never see the visita papers.[28]

By November 1584 the archbishop had seen enough of the audiencia to suggest a thoroughgoing housecleaning to the king. He recommended that the king send four oidores to replace the deceased Villanueva Zapata, and Farfán, Sande, and Robles. Farfán already had a license to return to Spain, and Moya thought it a good idea that he use it. Sande wanted desperately to return to Spain, as did Robles, because of what was turning up in the visita. Oidores were also needed to replace Sánchez de Paredes, who was elderly, in poor health, and wanted to die in Spain, and Diego García de Palacio, who had personal affairs to settle there.[29]

One result of the archbishop's recommendations was that by a royal order of 14 November 1584 the king authorized him to investigate any case arising from the oidores' ownership of lands, mills, and other properties they were forbidden to hold by royal order.[30] He did not, however, send any replacements.

There was one inclusive charge that was brought against all the oidores and of which all were eventually found to be equally guilty. This involved the use of improper influence to obtain favorable rulings in suits involving the family of Francisco de Sande. Sande himself had lost a lawsuit in the Philippines and had appealed to the king and the Council of the Indies. Instead of carrying through on the appeal, however, he brought the case before the audiencia of Mexico, which found in his favor even though it had no jurisdiction in the matter. Similarly, his brother, Bernardo, brought a suit before the audiencia over some encomiendas in the Philippines. Francisco, while governor of the Philippines, had granted some encomiendas to Bernardo. After Francisco's departure for New Spain, his successor, Gonzalo Ronquillo, annulled the grants on the grounds that the encomiendas were crown property. When Sande became an oidor in Mexico, the audiencia heard the case, despite a clear order from the king that it belonged to the jurisdiction of the governor of the Philippines, and found in Bernardo's favor.[31]

Of the individual oidores, the aging and ill Pedro Sánchez de Paredes seems to have been guilty of the fewest offenses. Besides his involvement in the Sande cases, he was charged for the most part with illegal purchase or extortion of Indian lands and abuses of repartimientos for personal benefit.[32]

Lope de Miranda was in Spain throughout the visita, but that did not prevent the investigation from uncovering some notable delinquencies. As with the other oidores there were charges that he favored friends in lawsuits and intervened on their behalf even in suits outside his jurisdiction. He was also charged with prejudiced behavior during court sessions and of handing down decisions that benefited him financially. He sometimes acted as advocate and judge in the same case. He seems to have been the most rowdy and ill-tempered of the oidores, for he was accused of disrespectful behavior in the courtroom during trials and of having abused his power by ordering the judicial torture of a person he suspected of having stolen his horse. He struck and verbally abused an alguacil and did the same to a seventy-year-old official of the municipal slaughterhouse. He also secured grants of Indian lands from Enríquez.[33]

As has been mentioned, Francisco de Sande had had a tempestuous career even before coming to New Spain. As a member of the audiencia he was still undergoing the residencia for his term as governor of the Philippines.[34] The same charges that had been made against him in the islands, such as illegal and shady business dealings, turned up again in the visita. Specifically, it was charged that Sande had been in complicity with Diego López de Montalbán, a merchant of Mexico City, who had shipped a consignment of cochineal to his brother, Esteban López, a merchant of Seville, in 1583. It was commonly supposed that the cochineal really belonged to Sande and that he had purchased it in Puebla and neighboring cities through two agents who claimed to be working for Diego López. One of these agents was Francisco Palao, Diego López's nephew.

Moya impounded the shipment while the case was being investigated. Little was learned, however, because people were still reluctant to testify against an all-powerful oidor. The archbishop finally allowed the shipment to leave for Spain, but only after Diego López had been compelled to post a bond against the anticipated sale of the cochineal. Then, early in 1584, the king ordered Sande to return to Spain. Reversing his earlier recommendation, Moya suspended the order because the audiencia needed its oidores and because he wanted to finish the investigation.[35]

The case was also under investigation in Spain. When the cargo arrived at Seville it was promptly impounded by the local authorities and sold at auction. The crown ordered all the papers dealing with the confiscation and sale and all the money made from it to be turned over to the Council of the Indies (4 October 1583).[36]

After a prolonged inquiry, Moya ordered the arrest of Diego López de Montalbán and his nephew, Francisco Palao (2 January 1586). It had been learned that López and Palao had also been involved with Sande in the importation of gold and silk from China by way of the Philippines. Palao had gone into the records of Diego López, which implicated both Sande and Pedro Farfán, and had removed the incriminating documents, despite the fact that they had been impounded by the alguacil of the visita. López and Palao were also accused of forging documents to prove that the original cochineal shipment did not belong to Sande.

Diego López denied all the charges and made out a list of enemies who might have denounced him.[37] Moya finally decided on more extreme measures. On 22 January 1586, he ordered Diego López and

Francisco Palao to be tortured. This was done on that same day by means of the cord and water torture.[38] Both denied any guilt. On 10 May, when the findings of the visita were about to be sent back to Spain, Moya ordered both men to send their legal representatives (*pro-curadores*) to Spain on the same flota.

The evidence against Sande was never as strong as Moya would have liked, and so Sande was not among the oidores he suspended. He was only able to get at the accomplices. The archbishop was convinced that the oidor was guilty, but on the basis of the documentary evidence now available, it seems that he was never able to prove it. Sande's future career was unimpaired.

Diego García de Palacio was charged with a number of offenses that by this time were becoming wearisomely familiar. He had put together a large ranch within the boundaries of the town of Tlalne-pantla in Oaxaca to the prejudice of the Indians. His servants mistreated the Indians there and dug up their maguey and maize lands for pasture for his cattle. It was also found that he had been remiss in keeping the accounts of the bienes de difuntos and had lent out money from that account, that he had abused repartimientos by using Indians for work on his home, that he had gone into debt, that he had borrowed money from merchants who could be the subject of lawsuits before the audiencia, and that he had forced the sale of Indian common lands (*ejidos*) to himself and his friends.[39]

Of all the oidores, the one most deeply involved in illegal business dealings and suspicious maneuverings was Pedro Farfán. There seems to have been almost no limit to his activities.[40] Irregularities were found in the visitas and residencias that he had conducted as oidor. He had secured a royal pardon for Luis Infante Samaniego, a relative by marriage, when the latter was accused of murder. For some seven years he had helped with the accounts of Martín de Irigoyen, one of the royal treasury officials who came under the scrutiny of Moya's visita.

Farfán was also accused of favoritism and partiality toward relatives and friends in cases that came before the audiencia. He extorted work from artisans and craftsmen in the city and then refused to pay them. He speculated in land, often through third parties, and traded in lands with persons with suits before the audiencia. He illegally obtained Indian ejidos. He gambled frequently for high stakes and neglected the business of the audiencia. He made his relatives executors for goods in the bienes de difuntos.

If he used his powerful position to work business deals to his personal advantage, he also used his power as a magistrate arbitrarily and capriciously. When a friend who was staying at his house accused a servant of having robbed him, Farfán sent for the public executioner and had the eighteen-year-old boy tortured. The boy was later found to be innocent. Farfán also accepted bribes in law cases, often in roundabout ways, as when he sold an elaborate coach to an encomendero of Jilotepec (who had no use for it, because the use of such coaches was forbidden by royal decree). When he was oidor in charge of the bienes de difuntos in 1578, he used the money as if it were his own. Likewise when he held that same position in 1583, he lent out some 4,000 pesos, which he hastily returned after the announcement of the visita. Together with Diego López de Montalbán and other citizens of Mexico City and Seville, he engaged in wholesale trade, contrary to royal orders and to the great scandal of the citizenry. And, of course, like so many others, he used repartimientos for private purposes.[41]

Farfán's marital activities, involving both himself and his son in intrigues and the forced marriage of minors, were bizarre enough to read like a bad novel. They also involved him in a bitter struggle with Viceroy Villamanrique, though the latter tended to close ranks with the audiencia against Moya. Although these nuptial adventures were in blatant violation of the law, they never formed part of the charges leveled against him in the visita.[42]

Hernando de Robles was found guilty of many of the same things, but there were additional charges stemming from his connection with the war on the northern frontier against the Chichimeca Indians. When the Chichimecas killed a rancher and his wife and carried off their children as captives, Robles, the senior military man on the scene, at first did nothing. When he later learned of an Indian cattle thief who was suspected of being a Chichimeca spy, he had him arrested and tortured. The Indian implicated numerous others, and on the basis of this information, Robles arrested twenty-four Pame Indians (a subgroup of the Chichimecas), whom he also had tortured. He promised them their freedom if they confessed. When they did so, however, he had them all hanged. At about the same time a captain named Juan Martín made a raid into Chichimeca territory and rescued the captive children. Martín tried to prevent the execution of the Pames but was unsuccessful. Robles then attempted to get hold of the rescued children in order to prevent the story from leaking out, but Martín and his men forcibly prevented this. Robles even had Martín arrested in order to keep the true story from being made public.[43]

Because Moya planned to return to Spain in April or May 1586, he hoped to have all the charges against the oidores finished by that time. His preoccupation with the office of viceroy and the provincial council prevented him from doing anything in the last part of 1585. Finally, on 18 January 1586, the charges against the oidores, the alcaldes, and fiscal of the audiencia were given to them and they were allowed sixty days in which to make their defense. The precise date on which Moya suspended the three oidores Farfán, Robles, and Palacio is uncertain, but it was probably no later than March 1586. The suspensions left only two active oidores, Sande and Paredes. The former was still under investigation, and the latter was in such bad health that the physicians had given up all hope. Moya continued to plead for new oidores, but they did not come.

The suspended judges were not without defenders. The Franciscans of the Holy Gospel province wrote to the king on their behalf, calling them "fathers" and "upright servants of the crown" for whom the entire country was weeping. As for Moya, they claimed that he was "motivated by the old antagonism that he has had against them and still has because they would not help his private cases." Farfán, they said, was suffering in a special way because he had sided with Enríquez against the archbishop. A more potent defender, however, was the new viceroy, Villamanrique. From the day of his arrival in New Spain he had been hostile to Moya and the work of the provincial council, and he sided with the audiencia in its disputes with ecclesiastics. The new viceroy was further irritated by the fact that he had learned of the suspensions only after they had been made and the oidores themselves informed. He asked Moya to send him the testimonies and records of the cases so that he would know how to proceed in choosing temporary replacements. Eventually he appointed Santiago del Riego and Eugenio de Salazar as temporary oidores and divided the work of the criminal chamber between the two.[44]

The new viceroy's descriptions of the audiencia meetings and the behavior of the oidores were completely different from those of Moya. Villamanrique claimed that the meetings were quiet and peaceful and that the judges were impartial, although he admitted somewhat reluctantly that there may have been grounds for the suspensions.[45] His pious view of the probity of the oidores suggests nothing so much as a conclusion in search of a premise. His attitude toward them and toward the entire work of the visita was formed both by his dislike for and antagonism to Moya and by the longstanding animosities between the civil and ecclesiastical arms. He, like the archbishop, had inherited his stance from his predecessors.

THE TREASURY OFFICIALS

In the organizational structure of New Spain, the exchequer or treasury officials (oficiales reales) occupied an important position, and this importance continued to grow throughout the sixteenth century. They had the overall care of the royal hacienda—that is, the collection and management of all royal funds. These funds were kept in a strongbox, or *caja*, a term that later came to refer to an entire administrative district.

Usually there were three such officials. First, there was the treasurer proper (*tesorero*), who had the special obligation of guarding the funds deposited in the strongbox to which he had one of the keys.[46] He was even required to reside in the building in which the strongbox was kept. He collected the income and made the various orders for payment (*libranzas*), for which he also kept the necessary books. It seems that he was also responsible for the collection of tithes. Second, there was the comptroller (*contador*), a very important official, whose principal task was the supervision of the custody and disposition of all the royal goods. He exercised control over what went in and out of the strongbox, certified all the papers, and wrote out the libranzas. Third, there was the general disbursing and royal business agent, who combined the two offices of *factor* and *veedor*.[47] He maintained constant contact with the Casa de Contratación in Seville and with other agents in New Spain. He was in charge of the royal warehouses that contained merchandise belonging to the crown and was responsible for the tributes in kind that were paid to the crown. He also oversaw the auctioning of those tributes and took care of the stores of arms and ammunition.[48]

These officials were nominated by the Council of the Indies and named by the king himself, an indication of their importance. Ordinarily a treasury official was appointed for life and was called a *principal* or *propietario*, as opposed to a *teniente*, who was a subordinate official with a fixed term. The office could be lost in penalty for dishonesty or incompetence, but a lifetime position was considered one of the perquisites of a treasury official. The treasury officials dealt with all the sources of royal income, including the king's share of the gold and silver mined in New Spain (*quinto real*) and the income from the import-export duty (*almojarifazgo*) and the alcabalas, though the collection of the latter was usually entrusted to a special *receptor general de alcabalas*.[49] They also had charge of expenditures, of which the most important was the payment of salaries to various government officials.

According to the royal ordinances of 10 May 1554 and 29 July 1560, the treasury officials were required to send a review of their accounts (*tiento de cargo*) to Spain each year and a full accounting every three years. Toward the end of the sixteenth century, as the power of the treasury officials increased, so did the regulations designed to keep control over their accounts. The general obligation of auditing and reviewing fell to the audiencias. Thus from 1585 to 1592 the audiencia of Mexico appointed oidores to supervise the accounts. The oidores were also present at all auctions of crown merchandise and tribute and supervised the collection of tithes, rents, and income. Because the oidores themselves often lacked expertise and were not always shining examples of fiscal probity, the results were inevitably uneven.[50]

For the treasury officials the temptations to graft and dishonesty were many, varied, and strong. The most common abuse was involvement in private business ventures, precisely the thing most stringently forbidden by royal decree. To avoid detection, they often made use of middlemen. Often enough, however, the problem was not dishonesty but incompetence. Some officials were simply not good bookkeepers, and their methods were haphazard at best. Not surprisingly, the alteration of books became common.[51] When Philip II was searching for means of increasing income from the New World in 1595, his secretary wrote that on examining the administrative organization of the Indies, he found "great defects in the method of administration, frauds against the hacienda, and carelessness or dishonesty in sending [in] the accounts for the last twenty to thirty-nine years."[52]

One of the precautionary steps taken by the Council of the Indies was the decree that all incoming money, without exception, had to be kept in the strongbox, which had to have three keys, each in separate hands. The flaw, of course, was the possibility of collusion among the various officials, who often took money for private business ventures and then hid the loss in their tortured bookkeeping. Another precaution was to compel the officials to put up bonds as a guarantee of their good performance in office, the money for which was often supplied by guarantors or underwriters (*fiadores*). It is easy to understand why visitas of treasury officials were common.[53]

In 1583 the oficiales reales of Mexico were Ruy Díaz de Mendoza (tesorero), Melchor de Legaspi (contador and son of the conqueror of the Philippines), and Martín de Irigoyen (factor).[54] There is evidence that complaints had been mounting against these men long before the visita, especially by the notary Gallo de Escalada, who had been bombarding Spain with denunciations since 1570. There is also evidence that Moya's visita of these men was not the first. In 1573 Philip II had ordered the oidor Arévalo y Sedeño to begin proceedings against them, and in that same year a letter from the audiencia made mention of a visita. Nothing much seems to have come of it. By a cédula of 19 May 1584, the king sent Moya a summary of all the charges and accusations that had been made against the treasury officials in the Council of the Indies. At first Moya contented himself with ordering an investigation and letting it proceed without disturbing the various officials in their work.[55]

That soon changed. The archbishop ordered a review of the accounts, which had been kept by Diego Ramírez, the royal accountant whom Moya had placed in charge of the visita archive. At least three audits were made by Hernando de Santotis, an accountant who was Moya's right-hand man in all the financial investigations. The first audit showed a shortage of more than 92,000 pesos. After a review of this audit, Moya ordered all three officials put under house arrest. Ramírez was replaced by Santotis and kept under guard in an apartment in the viceregal palace.[56]

Moya suspected that more frauds and shortages would appear in the accounts, especially in the collection of money from the auction of tributes and the government monopoly on mercury. He was equally confident that he could prove the guilt of the treasury officials. These men all put the blame on Diego Ramírez, who in turn blamed the notary who had witnessed and signed the closing of the accounts. This excuse collapsed when the handwriting in the suspicious entries failed to match the notary's.

Moya tried to use tact and leniency with Ramírez in the hope of obtaining information, but when this failed he resorted to more drastic measures. Ramírez refused to incriminate anyone, even under torture, and claimed that it was a case of simple error rather than of crime. The oficiales reales claimed the same thing, but the archbishop refused to believe them. Despite various obstructionist tactics on their part, another audit was taken up to 27 September 1584. The amount of the shortage was drastically reduced to some 25,000 pesos. If they were not guilty of any crime, Moya wrote to the king, they were certainly guilty of an almost criminal incompetence.[57]

It was clear that the officials themselves could never make good the deficit, and Moya demanded a list of their underwriters, so that at least the bonds could be recovered. Santotis drew up a summary of all that had been learned up to 2 March 1584 and prepared it for forwarding to Spain on the flota of December 1585. Irigoyen participated in this review and signed it. Mendoza and Legaspi refused to sign and entered appeals against the orders of the audiencia that directed them to do so. Eventually they gave in under compulsion and signed. For Moya their refusal was in itself reason enough for them to be suspended from office, especially if the rest of the investigation should prove successful. He also concluded that they were in no hurry to make good the shortage and that a final honest accounting would be impossible so long as they were in office. Hence, after lengthy deliberation, he suspended all three on 7 May 1585.[58]

The officials insisted that the audit of their accounts should extend to the very day of their suspensions, in the hope that the deficit might be lessened, but the extra audit merely proved them all the more guilty. They still complained loudly about both Moya and Santotis and the manner in which the audit had been conducted, despite Santotis's claim that there was a difference of only five *granos* between his audit and theirs.[59] Santotis's final survey of the accounts was drawn up for transmission to Spain on 24 October 1585. As of 7 May 1585, the shortage came to somewhat more than 29,000 pesos of clear obligation against the oficiales reales of New Spain.[60] Some time between November 1585 and February 1586 Moya ordered Mendoza, Legaspi, and Irigoyen and all their guarantors to be arrested. It was expected that the guarantors would not be able to make good the entire loss, and the property of the three officials was thus ordered sold as part of the restitution.[61]

Irigoyen was also involved in shortages and overpayments that were appearing in the provisioning of the port of Acapulco and the Manila galleons. Most of these frauds, however, were traced to the assistants of the three treasury officials, the tenientes, who were as dishonest or incompetent as their superiors. One, Juan de Aguirre, had retired to Spain a rich man. Despite Moya's urgent entreaties, he was never returned to New Spain to face charges. Another, Jorge de Arando, cooperated with Moya in the visita, although the archbishop fully intended to put him to the torture at a later date. The revelations of their underlings' dishonesty gave the oficiales reales an opportunity to blame them for all the shortages in the accounts.[62]

At the end of 1585, Moya turned these cases and all the other criminal ones over to Santiago del Riego for final determination. Despite all the permissions that had been given, he still refused to judge or pass sentence in criminal cases.[63] Arando was put to torture by Riego some time in early 1586 but refused to confess. He was then condemned to death and on hearing his sentence (which included the confiscation of all his property), he confessed that the accusations were true and that he and the other tenientes had defrauded the crown of some 24,000 pesos. All of his goods were sold at auction. Riego wanted to carry out the death penalty immediately but was dissuaded by Moya and Eugenio de Salazar, the crown prosecutor, who believed that Arando still had important information to give.[64]

Diego Ramírez and the three treasury officials were also implicated in another form of fraud, that involved in the weighing of silver. This weighing, which the treasury officials were supposed to oversee, was the occasion when the church's and the crown's share of the silver (the tithes and the fifth, or quinto) were collected. Gabriel Rodríguez de Bavia, the weigher (*balanzario*), in collusion with some of the silver merchants of Mexico City, had for some years been shortweighing the silver for his benefit and that of his friends. Moya had begun to receive denunciations of this toward the end of August 1584. He had hoped to see the fraud practiced firsthand, but the weight of denunciations forced him to move more rapidly.[65]

He took personal charge of the case, because he did not trust any other judges. Bavia was closely connected with Ramírez and the oficiales reales. The latter blamed Ramírez for the whole situation, claiming that the silver accounts were made out only once a year, sometimes practically from memory. "I am amazed that a matter so just and reasonable should have encountered so many difficulties in years past and provided the opportunities for the falsifications of the contador Diego Ramírez," Moya wrote to the king in 1585.[66]

Persisting in his refusal to become involved in criminal cases, Moya turned Bavia over to Santiago del Riego for judgment and sentencing. At the same time he gave Riego the case of Gregorio Ortiz de Velasco, who had committed frauds in the construction of two galleons that had been ordered by Enríquez for the Manila trade. Moya concluded that Ortiz de Velasco had defrauded the crown of some 26,000 pesos, but even though imprisoned under close guard, Ortiz refused to incriminate himself.

Ortiz de Velasco, Rodríguez de Bavia, and the latter's accomplice, Luis Díaz de Medina, were all found guilty and sentenced to death. Ortiz de Velasco's execution was set for 22 May 1586. In order to frighten Rodríguez de Bavia and Díaz de Medina into confessing and naming their accomplices, as Arando had done when he learned of his sentence, Riego ordered them brought out with Ortiz to stand at the foot of the gallows as the latter was hanged. He hoped they would think that he intended to carry out the sentences then and there. The ploy failed. The two were granted an appeal "at the very foot of the scaffold," and their cases sent back to the Council of the Indies. Ortiz de Velasco was not so fortunate and his sentence was promptly carried out.[67]

For all of his legal scruples in delegating these cases to Riego, Moya was still the authority ultimately responsible for the execution of Ortiz de Velasco and for the imposition of the other death sentences. However common or uncommon capital punishment may have been in the Indies, such a drastic step was not a normal feature of a visita, which was an investigative, not a punitive, process. That the archbishop should have permitted the execution of Ortiz de Velasco and come close to the execution of three others at a time when he was no longer viceroy appears to be unique in the history of sixteenth-century visitas. It is impossible to say why the penalty was inflicted in this particular case; others of both higher and lower rank had committed frauds equally as grave.

OTHER FRAUDS

The visita of Moya de Contreras reached every part of New Spain and uncovered a circus of corruption, fraud, and inefficiency at every level.

An area closely connected with Mexico City was that of the oficiales reales of Veracruz. These officials, who were tenientes of the treasury officials of Mexico, had the duty of receiving and forwarding to Spain all the gold and silver sent from the capital. Because of the importance of their work and the strategic nature of their location, they had less autonomy than subordinate treasury officials in other parts of the Spanish empire. The oficiales reales of Mexico were required to take turns living in Veracruz in order to supervise their operations. At the time of the visita there were only two treasury officials in Veracruz, the tesorero Luis Céspedes de Oviedo and the contador Alonso de Villanueva. There was no factor.[68]

On the basis of denunciations that had been sent to Spain by a certain Pedro de Chávez, Moya began an investigation of these officials between September and November 1584. It was discovered that in addition to the usual carelessness, they had been using crown money for private purposes and covering the shortages when they were audited by borrowing money from local merchants. It was found that Oviedo owed the caja some 7,000 pesos, and Villanueva 3,000. Both men were suspended from office and returned to Spain to answer a long indictment against them.[69]

Similar frauds were uncovered in the administration of the forts of the port of San Juan de Ulúa, a sensitive area because of its strategic value for the defense of New Spain. Luis de Arciniega, the majordomo of the *imposición*, together with the notary Mateo de Carmona, had sold to private citizens provisions that belonged to the forts. He was also guilty of illegal business dealings in selling ships' supplies to the imposición, using crown slaves for personal business, and buying supplies on credit rather than for cash, thus costing the crown extra money. Carmona, who was the official (*escribano de raciones*) in charge of notarizing the distribution of food rations, was found to have falsified his books by entering the distribution of rations to nonexistent slaves, to have falsified the records of military service for his creditors so that they could apply for favors from the crown, to have fraudulently issued viceregal licenses for the coastal trade, and to have held multiple offices to the neglect of his duty as notary.[70]

Another abundant source of dishonesty was the accounts and custody of the bienes de difuntos. As already mentioned, the oidores annually rotated the position of judge of these goods. In many cases the goods had to be collected by commissaries, who received their commissions from the judge for that particular year. Such collections were necessary because many of the goods reverted to the state or were sold at auction so that the returns could be forwarded to heirs outside New Spain. At the beginning of the visita, following a royal command, Moya had moved the entire operation into the viceregal palace. He then appointed a special accountant, who succeeded in recovering some 34,000 pesos owed to the *juzgado*. By this time even Moya, with his long experience with officials at all levels, was showing his amazement at the collusion of judges, notaries, and collectors in defrauding the government. "It is puzzling to see how wickedly they have carried on in this regard, because most of the hacienda has been consumed in expenses, costs, and frauds. . . . It seems that in general all of us who are in the Indies have as our only goal to enrich ourselves without fear of God or of our king."[71]

The investigation of these accounts continued well into 1585 and gave a number of people some hope that they might actually acquire the goods that they had inherited. This was one of the investigations that Moya turned over to Villamanrique by order of the king after the new viceroy's arrival in Mexico City. Consequently the outcome is not clear.[72]

The same wearisome pattern of carelessness and dishonesty turned up in the investigation of the collection of the alcabala. The archbishop began by recovering more than 30,000 pesos in uncollected taxes and promised not to stop until all had been collected, because "in this land it appears that as the years pass, the right to the debt is lost." He applied the same thoroughness in the dioceses of Tlaxcala, Michoacán, and Oaxaca. Final accounting of this investigation has not been located.[73]

Moya also sent the king an account of what was still owed to the crown as of 17 October 1584 from the mercury destined for the silver mines of Zacatecas. Coruña had ordered that one-eighth of all the silver that the miners brought before the treasury officials for stamping and the paying of the quinto should be taken to retire the miners' debt to the crown for the mercury. It was not a small one, for in addition to the cost of the mercury they had to pay the quinto and the tithes. This accounting has not been located, but a later one, covering the period from November 1576 to May 1586, found arrears of more than one and a half million pesos. Moya put pressure on the treasury officials to ensure their zeal in collecting the money and was confident that it would be recovered.[74]

An investigation was also made of the mint (*casa de moneda*), and as a result charges were brought against its tesorero, Francisco de Quintanadueñas. He was ordered to repay almost 5,000 pesos to the crown, and when he was unable to do so, he was arrested. The investigation continued well into 1587 and Quintanadueñas was eventually allowed to make a settlement on a percentage basis.[75]

It was not until November 1585 that Moya was able to turn his attention to the municipal cabildo, or town council, of Mexico City, and even then because of his many distractions, he had to delegate it entirely to a certain Dr. Alonso Martínez. The cabildo was no more eager than anyone else to be investigated and so threw up a number of obstacles. The regidores appealed to the audiencia against the delegation of powers to Martínez on the grounds that this exceeded the original commissions. The move failed, but it showed how strenuously officials of that age tended to defend their prerogatives.

The regidores were chiefly responsible for the care and distribution of public lands and the provisioning of the city, especially the supervision of the public meat markets (carnicerías) and the water supply. They also had the right to hear appeals from judges of the first instance in certain minor cases. The accusations brought against the regidores were usually that they had been too liberal in giving away public lands, but they were acquitted of these. In individual cases they were accused of having bargained down the fines of persons convicted by lower courts, thus robbing the royal treasury of money; of charging excessive fees; and even, in some cases, of failing to see that the streets and plazas were kept clean. The regidores had also been reluctant to supervise the carnicerías personally and without salary (as the law demanded) and had appointed one of their number (with a salary) to handle this distasteful chore. Of this they were found guilty.[76]

The investigation also touched the accounts of the tax (sisa) on meat and wine, the revenue from which helped to defray the expenses of the aqueducts that brought water to the city. An audit was begun in 1583, but because the auditor was transferred to Acapulco, it was never completed. Despite this, a number of shortages and uncollected debts did appear. One of the chief culprits was Guillén Brondat, who was both a regidor and the obrero mayor of the city. In this latter capacity he was in charge of public works, especially the building and maintenance of the conduits that carried water to the various parts of the city. Not only were his accounts short by more than 14,000 pesos, but it also was discovered that he was using repartimiento Indians to construct and improve buildings that he and his friends owned, and even to build private water conduits to them. Moya suspended Brondat from office on 10 May 1586 and ordered him to post a bond against his future sentencing by the Council of the Indies.[77]

At the king's order, Moya also directed an audit of the accounts of the obreros mayores of the cathedrals of Mexico, Tlaxcala, Michoacán, and Oaxaca, as well as of the paymaster of the Chichimeca war. In the accounts for the construction of the new cathedral of Mexico, a shortage was found against the obrero mayor and the architect of more than 15,000 pesos. In the accounts of the Chichimeca war, three accounts were found to have a shortage of almost 14,000 pesos. The visita of the mines of Zacatecas proved disappointing, as did that of Nueva Vizcaya.[78] In the collection of tribute from the Indian villages, Santotis discovered a shortage of some 96,605 pesos in gold and 45,765 arrobas of corn and tribute in kind.

Moya ordered the arrest of Andrés Vásquez de Aldana, the depositario general of Mexico. The audiencia had ordered a check of his accounts and found a shortage of more than 50,000 pesos, for which he was held responsible. Aggrieved parties who sued his underwriters were able to recover only about half that sum. A temporary replacement was appointed, but before the appointment of a permanent one, Vásquez's creditors demanded that the office be sold and that they be reimbursed from the sale, as if the office had been Vásquez's personal property.[79]

The visita reached down to the lowest level of government, often uncovering deep-seated abuses, sometimes bogging down in pettiness and excessive detail. Notaries at all levels were found to have charged excessive fees for their services and to have failed to enter these in their books. In addition to illegally leasing out the post of teniente, alguaciles were charged with overlooking gambling and the sale of pulque, and of mistreating innocent citizens on the streets. Public criers (*pregoneros*), one of whose duties was to act as auctioneers at the sale of tribute in kind, would neglect their duties and often sell themselves the choice goods at ridiculously low prices. Interpreters, who acted as go-betweens for the Indians with the government, were often guilty of overcharging their clients and of interfering in the election of Indian officials, a very serious crime in the eyes of the crown. The alcaldes in charge of the municipal and audiencia jails were found to have released prisoners in return for bribes, to have permitted gambling and prostitution, to have profited from the fees paid by prisoners for food (charging extra for the wine), and in general to have charged excessive jail fees. In cases of lawsuit and imprisonment for debt, so very common in the colony, officials at every level collected their fees before the creditors were repaid.[80]

THE ARRIVAL OF VILLAMANRIQUE

The arrival in New Spain of the marqués de Villamanrique on 28 October 1585 deprived Moya de Contreras of part of his power and made the work of the visita more difficult. The conflicting and overlapping jurisdictions so favored by the Spanish crown now worked against the

investigations. Visita and *gobernación* were now two parallel govern-
ments, involved in a struggle over respective areas of competence. The
new viceroy tended to side with the audiencia, and the longstanding
enmity between churchmen and civil officials again broke into the
open. For Moya and Villamanrique it was also a personal enmity,
based on arguments over points of etiquette and aggravated by excessive sensitivity on the part of each.

Moya and the new viceroy met at Chapultepec on 28 December
1585. The viceroy objected to the fact that Moya had ordered the alcaldes mayores and *corregidores* to turn over the accounts of the corpo-
rations (*comunidades*) of the Indian towns from 1580 on, as well as the
accounts of the Spanish towns (*villas*) and publicly owned lands. He
claimed that these matters did not belong to the jurisdiction of the
visita but to that of the regular government. Moya asked for copies of
the documents but refused to reply further, saying that he would
answer in writing from Mexico City.[81]

At a second meeting in Mexico City on 4 January 1586, Villamanrique and Moya had a heated argument over the visitador's jurisdiction
over the accounts of the Chichimeca war and the bienes de difuntos.
Moya produced numerous royal cédulas in justification of his authority, but on the basis of a specific royal command he did relinquish the
accounts of the bienes de difuntos to the viceroy. He also relinquished
the accounts of the Chichimeca war, which Villamanrique claimed in
his capacity as captain general (6 January 1586).[82]

The viceroy complained bitterly to Philip II about Moya's refusal to
tell him what he had learned in the visita. Even when he showed the
archbishop a royal order, Moya refused to tell him anything about the
situation of the oficiales reales. The viceroy had learned of the suspension of the oidores only after the fact, and Moya still refused to tell
what further he intended to do to them. In this way Moya was retaining control over these and many other affairs. Villamanrique claimed
that the archbishop should have let him know what was going on,
even though "he may not have any respect for the man who stands in
the place of the king." In the meantime, he declared piously, he would
suffer it all patiently and continue to work to serve the king.[83]

If Villamanrique was irritated over Moya's secretiveness, he was
outraged when he discovered that the archbishop was conducting a
secret investigation of his administration. In the spring of 1586 he
learned that Moya had issued an order that the governmental secretar-
ies should give him copies of all the decrees the viceroy had issued
since his arrival in New Spain. When Villamanrique investigated, he
found that the archbishop had done so in an oral order, which was put
into writing only after the fact. He demanded to know by what right

Moya had done this, and the archbishop replied that he had no special commission, but was acting within his broad powers as visitador. Villa-manrique then wrote a long and furious letter of denunciation, which traveled back to Spain on the same flota as the archbishop.[84]

OF CRIME AND PUNISHMENT

At the beginning of 1586 Moya thought that the entire visita would be finished by 20 April and that he would be able to leave for Spain on the flota scheduled to depart in May. May, however, found him still in Mexico City. He left for Veracruz some time in June and departed for Spain on the convoy that sailed on 12 July. In Spain he delayed for some time in Seville, in order to recover from the strain of the journey, and also in his native province of Córdoba.[85]

On 5 November 1586, while still in Sanlúcar de Barrameda, Moya drew up a report on the visita, which he forwarded to the king. He listed some twenty-seven officials whom he had suspended from office, including the four oidores. The oficiales reales of Mexico had been suspended, arrested, and their property sold. The other suspensions included the oficiales reales of Veracruz and a long list of majordomos, interpreters, notaries, lawyers, *receptores,* and three officials of the city government of Mexico. Four cases had been turned over to Santiago del Riego for judgment or appeal. Ortiz de Velasco had been put to death, and there is an indication that another official may have been executed in Spain.[86]

Actually his report touched only the surface of what had been done. There were far more charges than those that he listed, and the work of sifting and judging these took the Council of the Indies almost three years. The judgments were finally handed down from February to August 1589, with Moya joining the councilors in the majority of them.[87]

The first sentences, given on 22 February 1589, were the most important. First to be judged were the oidores. Pedro Farfán had been charged on 149 different counts, on 79 of which he was acquitted. Most of those of which he was found guilty involved illegal business deals and land speculation. The fines against him were confiscatory. The body of the charges included fines of 3,500 pesos, plus an additional 100 ducados. At the end of the judgment another fine of 4,000 ducados was added, the equivalent of somewhat more than five years of salary. He was suspended from office for ten years, to be reckoned from the day of his suspension by Moya, and he was required to give up all the lands he and his family had acquired.

In 1593 Farfán entered an appeal before the Council of the Indies to have his suspension revoked, but it was refused. Schäfer says that Farfán was named an oidor of Lima in 1594, but in view of the sentences and the refusal of his appeal, this hardly seems likely. He died in Madrid in 1594.[88]

The charges against Sánchez de Paredes were fewer and less severe. Out of twenty-eight counts he was acquitted in one way or another on sixteen. Most the verdicts centered on his illegal acquisition of land and the use of repartimiento Indians to work them. The only penalty was a fine of 50 pesos.

A total of seventy-two charges had been leveled against Diego García de Palacio. Of these he was acquitted of fourteen. For his illegal land holdings and for encroaching on Indian rights, he was fined 4,000 ducados and suspended from office for six years. For another incident of fraudulent acquisition of Indian lands, he was fined an additional 400 ducados. Because of other crimes involving the illegal possession of ranches, the period of suspension was lengthened to nine years and an additional fine of 2,000 pesos de minas applied against him. The total of the fines equaled a little less than five years' salary. On 26 May 1596 the Council of the Indies awarded 2,985 pesos to his children in spite of the wrongs he had committed.[89]

Hernando de Robles was sentenced to fourteen years' suspension from office and fined 2,100 pesos and 100 ducados, about a year and a half of salary. In 1593 his appeal for revocation of the sentence was refused.

Lope de Miranda, the absent oidor, was fined 1,500 ducados, but his suspension was revoked and he was restored to office with all his rights and seniority.

There is no indication of what the charges against Francisco de Sande were or of their outcome. He apparently emerged unscathed, for he went on to be president of the audiencias of Guatemala and then of Santa Fe. Accusations of dishonesty and graft, however, followed him wherever he went.[90]

The lesser officials of the audiencia were also sentenced on the same day. For the period when he had been alcalde del crimen, Santiago de Vera was found guilty of multiple counts of illegal land owning, but he was not removed from office. For the period when he had been fiscal of the audiencia, Santiago del Riego was convicted of numerous violations of legal procedure. Eugenio de Salazar, who later became an oidor, was acquitted of all charges.

A second set of six sentences was given on 27 April. Two cases are of special interest. Guillén Brondat was sentenced for delinquencies committed both as regidor and obrero mayor, but, like the other regidores, he was acquitted of excessive liberality in the distribution of city lands.[91] The other case was that of Mateo de Carmona, who had committed frauds in the distribution of rations at San Juan de Ulúa. He was the first of the officials of the fort administration to be sentenced, and his sentence, like those of the others, was severe: perpetual deprivation of this or any other office in the real hacienda and perpetual exile from the port of Veracruz and the island of San Juan de Ulúa.

On 26 May sentences were passed against six more persons, of whom the most important was Luis de Arciniega, the majordomo of the imposición of San Juan de Ulúa. He was sentenced to perpetual deprivation of office and fined 200 pesos. The sentences handed out on 28 June, 12 July, and 29 July touched a variety of interpreters, *relatores*, alguaciles mayores, tenientes, and notaries of every class.

The bulk of the sentences were given on 7 August. On that day Moya and the councilors signed an astounding 124 sentences of acquittal and guilt, delivered in 122 separate cases. Like the previous ones, they embraced almost every conceivable office in Mexico, including the entire municipal cabildo. On 30 August the last of the cases was settled. Alonso de Villanueva was sentenced for shortages in his accounts and other crimes and condemned to perpetual deprivation of all royal offices. In addition he and Luis Céspedes de Oviedo (whose charge and sentences are not in the visita papers) were fined 4,400 ducados jointly—that is, each was made responsible for what the other could not pay.

A total of 207 persons had been brought before the Council of the Indies by Moya's visita. Of these 163 had been acquitted of all crimes, although 7 were with the qualification that the charges had not been adequately proven (*por no probado*) and 1 with the qualification that the charges were too general. In some cases there was no determination because of the death of the accused.

The guilty verdicts were given the standard Spanish labels of *culpa, culpa grave*, and *culpa gravísima* or *muy grave*, and these offer some interesting indications of how the Council of the Indies viewed the seriousness of different crimes. Pedro Farfán's acceptance of a bribe to alter the outcome of a case before the audiencia and the shortage in Luis de Arciniega's accounts at San Juan de Ulúa drew the most serious verdicts. The designation *culpa grave* was attached to various abuses of office, such as Robles's execution of the Pame Indians and subsequent attempts to cover it up. Shady and illegal financial dealings, such as Farfán's trade with the Philippines and Peru, were also given this verdict. It should be noted, however, that some of these crimes were not so different in kind or degree from those of lesser officials. Higher officials were uniformly judged more severely than their inferiors. Farfán's illegal torturing of a young servant in order to find a thief was judged *culpa grave*. An alguacil mayor who had tortured a black as a suspected runaway slave was judged *culpa*. Undoubtedly the difference in degree depended on both the guilty party and the victim. The severity of the punishments meted out to the officials of San Juan de Ulúa undoubtedly reflected the importance attached to the safety of a port that was not only vital to the economy of New Spain but also vulnerable to the attacks of corsairs. One of the few lesser officials whose crime was labeled *culpa grave* was an *alcalde de la cárcel* who had permitted the attempted rape of a woman prisoner.

There is something of a mystery about Moya's participation in these sentences. He did not sign any of the judgments delivered on 22 February, 27 April, and 26 May, all of which were of higher officials. He signed all those handed down on 28 June, 12 July, 29 July, and 7 August, all of which dealt with lesser officials. He did not sign the 30 August sentence of Alonso de Villanueva. It is possible that for health or other reasons he was unable to be present at the meetings at which final decisions were given in these cases. It seems significant, however, that he should have failed to sign the sentences only of oidores, alcaldes del crimen, and those connected with San Juan de Ulúa.

THE RESULTS OF THE VISITA

Moya's visita took place when that institution was still in its formative stage in the New World. There can be no doubt that his work helped clarify and strengthen the visita as an arm of royal control. The numerous regulations issued by Philip II in 1588 dealing with the method and procedures to be followed must have owed much to the actions and recommendations of the archbishop. The *Recopilación* (lib. 2, tit. 34), contains no less than twelve ordinances issued in that year, stating, among other things, that visitas should be made public from the start, that all officials had to give information to visitadores, that officials were not to hinder the work of a visita, that the visitador needed a special commission to investigate the oficiales reales in a city with an audiencia, that all audiencia minutes were to be given to the visitador, that the visitador had the authority to name investigators, that the alguacil mayor and other officials had to obey the visitador, and that the visitador had the right to suspend officials.[92] This sharpening and increase of the powers of visitadores must surely reflect Moya's experience in New Spain and his influence in Spain after 1586, when he was a trusted advisor to Philip II and later president of the Council of the Indies.

As for the disputed question of the distinction between visita and residencia, Moya's visita indicates that at least in this one case there was a clear distinction between the two. One author believes that the archbishop's commission to inspect the mint, which included the right to pass sentence, was really a residencia, but that does not seem to be the case.[93] Moya did, however, take on himself the right to punish some of the offenders, either personally or through the alcalde del crimen, something that makes his visita unique.

The archbishop's investigation of the government and finances of New Spain was far more thorough and exhaustive than those of previous visitas. It left a strong impression on contemporaries, who believed that it caused a profound improvement in governmental efficiency and honesty. Yet at the same time it reinforces the common belief of historians that Spanish rule in New Spain was afflicted with chronic, almost wholesale, corruption.[94] Although the majority of those accused were acquitted, the number and quality of convictions revealed a rampant lawlessness at almost every level.

From the existing records it appears that the punishments meted out to the various delinquents were adjusted to their state in life and the gravity of their crimes. It seems further that the worst offenders were kept out of public life for extended periods of time. More study is needed before it can be said for certain that the Spanish crown was successful in permanently barring the more notorious offenders. Nor is it entirely impossible that the absence of Moya's signature on some of the sentences indicates his disagreement with the punishments given.

Did the visita produce any permanent good results? On the one hand, if the Franciscan Domingo de Talavera is correct, it actually did little to correct the deeply rooted abuses in New Spain, at least within the first few years after Moya's departure. His call for a new visita, made in 1596, appears to bear this out. On the other hand, a more recent investigator is of the opinion that the work of visitadores such as Moya de Contreras vastly improved Spanish administration; because of them, he believes, "the administrative machinery of the hacienda in the Indies formed a network that was up to a certain point perfect."[95] In some ways both views are correct.

Certainly Moya helped to uncover the worst excesses in the Spanish administrative system, and he at the very least checked the wholesale looting of public funds that had been taking place. It is clear, for example, that in the years following his visita the audiencia exercised more direct control over the oficiales reales. But there is little indication that Moya understood the structural causes of governmental corruption. His approach was symptomatic rather than organizational, and he seems to have been guided solely by the view that a choice between right and wrong was a matter of free will, a view that overlooked social and financial pressures. He was not alone in that respect: there is almost no indication in any of the documents of Moya's visita of a realization of the need for the reform of institutions as well as people. Recommendations by the Council of the Indies usually emphasized the need for greater surveillance and accountability by officials. The only solutions suggested in the sentences of the visita were that the king should send cédulas to remind the officials of those laws and procedures that were already in force. Moya himself suggested a continuation of the policy of deferring salary increases to enforce good behavior.

Nowhere is the ineffectiveness of the Spanish colonial system more clearly shown than in its attempts to collect some of the fines imposed by the Council of the Indies. As late as 1599 those levied against Santiago del Riego had not been paid, despite a specific royal command and a special messenger sent to the viceroy and the audiencia.[96]

The policies of deferred and insufficient salaries, overlapping jurisdictions, the failure of supervising agencies—all of these continued. The immediate interest of the Spanish crown was in getting its full revenue from the Indies, revenue that was being diverted into private pockets. The praise heaped on Moya for increasing the royal income is indicative of the crown's priorities. It wanted to uncover those who were stealing its money and, to the extent necessary, to punish them, but it was not looking for any wide-ranging program of reform in the administrative system that had helped nurture this corruption. It is tempting to speculate on what the outcome of the visita would have been had Juan de Ovando still been in power.

In general it would be safe to say that this energetic and able archbishop helped check official dishonesty and public corruption, even if he did not entirely cure it. He created no perfect system, but he certainly helped raise the standards of government and at least temporarily put the fear of God and king into public officials.

NOTE: THE VISITA OF THE UNIVERSITY

In addition to his other activities as oidor, Pedro Farfán was twice elected rector of the Royal and Pontifical University of Mexico (1570 and 1572). In that post he acquitted himself so well that modern historians do not hesitate to consider him a genuine founder of the university.[97] From 1579 to 1581 he conducted a visita of the university, out of which came the first statutes specifically for it, including one that prohibited students from bringing arms to class. A second visita was made by Moya, who was appointed to that task by a royal cédula of 3 May 1583.

The purpose was twofold: to investigate the financial condition of the university, especially how its income was being spent, and to investigate the educational level—that is, whether it had all the chairs that it was supposed to have and whether the faculty members were teaching as they ought.[98]

The cédula was shown to a plenary meeting of the administration and faculty (*claustro*) on 17 April 1584 and accepted without difficulty. One of the first things that Moya turned his attention to was the construction of the new buildings that the university needed. On 29 June 1584 he laid the cornerstone for a new building.[99] In his visita of the classes, he apparently began with the school of theology, which he inspected on 12 June of that year. After listening to two of the theology lectures, he gave the students an exhortation on developing their concentration and love of study. He then went on to inspect the chairs of law, liberal arts, philosophy, rhetoric, and medicine. The multitude of activities involved with the visita and the provincial council prevented his continuing this visita personally, and he delegated it to Luis de Villanueva Zapata, son of the late president of the audiencia, for whom he had a high regard. Apparently out of a desire to win favor, the university awarded Villanueva Zapata a doctor's degree, which was promptly annulled by the audiencia as contrary to the university's statutes; but the annulment perhaps resulted equally from a desire to retaliate against any partisan of the archbishop's. The degree was eventually sustained.

Although Moya de Contreras was keenly interested in the university, as well as in education in general, he did not play an active and important role in its development because of his preoccupation with so many other activities at the same time. The statutes that resulted from the visita, though commonly attributed to him, were mostly the work of Villanueva Zapata.

VII. The Viceroy of New Spain

Moya de Contreras's involvement with the civil affairs of New Spain began long before his appointment as interim viceroy in 1584. From the moment of his arrival in the New World he consistently reported his impressions and opinions of what was happening in New Spain to Juan de Ovando. He did not confine himself to the religious or ecclesiastical spheres, but commented on a wide variety of topics, many of which today might seem alien to the functions of an archbishop.

That he did so is not surprising in a society in which the functions of church and state often overlapped. It was only natural that prominent men in the one should be interested and involved in the affairs of the other. It was equally natural, given the situation in New Spain, that much of Moya's involvement with the civil government prior to 1584 should have been in the form of conflict, particularly with viceroys and audiencias. His attempts to resist the incursions of the latter into the church's jurisdiction were particularly strong, especially in regard to the via de fuerza whereby cases were appealed from ecclesiastical to civil tribunals. In these Moya was not just an observer but an active participant.

Beyond that Moya functioned as Ovando's man on the spot. His letters to his patron commented on the colonial situation in general, gave advice and suggestions on improving the local economy, recommended names for filling royal offices, and denounced viceroys and audiencias. Moya never hesitated to suggest to Ovando worthy candidates for the various offices that fell vacant or were for sale. Some of these nominees became pawns in the war of wits and status between the archbishop and Martín Enríquez. When Ovando appointed a certain Obregón as corregidor of Mexico City, Moya warned his patron that the viceroy would not like the appointment because he could not abide anyone who was not subservient to him.[1]

His reports to Ovando also commented at length on economic conditions, and although his ideas were no more profound or advanced than those of his contemporaries, he was consistently sympathetic to the problems of the colonists, especially the criollos. At the time he became archbishop, New Spain had been hit by two large financial exactions, the cruzada and the alcabala.[2] Perhaps his experience at the time of his consecration, when the viceroy and audiencia had reacted so strongly to the skit about the alcabala, had colored his attitude toward the tax, but the fact is that in his correspondence with Ovando he tried to soften the impact not only of the alcabala but of all the taxes in New Spain. He reported the general fear that the rate of the alcabala would rise. The miners were complaining that between the tithes and the cost of mercury they were being ruined. The merchants made the same complaints about the alcabala and the almojarifazgo. Moya suggested that the king write some placating letters (*cartas amorosas*) to the cities of New Spain to praise them and thank them for their obedience to the alcabala, and that he should also grant some special favors so that the effects of the various taxes would be blunted. It must be admitted that his suggestions fell far short of helping the beleaguered colonials in their efforts to escape the burden, real or imagined, of peninsular taxation.[3]

He was more specific and practical when discussing the mercury monopoly, a subject that consistently interested him during his years in New Spain and on which he held strong commonsense opinions. To Moya, as to most Spaniards, silver was the life's blood of New Spain. Without it the colony would collapse. Modern historians may debate whether or not the ore was as important as the archbishop and others believed, but there is no doubt that it ranked high. The silver mines, or better, the silver miners, depended on mercury. The amalgamation process used throughout the colonial period, awkward and slow as it was, was satisfactory for the needs of the colony—and for it mercury was essential.[4] Although the mother country produced a sizeable quantity of mercury, especially at Almadén, it was insufficient for the needs of the colonial silver industry. The discovery of silver at Potosí in

Bolivia and at Zacatecas in New Spain in midcentury had happily coincided with the discovery of large mercury deposits at Huancavelica in Peru. At first private merchants had been allowed to export and sell the mercury, but it soon was made a government monopoly, and prices were kept artificially high in order to increase the royal revenues. Moya insisted to Ovando that mercury was essential to the silver mines and that the silver mines were the mainstay of the colonial economy. Until the discoveries in Peru, the cost of mercury had been prohibitive. That, plus other costs such as shipping, tithes, and quintos, had caused most of the miners to go heavily into debt, with the result that at one time there had been no class in New Spain with a lower credit rating. Many had been driven out of business altogether. With the opening of the Peruvian mercury mines, the cost had gone down, the industry had revived, and the miners had improved their condition. Moya could point to positive results: in 1574 more silver than ever was leaving on the flota for Spain. That, of course, meant an increase in crown revenues.[5] Another advantage of cheaper mercury was that it became practical to work marginal mines whose output, while small in comparison with the others, justified the investment so long as the operating costs were kept low.

All of this had changed in 1574 when a ship arrived from Peru carrying some four thousand pounds of mercury and the news that the king had imposed a monopoly (*estanco*) on its exportation. With his usual diplomacy, Moya admitted that this move, with its increased prices, was justified for the sake of Peru, the more important colony, but he made no secret of the fact that he considered it disastrous for New Spain. The miners would be reduced to their previous status and the marginal mines would be abandoned. Worse still, the royal officials who sold the mercury were more demanding in their collection of payments than private merchants had been. The latter, in return for having steady customers, had been willing to carry the miners until after the silver had been processed and money was available. Competition tended to keep the price at a moderate level.

Moya admitted that the price set by Martín Enríquez, about 100 pesos per quintal (about 100 pounds) was not high, although shipping costs and other additions usually brought it to about 115 pesos. It was, however, a very sharp increase compared with the 90 pesos per quintal that had been paid before the monopoly was imposed. Worse, it had to be paid punctually and in cash. Moya pleaded with Ovando to allow the miners to pay in quarterly installments rather than weekly. His personal preference was to see the price returned to 90 pesos, and he argued that the money that would be lost from the reduction in price would be made up in the increased production of silver and the revenues generated by it.

In addition to these burdens the miners had to suffer the depredations of the Chichimecas, whose raids were raising the cost of goods, and hence the general cost of living, in the mining areas. Zacatecas, the richest mining region of New Spain, was the center of Chichimeca activity. Most miners could not afford to build machinery and dig mines in such dangerous country, and usually the ore they discovered was not rich enough to justify the risk. Most people in the mining districts preferred to cluster together in the safety of ranches and presidios and to avoid the more isolated and dangerous life of the miner. The archbishop could not resist adding his usual criticisms of Enríquez for failing to pacify the frontier.[6]

During his short term as viceroy, Moya was able to do something about regularizing the procedures for the distribution of mercury, but despite all his pleas he never succeeded in bringing about an actual reduction in price. As a result the economy of New Spain suffered from this throughout most of the colonial period. It was not until two hundred years after his death that the Bourbon dynasty put into effect the measures Moya had advocated in the sixteenth century and found that the results he had predicted did indeed come about.[7]

After Ovando's death in 1575, Moya's comments on the civil affairs of New Spain ended abruptly. Rarely again did he address a letter to the president of the Council of the Indies. He wrote to the king directly, and these letters were confined almost exclusively to ecclesiastical affairs, except in those cases when the inevitable conflicts with civil jurisdiction arose again. Not until he was made visitador did he reenter the civil and political arena. He again became free in making suggestions about appointments to offices and in commenting on the actions of the civil government, especially the audiencia. He sent the king a complete account of the discovery of New Mexico, written by Felipe de Escalante and Hernando Barrando, and in general gave the impression of a man who was abreast of things and increasingly sure of his own position.[8]

On 12 June 1584 Philip II issued a cédula that appointed Moya governor, captain general, and president of the audiencia of Mexico, with all the powers of a viceroy until such time as the king named a permanent one. Moya received word of the appointment on 15 September. He showed it to the audiencia twelve days later, and then took the oath of office.[9] There is no doubt whatever that he considered himself, and in fact was, an interim viceroy, appointed temporarily to complete his visita and to arrange the affairs of New Spain, or at least to hold them together until the arrival of a permanent viceroy. His letters throughout the latter part of 1584 and the first part of 1585 are filled with pleas to the king to send a viceroy and reminders of the need for a permanent leader. Consequently it is not surprising that his term was concerned mostly with the routine business of office. He was not able to establish new policies or make sweeping changes—though it must be noted that few permanent viceroys were able to do so either. In addition to the interim nature of his office, there was also the fact that his thirteen months in office coincided with the visita and the Third Mexican Provincial Council, either of which was sufficient to occupy him totally. The wonder was that he was able to do as much as he did. He did begin to show signs of independence and a greater control over his position, however, indications that he was growing increasingly self-assured.

It is a measure of Moya's stature and position with Philip II that he was given this imposing array of titles. The Spanish colonial system was built on an obsessive distrust of local officials and was designed to balance one against the other. Granting any sort of monopoly on power was not part of the system and was rarely done. Obviously, the temporary nature of some of Moya's offices and the fact that he was due to return to Spain in the immediate future made this delegation of power somewhat easier, but it nevertheless shows a high degree of confidence.

Whatever the nature of his office, Moya found himself immediately involved in the affairs of government. He now acknowledged receipt of all kinds of governmental documents, such as those dealing with judicial decisions in cases involving the almojarifazgo, financial matters, the implementation of the new Gregorian calendar, the sale of offices (such as the regimiento of Puebla), and the construction of new university buildings with money borrowed from the tax on drinking water. He forwarded with approval a request by the municipal cabildo of Mexico that the tax on wine, which had paid for the ordinary expenses and upkeep of the aqueduct from Sante Fe and had been repealed by the audiencia, be reinstated. At the king's order he collected all the firearms in the possession of the Indians. He reported on ships lost at sea. He forwarded with approval complaints from the merchants of the city that the loss of ships resulted from sailing too late in the season, when the weather was unfavorable, and he recommended that ships should be compelled to leave Seville on schedule whether they had full cargoes or not. He reported the suspicion in Mexico City that there was not enough surveillance of the ships in Seville, and that the masters and owners, who were often heavily in debt, sometimes falsified the values of ships and cargoes and then permitted them to be lost at sea. He sided with the merchants when they claimed that they should be allowed to choose which ships would be navíos de aviso on the return voyage to Spain rather than leave that decision to the Casa de Contratación. He suggested that in the sale of offices the buyers be allowed to pay in installments because, despite the risk of default, the crown would make more money in the long run.

In response to a query from the king, he suggested that there not be an entry tax on the salt that was shipped from Yucatán to Pánuco because the return would be meager and the Spaniards of Pánuco were living in a hot and poor land infested with hostile Indians. When Philip abolished the office of collector (receptor general) of alcabalas in June 1584 as a means of saving money, Moya opposed this because there was not that much money coming in from the tax and because the oficiales reales were too busy to take on the additional burden of collecting it. The salary of the collector, the only money that would be saved, was not that high, and so Moya invoked an old Spanish principle and said that he would put the order into effect "in its time and Your Majesty will be informed"—that is, he suspended it.[10] He even sent a report on an eclipse of the moon that he had watched with two cosmographers. It was also said that he tried to resume the policy of congregación, or resettlement of the Indians, but was prevented by the opposition of the audiencia and the religious.[11]

Moya's jurisdiction included the Philippines, and with it came an increasing interest not only in the islands but also in China and the geographical and maritime questions that involved both areas. He sent on to the Philippines the money ordered by the king for the construction of three galleons for the Manila–New Spain trade, and he also showed his concern for such matters as sending arms and ammunition to Manila, dispatching a mapmaker, and other often routine business.[12]

Moya was fascinated by China. In the sixteenth century the Spaniards had begun tentative trading with the Middle Kingdom, using Manila as the entrepôt. This trade was making itself felt while Moya was viceroy, and he became intrigued with the possibilities that China held, whether commercial or missionary. In 1584 Philip II sent some presents via New Spain for the emperor of China, but Moya was undecided about the proper form for delivering them. He suggested that in such questions the king's ministers should be given some latitude— that is, to decide whether it was better to send the presents to the viceroy of Canton as coming from the governor of the Philippines or from the king directly. Moya claimed that all that he knew about the Chinese was that they were an avaricious people who would lose no opportunity to make a profit.[13]

In December 1584 word reached New Spain that the mainland of China had been opened to Christian preaching, though not to the extent that had been hoped. This news must have referred to the entrance of Matteo Ricci and the first Jesuit missionaries. At the same time limited trading was undertaken with China, and the first galleons began sailing from Manila to the mainland. Moya forwarded to the king an account by the Jesuit Alonso Sánchez of a journey the latter had made to the Chinese mainland. Apparently the good father was of the opinion that Christianity would come to China only by force of arms, a position that would have put him diametrically in opposition to his fellow Jesuit missionaries. Moya suggested that the opinion of such a learned and holy man should be respected but was noncommittal about his own agreement or disagreement with it.[14]

When the governor of the Philippines sent Moya word that there were large quantities of cheap mercury in China, the archbishop was able to return to one of his favorite subjects. He used the occasion tactfully to repeat to Philip all the arguments he had previously used with Ovando in favor of a lower price for mercury. He was unsuccessful, because in 1590 the crown pegged the price at a high 187 pesos per quintal.[15] Moya also sought to eliminate some of the abuses that had arisen in the mercury trade. In order to encourage the mining of silver, Coruña had established a system whereby mercury was rented to the miners from the royal warehouses. To keep track of the amount lent, miners who came to declare the quantity of silver mined and to be assessed for the quinto would take an oath stating the amount of mercury used and pay for it. They would then be given a corresponding amount. Some were perjuring themselves, however, and were paying for a lesser quantity than they actually received. Needy miners were selling the extra mercury to the wealthier ones. As a result the supplies were diminishing. To prevent this, Moya issued a detailed set of instructions that established a fixed rate: payment for one pound of mercury for every *marco* of silver declared.[16]

Moya's interest in the Philippine-China trade led him to take a surprisingly independent step. He reported to the king that ships coming from the Orient ordinarily sighted land about seven hundred leagues north of Acapulco—that is, in the general area of present-day Oregon or northern California. They then followed the coastline, but there were no known harbors where they could reprovision, make repairs, or take refuge in bad weather. There were even occasions when they were forced to turn about and return to the Orient. Some experts believed that the coastline eventually extended to China, whereas others claimed that it stretched to the legendary strait of Anián, which was thought to reach across North America to the Atlantic Ocean. In spite of other expeditions that had gone up the California coast, such as that of Juan Rodríguez Cabrillo in 1542, the Spaniards had been unable to discover any port of refuge. Despite these initial failures, Spaniards of the late sixteenth century persisted in the belief that good harbors or a transcontinental strait was to be found on the California coast.

Moya decided to send an expedition led by a seasoned pilot and mapmaker, Francisco de Galí, to investigate and chart the coastline. He considered the matter so urgent that he arranged for the expedition without prior consultation with the king. He made the requisite apologies for so doing and explained that it would take some six to eight months and would cost no more than eight or ten thousand pesos. He also thought that the expedition might make contact with recently discovered New Mexico.[17] Apparently he was never able to put this expedition together, but he did send Galí on the ship *San Juan* with 10,000 pesos to the Philippines, with instructions to chart the mainlands of China and Japan and then the coast of California and New Spain on his return.[18] Galí made the trip, but despite other abortive efforts, it was not until 1602 that the Vizcaíno expedition discovered Monterey Bay.[19] It would be another century and a half before the Spaniards began the permanent occupation of California.

As mentioned earlier, Moya's short term as viceroy did not permit any startling innovations in government or the formulation of long-term policies. For the most part it was characterized by routine business, but it also showed an increasing grasp of the situation and a growing acquaintance with the needs of New Spain. One can only surmise what would have happened if Moya de Contreras had been given an extended term with the latitude to implement the ideas he had formed. Undoubtedly the subsequent history of New Spain would have been notably different.

VIII. The Archbishop Calls a Council

On 21 December 1574, just sixteen days after his consecration as archbishop, Moya de Contreras wrote to Juan de Ovando:

> I have learned from some persons that in the provincial councils that are now celebrated in Spain, there is a person present who is appointed by His Majesty. And because there is great need in this country to celebrate one, I ask Your Excellency to be pleased to name the person to be present at whatever may be celebrated here, in order that his absence may not cause delay.[1]

Although the archbishop had clearly made up his mind at the outset that a provincial council was necessary, it was to be more than ten years before one was actually summoned. Why the delay? There is no sure answer. Probably it was the strain of other work, the distractions of numerous duties, or even opposition to the idea of a council, for reform movements were not universally popular in either church or state. Whatever the reasons, when the announcement of the council was finally made, it came very suddenly and apparently without much warning. There is no indication as to whether the idea was Moya's alone or was developed in consultation with his suffragans.

The notion of a council was in the air and the need for one was obvious. In addition to Trent, whose influence all the bishops had felt, local councils that followed the Tridentine model had been successful in both Spain and Peru. The existing law of the Mexican province, dating from the first council of 1555, was inadequate for the new problems of the times. And the law itself was in a state of doubt. The provincial councils of 1555 and 1565 had never been approved by Rome, and the second, in particular, had been lost in the bureaucratic limbo of the Council of the Indies. Problems between church and state, the deplorable condition of the Indians, the problems presented by the ongoing conflict between bishops and mendicants, the need for a thoroughgoing reform of the church along Tridentine lines, Moya's own passion for organization and order, the new moral problems presented by an emergent capitalist and investment economy—all of these contributed to the climate of thought in which a provincial council became a pressing necessity.

On 1 February 1584 Moya sent a Latin edict throughout his archdiocese and to all his suffragan bishops announcing the convocation of a provincial council for the province of Mexico for 6 January 1585.[2] When traveling conditions made it impossible for some of the bishops to reach Mexico City by that date, the opening was postponed to 20 January.

Most of the year 1584 was given over to the preparations for the council. These included an almost complete rebuilding of the old cathedral—that decrepit old building had to be made more fitting for what was regarded as the religious event of the century. Its small size and unpretentious ornamentation had long been an affront to the civic pride of the city, and since the construction of the new cathedral, begun some twenty-one years before, was lagging, Moya resolved on an almost total reconstruction of the old one. The work was entrusted to Melchor de Avila, the architect of the new cathedral (whose books were found by the visita to contain sizeable shortages). After his death in an accident in December 1584, the task was turned over to his nephew Rodrigo. Moya himself donated several works of art to the refurbished building. As far as can be ascertained, the restoration was finished just in time for the opening of the council.[3]

BUILDING ON THE PAST

If Moya and the other bishops of New Spain were moved by the example of Trent, they could also look back on the work of their predecessors in New Spain. There was a long history of groping and working toward a comprehensive set of laws for the church. The colony had seen many antecedents to the Third Mexican Provincial Council, but none of them equaled it in thoroughness, breadth, or profundity of reform.

From the earliest days of the Spanish conquest, the leading church-men of New Spain had met together in various *juntas apostólicas* to dis-cuss common problems. These were not ecclesiastical councils in the canonical sense of the term and so did not have the same binding force. As far as is known, these juntas were held in 1524, 1532, 1539, 1544, and 1546. In the beginning they were concerned with the fundamental prob-lem of Christianizing the Indians, but the questions and decisions be-came more complex and more lengthy as time went on. The junta of 1532 made an important statement in favor of the Indians' ability to receive Christianity and seemed almost an anticipation of the *Sublimis Deus* of Pope Paul III (1537). The junta of 1539 even made the first tentative steps toward approving the ordination of Indians to the priest-hood. A less favorable view of the Indians was to be found in the junta of 1544, which was attended by such important personages as Juan de Zumárraga, Alonso de la Vera Cruz, and Domingo de Betanzos. It went on record as opposing the New Laws of 1542 and declared that the Indians were incapable of civilization or Christianization without the tutelage of Spaniards, whether ecclesiastical or lay.[4]

In 1542 Paul III made the dioceses of New Spain independent of the metropolitan of Seville when he raised Mexico to the rank of an archdiocese. New Spain was now a true ecclesiastical province with the right to hold its own provincial councils. In 1554 Alonso de Montúfar arrived to take up the government of the archdiocese, and in the fol-lowing year he summoned the First Mexican Provincial Council "desir-ing to imitate our predecessors and in fulfillment of what is com-manded us by the sacred canons."[5]

The first council was attended by five bishops, among them the great Vasco de Quiroga, and by numerous other churchmen and civil officials. It dealt with a wide variety of issues, including the catechizing of the Indians and the administration of the sacraments to them. A special chapter was devoted to the obligations of parish priests of the Indians. The natives were also exempted from the celebration of certain feasts and from some ecclesiastical penalties. One famous decree or-dained the establishment in every village of a hospital for poor Indians that was also to serve as a hospice for travelers.[6] The council fathers also reinforced the policy that the instruction of the Indians was to be carried out in their native languages, and means were set up to assure that such instruction was actually given.

On a less happy note the council, in what was almost an *obiter dictum,* prohibited the ordination of Indians to the priesthood. Going still further, the council revoked the decision of the junta of 1539 that permitted the Indians to be ordained to the minor orders and even forbade them to handle sacred vessels. In general, Bishop Llaguno is probably correct when he states that the First Mexican Provincial Council reflected a concept of the Indian as "an inconstant being, inclined to evil, with little intellectual capacity, weak, with all his rights as a Christian but under the tutelage and protection of ecclesiastics and missionaries."[7] It is equally true, however, that the euphoria of the early years was beginning to fade and that the original grand vision of Christianized Indians was yielding to disillusionment over the failure of the missionary enterprise either to make a deep imprint or to take hold permanently. Perhaps, after years of effort, organization, and frustration, the churchmen would have been more than human if they had not tended to blame the Indian and his shortcomings for this lack of response.

The first council made an honest effort to draw up a more or less comprehensive code of legislation for the newly independent church of New Spain. It dealt with the administration of parishes, the instruction of the Indians, public worship, the extirpation of idolatry, and similar matters. The conciliar decrees contained ninety-three chapters; much of its legislation was taken over in toto by the third council. Like the third council some thirty years later, it addressed a letter to the king, written by Archbishop Montúfar, asking for remedies for the various necessities of the church. The decrees were publicly proclaimed on 6 and 7 November 1555. They were printed by Juan Pablo Lombardo, first printer of the city, in February 1556, and all parish priests were ordered to have a copy within six months.

The Council of Trent concluded its sessions in 1563, and Pope Pius IV promulgated its decrees for the universal church as of May 1564. On 12 June of that year Philip II issued a cédula that the decrees of Trent were to be obeyed and put into execution. At that time Jerónimo de Valderrama was conducting his visita of New Spain, and among his orders was one to convoke the bishops in a council "to deal with the things necessary for the good of their churches and bishoprics."[8]

And so Archbishop Montúfar once again gathered his bishops in council. They reviewed the legislation of 1555 and found it acceptable. It was renewed with only minor changes, designed to bring it into full conformity with the decrees of Trent. They also published seven bulls of Pope Pius IV "for the usefulness and consolation of the Spaniards and natives of this aforesaid New Spain."[9]

On 11 October 1565 the bishops of the council directed a solemn petition to the audiencia. They recalled the royal orders that the decrees of Trent were to be observed, among which were some that dealt with the church's liberty and immunity. They demanded that the audiencia observe the immunity of clerics from civil courts and that it not interfere in the choice of pastors or parish priests, an area that belonged exclusively to the prelates. They also said that priests and friars should be paid a sufficient salary by the audiencia. The oidores were not to give any orders to religious or ecclesiastical persons respecting their religious duties, because that power belonged to the bishops and superiors alone.

Regarding the repartimiento, or conscript labor system, which was still in its early stages, the bishops pointed out the abuses that were already creeping into it. The Indians, the bishops said in complaints that were to be echoed even more forcefully at the third council, should not be brought from long distances, they should be paid for their journeys to and from work as well as for the days they actually worked, they should be paid at the beginning of the week, and they should not be forced to work before sunrise or after sunset.[10]

The constitutions of the Second Mexican Provincial Council were read and promulgated on 11 November 1565. According to Domingo de Salazar, a Dominican who later became bishop of Manila, the *acta* of the council were sent to Spain to the Council of the Indies for approbation and were never heard of again. They were not printed until 1769, when Archbishop Lorenzana published them in Mexico City.[11]

In the progression of juntas and councils between 1524 and 1565 it can be seen that the church in New Spain was moving toward a coherent and uniform ecclesiastical policy. In the beginning it was more a question of defining the problems than of finding solutions. As the years went by, with their accompanying disappointments and frustrations, the solutions tended to show an adjustment to reality and with it a lower esteem for the capacity of the Indians. With the first council of 1555 the church had come close to a comprehensive set of laws for the ecclesiastical life of the colony, but the work was far from complete. The organizing impetus of the Counter-Reformation had not yet come to full term, and the reforms of Trent had not had the time to implant themselves solidly in the New World. By 1585 the time had come.

BLUEPRINTS FOR REFORM

One of the most important tasks in preparation for the council was the formulation of an agenda. Among other things this meant soliciting and receiving opinions from everyone who felt any concern for the needs of the church and the colony. Of special importance were the memorials or reports submitted to the bishops for consideration in the conciliar meetings. Those that dealt with the Chichimeca war and the repartimientos will be treated later. Of the others the most significant were those of the Jesuit Juan de Plaza, Bishop Pedro de Feria of Chiapas, Bishop Domingo de Salazar of the Philippines, and, to a lesser degree, of the canon lawyer Hernando Ortiz de Hinojosa and the Franciscan Gerónimo de Mendieta. All of these are enlightening as far as colonial and reformist attitudes are concerned, and from them alone it would be possible to write a comprehensive monograph on the status of church and state in New Spain in 1584.

Juan de la Plaza. In October 1574 Juan de la Plaza was named visitor of the Jesuits of Peru, and he arrived in the New World the following year. In 1576 he went to Cuzco for a provincial congregation of his order and then traveled through the Jesuit mission stations in Peru. In 1580 he left for New Spain, where he acted as both visitor and provincial.[12]

Plaza's first memorial, which was submitted to the council and discussed on 6 May 1585, concerned seminaries. As remarkable as it may seem to the modern reader, there was at that time no systematic structure for the education and preparation of priests, and neither were there any educational prerequisites. A man could take his degree at a university and then present himself to a bishop for ordination. An individual could be ordained, as happened in Moya's case, without ever having studied theology. Often preparation took no other form than that of simple apprenticeship to a priest or bishop. In 1563, in one of its last sessions, the Council of Trent had decreed the establishment of seminaries in all dioceses that had nothing comparable for the formation of priests (session 23, chapter 18). One of the bishops present at Trent later said that the bishops considered this the single most important reform action of the entire council.[13]

Plaza began his discussion with one of the comparisons that was most popular in Counter-Reformation thought, that of rebuilding the temple of Solomon. Good priests were the stones with which the new temple—that is, the church—would be rebuilt. In support of this, he quoted in its entirety the Tridentine decree on seminaries and also gave a good brief historical summary of how priests had been trained up to that time. From the time of Saint Augustine on, the commonest and most effective method had been to have the candidates live in the homes of bishops and learn from them. He encouraged the bishops to continue this practice as a means of personally inspiring their future priests.

This method, however, had not always proved practical because of the lack of space and money, and so the Council of Trent had decreed the erection of seminaries. The biggest obstacle to implementing this decree was still the lack of funds, which was the principal reason why seminaries had not succeeded up to that time. Still, he considered New Spain ripe for such a seminary and suggested that the college of San Juan Letrán would be suitable for conversion into one. There was also a college attached to the cathedral of Michoacán and a Jesuit college in Oaxaca that could be used for the same purpose. As it turned out, the bishops at the council did not accept his suggestion and continued to depend on the university as a source of priests. It would be many years before a conciliar seminary would be founded in Mexico.[14]

Closely connected with the question of how priests should be prepared was that of the kind of men who should be admitted to ordination. This subject formed a separate memorial, submitted and discussed on 6 June 1585. Basically, said Plaza, they were to be only those who were truly called by God. The candidates were to be carefully scrutinized, especially as to motivation, because all too often men entered the priesthood for less than lofty motives. The signs of vocation were prayer, "because it is the office of a priest to pray," and the living of a holy and pure life. It was not enough that the individual merely avoid scandal; he must be positively virtuous and involved in works of mercy and charity. He met the implicit objection that this would mean fewer priests by citing the famous statement of Saint Thomas Aquinas that if only worthy men were ordained, God would never desert his church and would always supply the ministers needed.

So far as priestly studies were concerned, he again cited Trent (session 23, chapter 16), which warned against ordaining men who were not necessary or useful to the ministry. He pointed out that the Jesuit college was able to prepare good ministers even if they did not have a benefice or patrimony. Clerics ought to be in a college like that for at least two years, both for academic and spiritual preparation. He suggested a program of studies resembling the one usually followed by Jesuits—that is, theology, canon law, and cases of conscience.

He also showed a concern for what today would be called continuing education of the clergy. Those already ordained whose learning or abilities were in doubt should be compelled to attend sessions of cases of conscience for at least two years. Such classes should be offered in every city in which there was a cathedral. Those who were deficient should not be allowed to say mass in parish churches. In addition the bishop or one of his assistants should gather all the clerics together at least once a month and give them an exhortation on holiness of life. That, of course, was precisely what Moya had been doing for years with the help of the Jesuits.

Plaza's third memorial, which was submitted and discussed on 18

July 1585, dealt with parish priests. It was especially important, he wrote, that these men be good, because they were the ones who had the most immediate contact with the people. A parish priest did not fulfill his obligations by waiting for the people to come to him but must seek them out and help them.

He went on to give an extended commentary on the superficiality of much religious faith. For most of the Catholics of New Spain, their faith was not deep. It was more like human opinion, or an inheritance that came from family and background, just as the Moors were Moslems primarily because their ancestors had been. For this reason Plaza felt that the council should pay specific attention to religious education, especially that of children. Of particular concern were those who lived in isolation on ranches and at the mines.

The Indians were a special problem because they had been so poorly instructed and because, by and large, the parish priests did little to rectify this. This was the fault of the priests, not the Indians. He cited with approval the opinion of Francisco de Vitoria that the gospel had not been preached to the Indians in such a way that they were obliged under penalty of sin to believe it.[15] A major reason for this was that the parish priests did not know the native languages. The First Mexican Provincial Council's legislation on the subject had remained a dead letter. Plaza had a simple solution: the salaries of parish priests should be withheld until they learned the necessary languages. They should also be examined on this point, not with the formality of three or four questions, but with a thorough examination of their fluency. He also suggested the establishment of a seminary for young men who had been raised among the Indians and knew their languages. These boys, because of their background, could easily be supported on a diet of tortillas and a little beef, so the expense would be minimal, he claimed.

One of the principal concerns of Trent had been the improvement of the quality of preaching, and it was to this question that Plaza dedicated one of his longest and most detailed memorials (30 July 1585). Trent had decreed that the office of preaching belonged primarily to the bishop, but it was a responsibility that the bishops of New Spain had not yet fully accepted. Although they were quite scrupulous about other Tridentine decrees, such as residence, they too easily excused themselves from the obligation of preaching. A bishop could not shirk this duty by alleging his lack of learning. Even if his degree was only in canon law, he still had enough books at hand and had listened to enough sermons himself to be able to preach the gospel.[16] Nor could he delegate the preaching to the religious orders, whose preaching was usually without much effect and was not in accord with the wishes of the bishop. He concluded by suggesting that sermons should be improved so that the people would not grow tired of them.

Plaza devoted an entire memorial to the visitations that a bishop should make of his diocese, which he called "the soul of the government of a diocese" (8 August 1585).[17] The visitation should be made by the bishop personally, not through a vicar. It should, like charity, begin at home—that is, the bishop should put his own household in order before presuming to visit others. He should assemble all his clerics at least once a month, consult with them about whatever was necessary, and exhort them to virtue. Sin and scandal should be corrected by fraternal warnings rather than judicial proceedings, which rarely worked any permanent good. Public condemnation and punishment could be effective in some cases, however, and he suggested that the bishops make an example of some of the more infamous clerics of New Spain for concubinage, greed, and gambling.

The bishop's visitation should extend to the principal civil officials, for they were particularly prone to notable and manifold public sins. He should investigate the confraternities and charitable groups that were organized for the sick, the imprisoned, the orphans, and other needy cases. He should set the foremost example in visiting hospitals and jails. The visitation would be far more effective if the bishop knew the native languages. If he did not, he should take along religious to act as interpreters, preachers, and confessors. He should be especially vigilant about drunkenness among the Indians. Kindness and concern were the best ways to win over the Indians, as the life of the saintly bishop Vasco de Quiroga had amply proved. In summary, the ministry to the Indians consisted of curing their drunkenness, seeing that they were well instructed in religion and good morals, and making sure that priests treated them with charity and care.

The last of Plaza's memorials dealt with confessors. If all confessors had been the type of men that they ought, he wrote, the work of reform would have been much further advanced than it was. The lack of good confessors was the reason for so many sins and such disorderly lives among Christians. For this reason the Council of Trent had decreed that religious who were confessors should be examined for suitability by a bishop (session 23, chapter 15) and that it was not enough that the religious superiors grant faculties for hearing confessions.[18]

Plaza's memorials were a clear blueprint for the kind of pastoral reform envisioned by both Trent and the Third Mexican Provincial Council. The heavy indebtedness to Trent and to the entire Catholic Reformation movement are so clear as to need no comment. His memorials had a strong influence on the council and many of his recommendations were incorporated into its decrees.[19]

Pedro de Feria. The bishop of Chiapas had been born Pedro González in Feria, Extremadura, about the year 1524. In 1545 he was professed in the Dominican order at the convent of San Esteban in Salamanca, where he was under the direction of Domingo de Soto. As was common among the mendicants, he took the name of his birthplace as his name in religion. After six years spent in the study of theology, he was sent to New Spain to work in the Zapotec missions. In 1557 he was made prior of the Dominican house in Mexico City. Three years later he was sent to Florida as provincial vicar, and seven years after that, in 1567, he was elected provincial of the Dominican province of Santiago in New Spain. At the conclusion of his term he returned to Salamanca to be master of novices and vicar. In 1575, while living in retirement, he was nominated to the bishopric of Chiapas. He returned to New Spain in that same year and governed the diocese for fourteen years until his death in 1588. He was buried in the Dominican church in San Cristóbal de las Casas (formerly Ciudad Real).[20]

Feria was one of the bishops absent from the council. On his way to Mexico City he fell from the mule on which he was riding and broke a leg. He remained in Oaxaca to recuperate and sent ahead a well-known Dominican theologian, Juan Ramírez, with a packet of letters and memorials. These included a Zapotec dictionary, a directory for confessors in the same language, and a Zapotec catechism. More important were a memorial on the ministry to the Indians, a short memorial on some special problems, and a treatise on the difficulties being encountered by ecclesiastical immunity and freedom.

Feria treated some of the same problems as Plaza, but his approach was quite different. Although he was a trained theologian of the Dominican school, his memorials were less well organized, less planned, more personal, and, most of all, based on personal experience of long standing. Feria was not the post-Tridentine reformer that Plaza was. Rather, he had been a missionary for some thirty years, and his memorials were a summation of his attitudes and outlook as they had developed during that time. They were also strongly in favor of the mendicants' ministry to the Indians.[21]

Feria began his treatment of the ministry to the Indians by facing the reality of the New World—that is, that this ministry was entirely distinct from that to the Spaniards. The Spaniards were Old Christians, the Indians were New Christians.[22] In dealing with the Spaniards the church had centuries of experience to fall back on. In ministering to the Indians the church was making a beginning and also had a language barrier to overcome. He considered it an error to think that the Indians were now advanced enough in their new religion that they no longer needed ministers as learned as their first ones. It was also wrong to believe that all that a priest needed to know was how to teach the Indians the basic prayers and that this would satisfy the consciences of the bishops. Daily experience proved again and again that despite baptism the Indians still retained their old beliefs and customs.

Feria singled out his own diocese as one that had some of the best priests in New Spain and a reputation for Indians who were most advanced and most committed to Christianity. Yet as recently as 1584, when making a visitation of his diocese, he had discovered that many of the Indians were still worshiping idols and that one of the principal converts, who had been baptized some forty years before and was considered an outstanding Christian, was a crypto-pagan. Because of the conflicts between diocesan and religious priests, some Indians believed that the religious would eventually leave and take Christ with them. In everyday practice the Indians identified Christ with some of the local gods (whom Feria called by the Latin *lares*, the Roman name for household gods). They were even guarding the ruins of an old temple in expectation of the day when the religious would depart and they would be able to use it again.

Missionaries, then, had to realize that they would be beginning anew, almost literally starting from scratch. The new missionaries, the bishop said, had to be free of all kinds of business and money-making activities. They should not only be spiritual fathers but also temporal ones who would defend the Indians against injustice, care for the sick, and teach their charges to live in a civilized fashion.

In his opinion the only ministers who really met these qualifications were the mendicants. They were the only ones who from the first days of the conquest had learned the languages, worked hard, and suffered much. Without them there would have been no Christianity in New Spain. He asked that the council favor the religious, publicly declaring their virtues and interceding with the king on their behalf—a request that in the light of previous events was rather naive.

Feria's briefer, second memorial dealt with certain isolated questions. He suggested that the council try to see to it that the decrees of Trent allowing ecclesiastical judges to impose monetary fines on lay persons in some cases be implemented. Secular judges had almost completely nullified this provision. He also asked that the council look at the privileges of the mendicants and order those that were no longer useful abrogated. This was rather surprising in view of his ordinarily proreligious stance. He also suggested that the council abolish the custom of formal promises of marriage (*desposorio por futuro*) among the Indians because of the abuses that arose from it. Because of the shortage of priests in New Spain, he felt that there would be justification for abbreviating some of the church's ceremonies, such as marriage, baptism, and extreme unction. He concluded this second memorial with suggestions for the arrangement of ecclesiastical court procedures for the outlying Indian districts.[23]

More important than this second memorial was a lengthy treatise on ecclesiastical immunity that Feria sent to the council.[24] The author was identified only as a Dominican but was probably Alonso de Noreña. It was a closely reasoned, well-organized canonical treatment of the intrusions of secular judges into ecclesiastical affairs. It is second only to Salazar's memorial as an attack on the abuses of the patronato and a criticism of the bishops for their reluctance to take a stand. The author complained that secular judges were making formal investigations of prelates and clerics, complete with oaths and witnesses, and then forwarding the evidence to the viceroy and oidores. When parishes were subdivided the secular judges took it upon themselves to allot the ornaments or appurtenances between the two new divisions.

The author dwelt at length on the provisions for beneficed clerics that had been established by the Ordenanza del Patronazgo. These provisions were now undoubtedly the law of the Indies, but they raised as many problems as they resolved. The fact that a parish priest was no longer permanent, but removable at the will of the viceroy and bishop, meant that his bond to his people was weakened. The author appealed to his own forty years of experience in the Indies to prove this. Another difficulty was that there was no room in the procedures for bishops to examine nominees on their knowledge of the native languages, nor could bishops reject candidates for not knowing these languages. Aspirants could merely appeal to the audiencia. Finally, a bishop alone could not remove a parish priest; the viceroy or some other secular authority was always involved. This presented special difficulties if the pastor had fallen into any sort of secret or serious sin.

The author expressed his amazement that these things had not been made clear to the king or that recourse had not been had to the pope. "I remember that in an arduous case very much like these, when some bishops were puzzled over what should be done, one most reverend bishop stood up and said, 'Why do we have a pope in Rome if not so that everyone can go to him?' " It was a good question, but despite all the memorials and complaints, the bishops had accepted too much of the patronato to turn back. The author realized this and politely rebuked the bishops, "because the bishops have done nothing, no one can say for sure that humble opposition and supplication will be futile and without effect."

One of the most serious intrusions was that the audiencia might exile a bishop when he failed to obey one of its orders. No specific case was mentioned, but the author may have been thinking of Antonio de

Hervías, bishop of the neighboring diocese of Vera Paz. As might be expected, the author cited the example of Thomas Becket as one who had resisted the unjust intrusions of civil authority.

The themes covered in this small treatise were also taken up at greater length and with greater passion in the remarkable report sent to the council by Domingo de Salazar, the first bishop of Manila.

The Salazar Memorial. Domingo de Salazar (?1512–1594), the first bishop and archbishop of Manila, was a Dominican from San Esteban in Salamanca. He had studied there under Vitoria and been professed in 1546. Two years later he went to New Spain to join the Dominican province of Santiago. He labored as a missionary in Oaxaca and then joined the ill-fated expedition of Tristán de Luna y Arrellano to Florida, after which he returned to Mexico City to be vicar and provincial of the Dominicans. He was also appointed as the first consultor and censor of books of the Inquisition by Moya. The part he played in the disorders attendant on Moya's consecration has already been seen. In 1576 he returned to Spain to be provincial treasurer of the Dominicans, and three years later he was nominated first bishop of China, as the bishopric of Manila was then called. He served in the Philippines from 1581 to 1591 and then returned to Spain, where he died in 1594.

His memorial to the bishops of the Third Mexican Provincial Council is one of the most important and valuable of all the conciliar documents. It dealt with only one topic: the encroachments of the civil government on the freedom of the church. It was a criticism of the patronato as it existed in practice, a denunciation of the civil officials whose interference and obstructionism were hindering the work of the church, and a rebuke to his fellow bishops, whom he did not hesitate to accuse of cowardice.[25]

He began on an aggressive note by criticizing the bishops. While in New Spain he had often complained about the wrongs committed against the freedom of the church and about the fact that the bishops ignored them. Had he then been a bishop, he wrote, he would have preferred to die rather than submit to them. At the time of the Second Mexican Provincial Council he had discussed this question with some of the bishops, but he had been disgusted to see how timorous they were. Only Fernando de Villagómez, bishop of Tlaxcala, had shared his opinion and said that he would like to approach the king personally and, if that did no good, to appeal to the pope. The views Salazar had held as a friar he still held as a bishop. Yet he was deeply disturbed because the bishops preferred to keep silence and to ignore what was happening.

Salazar's first specific complaint was about "how much the secular power continues to meddle in the affairs of the church." This was particularly true of viceroys and audiencias. It seemed that almost every ecclesiastical case ended up before the audiencias. Thus, for example, many cases had arisen from the papal bull *In Coena Domini* and the audiencias were intruding themselves into these.[26] To prevent this Pope Saint Pius V (1566–1572) had issued a *motu proprio* excommunicating those who were guilty of such intrusions. Further, the audiencias had been calling ecclesiastical persons before their courts to give information against clerics and friars. Salazar predicted that the audiencias would soon become the courts of first instance in ecclesiastical cases; already some ecclesiastics were beginning to look on the oidores as their superiors. The bishops were aware of this, but they kept silence. "I am astonished at how the church suffers a servitude like this."

A second complaint was about Philip II's recent order that the bishops not appoint more than one alguacil, and that one only for the chief city of the diocese. "And because it is His Majesty's command, there is no one who dares to speak." Salazar was unable to understand why a corregidor was empowered to appoint all the alguaciles he wanted and the bishop was permitted to name only one. The justice of the church was superior to that of the state and bishops were the princes of the church.

Another intrusion was found in the royal order that the decrees of provincial councils be sent to the Council of the Indies for approval prior to publication.[27] Salazar cited the fate of the second provincial council, whose acts had been sent to Spain and never heard of again. To him it seemed incredible that the bishops who gathered together for the good of their flocks should have so little authority that they could not publish their decisions until such decisions had passed through the hands of four councilors "who are usually no more learned or holy than the bishops who have celebrated [the provincial council]." The only reason why the government and civil officials had been able to do these things was that they had no opposition. If a stand were not taken at the beginning, such intrusions would take on the force of custom, and then they would become virtually ineradicable. "Let us know, gentlemen, by what law we live and if we are to take as our rule the Council of the Indies." The Council of the Indies, he declared in another context, was not a church council; nor did its decrees have the force of canon law. When it tried to be such, it should be resisted.

As a bill of particulars, Salazar cited the actions of Viceroy Enríquez, especially as they were directed against Moya. Patience, he wrote, was praiseworthy, but there were limits, and there were times when it was necessary to take a stand against wrongs and to defend the rights of the church. Archbishop Montúfar, because of his meek spirit, had endured such things despite Salazar's advice to the contrary. Moya had no such excuse. Salazar reported a rumor that during the third provincial council of Lima, Enríquez had attended the sessions and sat at the right hand of the archbishop. Salazar would have called off the council before enduring that. Viceroys and oidores had usurped precedence over bishops in ceremonies and processions. Such things had been done by Robles and Farfán, whom Salazar called "enemies of the church." As in the Noreña treatise, the bishops were reminded to take Thomas Becket as their example.

Salazar criticized the Ordenanza del Patronazgo as containing many clauses in violation of the church's freedom; yet Moya had accepted it without even consulting his suffragans. The bishops in council were now in a position to do something if they wished. The condition of the church showed that the bishops had failed to live up to the oath taken at their consecrations to support the sacred canons. For example, canon law stipulated that bishops could intervene in judicial cases involving poor persons when the civil judges failed to give justice. Yet this was so forgotten that if a bishop were to attempt it, he would be laughed out of court.

The situation was even more lamentable in regard to the ministry to the Indians. In this the royal officials paid no heed whatever to the bishops. The most they did was to ask for a priest to accompany the soldiers who went out, not to convert, but to conquer. Salazar suggested that the bishops write a joint letter to the king and to the pope and give a complete account of this. Similarly, the church received only a scant share of the tribute and the money that belonged to it by right. Those who went among the Indians to kill and rob received the major portion.

It was well known, he wrote, that the gospel had made little headway among the Indians. Some claimed that this was because of the way in which it had first been brought to them—that is, with war, violence, and murder. Others blamed the bad example given by the Spaniards and their oppression of the Indians. Salazar added another reason: the imperialism of the religious orders, which had divided up New Spain so that there were not enough ministers and that sometimes one friar had to minister to ten or twelve thousand Indians. This system had become fixed. The religious believed that if in a village of some five or six thousand Indians there were two friars, one of whom might know the native language, then that village was well served. The situation was little better among diocesan priests. It was a rather damning accusation, especially as Salazar himself was a Dominican.

The Salazar report was a blunt attack on the religious situation as it existed in 1584 and on the reluctance of the bishops of New Spain to face some of the realities of that situation. He understood the power of corporate pressure groups in the Spanish governmental system. Even more important from the point of view of this study were the criticisms leveled against Moya personally. From the perspective of the twentieth century, there can be no doubt that most of these were valid. Moya was a regalist. He seems, moreover, to have been overly cautious and yielding at times. It should be noted, however, that the Council of Trent itself did not squarely face the growing problem of regalism and church-state relations throughout Europe. If Moya had had guidelines from Trent, his conduct might have been different. In hindsight, his approach was probably too cautious, but it is difficult to fault his subjective dispositions.

Ortiz de Hinojosa. Hernando Ortiz de Hinojosa was a native of Mexico City and a descendant of conquistadores. He had a master of arts degree as well as a doctorate in theology and canon law. He held the *prima* chair in philosophy and a chair in theology at the Royal and Pontifical University. A linguist, he was proficient in Latin, Greek, Chaldaic, and Nahuatl. At the time of the third council he was the vicar general of the archdiocese of Mexico and a canon of the cathedral. In 1596 the king named him coadjutor bishop of Guatemala with the right of succession, but he died the following year before he could take over the office.

Ortiz de Hinojosa was an active participant in the council and submitted a number of memorials, some of which will be noted later. Three of immediate concern dealt with the situation of the Indians and the general state of religion in New Spain.[28] Though it is clear that Ortiz de Hinojosa was a learned and sincere man, his writings were verbose, tautological, pedantic, and often petty. Here and there some genuine concern for the Indians can be found, but this is coupled with a true conquistador-criollo mentality. He discusses practically every aspect of Indian and church life, but with a multitude of details that can only bore the modern reader and, one suspects, bored the bishops of the council.

Ortiz de Hinojosa disposed of the question of native languages very quickly. Taking a stand contrary to the policy already adopted by the church in New Spain, he said that the only solution to Indian ministry was to have all the natives learn Spanish. The native tongues were too many and too difficult for the religious or other priests to learn. "They do not seem to have been developed by men but by nature, like the illiterate sounds of birds or brute animals, which cannot be written with any kind of letters and scarcely even pronounced because they are guttural and stick in the throat and are almost impossible to learn."[29] It was a harsh judgment from someone who supposedly knew Nahuatl, and it seems to echo the ideas of Juan Ginés de Sepúlveda. Ortiz de Hinojosa saw the Spanish language as the Christianizing and civilizing force for the Indians. He suggested that the school of Tlaltelolco would be the ideal place to begin this instruction. Ortiz de Hinojosa's concept of the primacy of the Spanish language seems to have been incorporated, at least in part, into one of the decrees of the third council.

Despite his low opinion of their languages, he did not think that the Indians should be kept from the sacraments. Rather, they should be compelled to receive them. He condemned the practice of having the Indians bring their sick and dying to the churches for communion and the last rites, because that was a way of killing them. He favored the policy of congregación. He suggested that religious be sent into the provinces to ferret out crypto-idolatry and punish the relapsed with exemplary punishment. Religious art, he wrote, should not depict demons or animals, as sometimes happened in Christian art (for example, in pictures of Saint James) because the Indians were thus tempted to fall back into idolatry. He advocated the use of hymns and songs in the native languages, such as those to be found in Sahagún's collection.

In the Indians' favor, he recommended moderating fasting laws because of their poverty and not increasing the number of feast days. Indians should be paid a just wage for their work. As it was, he said, they were underpaid for their labor, which was often skilled. He suggested visitations of ranches, mines, and *obrajes* to make sure that the Indians were not being forced to live apart from their families. He advocated measures against Indian drunkenness and noted that because tavernkeepers served the Indians an inferior product, the Europeans referred to any cheap wine as "Indian wine." He condemned the exploitation of Indians by priests and noted that among some of the natives both secular and religious clergy were called *tetolinique,* which meant mistreators.

Many of Ortiz de Hinojosa's ideas were sound, and some were adopted by the bishops. Yet even some of his trivial or ridiculous suggestions were incorporated into the conciliar decrees. These included his recommendations that the Indians not be allowed to choose Jewish names, such as Moses or Abraham; that they not have double names, such as Juan Pablo; and that priests not demean themselves by accepting dinner invitations at the homes of Indians, even those of chiefs.

In general, he had a low opinion of the Indians and their capacities.[30] He did not consider the Indians intelligent enough to take the same course of studies as Spaniards. They should be taught only Spanish at the school in Tlaltelolco, because no other course of study was of any use to them. However, he also denied that they were idiots or imbeciles, saying, "They have the same intelligence as many unlearned Spaniards."

His overall evaluation of Indian capacity was a low one, tempered at times with a realization that there was more to the question than was commonly supposed. But he had an even worse opinion of their sense of responsibility. He viewed Indians as minors, to whom one hesitates to entrust important matters. They rarely fulfilled the laws of the church about fasting and abstinence, not just because of their poverty, but because of a certain fickleness of spirit. So true was this that he advocated that the church accommodate itself to this reality and lighten these obligations.

In a real sense Ortiz de Hinojosa was caught between two realities. One was the poor and miserable state of the Indians, which led him to view their capacities in a bad light, a tendency reinforced by his own criollo background. The other was the reality that the Indians had innate capacities that even he had to recognize. They also had rights, among which he enumerated the right to just wages, the right of native rulers to have authority, the right to make wills and testaments, and the right to receive the sacraments. He took a strong stand in favor of the free labor of the Indians and against the repartimiento.

Mendieta. Gerónimo de Mendieta (1525–1604) was one of the most famous of the early Franciscan missionaries in New Spain. By the time of the Third Mexican Provincial Council he had been a missionary there for over thirty years. His best-known work was the *Historia eclesiástica indiana,* which, probably because of its harsh criticisms of Spanish colonial policies, did not see the press until the nineteenth century. Mendieta is most famous today as having been one of the chief exponents of the apocalyptic and millenarian school of Franciscan thought.[31]

Mendieta did not attend the council, but he did send a short set of recommendations with Bartolomé de Ledesma, the bishop of Oaxaca. His first suggestion was one that set the tone for the Franciscan contribution to the council, "that a remedy be found for the ruin and insupportable vexation which at the present time the Indians have from the forced personal service," that is, the repartimientos, "which are destroying and putting an end to their towns and republics and even giving reason for the name of Christian to be hateful to them."[32] This was to be one of the overriding concerns of the bishops at the council, and the Franciscan contribution on the subject was to be of supreme importance.

His other recommendations were less sweeping. He asked the council to eradicate the "pernicious abuse" whereby distinctions were made when applying the name of Christian to Indians and Spaniards, almost as if they were two different species of Christian. He also complained about Spaniards who lived among the Indians and set bad examples by their slovenly attendance at mass and other services. This was especially true of women, who talked during mass and made so much disturbance that the celebrants could scarcely carry on the ceremonies.[33]

Mendieta was more conciliatory when broaching the question of the religious and their privileges. He pleaded with the bishops to look favorably on the past and present works of the mendicants and asked them to avoid undue confrontation in their visitations. He also said that the examination of religious candidates for the priesthood should be carried out by their own superiors.

In general Mendieta's contribution to the council was negligible. The times were moving away from the kind of impassioned and apocalyptic approach that had characterized the Franciscan attitude in earlier days of the missionary enterprise. The Franciscans made great and important contributions to the thought of the council, but they did so as part of a transition to a new age.

Miscellaneous Memorials. On the opening day of the council (20 February 1585), Moya had an edict read that invited any and all to submit suggestions, requests, recommendations, and petitions to the bishops. He promised secrecy and protection to everyone who did so and said that all would receive a fair hearing.[34] Not surprisingly, materials of all sort rained down on the council. Some were frivolous, some self-seeking, some purely personal requests, and others the results of sincere devotion to religion. Viewed as a whole they offer still more insights into the problems of colonial life.

The municipal cabildo of Mexico City was responsible for some of the more important suggestions, all of which were given serious consideration by the bishops and many of which found their way into the conciliar legislation and acta. Its most important request sought an opinion on the morality of the war against the Chichimeca Indians. It also made suggestions about implementing the Ordenanza del Patronazgo, especially in regard to beneficed clerics, and about the life and conduct of the clergy in general. The regidores protested against anti-criollo legislation among the Franciscans and asked for assurance of greater freedom for girls about to be professed in the city's convents. They came out in opposition to an attempt that was being made to incorporate the college of San Juan Letrán into the Royal and Pontifical University, a move they considered disastrous for the boys attending the college.[35]

The chapter of the metropolitan cathedral was less idealistic and more self-interested. Most of its memorials concerned the canons' salaries and the right they had to a certain share of the cathedral's income. Juan Zurnero, the sometimes troublesome archdeacon, submitted two reports defending some of the rights of the canons and other *prebendados*. The first dealt with the right that chaplains and various ministers of the chapter had to a salary from the chapter's income, and the second with their right to take a paid vacation from choir.[36]

Memorials by individuals covered a vast number of topics. Pedro López, a charitable physician known for his interest in helping blacks, submitted two memorials on the need for a confraternity and regular catechesis for the blacks of Mexico City. Pedro Tomás de Denia complained of the wrongs involved in building a new convent for Jesús María. Francisco de Olivares wrote about the dangers of gambling and cardplaying. Diego Jiménez de San Román discussed the publication of indulgences without the bishop's sanction. Diego de Muñón petitioned that the feast of Saint Anthony be made a holyday of obligation so that people would frequent the church he had built in the saint's honor. Pedro Rodríguez, overseer of the art of painting in Mexico City, wanted closer supervision of the manufacture and sale of religious art. Pedro Velásquez, a prisoner in the municipal jail, wanted the council to compel a friar to whom he had given a stone with great curative power to return it to him. Dr. Urbina Zárate, a pastor who had been driven out of his parish by the Franciscans, made numerous suggestions about the ministry to the Indians.[37]

Each of these items was duly received and notarized by the bishops and their secretary and undoubtedly received some sort of hearing.

THE OPENING OF THE COUNCIL

As the opening day of the council approached, last-minute preparations multiplied. On 3 January Moya issued a list of the officers he had appointed to handle the various aspects of conciliar business, the most important being the consultors and the secretary. The theological consultors were the Dominican Pedro de Pravia and the Augustinian Melchor de los Reyes, both *catedráticos* in theology at the Royal and Pontifical University; the Franciscan Juan Salmerón; the Jesuit Juan de la Plaza; and Hernando Ortiz de Hinojosa. Moya named Pedro de Ortigosa of the Jesuit college as his personal theologian. The canonical consultors were Juan Zurnero; Fulgencio de Vich; the Jesuit Pedro de Morales; and the diocesan priest Juan de Salcedo, who was also appointed the council's secretary.

On 18 January all these men took an oath before Salcedo that they would fulfill their offices according to the orders and directions of the archbishop.[38] On that same day Moya issued an edict in Spanish that formally proclaimed the opening of the council and outlined the ceremonies that were to inaugurate it.

Of all the officials involved in the council, the one to whom the modern historian must be especially grateful was Salcedo. This energetic and dutiful secretary, who doubled as a consultor in canon law, kept copious notes on the proceedings, saved and filed away documents, and made sure that, despite the inevitable losses of time and human carelessness, a substantive history of the council could be written. Salcedo was a criollo, a native of Mexico City, and at the time of the council was about forty-four years of age. He was a licentiate in canon law and had first been *catedrático del decreto* (that is, teaching Gratian's Decree, one of the texts of canon law) and then *catedrático de prima* of canon law at the university. In 1575 and 1576 Moya had described him as a man of ability and good memory who had studied well and was known to be virtuous, clever, and sharp-tongued, "free and proud, a little arrogant." In all probability he did not suffer fools gladly. The bishops were so impressed by his performance at the council that in the course of it they nominated him to the vacant post of *chantre* in the chapter. About the year 1590 he was named archdeacon and held that post into his old age. It is not certain when he died; he was still alive, aged seventy, in 1618.[39]

In addition to the officers there were also present at the council representatives from the ecclesiastical chapters of Mexico, Guatemala, Puebla, Guadalajara, and Oaxaca. The Dominican provincial, Domingo de Aguiñaga, and the vicar of the Augustinians, Juan Adriano, also attended. Alonso Ponce, the Franciscan commissary, had demanded, but not received, the right to vote at the council, and as a matter of fact was absent from Mexico City for the greater part of it.[40]

The most important participants in the council were, of course, the archbishop and the six suffragan bishops who were able to attend. These were Fernando Gómez de Córdoba of Guatemala; Juan de Medina Rincón of Michoacán; Diego Romano of Tlaxcala; Gregorio de Montalvo of Yucatán; Domingo de Alzola (or Arzola) of Nueva Galicia; and Bartolomé de Ledesma of Oaxaca. Three bishops could not attend: Domingo de Salazar of Manila; Pedro de Feria of Chiapas; and Antonio de Hervías of Vera Paz. It is scarcely credible that Moya expected Salazar to make the long journey from the Philippines; the bishop sent a delegate who brought the report previously mentioned. As noted, Feria suffered an accident on the journey to Mexico City, and Hervías had embarked for Spain to lay his troubles before the king.[41]

It is significant that of the seven bishops at the council, three were doctors of the University of Salamanca and a fourth, Ledesma, had studied there under Vitoria. Three of the seven were Dominicans (two of them from San Esteban in Salamanca), one an Augustinian, and one a Jeronymite. Despite this, all showed themselves consistently hostile to the claims of the mendicants. The background of these bishops put them very much in the mainstream of the humanitarian and pro-Indian tradition represented by such persons as Las Casas and Vitoria.

The Third Mexican Provincial Council opened at 6:30 A.M. on the feast of Saint Sebastian (20 January 1585). A large crowd, including the various confraternities (religious associations of laypersons) with their insignia, turned out for the ceremonies—all having been invited to do so under threat of excommunication.

Prior to the opening ceremonies, Moya summoned the audiencia, Salcedo, Santiago del Riego, and Eugenio de Salazar to the viceregal palace. In their presence he took an oath that constituted him the king's delegate at the council. In so doing he fulfilled the law and perhaps prevented the audiencia from taking a similar step or claiming a like role. At first it put him in an advantageous position to ward off outside interference, but it also, in the end, created a definite conflict of interest.

The bishops were now ready to turn their attention to the nine months of labor that would leave a permanent impress on the church of New Spain.[42]

IX. *The Mexican Trent, I*

It is very difficult to reconstruct the day-to-day operations of the Third Mexican Provincial Council or specify its modus operandi. Only a small part of its labors was recorded in writing. The usual procedure was the formulation of *consultas*—that is, cases of conscience, doubts, and important questions—which were then submitted to the consultors and the religious orders. These responded with written opinions, after which the bishops met and voted on the questions and the opinions that had been submitted.[1] It is noteworthy that in the written votes that have survived, Moya was the most frequent dissenter. Usually he shied away from the more rigorous penalties favored by his suffragans, such as frequent excommunications, and not unexpectedly he adopted a conciliatory stance toward the civil government.

THE CONSULTAS

The consultas, as the name indicates, were formal consultations with all the conciliar advisors, as opposed to memorials, which were individual opinions, solicited or otherwise. In all there were seven consultas, two of which dealt with the Chichimecas and the repartimientos.

These will be treated in the next chapter. Some of the questions proposed were narrow in scope—for example, whether a particular priest had incurred an excommunication for being involved with a suspect woman or what foods were permitted on days of fast and abstinence.[2]

The rest of the questions arose from the constitutions of the first council. These questions were disparate, without any connecting theme, yet they did have a direct bearing on the pastoral practice of the church. Thus the consultors, with the exception of the Franciscans, favored retaining the same legal age for marriage for both Indians and Spaniards. The Franciscans favored lowering it as a means of keeping native marriages more stable. The consultors agreed unanimously that there was no penalty in canon law for baptizing an adult Indian without proper instruction, but they vehemently condemned the practice and suggested remedies for it. They unanimously rejected the proposal to read a list of sins carrying the penalty of excommunication to the Indians prior to Lent and urged that the bishops keep "a thousand leagues" away from such penalties in the case of the natives. They pondered the question of Indians' confessions (when they should be made, whether an interpreter could be used) and the time for making the Easter duty. Finally, they answered twelve highly technical questions about the justice of the more common silver contracts in New Spain.[3]

THE DECREES

The real purpose of the council was legislation. It was in this area that it made its most important and lasting contribution to the life of the Catholic Church both in New Spain and in independent Mexico, for it drew up a veritable constitution that endured until the twentieth century.[4] Most of this legislation was taken from previous councils and adapted to the needs of New Spain. The most obvious influence was Trent, whose legislation was the underpinning of almost everything that the third council did. Besides Trent, the bishops were most influenced by the acts of the first two Mexican councils. The decrees of these councils were carefully examined and those deemed still valid were incorporated, often with little or no change, into the legislation of the third council.[5] Of those two councils, the first, which had been held in 1555, had the stronger influence. The bishops also had at hand the acta of the numerous provincial councils held throughout the Spanish dominions in the wake of Trent. The most frequently cited were those of Lima (1583), Guadix, and Granada.[6] Of the third council's legislation, only a small percentage was original. For a council whose work, as it turned out, took almost a full year to complete, such borrowings were an eminently sensible procedure.

The decrees of the council, with all that was original and all that was borrowed, were composed in Spanish and then translated into Latin by Juan de Salcedo and Pedro de Ortigosa.[7] Written in the Ciceronian style popular at that time, the translation often seems verbose and long-winded. At times it is closer to a paraphrase than to an exact translation. Often, too, the paragraphing of the Latin is different from that of the Spanish. The need to translate contemporary concepts into a classical language sometimes led to odd phraseology, such as *toga* for cassock or *qui ex altera parente Aethiope nascuntur* ("those who are born of one Ethiopian parent") for mulattoes.

The Latin translation underwent further changes when it was submitted to the Congregation of the Council for approval, probably around 1587. This congregation, a department of the Roman Curia, had originally been established to provide authentic interpretations of the decrees of Trent. Generally speaking, the changes it made were minor, often consisting merely of grammatical corrections, but on occasion the changes were more substantial. The congregation consistently tried to moderate the regalism of the Mexican bishops, as when it suppressed the references to Moya's civil offices. They were also baffled by some Hispanic prejudices, such as the prohibition against ordaining Indians to the priesthood. In general they also tried to mitigate some of the rigorism of the conciliar decrees, especially the excessive readiness of the bishops to pronounce excommunication for almost every delinquency.[8]

Unfortunately, this is not the place for a detailed consideration of the conciliar legislation, which was so illustrative of the bishops' attitudes and so important in the formation of the religious mentality of the Mexican people. Bernabé Navarro has written a valuable summary of the decrees, but he focuses on those that concerned the Indians.[9] There is need for a study in English of the attitudes and ideas that lay behind the decrees and of the impact they had in the course of the almost three centuries during which they were in force. Two specific decrees merit special attention here.

The first of these is found in book 5, title 7, and deals with "injuries and damages." Ordinarily this would have been a rather dry canonical treatise, but in this case it was not. It began by forbidding clerics under severe penalty of automatic excommunication to accompany military expeditions against non-Christian Indians without the express permission of their bishops. Then the bishops turned to the question of injuries to the Indians. They broke out of their legal terminology and pleaded eloquently for the Indians with an intensity that shines through the Latin.

The bishops and governors of these provinces and kingdoms must be convinced that no greater care has been entrusted to them by God than that they should protect and defend, with the deepest feelings of their minds and with a father's heart, the Indians who have recently been born into the faith. They should always be concerned with their bodily and spiritual good. The innate meekness, submission, and assiduous labor of the Indians, by which they serve the utility of the Spaniards, would lead the hearts of even the most savage people to take up their defense and to have compassion on their misery instead of afflicting them with the grievances, injuries, and violence with which they are daily afflicted by every kind of person. Considering these things, and grieving deeply that there is no piety or humanity in those in whom it ought especially to be found, this synod to the extent of its power exhorts the royal governors and magistrates of this province in the [name of the] Lord to deal piously and benevolently with the poor Indians, and to restrain the insolence of their officials and of those by whom the Indians are afflicted with grievances and burdens, so that the Indians may be considered by them not as slaves but as free men. All kinds of different burdens by which the Indians are afflicted in both person and property have come to the attention of this synod. These are all presented and declared in the Directory for Confessors approved by this synod. And the same things are made known both to the magistrates, in order that they may consult learned men from whom they can learn in the forum of conscience about the restitution and satisfaction to be made for the harm done to the Indians and that [the offenses] may be corrected in the future. These are also [made known] to confessors, in order that if they find anyone to be contumacious and unwilling to correct himself or to make the required satisfaction, they should not in any way give [that person] absolution. . . . In carrying out all these things this synod burdens consciences and threatens the perpetrators [of such offenses] with the wrath of Almighty God on the fearful day of judgment.[10]

As clear and uncompromising as this decree may appear, it is difficult to evaluate. Does it demonstrate that the spirit of Las Casas and Montesinos still lived, that the church still stood by the Indian against Spanish oppression, and that the earlier humanitarian movements were not dead? Or was it the last gasp of a dying movement that was about to be submerged by the "American reality"? A brilliant torch in stygian darkness or a sputtering candle about to die? Probably something of both.

One thing this declaration showed clearly was the dependence of the bishops on the council's *Directorio para confesores*. Like Las Casas they saw the spiritual ministrations of the church, and especially its power over consciences in the confessional, as the best and ultimately most effective weapon for altering or improving the condition of the Indians. It was an outlook that had an ancient lineage, reaching back to Canossa and beyond. In an age when the overwhelming majority of people believed literally in God, the devil, sin, and hell, this approach had validity. Yet it was not without its dangers, because it implied a unity of action and unanimity of opinion by confessors—and the confessional by its very nature was a situation in which such unanimity could not be guaranteed. Not only in this statement but also throughout their decrees, the bishops showed an almost excessive faith in the effectiveness of their *Directorio*. If this failed, then a good many of their statements and actions failed with it. And that was precisely what happened. The *Directorio* was never published or printed. It had no impact on the ordinary confessors of the Spaniards.

The other decree of special interest is the famous one that appears to ban the ordination of Indians to the priesthood. This decree has been treated in detail in a separate study.[11] The actual wording read as follows:

> In order that honor and reverence may be paid to the clerical state, it has been laid down in the sacred canons that those who suffer from certain natural defects, or others unbecoming to the clerical state, even though these do not involve any personal fault, should not be ordained. The reason is that those advanced to sacred orders should not be held in contempt, nor their ministry be held up to censure. Therefore this synod forbids that those descended from persons who have been condemned by the Holy Office of the Inquisition in the first and second degree on the father's or mother's side be admitted to holy orders, because they are under [the impediment of] common infamy. . . . Whence also, neither those of mixed blood, whether from Indians or Moors, nor mulattoes in the first degree are to be admitted to orders without great caution.[12]

The wording of the final paragraph underwent several changes and is garbled in its present form. The original intention of the bishops had been to disqualify Indians and castas from the priesthood. The consultors of the Congregation of the Council confessed themselves baffled by the decree, and it was apparently for this reason that the wording was changed and the proviso "without great caution" added. Contrary to the commonly accepted belief, the final wording of the council's decree did not actually prohibit the ordination of Indians, but merely advised great caution in doing so.

Even a cursory reading of the conciliar decrees gives the initial impression of a numbing complexity and detail. The bishops provided for almost every contingency that could occur in the church of their province. When the statutes or decrees of a more particular and temporary nature are added, the weight of legislation is almost overpowering.

Obviously the religious lives of both Spaniards and Indians were closely and minutely regulated. Little was left to individual initiative or decision. In part this reflected the tendency of the Catholic Reformation to be suspicious of spontaneity and to rely on law as a support of the Christian life. The frequency of excommunications and the monitoring of such individual matters as private confession exemplified this. The bishops of New Spain, like those of Trent, sought discipline in religious observance.

The decrees of the third council can also be read as an indication of the religious ignorance of the average inhabitant of New Spain, whether Spanish or Indian. Certainly in the case of the Indian the supposition was that Christianity had only a tenuous hold. The regularity with which the council drove home the need for fundamental and basic instruction indicates that the bishops did not have a high opinion of the religious mentality of the peoples of New Spain.

The attitude toward the Indians was ambivalent. The decrees viewed them as having less capacity than Europeans. They were called *rudes*, a Latin theological term indicating persons incapable for some reason of learning more than the rudiments of religion, on a par with the lowest level of European peasantry (*rudes* in fact translated the Spanish *de menor capacidad*). The Indians were seen as inconstant, in need of tutelage and instruction, forgetful of what had been learned; they fell easily into sin, it was thought, because they were fickle by nature.[13]

Yet at the same time, from the religious point of view, there was also a basic equality with Europeans. In their fundamental religious rights and obligations, such as instruction, the sacraments, the validity and form of marriage—even perhaps, against the will of the bishops, in regard to ordination—they were the same. Despite this fundamental equality, they were, in the oft-repeated phrase, "new plants," and so had to be treated tenderly. The rigorous fast days of the Spaniards and the numerous holydays of obligation did not apply to the Indians. They were exempt from excommunication and other censures because of their lack of understanding and lack of malice. In general, the Indians were seen as true Christians who in most ways were still to be treated like children.

There was no such ambivalence when the bishops discussed the exploitation and degradation of the Indians. They were unequivocal in declaring that the Indians were free persons with rights to free wages and that both civil and ecclesiastical government, clerics and laymen, were bound to respect their God-given rights.

True to its Tridentine inspiration, the Third Mexican Provincial Council was reacting against the problems and abuses that had plagued the church prior to the Catholic Reformation. These included simony, clerical ignorance, and the generally disreputable lives of many clergy. The third council emphasized liturgy and ceremonies, the correct implementation of which had been sadly neglected in the years before Trent. The reaction to the loose, almost chaotic, situation of the pre-Tridentine church expressed itself in a strong move toward law, order, and regimentation. In a real sense the third council exemplified the rule of law in the period of the Catholic Reformation.

It can be misleading, however, to draw conclusions that are too far-reaching from the wording of the legislation. Laws and decrees such as those of the third council were directed primarily against abuses and wrongs. Hence they give a one-sided picture and by their very nature cannot illuminate the more positive aspects of life in New Spain. Just as a reading of the conciliar decrees can lead to the conclusion that the bishops regarded all Indians as inferior and inconstant, so one can also conclude that they regarded all clerics as concubinate, lecherous, greedy, ignorant, and unworthy of confidence.[14] It is to be doubted that such was their meaning.

In addition it is essential to bear in mind the attitude toward law of people of that time and place. To the Anglo-Saxon mind, law is the result of practice and custom and ought to reflect the way in which things are actually done. To the Roman and canonical legal mind, law is primarily a set of principles expressing an ideal to be striven for. These principles must be interpreted in concrete situations according to other principles and rules of law. A people as legalistic as the Spaniards of that century were accustomed to interpreting law and turning it to their advantage. The rigidity of the legislation must not be exaggerated so far as daily life is concerned. Not even the bishops honestly believed that their decrees would be observed and obeyed in exactly the same way at all times, for such was not their concept of law. Even when these cautions are borne in mind, however, it is still clear that some of the conciliar legislation was too strict, even for Rome.

The conciliar decrees were a true constitution of the Mexican church. They were extended to the Philippines in 1626 and were retained by Guatemala when it became an independent ecclesiastical province. They governed the archdiocese of Mexico down to the provincial council of 1896 and the rest of the church in Mexico down to the promulgation of the revised Code of Canon Law in 1918.[15] As such they had a lasting and permanent impact. The irony, of course, was that they were never intended to last that long. Although Trent had decreed that provincial councils should be held every three years, and the period had been extended for American dioceses to five and then to twelve years and finally left to the discretion of the bishops, the fact is that the Third Mexican Provincial Council was the last such meeting with any authority held by the archdiocese of Mexico for over three hundred years.

THE LETTER TO THE KING

On 16 October 1585 the six bishops of the Third Mexican Provincial Council affixed their signatures to a joint letter to Philip II. It dealt with topics that did not properly fall within the scope of the decrees or statutory law. Rather, it was a wide-ranging, diversified document that today offers an interesting view, sometimes comprehensive, sometimes sporadic, of the chief problems that faced the church in New Spain. The letter was occasioned by a royal cédula of 6 December 1583 that ordered the bishops to give their collective opinion on the question of control of the doctrinas by the religious. The bishops did not confine themselves to that single issue, however, but covered every point they felt should be taken up with the king. Sometimes petty and legalistic, sometimes fiery and bold, it is one of the most important ecclesiastical documents of that century.[16]

Three of the topics covered by the bishops—that is, the opposition to the council, the repartimientos, and the Chichimeca war—will be covered in the next chapter.

The bishops began by citing the king's request for an opinion on the doctrinas and then went on to give a brief summary of the work of the council and a list of the bishops attending it. They urged the king to be speedy in approving it so that the church of New Spain would not be left without laws. They also asked that he reject the appeals of those "who have sought to frustrate and weaken it."

The first part of the letter discussed questions arising from the constitution that governed the church of New Spain. This constitution was embodied in the so-called "erection" of the church—that is, the papal bulls and other documents that established the ecclesiastical province and its laws when it was first set up. These were all included in a brief issued by Pope Clement VII and had some additional norms drawn up by Archbishop Zumárraga. Because of the passage of time and the change of circumstances, many of these were no longer practical, and the bishops asked the king (rather than Rome) for some clarifications.

Some of the questions they asked concerned procedural matters that did not have long-term or permanent significance—for example, the precise duties of some chapter members or the academic degrees necessary for holding certain offices. In other questions they pointed out the contradictions between the erection and the Ordenanza del Patronazgo, such as the provisioning of benefices, over which the king now had more power. Similarly, the constitutions gave the bishop and the chapter the power to appoint certain lesser ecclesiastical ministers, such as acolytes, but the viceroys and governors, citing a clause in the Ordenanza, demanded that right for themselves. Again, the bishops asked for a clarification. Some complex questions of financing and tithes were also dealt with.

The bull of Clement VII that erected the ecclesiastical province of Mexico had given to the king the power to fix the boundaries of dioceses. From this the audiencias had deduced that they had the power to draw the boundary lines of parishes. The bishops had originally intended to issue a strong statement on this, but ended by accepting this intrusion, being content to object that it was being done without consultation of the bishops. They mildly requested of the king that in the future they always be consulted before such decisions were made.

The final section of the letter, titled "Matters of Advice and Request" (*Cosas que se avisan y suplican*), ranged over a variety of topics. It was not as logically organized as the first part, and often the expression of opinion was more personal. In it the bishops came to grips with some of the practical problems of New Spain and in so doing often broke out of the more formal mold in which the first part of the letter was composed.

They began this section by pointing out the virtual impossibility of implementing Trent's decrees on the establishment of seminaries because of the lack of funds and resources. They then requested that there be a uniform method of paying priests who worked in parishes, whether diocesan or religious. They asked that only the bishop be involved in the process of removing a *beneficiado* in Indian parishes because of the danger of injured reputations and scandal. They complained about the appointments made to vacant benefices in New Spain by the Council of the Indies and asked that these appointments be reserved to the bishops and chapters. They requested that when the king appointed anyone to these posts, he be very careful about *limpieza de sangre,* or purity of blood. The request was rather oblique, and it was the only time in all the conciliar papers that any direct reference was made to this subject.

With regard to the Christianizing of the Indians, the bishops pointed out that one of the greatest difficulties was the diversity of languages. For this they offered a somewhat simplistic solution, which though not as drastic as that of Ortiz de Hinojosa does not seem to have been entirely practical. They suggested that schools for Indians be established in every diocese where the children and the young could learn Spanish. Because of their youth this would not be difficult for them. For the rest, the principal Indian tongue of the region should be designated the official one in each diocese, and all the older natives should be required to learn it. This, the bishops felt, would not be so difficult for them as it would be for a European priest to learn all the native languages of a region. In addition, they must have realized that the repeated legislation of juntas and councils had been ineffective in prodding the clergy to learn the languages of the peoples they served.

This part of the letter was followed by an appeal to the king to restrain the audiencias and civil judges from interfering in ecclesiastical trials and from too lightly using the via de fuerza. This section appears to depend on both the Noreña and Salazar memorials in outline. The judges had involved themselves in all sorts of cases where they had no right, and the result had been the increase of sins because of the diminution of ecclesiastical authority. The same was true in a special way of the audiencias, which often interfered even though they had no accurate knowledge of the litigants or the matter of the case. They had all but obliterated the immunity and exemption of clerics and treated them in general no differently from the laity. In contrast, they did not permit lay people to testify in ecclesiastical courts—for them jurisdiction was a one-way street. Ecclesiastical judges had been intimidated. The oidores who acted as judges of the bienes de difuntos interfered with the wills of clerics, although this was against all canon and civil law. The audiencias meddled in cases involving clerics and concerning tithes and they appointed Indian *fiscales,* although all of these things belonged by full right to the bishops. Both the viceroys and the audiencias prevented the bishops from making visitations of hospitals, even though there was no legal basis for this. Moya had previously complained about this to the king.

There was an especially long indictment of the oidores and their abuses of power, with particular emphasis on the bienes de difuntos. They used up so much of the property and funds in this court that the actual bequests and legacies could never be carried out. This was a gross injustice, against which the bishops cried out. They also complained about the practice of the Council of the Indies of appointing men of inferior capabilities to the various chairs in the university or of making such appointments without knowing the beneficiary's qualifications. This practice was harmful to the church and state, because the university was the prime source of candidates for the priesthood.

They then turned to the ministry to the Indians. Because music and song were among the best tools for the apostolate to the Indians, it was vital that they be maintained and be of high quality. The quality was declining because of difficulties in paying the Indian musicians and singers. Between the tributes to the crown and the encomenderos on the one hand and the repartimientos on the other, the Indians could barely support themselves. The bishops asked that these musicians and singers be exempted from the repartimientos and that they be paid a salary from the common funds of the Indian villages.

The bishops asked that the policy of congregación be continued. Enríquez and Coruña had not carried out the royal orders in this regard, and the bishops had already urged in a public decree that these orders be fulfilled immediately. Similarly, they asked that the custom whereby Indians gave a certain amount of food to their parish priests be continued and standardized. The oidores and others used this as a means of intimidating the clergy; they would suggest to the Indians that they not give food to clerics or order them not to do so. As a result the clergy became wary of correcting the Indians' faults or alienating them in any way. The audiencias should be forbidden to interfere in these matters.

After a long and fiery condemnation of the Spanish war against the Chichimeca Indians, the bishops turned to a condemnation of the almost universal vice of gambling and asked for stricter royal control. They went on to complain that the prebends of some of the canonries of New Spain had been diverted to pay the salaries of inquisitors and that diocesan priests who were appointed notaries of the Inquisition immediately considered themselves exempt from the jurisdiction of their bishops. They also discussed the various contracts used in the sale of silver and the unjust and usurious aspects of these, especially the practice of selling low-grade silver for the price of better.

Abruptly they returned to the ministry to the Indians and discussed the problems of residual idolatry. The ambivalent attitude of the bishops toward the Indians shows itself in the somewhat inconsistent phrasing of this paragraph. The bishops complained that their hands were tied because they could not proceed against the leaders of crypto-idolatry with full vigor, even, if necessary, with capital punishment. Hence they had to content themselves with a generic decree that each bishop should do what was best for his diocese. They concluded by saying that until the king ordered otherwise, they would proceed with meekness and mildness, because the Indians were a new people and weak in the faith.

The letter concluded with a long and harsh condemnation of the various kinds of repartimientos.

The letter to the king manifests the same outlooks, attitudes, and themes as the decrees of the council, but often in a more personal and intense form. Both illustrate the status and problems of the church in 1585 and the mentality of the men who guided it.

First, there was the inevitable Counter-Reformation desire for law and order, for standardization and regularization of procedures. Only the restoration of proper authority and the imposition and maintenance of some kind of system could uproot abuses and prevent their recurrence. To the bishops one of the greatest dangers the church of New Spain faced was that of finding itself without laws, even for a brief period. Such a situation was the enemy not only of reform but also of the Christianizing of the Indians and the good order of the state. This outlook was natural for Spaniards of the sixteenth century, and especially for men whose backgrounds were predominantly legal, as those of the bishops were.

A second theme was an intensely personal dedication to ending the exploitation of the Indians. In dealing with the injustices committed against them, the bishops broke out of the formal, restrained legal language that characterized the rest of their work. They spoke with the apocalyptic overtones usually associated with the Franciscans. They harshly criticized their countrymen in terms that, although more restrained than those of Las Casas, reflected the same line of thought. Those sections of the letter that dealt with the exploitation of the Indians and war against them placed the bishops of the third council squarely in the mainstream of the great humanitarian movements of the sixteenth century.

The third theme may be called the triumph of regalism. The joint letter was an ideal opportunity for a reasoned and orderly attack on abuses associated with the patronato. Instead, at every step, the bishops accepted the supreme decision-making power of the king in religious matters. Although at times lengthy, their criticisms of the intrusions of the civil power into the ecclesiastical sphere did not reflect the stronger stands of Salazar and Noreña. The bishops were in an inconsistent position, for they demanded and accepted the support of the government in almost all areas of the church's life and the position of the king as arbiter. They were in no position to attack the Ordenanza del Patronazgo from which so much lay control flowed. What criticisms they did have were based on its contradiction of passages in the constitutions. And even these were turned over to the king for final determination. Undoubtedly Moya contributed abundantly to this attitude. Yet there seems no reason to doubt that just as the third council put the church of New Spain fully on the road of the Catholic Reformation, it also put it fully on the road to unrestrained regalism.

THE LETTER TO THE POPE

Striking proof of this can be found by comparing the matters submitted to the judgment of the king with those submitted to the judgment of the pope. There is evidence that the bishops sent two letters to the pope. The first was a brief note of congratulations to Sixtus V on his election (1585).[17] The other, of which no copy has yet been found, was to parallel the letter sent to the king, asking the pope for solutions to various questions that only he could give. A copy of this was sent to Philip II together with the bishops' letter to him.

The working papers for the papal letter indicate that most of the questions submitted to Rome for clarification or resolution were minor ones.[18] They included a request that the religious be compelled to pay tithes on the lands and ranches that they owned and that a dispensation be granted to allow the use of lard, butter, and any form of animal fat on abstinence days. There were complaints about the religious, especially the fact that they had performed marriages even after Trent had denied them that faculty. There was also a request for the publication of the bull *In Coena Domini* as a means of attacking interference in ecclesiastical jurisdiction.

It is quite easy to see where the bishops looked for leadership. The substantive issues, those that touched the daily life of the church, went to the king. These were often totally and completely ecclesiastical in nature. Lesser issues were submitted to the pope, who clearly did not loom as that large a force in the life of the Mexican church.

OTHER WORKS

The Third Mexican Provincial Council was also responsible for the formulation of a number of books and manuals that were considered necessary for the proper functioning of the church in New Spain. Trent had ordered the composition of a universal catechism and the revision of liturgical books such as the Roman Missal and Breviary and even a revision of the Vulgate, the official Latin Bible of the church. The third council followed this example by drawing up a directory for confessors; a ritual, or book of ceremonies; and two catechisms, all for the use of the ecclesiastical province of Mexico. All of these books had difficult or obscure histories.

Foremost among them was the *Directorio para confesores*. Such directories were common in the period of the Catholic Reformation and were handbooks intended to guide confessors in dealing with their penitents (*praxis confessariorum*). The third council's directory was a lengthy manual that was a digest of all the pertinent material from dogmatic and moral theology, canon law, and the decrees of the council itself, together with guidelines on pastoral practice. It was clearly intended to compensate for the lack of education among the clergy and to give them a readily available synthesis of all they were required to know for this important and delicate ministry. Much of it was in question-and-answer form, like a catechism. Different sections dealt with the qualities needed for the reception of holy orders, the qualities of a good confessor, the knowledge that he should have, and a summary of the sins that could be committed against the Ten Commandments. After that were given the procedures for administering the various parts of the sacrament, motivations for contrition, and a consideration of the seven capital sins.

A standard part of such directories was a summary of the obligations of different states of life and the sins that could be committed by the persons who held various offices and ranks in society. Also standard were cases of conscience that dealt with practical moral problems, presented in story form. In the case of the third council's directory, these sections make it an invaluable source for social and economic history. The states of life included feudal lords, bishops, clerics, physicians, students, judges, lawyers, royal officials at all levels, witnesses in court, pharmacists, teachers, city officials, soldiers, merchants, and diverse classes of artisans. The cases of conscience, which were based on those submitted to the bishops, described in detail the business procedures and contracts in use in New Spain, especially those in the silver industry.[19]

The bishops stressed repeatedly that because of the opposition the council had encountered and because of other obstacles, they had to rely on the directory as a means of helping to improve the lot of the Indians. In view of these repeated protestations, it is surprising that the section dealing with "the Indians, the vexations, grievances, and other injustices that are committed against them" is rather short. Like the cases of conscience, this part is a summary of the different questions, such as the repartimiento, that had been submitted to the council and was not taken from the legislation as such. Because the repartimientos were the chief question at issue, this section of the directory will be dealt with in the following chapter.

The directory was never printed, and neither, so far as is known, was it ever circulated in New Spain. It is possible that it was suppressed, but it is more likely that it was forgotten, a common enough fate for conciliar documents in the stormy aftermath of the bishops' meeting. In the thirty-seven years that intervened between the end of the council and the printing of its decrees, many of its works were forgotten. The directory disappeared into the archdiocesan archives. In the eighteenth century it was seen by Beristáin de Sousa, who lamented that such an important work had never been published. After that it was unseen again until it was rediscovered by John Frederick Schwaller within recent years. The hope of the bishops that it would be an effective instrument for ecclesiastical reform and for helping the natives was never realized.

The Third Mexican Provincial Council also decreed the writing and publication of a greater and a lesser catechism. Their fates, too, have been obscure until comparatively recent times. Although the task of writing the major catechism was originally entrusted to a group of consultors, the final work was actually authored by the Jesuit Juan de la Plaza.[20] According to Father Ernest Burrus, the catechism was held in abeyance, like the other conciliar works, in the period between the end of the council and its printing in 1622. During that time the catechism of the Jesuit Father Martínez de Ripalda had established itself almost universally throughout the Spanish dominions and the catechism of the third council was superseded before it could be printed. The Fourth Mexican Provincial Council of 1771 revised and published the third council catechism as a replacement for Ripalda's as a result of the anti-Jesuit movement in the Mexican church following the expulsion of that order in 1767.[21]

As for the ritual or ceremonial book, Fortino Hipólito Vera says that in 1600 there was in use in New Spain a ritual that had been printed in Salamanca in 1585 by order of Moya de Contreras.[22] Outside of that nothing is known of it.

The publication and formulation of works such as these, so characteristic of the Catholic Reformation, were an important part of the work of consolidation and organization undertaken by the third council. Yet in this area as in others much of the conciliar work was frustrated. One of the tragedies of the Mexican church was that in so many ways the task of the Third Mexican Provincial Council of 1585 was left incomplete.

Pedro Moya de Contreras as inquisitor, burning heretics. Mural by Diego Rivera, National Palace, Mexico City.

Pedro Moya de Contreras as archbishop of Mexico. Original in the Metropolitan Cathedral, Mexico City. Courtesy of the Instituto Nacional de Antropología e Historia.

Pedro Moya de Contreras as archbishop. Courtesy of the de Young Museum, San Francisco, California.

Pedro Moya de Contreras as viceroy. Original in Chapultepec Castle, Mexico City. Courtesy of the Instituto Nacional de Antropología e Historia.

Martín Enríquez de Almansa, fourth viceroy of New Spain. Original in Chapultepec Castle, Mexico City. Courtesy of the Instituto Nacional de Antropología e Historia.

D. Laurentius Xuarez D. Mendoça Comes Coruñæ S'Prorex Et Dux Gnälis
1580

Lit de la V. de Murguia é hjos.

Lorenzo Suárez de Mendoza, Conde de Coruña, fifth viceroy of New Spain. Original in Chapultepec Castle, Mexico City. Courtesy of the Instituto Nacional de Antropología e Historia.

D. Aluarus manrriqz Ð sfunica Marchio Villæ-Manrrique. Pro-Rex et Dux
gtts año 1886.

Alvaro Manrique de Zúñiga, Marqués de Villamanrique, seventh viceroy
of New Spain. Original in Chapultepec Castle, Mexico City. Courtesy of the
Instituto Nacional de Antropología e Historia.

GEROGLIFICOS RELATIVOS AL CONCILIO III MEXICANO,
tomados del Facsímil de los

"ANALES MEXICANOS,"
pág. 126.

1585 Años.
"Y Inoxitin yglesia mayol
axcanlones a xo de Enero 1585
as."

1585. El lúnes á diez del
mes de Enero se concluyó la
Iglesia mayor.

"I Inic xxii Enero domingo-
tica ynotlayaualloque obispos
ynic cñic moyetzticate y iii y
van yntlatoque Auh y pan octubre y movicaque y nin tete-
quiuhpa."

El domingo XXII de Ene-
ro hubo una procesion con a-
sistencia de tres obispos y de
los principales personajes. Y
en Octubre del mismo año lle-
varon á cabo el trabajo que ha-
bian comenzado.

"I domingo a xviij de no-
viembre ovalla in visorrey don
franco. de alvaro."

El domingo á diez y ocho
días del mes de noviembre lle-
go el virrey don Francisco de
Alvaro.

Description in Nahuatl and Spanish of the opening of the Third
Mexican Provincial Council. From the *Anales Mexicanos,* reproduced in
Fortino Hipólito Vera, *Compendio histórico del tercer concilio provincial mexicano.*
Courtesy of the Bancroft Library, University of California, Berkeley.

X. The Mexican Trent, II

THE GREAT QUESTIONS

In addition to enacting laws and decreeing the publication of various works, the bishops of the Third Mexican Provincial Council were called on to address issues of the highest importance in New Spain. Their responses were given in a variety of ways and circumstances. One of the issues was the familiar one of the privileges of the religious. Two others were moral questions of the first rank: the war against the Chichimeca Indians and the repartimientos. Finally, the bishops had to struggle over the fate of their own council when a concerted effort was made to prevent publication of its decrees and undo its work.

THE ASSAULT ON THE MENDICANTS

It was clear from the beginning that the question of the mendicants and their privileges in regard to the ministry to the Indians would come before the council. It was equally clear that each side would take the same stance that had been taken for decades, and that the council would be an open forum in which the question would be thrashed out. Each side hoped that a final resolution would be forthcoming. A struggle there was, but a solution was not so easy to find.

The canonical aspects of the question had become so tangled by 1585 that legal proof could be found for almost anything. There was no question of the validity of the privileges granted by popes and kings to the religious prior to the Council of Trent. Trent, however, was dominated by European bishops who had no more love for the religious than their brethren in the New World and who sought to put an end to what were judged to be the exorbitant privileges of the religious orders. As a result they enacted two decrees of supreme importance for the mendicants. In chapter 11 of session 25, the council decreed that in religious houses to which parochial responsibilities were attached, those who exercised such responsibilities and administered the sacraments "shall in all things that pertain to the *cura* and to the administration of the sacraments be subject immediately to the jurisdiction, visitation, and correction of the bishop in whose diocese they are located. Neither may anyone . . . be appointed thereto except with his consent and after having been previously examined by him or by his vicar." Chapter 14 of that same session gave the bishop, in certain circumstances, the right to punish individual religious for offenses committed outside the religious house.[1]

The situation did not long remain so clear. In 1565 Pius IV issued a brief that revoked all privileges of the religious that were in any way contrary to the decrees of Trent. His successor, Pius V, a Dominican, restored those privileges by a series of briefs from 1567 to 1571. His successor, Gregory XIII, issued a new order in 1575 that reduced the privileges of the religious to those accepted by Trent and the universal law of the church. Gregory had also issued many new privileges to the Society of Jesus, however, and these were claimed by the mendicants on the basis of the time-honored custom of communication, by which the privileges granted to one religious order were shared by all orders. In addition, the various briefs and instructions contained so many escape clauses, conditions, and exceptions that they formed a veritable canonical jungle—a paradise for the lawyer, but impenetrable to the person who sought to ascertain the true status of the religious in New Spain.

The council plunged into the question almost at its beginning. On 16 February Moya de Contreras issued a directive that the religious provincials were to submit copies of their various privileges for consideration by the bishops. Within a week the Dominicans presented seven different documents, the Franciscans nine. It is not certain what the Augustinians submitted or when.[2] The Jesuits also submitted their privileges, but because these were of a later date, more certain, and less threatening than those of the mendicants, they were treated somewhat differently. An ad hoc committee consisting of Bishops Montalvo of Yucatán and Alzola of Nueva Galicia was appointed to study the documents and make recommendations. Both bishops were Dominicans, but their sympathies lay with their fellow bishops.

They made their report on 8 May and it was an overall rejection of the claims of the religious. The various briefs of Pius V that had not only restored privileges but also granted new ones were judged not pertinent because they had been superseded by the reduction of Gregory XIII. Others were rejected as having been personal in nature and thus terminated by the deaths of the individuals to whom they had been granted. In general the verdict was that the reduction by Gregory XIII in 1575 had settled the question permanently.[3] However, the two bishops deferred any consideration of the bull Omnímoda to a later time.

The Jesuit privileges were treated more leniently. Aside from the fact that the Jesuits had not yet begun to feel the hostility of the bishops and were still considered allies, most of their privileges had been granted by Gregory XIII after the 1575 reduction. There could be no question of communication of privileges with the other orders, however, as the pope had declared in a brief of 3 May 1575 that they were granted to the Jesuit superior general to be used only at his order and discretion.

The bishops did not make a final determination on these recommendations until October. In the meantime, just a few days after Montalvo and Alzola had made their recommendations, the question was submitted to the religious and other consultors as one of the doubts that had arisen from the constitutions of the first council of 1555. The sixth of these doubts asked the consultors for their opinions about the privilege the religious had of administering the sacraments to the faithful, and the seventh asked about the correct interpretation of the clause in the Omnímoda that specified that religious had to be two days' journey from the place of residence of a bishop "or any vicar of his."

Pravia and Zurnero refused to answer on the grounds that they did not have sufficient knowledge of the documentation involved. The Franciscans, of course, defended the privileges of the religious to the hilt. Melchor de los Reyes held for the validity of the privilege of administering the sacraments. The Jesuits and Salcedo did not answer the entire question, because they had not yet seen all the documents. Fulgencio de Vich said that the sixth question was too general and, while giving abundant legal citations, never got around to answering the seventh. The consulta, on the whole, was not very enlightening.

The bishops, however, forced the question of the religious administering the sacraments when Salcedo gave the consultors two documents. One was the revocation of mendicant privileges by Pius IV and the other was the reduction of the restored privileges by Gregory

XIII.[4] To these the Jesuits and Fulgencio de Vich replied that all the privileges of religious had been reduced to the law of Trent and that the only valid ones were those granted after the reduction of Gregory XIII. Ortiz de Hinojosa gave a similar answer, but in much more detailed form. The Dominicans, through their provincial, Domingo de Aguiñaga, answered that they did not believe that their privileges had been revoked, but that they would follow the safer course and not administer the sacraments without the permission of the bishops until the matter had been finally decided. They asked the bishops to grant them this permission, which was done on 3 June. On 17 June the bishops issued a statement of their belief that all the privileges of the religious had been revoked, but for the good of consciences and of the faithful, they were extending faculties to all the religious of New Spain. The provincials of the mendicants responded jointly and asked the bishops to decree that nothing be done until both king and pope had been consulted.

On 27 August the bishops voted on the advisability of a public decree that religious did not have the privilege of administering the sacraments without the permission of the bishop and on whether they should adopt as their own the wording of the third council of Lima in that regard. All the bishops save Moya voted to accept it verbatim. Although Moya said that he understood from all the evidence submitted to the council, including evidence given by the mendicants themselves, that they did not have such privileges, he felt that a public decree would cause difficulties (the inevitable inconvenientes) and that it would solve nothing. He voted against a public decree in favor of seeking the advice of king and pope. In a sense both sides prevailed. The conciliar decrees consistently rejected the idea of religious privilege and subjected them in everything to the bishops and the universal law of the church. The question, however, still went to the king. On 16 October, the day they signed the letter to the king, the bishops voted to accept as their own the recommendations of Montalvo and Alzola.[5]

In their letter to Philip II the bishops began with a wholesale assault on the ministry of the religious to the Indians. They expressed their general belief that the evangelization of the Indians and the good of the church would neither continue nor improve until the religious followed the order and law of the universal church. "With absolute dominion [imperio], without recognition or dependence on the bishops (to whose sheep they minister), they have proceeded according to the order and means that seemed good to them, without the bishops' being able to know who their ministers are, their goodness and qualities, nor the good that their sheep obtain, whether it be positive or negative."

The religious, wrote the bishops, were not meant to be parish priests. The parochial life was inconsistent with their vocations as religious and their daily life of prayer. The diocesan clergy should dedicate themselves to the active ministry, the religious to their contemplation. The bishops claimed that the role of the religious in the doctrinas was that of substitutes until there was a sufficiency of diocesan clergy. Within a few years, they hoped, there would be more than enough diocesans to staff all the doctrinas. So they recommended that the orders relinquish half of their houses and be forbidden to build or take on new ones. The diocesan priests would move into the vacancies, which would encourage many of those studying at the university to persevere in their purpose. If any of the houses that remained to the religious were parishes or doctrinas, then the religious in them should be subject to the bishop in accord with the dictates of Trent.

Clearly what the bishops were advocating was a wholesale negation of the presence of the religious in New Spain. Whatever may be said about their arguments either from law or fact, there is no doubt that their proposals were unrealistic, both because of the continued need for the religious and because of the inevitable uproar that would have followed an attempt to implement this plan. As observed in chapter V, the pressure exerted by the bishops had only a limited effect. The crown continued its devious, but ultimately successful, policy of both restricting the religious and gaining control over the bishops.

THE MORALITY OF THE CHICHIMECA WAR

Contemporary accounts agreed on the principal characteristics of the several Indian tribes called the Chichimecas. The term had been used at different periods in pre-Hispanic times to designate wild, barbarian tribes that swept down from the north and either destroyed or displaced existing civilizations. The origin of the name is uncertain. The most commonly accepted derivation is from the Nahuatl word for dog, which may have had a totemic significance. According to Nigel Davies, it originally meant young people or newcomers. P. W. Powell says that by the sixteenth century it was a pejorative term synonymous with "dirty, uncivilized dog."[6] Whatever its origin, in the sixteenth century it designated the various "nations" that lived in the central plateau north of Mexico City, specifically the Pames, Guamares, Zacatecos, and Guachachiles.[7] They appear to have been the original inhabitants of the regions around Guadalajara, Compostela, and Santa María de los Lagos, who had been displaced by the Mexica during the latter's southward march.[8] They were in no sense uniform, for they differed as to customs and language, although they also had much in common. Of these tribes the largest and fiercest were the Guachachiles; the least warlike were the Pames.

All of them were stone-age aborigines. They were food gatherers and hunters and lived especially on the fruit of the prickly pear cactus (*tuna*). One of the less attractive aspects of their culture was cannibalism, which seems to have been widespread and was remarked on by most observers. Chichimeca shelter was scarcely more advanced. They lived in caves, holes, or rude thatch huts, which they constructed as the need arose. These were frequently situated in canyons or other inaccessible areas in order to avoid surprise attack. Their nomadic way of life made them difficult to conquer.

In personal appearance most of the Chichimecas were not particularly ferocious. Physically they were an attractive people, being described by Alonso Ponce as "well built, dark, robust, graceful, and capable of great exertion."[9] The most startling facet of their personal appearance, at least to the Spaniards, was their habit of going partially or completely nude. This especially struck European observers and was reported again and again by the chroniclers of the period, but it seems, however, to have been something of an exaggeration.[10] At times both men and women wore some sort of covering. Complete nudity was reserved for war, when it was used as a means of startling enemies. With the Spaniards this tactic seems to have been effective.

"A most warlike people," wrote the Jesuit Alegre, and indeed war seems to have been almost their life's blood.[11] They were born warriors, and their courage, nudity, war shrieks, and extraordinary prowess with bow and arrow made them formidable opponents, both militarily and psychologically. They were trained to the bow from childhood and were such expert marksmen that, according to Ponce, "if they aim for the eye and hit the eyebrow, they consider it a bad shot."[12] Their favorite method of attack was the ambush, usually from higher ground, during which they would unleash an incredible number of arrows at their victims. The attack over, they would melt back into the protecting wilderness of the Gran Chichimeca. Added to this was a deep-seated hatred of Christianity: "They are very given to killing Christians, whether Indians or Spaniards, with whom they carry on continual war."[13]

The Chichimecas first became a problem as Spanish expansion began to move into the territory directly to the north of Mexico City, especially after the discovery of silver in Zacatecas in 1546.[14] The first raids, which began rather abruptly around 1550, were directed against the silver traffic on the highways, something that interfered directly with one of the most important areas of the colonial economy. Little, however, was done toward formulating a coherent policy to deal with the problem. The period from 1560 to 1570, which one modern historian has called "the indecisive decade," saw little done to counteract the increasing Indian activity in the Gran Chichimeca.[15] During the viceroyalties of the marqués de Falces (1566–1567) and Martín Enríquez (1568–1580) attempts were made to achieve peace by conciliation, but without success.

By 1570 the clamor of Spanish settlers and the chaotic condition of the silver frontier brought the first demands for war by fire and blood (*a fuego y a sangre*), that is, total war to the point of extermination if necessary, but very definitely to the point of enslaving all captives. The latter was the more attractive alternative because it combined peace with profit. Enríquez's first moves in that direction were unsuccessful, because total war against the Chichimecas was impossible. As many nations before and since have learned (or sometimes failed to learn), massed armies and formal battles are ineffective against nomads fighting on their own terrain. This elementary fact did not halt the demands for total war. They were as strong in 1585 as they had been ten years before.[16]

Peace eventually came to the northern frontier through a "combination of diplomacy, purchase, and religious conversion."[17] In the latter, the efforts of the Jesuits played an important role. By the year 1600 the people of the Gran Chichimeca had been pacified, converted, and were in the process of amalgamation that would result in the typical Mexican of the central regions. Before that happy outcome, however, the question of total war had been thoroughly thrashed out before the Third Mexican Provincial Council.

From the moral point of view, war with the Chichimecas had disturbed consciences from the beginning. It was, however, the question of total war, with death, destruction, and permanent enslavement, that aroused the greatest theological and moral controversies. Priests, religious, theologians, and jurists all considered the problem and often arrived at different conclusions. One of the more intriguing aspects of the consultations presented to the third council was the diversity of opinion the question provoked.

In this regard, one of the more remarkable about-faces was that of Moya de Contreras. In 1574 he had expressed his approval of small individual expeditions that would hunt down the Indians for extermination, enslavement, or the best possible combination of both—an idea much in favor among the colonials. Moya wrote to Ovando that each day new reports arrived of murders and robberies in the northern region. He repeated the persistent refrain of the colonials that more Spaniards had died in the war against the Chichimecas than in the entire conquest of New Spain. The roads to the north were closed, and the cost of living had risen to such an extent that miners and workmen could scarcely support themselves. He quoted with approval the opinion of some that perpetual enslavement was the only adequate means of pacifying the frontier, but he was insistent that such a drastic move could be carried out only against those who were proven guilty.

> I understand from persons in that land that if only they [i.e., the Chichimecas] are made slaves for the rest of their lives, by that fact alone will they all be captured. There are many who will join in groups and companies for the sake of profit . . . but since they cannot do this [enslavement], except in the case of individuals who by [judicial] process may seem guilty—and that for a limited time only—and because if they do capture any, they are taken away from them and given to others on deposit, there is no one who wants to spend his time and money in going to war, especially since the investigations and processes would go on forever.[18]

He added that a junta of learned men convoked by Enríquez had met a few days before to discuss the justice of the war and the enslavement of the captives. All had agreed to both, except the Dominicans, who had accused the Spaniards of being the aggressors.

Not all the bishops agreed with Moya. In 1584 Domingo de Alzola of Nueva Galicia, a man living close to the scene of the war, wrote to the archbishop about the futility of Spanish methods against the hostiles.[19] The war was "costly and difficult." The presidios were not working; "they really serve to prolong the war because of the harm they do the natives, capturing their women and children." Total war against the Indians would never work, "because the costs of such a war would end by driving the Spaniards out of the land because of the heavy taxation." The only answer was small settlements of Spaniards with a few Franciscans and soldiers (for defensive purposes only). Likewise some Mexican and Tlaxcalan Indians could be used. The good example of the Spaniards and the Indians and the preaching of the friars would bring peace to the troubled frontier. This proposal, of course, was similar to the peaceable colonization advocated by Las Casas and to the policy later advocated by the third council. It is significant that peace was eventually brought to the Gran Chichimeca by an almost identical system.

A similar opinion was voiced by Juan de Medina Rincón of Michoacán, who wrote a lengthy letter to Philip II giving an account of his diocese and its problems. A large part of it was taken up with the Chichimeca question.[20] The bishop blamed the war on the aggravations and atrocities of the Spaniards. The military effort had been a failure because it had not been entrusted to the right men. He went through a list of the various captains who, despite treachery and ruthlessness, had been unable to curb the Chichimecas. The only solution, he maintained, was to populate the four main villages of the area (Celaya, San Felipe, San Miguel, and León) so as to fill out the empty stretches between populated areas and thus hinder the Chichimecas' lines of communication. He had, he wrote, recommended this plan to Enríquez, who approved of it in principle but claimed that it would be impossible to persuade anyone to migrate to the war area. Medina Rincón suggested tartly that if the Spaniards were to take this as much to heart as they had other aspects of life in New Spain, something might be accomplished. At the time of his writing there was danger that friendly Indians, negroes, and mestizos might rise and join the hostiles, a constant, pervading fear of the Spaniards. He concluded his letter with some sharp observations on how life in the New World had corrupted even the most virtuous of Spaniards and dulled their sense of justice.

It is clear that at least some of the bishops had pondered the question prior to the third council and had already formed opinions on how to deal with it.[21] By the time the council met, the situation was more desperate than ever, and while its deliberations were going on, the town of Zimapan, in the modern state of Mexico, dangerously close to the capital itself, was razed by the Chichimecas and one Spaniard and twelve Christian Indians were killed (March 1585).[22] Obviously the consideration of the morality of war by fire and blood and perpetual enslavement of the captives acquired a special urgency.

In December 1584, shortly before the opening of the council, Moya, then acting viceroy, requested and received from Hernando de Robles a complete report on the Chichimeca situation, evidently as part of the preparation for the conciliar agenda.[23] Although Medina Rincón had listed Robles as one of the incompetents who had accomplished little or nothing on the Chichimeca frontier, this oidor seems to have enjoyed a certain reputation as an expert on the Chichimeca problem. It is certain that at the beginning of 1577 he had been acting as lieutenant captain-general for the Santa Ana mining camp in the Guanajuato district and that by the spring of 1579 he had left the Chichimeca frontier to pursue Francis Drake. Despite the unflattering references by the bishop of Michoacán, he was apparently very influential.

The Robles report was important because it was the basis on which many of the opinions submitted to the council were formulated. In general, it was a brief in favor of war by fire and blood. Robles gave an extended history of Spanish settlements in the north and the depredations caused by the Indians. He repeated all the standard accusations against the Chichimecas and added another, that they "use their women barbarously without observing any order or relationship and committing incest at will."[24] Despite the efforts of Luis de Velasco the elder and Enríquez, the Chichimecas had not only not been conquered but also had become more powerful. They sought out neighboring tribes as allies. There was a danger, Robles wrote, that natives hitherto regarded as peaceful would apostatize from the Christian faith and join the hostiles. So great was the damage caused that it was estimated that between 1579 and 1582 the Chichimecas had killed more than a thousand persons. Robles detailed a long list of Chichimeca atrocities, of which cannibalism was one of the less barbarous. He also repeated some of the common complaints—for example, that the cost of defeating the Chichimecas was exceeding the cost of the original conquest, that the highways to the north had been closed, that profit from the silver mines was slowing to a trickle and life in the provinces coming to a standstill. "There is no safety anywhere since these common enemies of the human race have become so powerful."

"Enemies of the human race." This term is significant and gives a clue to what Robles considered the only solution to the problem—total war by fire and blood, with permanent enslavement of all captives. To his credit, it must be mentioned that Robles added the condition that care should be taken that no excesses be committed and that some limitation of territory and method be placed on the war. The enslavement of the Indians was justified only by the need to avoid greater evils. It is not too much to say that Robles reflected the common colonial point of view. The Spaniards, legalistic and theological, demanded further justification of total war against the savages.[25] It was quite in keeping with the temper of the times that the official request for a theological opinion on the morality of such a war should have been made to the third council by the cabildo of Mexico City.

Presented by Juan Velázquez de Salazar and Alonso Valdés Volante, regidores of the city and its representatives at the council, it was another long recital of Spanish grievances against the Chichimecas. It included mention of the raid at Zimapan and repeated the now hoary charge that more Spaniards had died fighting the Chichimecas than in the entire subjugation of New Spain.[26]

The request paralleled the Robles report in general outline, but one paragraph stood out because it clearly showed the more lenient and tolerant attitude of the Spanish crown, an attitude that must have irked the colonials no end.

Nothing has been done as it should have been because this perverse nation of the Chichimecas has not been declared enemies by fire and blood, as they really are. Rather, there have always been safeguards that they should not be fought as enemies but that attempts be made to punish them as delinquents.[27]

The request concluded by asking that the Chichimecas be declared "enemies of our Catholic and Most Christian Lord, Don Philip, and of all his vassals and of the church and the Christian religion, and that war by fire and blood can and ought to be waged against them."[28]

The request was submitted on 6 April 1585. Copies of the Robles report were given to the consultors and religious orders five days later, with instructions that their opinions be turned in by 29 April. Most did not meet the deadline.

The opinions that were eventually given to the bishops fell into two categories, those of the religious orders and those of the consultors. In general the religious adopted a reserved attitude based on a lack of firsthand knowledge or personal experience of the question. The Dominicans gave a cautious answer that basically did not resolve the question. They said that such a war would be lawful if the material in the Robles report were true. They did not, however, attempt to decide the question of fact.[29] The Augustinian report was a simple confession of perplexity: "We openly admit that we do not know how to arrive at a solution in giving our opinion on what has been proposed."[30]

The strongest stand in favor of the Indians, outside of the actual decision of the bishops themselves, was taken by the Franciscans. Their report admitted that the damages and disturbances that had been caused by the hostiles could have been stopped. For the Franciscans the troublesome fact was the means to be used. One expedient had not yet been tried—that is, settlements of Spaniards and natives in the hostile areas, together with just enough soldiers for their defense and the security of the highways. These soldiers were to be forbidden to make raids into Chichimeca territory. Rather, the religious should enter, subduing the Indians and ending their raids by preaching and catechizing. Only when this approach had been tried and proven a failure could the crown begin to think of total war. And even then an accurate investigation had to be made of the justice of the Indians' grievances against the Spaniards. "We think that there should be an investigation of the injuries that these barbarians have received from our people, just as there have been investigations of those which they have caused and are still causing."[31]

The Jesuit opinion was a capsule version of that given by the Franciscans.[32] The justice of the Indian cause must be investigated, and before any war could be undertaken, settlements of Spaniards and religious should be attempted, of a number and quality that in the

opinion of prudent, experienced, and Christian men would be sufficient to stop the raiders.

Of the consultors only one, Juan de Salcedo, indicated his agreement with the religious. Juan Zurnero simply stated his agreement
with Hernando Ortiz de Hinojosa, who, together with Fulgencio de
Vich, gave complete approval for war. Ortiz de Hinojosa's opinion was
long, verbose, and pedantic. It borrowed heavily from Father Juan
Focher's *Itinerarium Catholicum* (1579). He saw no room for any justice
in the Indians' cause and even justified visiting the sins of the fathers
on the children. At the end of his report he added a codicil that seems
to have been intended to answer any further objections that could
arise. In it he urged further investigation of the justice of the Indian
cause, though he was convinced that there was none. The memorial of
Fulgencio de Vich was strikingly similar to that of Ortiz de Hinojosa,
displaying the same weakness for length, verbiage, and ponderous
quotations from Roman law. Like Ortiz de Hinojosa he appended a
brief second opinion to the effect that, although there was nothing
wrong with the theory behind what he had said, he had been operating on the supposition that the Spaniards were the injured parties in
the case. Discussions with the other consultors had shaken his certainty. Hence he suspended his opinion and hastened to write to the
bishops that his entire report was based on the hypothesis that there
was no justice in the Indian cause.[33]

Thus it happened that two of the strong proponents of total war
had already modified their positions even before the bishops considered the question.

According to a notation by Juan de Salcedo, the council reached its
decision on 31 July and wrote a formal opinion to be included in the
letter that was to be sent to Philip II at the conclusion of the council.[34]
That decision was remarkable in that it went far beyond the opinions
that had been submitted. Perhaps the oral discussions in the conciliar
meetings served to crystalize opinion far more than the written reports,
or perhaps the bishops had already formed their opinions and were
not shaken by advice to the contrary. Vich mentioned a junta at which
one of the consultors (unidentified) had steadfastly refused to give an
opinion until a complete report on the justice of the Chichimeca cause
had been made. Be that as it may, the bishops' stand was an uncompromising condemnation of total war, an equally uncompromising condemnation of the Spaniards as the cause of the war, and a stirring plea
for peace.

After mentioning the circumstances of the request by the municipal cabildo and noting the opinions of the orders and consultors, the
bishops launched into a bitter attack on the colonial Spaniards. Royal

instructions regarding the Indians had not been observed, they wrote. The Spaniards had committed—and every day still committed—intolerable acts of injustice, tyranny, and robbery, making captives of Indians who were still pagans because they had never had the gospel preached to them as the king had commanded. The Indians had been sold into slavery and treated like animals, all on the pretext that they were murderers and raiders, all because of "imagined grievances."[35] The natural result was that the Indians went on the warpath and caused the destruction so vividly described in all the reports.

The raids and incursions made by the Spaniards into Chichimeca territory were therefore *"tyrannical, impious, and to the injury* and discredit of the gospel."[36] This was a remarkable sentiment in view of the reports handed in to the council and the almost universal opinion held by Spanish colonials. To say that the bishops were championing an unpopular cause would be a marvel of understatement. They went on to refer to the Chichimecas as innocent and meek, persons who had never injured the Spaniards and who did not deserve slavery and captivity. It is difficult to think of a description more at variance with the Robles report, the cabildo's request, the memorials of Ortiz de Hinojosa and Vich, and common opinion. "It is pitiful to see how openly they are brought naked to a nation that professes the gospel, chained and yoked, for public sale—and there is no one to stop it."

Behind the solicitude of the bishops lay one simple motive, summed up in a moving appeal to Philip II to alleviate the lot of the Chichimecas:

They are souls redeemed by the blood of Christ . . . by whose passion we humbly beg Your Majesty with heavy sorrow and tears to turn your face to this matter and, fulfilling your obligation and royal patronato, discharge your royal conscience and apply a remedy to this contagious evil.

The bishops then turned their attention to a positive solution to the question, a plan of peaceful colonization. The crown should provide a number of settlements populated with sufficient settlers to hold the land permanently. These should be both Spaniards and Christian Indians, persons who lived and supported themselves after the fashion of the Spaniards, *políticamente,* and who should be exempt from taxation and other obligations. Total war would not work, because the nomadic nature of the Chichimecas made it impossible to wage effective war against them. Better to spend the money on the settlements. This, of course, was the solution finally adopted by the Spanish crown with the help of Christian Indians and particularly of Jesuit missionaries.

How responsible were the bishops for this ultimate policy? The extant documents do not allow us to know for sure. It is certain that the crown did not adopt the policy of war by fire and blood and that its practice closely followed the bishops' suggestions. Both crown policy and the bishops' stand went against heavy pressure from almost every quarter of the colony. It must be admitted that the crown seems to have been intent on such a policy even before the Third Mexican Provincial Council. Still, it is quite possible that at least for one bright moment in human history moral considerations had an impact on political policy. The answer of the bishops was unequivocal, a dramatic cry for peace and justice: "We do not find nor do we feel any justification for making war by fire and blood."

THE MORALITY OF THE REPARTIMIENTOS

If, as has been asserted, the Mexican Indians owed their daily wages to the Third Mexican Provincial Council, then the attitude of that council toward the sensitive question of native labor must be of surpassing importance for Mexican history. This assertion was first made by the nineteenth-century priest-historian Fortino Hipólito Vera.[37] It was quoted with approval by Bernabé Navarro, who referred to the council securing the payment of just wages to the Indians as "a genuine glory of the church."[38] Such assertions should not be accepted unreservedly because the facts were not that simple. Any stand the bishops may have taken in favor of just wages for the Indians and against the abuse and exploitation of their labor must, however, be regarded as having deep significance.

The question of Indian labor is as controversial today as it was in the sixteenth century. It was, and is, the central issue around which all other aspects of exploitation revolved. The Spaniards' treatment of the Indians as workers and as the foundation of the economic structure of colonial society was the stuff of which black legends were made, as the Spaniards themselves realized in the sixteenth century. The question of labor was also the storm center of most of the controversies that swirled around the Indians in the colonial period.

A forced labor system of some kind was part of the economic and social structure of both conquistadores and conquered.[39] In Spain, from the early days of the Reconquista, Christian warriors had been rewarded with large landed estates called *latifundios*, the possession of which also carried the right to certain services from the tenants. In the pre-Hispanic period the Mexica had demanded services from subject or conquered tribes, impelled perhaps by the scarcity of arable land in the

Vale of Anáhuac. To such an extent did they depend on forced labor that it has been said, albeit with exaggeration, that the Spaniards merely adopted the existing system.

The first form of compulsory labor was the encomienda, or assignment of certain Indian towns or populations to designated Spaniards in reward for services rendered to the crown or for other reasons.[40] This carried with it certain rights and obligations. The rights were usually two: to receive tribute and to utilize the labor of the natives in certain circumstances. The obligations were those of Christianization (especially by building churches and paying clerical salaries), good treatment of the Indians, and, in emergencies, service in the militia (there was no standing army). Encomenderos did not live in the towns from which they drew their tributes, and their rights over the Indians were theoretically limited. Though the encomienda was not synonymous with feudalism, it was close enough to trouble the Spanish crown, which had but recently quelled the independence of its feudal nobility. The encomienda became a legal part of Spanish administration by the Laws of Burgos (1513), which, while attempting to deal justly with the Indians, also fastened the system on Spain's New World possessions.[41]

The question of the encomienda and attempts to introduce a free labor economy were a central part of the ideological and humanitarian controversies of the following thirty years. The crown used the protests of the pro-Indian and humanitarian factions, especially those of Las Casas and the mendicants, as leverage for a legal dismantling of the encomienda, just as it later used the bishops and diocesan clergy to attack the independence and power of the mendicants. The New Laws of 1542, an amazing combination of humanitarian vision and political centralization, attempted to bring the system to a gradual end. The frontal attack failed, causing a revolt in Peru and the suspension of the New Laws in New Spain. Eventually some of the more stringent enactments were repealed, but enough remained on the books to provide a legal framework for emasculating the encomienda system.

The New Laws, together with the graduated abolition of Indian slavery in the years leading up to 1558, spelled the end of the old order. The coup de grace was administered by the drastic decline of the Indian population, especially in the epidemic of 1576. As entire villages were depopulated or deserted, their value for tribute and labor dropped, and some encomenderos found themselves reduced almost to the poverty level. In addition, the encomienda, as an economic institution, failed to meet the needs of the expanding economy of New Spain, if only because the majority of the white population was excluded from it.[42] Indicative of the crown's priorities is the fact that once the encomienda had ceased to be a threat to the power structure, the government lost interest in totally eliminating it and it endured in some form for another century or more.

As a result of the epidemic of 1576, the cost of free labor skyrocketed. In addition, the Spaniards were convinced that despite the depopulation there were still entirely too many idle Indians. These factors, operating together in the period from about 1550 to 1580, gave birth to the repartimiento as it was known to the bishops of the Third Mexican Provincial Council.

The problem that faced the Spaniards was how to force the Indians to work for them while still paying lip service to the natives' rights and liberty as defined by the law. The repartimiento met this dilemma by an appeal to the principle that the state had the right to coerce citizens to perform work for the good of the commonwealth, just as it had the right to conscript them into military service. Hence, from the middle of the sixteenth century, the repartimiento may be defined as a temporary allotment or distribution of paid Indian labor on a rotating basis to individuals judged to be performing work that contributed to the common good.

The conditions of a repartimiento were that the labor of the Indians was (1) allotted by a governmental agency, (2) spaced at intervals, not continuous, (3) paid a just wage in cash according to a prevailing scale, and (4) a contribution to the common good (*bien común*). This last condition came to have a wide definition and eventually included silver mines, food production, public works, construction and maintenance of harbors, irrigation projects, drainage, the building of new towns, and almost any task connected with the building and maintenance of churches and schools. It was often difficult to find work that was not for the common good as Spanish entrepreneurs understood it, and they soon came to consider conscripted native labor as their right.

A Spaniard who wanted Indian labor first applied to the local corregidor, or more commonly to the special *juez de repartimientos,* to whom it was customary to pay a fee, often a disguised bribe. The applicant declared that he was engaged in work for the common good and specified the number of Indians he wanted. He also agreed to pay them the prevailing wage, which in most cases was supposed to be a real a day, though in practice it was less. On a specified day, usually Sunday, a percentage of the Indians from a town or district were brought together and assigned the tasks for their period of service. Supposedly each Indian had to serve only once in four weeks, but the rotation of work could be more frequent and even continuous.[43]

It is hardly surprising that the system was riddled with abuses. Repartidores could be easily bribed and the Indians cowed into accepting longer service and lower wages. The most frequent abuse arose from the blurred distinction between common good and private profit. In addition, the Indians were compelled to travel long distances, they were called up more frequently than the law permitted, and they were forced to work in unhealthy conditions, especially in the mines. Not the least abuse was that they were often defrauded of their just wages. The Jesuit Juan de la Plaza vividly described how in the textile workshops (obrajes) the system of debt peonage was already being used to shackle the Indians to a new form of involuntary servitude.[44]

Churchmen and other reformers were quick to point out and denounce these abuses. The Franciscans were especially hostile to the system, and in 1575 Gerónimo de Mendieta wrote a long denunciation to Philip II. His protests were echoed by Alonso de Zurita in that same year.[45] Most churchmen, however, seem to have been able to accept the basic concept of the repartimiento and to view it as theoretically justifiable or as a lesser evil. Many more simply profited by the system in the same way as other Spaniards. How many did so and to what extent is not clear. That the church had an economic stake in the repartimiento is undeniable, a fact that makes the third council's condemnation stand out all the more.[46]

The repartimiento system lasted into the 1630s. The crown was never entirely at ease with it and attempted to regularize it through a series of cédulas. The *real ordenanza del servicio personal* of 24 November 1601 attempted to remove all compulsion from the repartimiento and marked a genuine attempt by the government to bring it to heel.[47] It abolished the position of juez repartidor (as the bishops of New Spain had suggested) because of the flagrant bribery and abuses connected with it. Despite this ordinance, and another attempt to end the system in 1609, the repartimiento endured. After that the crown settled for a policy of attrition. Again, however, economics came to the rescue of humanitarianism. The growth of the hacienda, which offered greater security and better treatment to the Indians, siphoned off the labor force that would ordinarily have gone into the repartimiento. The hacienda and the conscription of labor for the desagüe together spelled the end of the agricultural repartimiento, the most important part of the system, and left the other parts exposed and weakened. The other forms were gradually abolished by viceroys and audiencias, though it was still possible to invoke them in emergencies. As John Leddy Phelan has said, "Mexico had simply outgrown the repartimiento."[48]

As has been noted, some churchmen could justify the repartimiento in the abstract. Even some modern authors have been sympathetic to it as a stopgap, a temporary expedient that helped prepare the Indians for entrance into a free-wage economy, a short-term evil that had to be tolerated until a better situation could be devised.[49] Such toleration is not easily found in the reports and memorials to the third council. Whatever theoretical justification could be found for it, the men of the council could not justify it in the form in which it was then being employed. Some, like the Franciscans, went further and con-demned the entire system as intrinsically evil because it involved a violation of the fundamental right of free persons to bargain for their labor.

One of the first actions that the bishops took in regard to the repar-timiento was to forbid preachers to attack or criticize it until the council had seen and approved the material in their sermons. This order was almost immediately disobeyed by the Dominican Juan Ramírez, Pedro de Feria's delegate to the council, who delivered a scathing sermon in favor of the Indians and against the governors of New Spain. On 6 April 1585 the bishops decided against revoking Ramírez's license to preach and left the question of disciplining him to his provincial.[50] Although a minor incident, this is illustrative of the difference between what might be called the "old" and the "new" churches of New Spain. The position of most of the religious, especially the Dominicans and the Franciscans, was clearly more extreme than that of the bishops. It was the difference between the charismatic, apocalyptic, and sometimes inflammatory ap-proach of the earlier religious (such as Ramírez's fellow Dominican An-tonio de Montesinos) and the more cautious, restrained, and organiza-tional approach of the bishops.

In approaching the question, the bishops drew up a list of doubts about the morality of the repartimiento, based on a number of observa-tions submitted by Ortiz de Hinojosa on 9 February 1585. Although his observations were phrased as doubts, it is clear that he was condemn-ing the repartimiento as it was then practiced, with special emphasis on abuses by churchmen.[51] Without giving credit to Ortiz de Hinojosa, the bishops took his treatment of the subject and formulated their own list of doubts, which were not sterile legal propositions but strong condemnations of the abuses of the repartimiento. In asking the simple question of whether it was licit to allot the Indians to the mines of New Spain, for example, the authors of the doubts launched into a bitter description of the sufferings of the natives.

> It is a pitiful thing to see them come from six, eight, ten, or more leagues . . . and they make them work all day and a good part of the night or the whole night, making them haul the ore up steep cliffs and putting them in mines that are usually so deep that the said Indians can make their way only with torches and lighted lamps. And they go into the water, submerged up to their necks for a whole day, in order to take out the ore or to drain it. As a

result, the cold and excessive work kill them, and the wage that they take away is only half a real a day.[52]

After this formulation of the doubts, there is no documentation in the conciliar records on the question of the repartimiento until the following May. In their letter to the king the bishops mentioned that they had received opinions from the Jesuits, Dominicans, Augustinians, and the municipal cabildo. Of these only that of the Franciscans and a unanimous opinion of all the consultors are still in the conciliar documents. It was not until 2 May that the bishops circulated their list of doubts to the consultors. The bishops' concluding statement clearly shows that they were interested in condemning the abuses attendant on the repartimiento, not the system itself: "We are looking for some way that, though we still have the repartimientos, the evils and consequences mentioned should cease."

What most concerned the bishops was the abuses that had crept into the system. One can detect here a note of resignation to the fact that the repartimiento, like the poor, would always be with them. Their limited objective was to render it as harmless as possible. Not all the consultors, however, saw the problem in that light. The Franciscans took up the challenge of the first doubt—whether, aside from its abuses, the repartimiento was licit or not—and answered with a resounding condemnation of the entire system as intrinsically unjust and inseparable from the abuses associated with it.

The Franciscan report actually consisted of three memorials. Two were shorter documents of lesser importance, the third a longer one that was a detailed, unequivocal theological condemnation of the entire forced labor system. The third memorial also incorporated verbatim two reports written by Fray Gaspar de Recarte as part of a statement on the morality of the repartimiento that had apparently been prepared for Moya in 1584.[53] As might be expected, many of the ideas common to the Franciscan controversialists of the sixteenth century, especially Mendieta, are to be found in this memorial—for example, the comparison of the Indians with the Children of Israel in bondage in Egypt, the fact that Indians were forced to work while New Spain was full of lazy vagabond Spaniards, the idea that only the gift of faith justified the Spanish conquest of the New World, and the apocalyptic and prophetic tone that saw temporal misfortunes such as epidemics and wars as punishment for the injustices committed against the Indians.

The Franciscans plunged directly to the heart of the matter, asking whether the repartimiento was "in itself a good and licit moral act," even with the abuses removed. The answer was that the repartimiento as such was "illicit and evil and full of cruelty." They went on to refute the standard reasons given for the repartimiento: the laziness of the Indians (the Spaniards, they said, were worse), Aristotle's theory of natural slavery, the fact of longstanding practice, and the various needs of the commonwealth. The Franciscans condemned the repartimiento because Indians had to work while vagabonds did nothing, the repartidor did not defend the Indians ("We say that he is the best executioner they have"), and the Indians were being destroyed. The worst were the repartimientos to the mines. "To send them to the mines is nothing else than to send them to death."[54] Their arguments even included a remarkably prescient vision of the Black Legend—the picture of Spanish rule in the Indies as a period of unrestrained exploitation and cruelty.

> What greater infamy can endure for the Spanish nation during the next centuries than to say that by its greed and cruelty it destroyed and devastated a new world of innumerable and docile peoples, whom God had put into their hands so that they might care for them as children, protect them, and put them on the road to the salvation of their souls? And as for the kings and princes who consent to such a thing, what Christianity and fear of God could they have had?[55]

Toward the end the Franciscans took up a favorite theme of apocalyptic preachers—that the Spanish oppression of the Indians was similar to Pharaoh's oppression of the Chosen People in Egypt: "To the letter this is happening among the Spaniards. In order not to lose the temporal profits that they receive from the service of the Indians, they turn their faces from whatever laws there are, whether human or divine."[56]

The two shorter memorials paralleled this one exactly. They emphasized that the repartimiento could not be separated from its abuses, which, it was claimed, followed naturally from the very nature of the system. "We say that . . . it is impossible, morally speaking, to strip them of their evil circumstances, except by abolishing them altogether." In the most basic sense the repartimiento was "evil, vicious, unjust, and dangerous because it is making partial slaves of those whom God and nature make free."[57]

On Saturday, 18 May 1585, the consultors and representatives of the mendicant orders appeared in the conciliar hall and presented a common opinion (*parecer concorde*), signed by all, on the morality of the repartimiento.[58] In the name of all present Juan de la Plaza reiterated to the bishops the grave necessity and obligation of remedying the injustices enumerated and condemned in the opinion. It was then seen and read by the entire council, which declared itself gratified by the zeal and wisdom shown, and it was decided that provision should be made for whatever was necessary for the service of God and the increase of the faith among the Indians.

The parecer concorde itself was basically a summary, but despite its brevity it went to the heart of the question. It was composed of twelve points of condemnation and four positive suggestions for ensuring the liberty of the Indians. Though not so strong as the Franciscan memorials, it went beyond what was found in those of Ortiz de Hinojosa or in the questions originally formulated by the bishops. Still, it seems almost certain that the Franciscan influence was the determining factor.

The opinion began with a blanket condemnation of the repartimientos "in the manner in which they are now carried out," because they were "unjust, prejudicial, and harmful to the souls, possessions, health, and life of the Indians." The reasons were many. Free men were forced to work against their will and were paid only half of what they should have been. Indian tradesmen and skilled workers were forced to work for a fraction of what they could earn in free labor. Those conscripted often included the very young and the very old, even the sick, who sometimes died at work or on the way to it. Indian wives and children were left unprovided for. The Indians were conscripted at harvest and seeding time, when they should have been tending their fields (milpas). The workers were called up more often than was legal. The repartidores were dishonest and open to bribes. The Indians were forced to travel long distances, even journeys of four days, for which they were not paid. They were also compelled to work on Sundays and holydays. In the work situation they were also badly treated. This section of the opinion concluded with a declaration of the "obligation under pain of mortal sin" that bound civil officials to put an end to the situation.

Ironically, the positive suggestions made by the consultors were much less satisfying than their condemnations. The first and obvious one was that the Indians should be paid just wages for their work. The nagging problem, however, was how to provide for the public good and necessity once the repartimiento had been abolished. As a first step the consultors suggested abolishing the office of repartidor and instituting the following system:

> The viceroy will give a cédula to the applicants to be given to the governors of the Indians, just as he now gives one for the repartidores. The said governors will give the applicants [Indians] from their villages, in the same numbers as they now send to the repar-

timiento. And if the governor fails to take action to give the Indians to the applicant, the applicant should have recourse to the *alcalde mayor* of the area so that he will order them given.

It is difficult to see a real distinction between this proposal and the system the consultors had just condemned. Obviously they saw the office of repartidor as the chief source of abuse. The governors and alcaldes, who were on straight salary, would not be paid according to the number of Indians allotted. They were desperately trying to salvage a bad situation, but they had to face the inescapable fact that in New Spain everything ultimately depended on the labor of the Indian. They could condemn the repartimiento, but they were hard put to find a viable replacement.

Ten days later, on 28 May, the bishops met to vote on the repartimiento. Gómez de Córdoba of Guatemala said that he agreed with the opinions expressed by the consultors and believed that the repartimiento should be condemned as it then existed, and that a decree to that effect should be published as soon as possible. Medina Rincón of Michoacán agreed with the opinions of the consultors and asked for a decree that would condemn the repartimiento to the mines absolutely and without qualification. With regard to the other repartimientos, he asked that Moya, in his capacity as viceroy, take steps to correct the abuses that accompanied them and that he make sure that the Indians received just wages. Diego Romano of Tlaxcala believed that the repartimiento should be condemned as it then existed, without reference to the past, when there might have been just reasons for it. Gregorio Montalvo of Yucatán condemned the repartimiento to the mines absolutely and without qualification and asked for a decree that would condemn the other forms as they then existed. Domingo de Alzola of Nueva Galicia agreed with the consultors and asked for the immediate publication of a decree that would condemn the repartimiento as it then was. Bartolomé de Ledesma of Oaxaca considered it necessary that the repartimiento to the mines be stopped and that it be forbidden without limit or exception. The other repartimientos, he believed, were wicked and wrong in the way in which they were then being employed and should be condemned by the council.

In general the suffragan bishops were willing to leave aside the question of the justice of the repartimiento system considered in itself, but they were unanimous in condemning it as it then existed. They were also unanimous in condemning the repartimiento to the mines without any qualification. There was also general agreement that their opinion should be incorporated into a decree of the council and published immediately. Although they were unwilling to go as far as the Franciscans urged, they accurately reflected the opinions of their consultors.

Once again Moya acted as a restraining and regalistic influence. He agreed that the repartimiento in its current form was unjust, but he also defended the principle that some sort of compulsion was necessary because of the Indians' natural propensity toward idleness. He disagreed with the Franciscans, saying that the repartimiento in itself (*simpliciter*) should not be condemned, because it did not involve any injustice, but rather good Christian and civil government "if used properly." The matter was so important that the publication of a conciliar decree would result in many insuperable problems (the ever-recurring inconvenientes) because it touched all the inhabitants of New Spain. His recommendation was that the matter be submitted to the king and the Council of the Indies.[59]

The archbishop's influence carried the day, and his suggestion of writing to the king was accepted by the other bishops. Moya again showed himself the regalist, unwilling to take action without consulting the king, a cautious man both as archbishop and viceroy, reluctant to upset all of New Spain with a public decree. In taking this stance, however, he also weakened the force of the condemnation.

In their letter to Philip II the bishops began the discussion of the repartimiento by recalling the solicitude that the king's predecessors, especially Queen Isabel and the emperor Charles V, had had for the well-being of the Indians. This concern had been shared by the various popes who had granted the rights of the patronato because Christianizing the Indians was impossible without the help of the royal power. The experience in the Antilles, where the native population had almost been destroyed by Spanish exploitation, made it imperative that steps be taken to prevent a like occurrence in New Spain. That was done by the New Laws of 1542, which raised the Indians to the status of free men and rational citizens. Where the New Laws had been obeyed, only good, both spiritual and temporal, had been the result.

The bishops then gave a ringing condemnation of the repartimiento to the mines, listing the abuses that had been reported to them in the course of the council: the lack of just pay, the greed of royal officials, the long journeys that the Indians were forced to make, and the intolerable living conditions. Not even during the epidemic of 1576, which killed almost half the Indians, did the repartimiento to the mines stop. The bishops also admitted their own helplessness. They would have liked to charge the consciences of royal officials and the audiencia by a bold public decree. Yet they had to be content with a generic one, reminding the officials that some day they would have to face God and render an account for those things that cried to heaven for vengeance. They had to be satisfied with this feeble alternative, they wrote, because, in the mad rush for riches, profit, and silver that had seized New Spain, their authority had come to be so despised and ignored that a public decree would simply have incited the Spaniards to further hate, anger, and indignation. "Glutted with the blood of these poor people, they are only carried away all the more by their greed and desire to be rich in violation of our faith and in injury to their neighbors."[60] The bishops' only recourse was to appeal to the king.

The bishops took up the question of repartimientos to public works and detailed the abuses attendant on them. They did the same for the other forms of repartimiento. They cried out in particular against one form of exploitation, "worse than the slavery and harsh oppressions that the people of God suffered in Egypt," that was not mentioned in the other conciliar documents. This was the system of debt peonage found in various industries, especially in the textile mills, hat factories, bakeries, and iron works. The system was quite simple. A Spaniard lent money to an Indian, and when the latter was unable to pay, he was summoned before the courts, which, on the pretext that he might run away, turned him over to the charge of his creditor, a virtual prisoner, to spend the next eight, ten, or more years working off the debt.

Worse still, employers would seek out and kidnap Indians, throwing them into their private prisons and there laying the foundations of debt peonage. They called in judges to pass sentence on the poor natives, who were unable to defend themselves, knowing little or nothing of the judicial farce going on around them. The judges, who were poorly paid, were an easy target for bribery, and the entire proceedings became "a condemnation based on money, without examination of whether the Indian is innocent or guilty or the reasons for his oppression."[61]

How effective was the bishops' protest? It is impossible to say for certain because of the lack of data about the later history of the repartimiento. There is no doubt that the system was modified and changed in later years, but this was probably owing to economic conditions as much as to moral considerations. In light of the Franciscan condemnation of 1594, it is likely that the conciliar letter had little immediate impact. Aside from economic considerations and the "American reality," there was the fact that neither the bishops nor their consultors had a workable alternative to the repartimiento.

The council's condemnation of the repartimiento, with the full consent and agreement of its consultors, was paradoxical. Beyond doubt the church, including the religious orders, made use of Indian labor and in a real sense could not do without some form of repartimiento. The bish-

ops were opposing the actions and profit of many of their fellow churchmen. Probably they saw the reformed institution as still beneficial to the
church and, perhaps, even to the Indians. To some extent, now probably unknowable, the condemnation was a self-denying action on their
part. At the very least, it helped put the church's attitude toward Indian
labor into better perspective and showed that it was not all of a piece. It
should also be noted that the bishops and religious displayed a consistent anti-Spanish prejudice and an alienation from the interests of their
countrymen that is usually associated with the more extreme reformers,
such as Las Casas.

Would a public decree have been more effective? That is debatable.
In view of the increasingly limited influence of the bishops on public
life, it probably would not. As in other cases of exploitation of the
Indian, the bishops pinned their hopes on a direct appeal to the king's
conscience and on the effectiveness of their *Directorio para confesores.*
The language of the *Directorio* was very strong. It spoke of how "this
tyranny . . . cries out before Our Lord against the governors and
judges whose responsibility it is to remedy it and they do not do so."
In apocalyptic tones it warned of the obligation of king, officials, and
churchmen "to cry out and raise an outcry under pain that they will
have to give a very strict account of this to God, whose terrible judgment awaits them if they do not immediately provide a remedy for
this."[62] Remarkably, the *Directorio* also incorporated the idea that if the
civil officials had continued the use of black slaves in the mines, the
Indians would not have been suffering as they were.[63]

Whatever the final impact of the council's condemnation of the
repartimiento, it is to the everlasting credit of the bishops and consultors of the third council that they spoke with such fervor on behalf of
justice and liberty for the Indians.

THE STRUGGLE OVER PROMULGATION

As the council drew to a conclusion, the bishops had to turn their
attention to the questions of promulgating the decrees, of seeking papal and perhaps royal approbation, and finally of seeing the decrees
through to the printing press. All of these generated a crisis in which
the bishops, with the exception of Moya, decided to draw a line in the
sand against regalist interference. The last act of the Third Mexican
Provincial Council was also its stormiest.[64]

On 7 September 1585, at a meeting of all the bishops, Fernando
Gómez de Córdoba of Guatemala, the senior suffragan bishop at the
council, notified Moya in the name of the other bishops that the busi-

ness of the council had been finished and that there remained only that of promulgating it—that is, publicly reading and approving the decrees in the manner and form customary. By this act the decrees would take on the force of law for the ecclesiastical province of Mexico. Moya answered that he had assisted at the council not only in his capacity as archbishop but also as governor, visitador, and viceroy of New Spain— that is, as agent and representative of the king. In 1560 the latter had issued a cédula that all conciliar legislation should, before promulgation, be forwarded to the Council of the Indies for approval. Hence, Moya said, the acts of the council should be sealed immediately and sent to Spain. The bishops replied unanimously that the 1560 cédula used the terms *sínodos,* which referred to diocesan synods, not provincial councils. They added that they had met in council at the request of the archbishop himself, who had declared that one of its purposes was to enact legislation and to put into execution the decrees of the Council of Trent. Trent had been accepted and subscribed to by the king of Spain. As there was nothing in the third council's legislation that was not Tridentine in spirit or derived in some way from the legislation of Trent, it was ridiculous to think of sending it to the king for approbation. Furthermore, failure to promulgate the decrees of the council would cause great scandal throughout New Spain and would burden the conscience of the king for interfering with the means the Holy Spirit had chosen for reforming the church. The bishops then voted that the decrees of the council be promulgated on 29 September.[65]

The 18th of September found the bishops in full council again, and they resolved once more on immediate promulgation, reaffirming all that they had said before. They also resolved that promulgation should take place with all proper solemnity, something that would require the presence of the audiencia. And again they set the 29th as the date.[66]

The promulgation did not take place on the day chosen. It is not clear what stopped it, but on 2 October the bishops met again. They were still at an impasse with Moya on the subject of royal approval. They made reference to the need to return to their dioceses and to Moya's resistance to promulgation. Together they begged him to see to the promulgation with all proper solemnity. They proposed that the decrees be publicly read over the weekend of 18 October. They also threatened that if this were not done, they would refuse to sign the decrees and would return to their dioceses, leaving the entire council in abeyance, an act that would cause great scandal throughout the realm and leave it without effective legislation. The discussion grew warm as the bishops threatened Moya "with the terrible judgment of God and of his duty to his pastoral office and his consecration and the oath by means of which they all promise not to falter, insofar as it shall be possible to them, putting aside every human consideration and attending only to what God and his holy laws oblige them in the publication of the Holy Council." The archbishop, "desiring to avoid scandal and seeing the resolute and determined wills of their excellencies," tried to compromise by suggesting a reading of the decrees before the bishops alone or before canonical witnesses, without any public solemnity or ceremony. This was his concession prior to royal approval, because as the representative of the king at the council he had to carry out the royal cédulas. The bishops rejected the proposal and remained adamant in their previous stand.[67]

Five days later the bishops returned to the attack when Gómez de Córdoba, again speaking for the group, pointed out the harm that was being caused to the various dioceses by the absence of their bishops. He repeated the demand that the promulgation take place on 18 October with all due solemnity and publicity, including an announcement by public herald. After him, the other bishops, each in his turn, insisted on the same thing. Moya answered that he had precise instructions from the king, sent on the most recent flota, that the decrees of the council not be published without prior royal approval.[68] Because of the determination of the bishops, however, and because of the harm that would follow if they were to disperse without signing the decrees, Moya yielded and said that he would have them published in the way and on the day requested by the bishops. At this they made a great demonstration of gratitude and the meeting concluded. The bishops had triumphed on this particular point, but many trials still awaited them. Their conflicts with Moya were over, but those with the civil authorities were just beginning.

Just four days before the decrees were scheduled to be read publicly, Eugenio de Salazar, the fiscal of the audiencia, appeared before that body to protest the coming promulgation. Armed with the cédulas of 1560 and 1585, he declared the proposed promulgation illegal. The oidores agreed and commissioned the audiencia's secretary, Sancho López de Agurto, to inform the bishops of this and to direct them to carry out the orders in the cédulas.[69] The following day López de Agurto met with the bishops in the viceregal palace and delivered the instructions of the audiencia, together with copies of the cédulas. The bishops responded with the same arguments that they had used with Moya and repeated their threat to return to their dioceses without signing the decrees, "from which would follow infamy and scandal and much disservice to God Our Lord and to His Majesty and great harm to this province."[70]

One of the principal duties of a fiscal was to see that the rights of the patronato were observed. Eugenio de Salazar rose to this duty with zeal. When the bishops' answer had been carried back to the audiencia, he entered a detailed account to refute it (16 October). He alleged many reasons why the bishops were wrong, but his bluntest argument, one that exposed the starker side of the patronato real, was simply that they were creating a power superior to the king's, one that the king could not suspend. He concluded by saying that a private promulgation in the conciliar hall before the bishops alone would be sufficient. This was Moya's compromise, probably made in his capacity as president of the audiencia. Salazar also pointed out that having acted as the royal delegate, the archbishop, who was presiding over the audiencia, had all the more obligation to see to the fulfillment of the royal orders and the observance of the royal prerogatives. He concluded that he had heard that the new viceroy, the marqués de Villamanrique, now on his way to Mexico City, was bringing more specific instructions regarding the council.[71]

According to the later testimony of the bishops, contained in a letter they wrote to Philip II on 1 December, this was the point at which the audiencia acquiesced in the promulgation of the decrees of the council. That this was so is supported by the fact that on the same day Salazar sent an agent to the bishops with a formal appeal against promulgation. All the bishops were present, though the petition was addressed only to Moya. Salazar accused the archbishop of failing to halt the promulgation even after being informed of the pertinent cédulas, and he announced his appeal in the king's name against anything that could in any way prejudice the patronato and the prerogatives of the king or his vassals. He likewise interposed the same appeal before the pope. The bishops answered with the standard formula that they would do what was appropriate.[72]

The next day, 17 October, the audiencia formally received Salazar's petition, but it came too late to do any good. On the following day, after notice had been given by public herald, the promulgation of the decrees was begun in the cathedral. For three successive days, after one of the bishops of the council had celebrated mass, Salcedo ascended the pulpit and "in a loud and clear voice" read the decrees of the provincial council and received the final *placet*, or vote of approval, of the bishops.[73]

With the promulgation an accomplished fact, opposition began to take new forms. Generally these consisted of appeals of nullity against the actions of the council, mostly on the part of the secular clergy and the chapters of the various dioceses, and an attempt to prevent further spread of the council's work by impounding the original decrees and any copies that had been made. The opposition also claimed that since the promulgation was illegal, the decrees of the council could not be put into effect or executed until royal approbation had been secured.

On 24 October, less than a week after the promulgation, an appeal was lodged before the bishops by the diocesan clergy of New Spain. It was presented in the names of the deans and chapters of Mexico, Guatemala, Tlaxcala, Nueva Galicia, Michoacán, and Yucatán. They began their appeal with the claim that the council's consultors had been ignored and that many, such as the cabildos, who had a right to be heard had not been called before the council. The decrees of the council had been promulgated "although because of the crowd and the noise of the people and the smallness of the place they could not be generally heard or understood." For this reason the appellants requested copies of the decrees from which they could draw up their appeals. They considered themselves aggrieved "both in regard to those things that oppress priests and the beneficed clerics and persons . . . and also because of the many penalties and censures that are placed at every step in matters that are difficult to carry out." In conclusion, they announced their appeal from the decrees of the council and asked the bishops to receive their petition. Should they be refused, they would automatically appeal to the next higher tribunal.[74]

This appeal was given on the 24th to Juan de Salcedo, the man who was destined to be the storm center of much of the ensuing strife, with the request that he forward it to the bishops. He refused on the grounds that the council had been concluded and he no longer held any official position. This was to be the standard ploy of both Salcedo and the bishops in rejecting the appeals of the clergy.[75] The appeals were also refused by a royal notary, who claimed that he had no authority to carry their appeals to the bishop. The clergy then turned to an ecclesiastical notary, who, after securing permission from Moya, conveyed the appeal to the bishops. The replies followed the same pattern as Salcedo's—that is, the council was over, the matter was concluded, the bishops no longer had any official conciliar positions, and hence they could not act as judges of appeals. In addition, they said, the appeals of the clergy could not and did not suspend the execution of the decrees.[76]

At some unspecified time after this the clergy returned to the attack. After detailing the rebuffs they had received, they asked that the bishops hear their cause and receive their appeals to be taken before the pope, that the bishops not proceed to the execution of any of the things against which they were appealing, and that the bishops obey the royal cédulas regarding the publication and execution of the decrees of synods and provincial councils.[77]

Another appeal had been entered on behalf of the clergy by Juan de Salamanca and Alonso Muñoz. As delegates of the clergy they protested the rigor of some of the legislation, "which is harmful and prejudicial to us and contain[s] many rigorous penalties." These penalties, they maintained, were so easy to incur that, given human frailty, they would cause great harm to the church in those provinces. Trent had said that such penalties should be applied rarely and with discretion. The very words with which the legislation had been formulated slandered the entire clergy of New Spain. They appealed from the council to the pope and asked the bishops to receive their appeal.[78] Appeals such as this were obviously self-serving, and many of the diocesan clergy were resisting reform, but there was justice to their complaints about the excessive rigorism of the conciliar penalties.

This petition was presented to Salcedo, who refused to accept it for the reasons he had given before. Salamanca and Muñoz then went before the bishops personally and asked them to suspend the execution of the council until such time as it had been approved by the pope, the Council of the Indies, and the king.[79]

Events now began to move faster. On 26 October Moya summoned three of the oidores to the viceregal palace to inform them that he had just received two letters from the new viceroy, Villamanrique. One was addressed to him, the other to the audiencia. The letter to the audiencia, written from Perote on 22 October, was read jointly by the archbishop and oidores. Villamanrique said that he did not believe that the decrees of the council had been promulgated, but if they had, "under pain of their [the bishops'] temporalities no decree or section or other part should be put into execution, nor should they consent to such execution until His Majesty should see it first and give permission." Further, the legislation was to be gathered together and impounded. It was then to be closed, sealed, and delivered to the audiencia.[80] The letter to Moya was substantially the same. With the letters came a copy of a royal cédula dated 22 May 1585, directing Villamanrique to participate in the council as the royal representative, as Moya had already done, and to see that all the royal prerogatives were respected. At the end the king commanded "that nothing be put into execution until I see it and give permission for it."[81]

The new viceroy had stepped into the dispute with a heavy regalist foot and a crude threat that could have no other effect than to stiffen the bishops' resistance. His order to impound and neutralize the conciliar documents, no matter what its basis in royal orders, set the stage for new struggles. It is hardly surprising that from the beginning his relations with the bishops were strained, if not outright hostile.[82]

The archbishop and the audiencia immediately obeyed the new

orders and directed that the conciliar decrees were not to take effect until the royal cédulas had been complied with. Moya himself signed this order as president of the audiencia, but, as an indication of the ambiguous situation in which he found himself and the entrenched legalism of the Spaniards, the audiencia's secretary immediately informed him of it in the presence of the oidores, this time in his capacity as archbishop of Mexico. The other bishops were notified that same day.[83]

In the meantime the diocesan clergy entered an appeal por via de fuerza before the audiencia, which, with the expected arrival of the new viceroy, began to intrude more actively in the struggle. The clergy based this appeal on the bishops' failure to obey the royal cédulas on promulgation, although they knew full well that the new viceroy was bringing specific orders in that regard. They asked the audiencia to compel the bishops to obey the royal orders and to declare that the bishops had exceeded their powers both in promulgating the decrees of the council and in refusing to accept appeals against it. The clergy were not alone. Everyone who felt aggrieved by the conciliar decrees, from physicians to *beatas*, began to rain appeals on the bishops.[84]

On 28 October the opposition was strengthened by the arrival in Mexico City of Alonso Manrique de Zúñiga, Marqués de Villamanrique, the seventh viceroy of New Spain, a man with whom Moya had already had his first altercations. The archbishop's power in the civil sphere was now curtailed, and the audiencia and other opponents of the council had a powerful new ally. A determined effort was now made to secure the originals and all copies of the acts of the council.

Thus fortified, Salamanca and Muñoz presented themselves before the audiencia and its new president on the day after his arrival and again related the difficulties that they had encountered with the bishops. They asked the audiencia to summon Salcedo to make an accounting of the actions he had taken against the appellants and also to see that all excommunications and penalties that might have been incurred in the course of the appeals were lifted. The audiencia complied and a summons was sent to Salcedo.[85]

While this was taking place, all the bishops except Moya met in the viceroy's palace to answer the demand that they obey the royal cédulas concerning promulgation of the decrees of the council. The bishops replied by asking to see the cédulas and saying that until they had done so, they would not be bound to any deadline for carrying out the directive, nor did they consider that its contents would affect them.[86] Two days later, on 31 October, Salazar informed the audiencia that he had learned that the bishops were having copies made of the conciliar decrees with the intention of taking them to their respective dioceses for implementation. This, of course, would have been directly contrary to the orders of the audiencia. Salazar asked the oidores to serve notice on the bishops that any copies were to be surrendered and no steps taken to put the decrees into execution. In two meetings the audiencia decided that the bishops should be notified of this and that all copies of the conciliar decrees should be collected and brought to the audiencia.[87]

On 2 November, again without Moya, the bishops met to answer the appeals of the various diocesan chapters that had been presented to them on that day. They repeated their claim that they could not act as judges after the conclusion of the council. They described as "frivolous" the contention that the petitions were based on canon law or the decrees of Trent. Furthermore, because the decrees of the third council were entirely in conformity with these, the appeals did not have the force of suspending the execution of its acts.[88]

On 9 November the audiencia demanded that Salcedo give it the original of the conciliar decrees, together with any copies that had been made. Salcedo gave the usual response about his lack of authority. Moya had turned the documents over to Salcedo for safekeeping, and the secretary said that he would not release them without Moya's permission. When the audiencia demanded that Salcedo come before it to give an account of any copies that had been made, Salcedo refused on the grounds that as a cleric he could not do so without his bishop's permission.[89]

Moya apparently agreed to the delivery of the original, because Salcedo handed it over to López de Agurto on 21 November. That did not satisfy the audiencia, which continued to demand that Salcedo appear before it in person, as three representatives of the diocesan clergy had complained that what Salcedo had turned over was not really the original. They asked that the secretary be summoned to take an oath as to the authenticity of whatever it was that he had delivered.[90] The audiencia agreed and sent the demand to Salcedo on 22 November. Salcedo did not appear before the audiencia but took the oath before López de Agurto, swearing that he had delivered the authentic copy and that he still had the minute book (*registro*) from which it had been made. He then gave the book to López de Agurto.[91]

Despite this the clergy reiterated their demand that Salcedo appear before the audiencia to give an account of any copies that might have been made. Despite his oath, they claimed, they knew that the contrary was true and that Salcedo knew how many copies had been made and to whom they had been given. In the name of the clergy of New Spain, they asked that any accounting by Salcedo be in a public place, so that their letrados could be present. They concluded by saying that they considered Salcedo "odious and suspect."[92]

The whole affair approached a climax on 28 November, when all the various threads of appeal and conflict began to weave together. On that day Sancho López de Agurto informed the audiencia that Salcedo had turned over the registro of the council. At the same time the bishops, this time with Moya, requested that the cédulas governing the execution and promulgation of councils be shown to them. The audiencia replied that the cédulas were to be obeyed, and that if the bishops insisted on seeing them, then the viceroy would show them. The bishops had no intention of abiding either by that response or by cédulas they had not seen and began to make preparations to return to their dioceses. Juan de Salamanca hurried to the audiencia to warn them that the bishops would start implementing the decrees in their home dioceses. Salamanca and Muñoz also warned the audiencia of the existence of the ritual and the *Directorio para confesores* and urged the oidores to order that these be brought to it by Salcedo for inspection. This was done. Finally, on that same day, Juan Hernández reported to the audiencia that all the acts and appeals relating to the council had been gathered together as the audiencia had ordered and were now in the possession of Sancho López de Agurto. On the following day the audiencia sent a relator to get them.[93]

On 2 December a new figure entered the controversy. Francisco de Beteta was the maestrescuelas of Tlaxcala and had been appointed as the official representative of the bishops in the forthcoming struggle for royal and papal approbation.[94] In a petition to the audiencia he began by citing its orders to Salcedo and the bishops concerning the original and the copies of the council's decrees. He then went on to insist that the bishops had never had any intention of doing anything contrary to the patronato or royal jurisdiction. Rather, they had been zealous in upholding and promoting it. He emphasized the legal nature of the council, with the archbishop assisting in the name of the king, and that the audiencia itself, which had been present at the promulgation, had realized that all this was for the good of the church and the civil government of New Spain. He reiterated the reasons given previously for immediate implementation of the decrees. The audiencia replied that Beteta might go to the king, but that in the meantime its orders were to be obeyed.[95] From 3 to 5 December the royal notaries were kept busy informing the bishops of the various orders of the audiencia concerning the execution of the council's decrees. The audiencia was demanding adherence to its orders without feeling the need to show the basis for them. Most of the bishops answered that they would obey the cédulas when they saw them, provided they were not contrary to canon law, the decrees of Trent, or their consciences, a formidable list of conditions. Even Moya answered that he would obey them "insofar as there would be in it [*sic*] what was fitting to the service of His Majesty." The longest answer was given by Domingo de Alzola of Nueva Galicia, who very properly pointed out that he was not subject to the audiencia of Mexico. He expanded his answer with a rejection of patronato rights in this case.

> Besides this the matter of the execution is not subject to temporal power, because it is purely spiritual and subject immediately to ecclesiastical prelates, especially to the pope. No matter how the [decrees of the] council may have been published [i.e., promulgated], it began to obligate both the prelates and all the subjects touched by its decrees to obey them. Only the pope can hinder or suspend its obligation.[96]

Like Eugenio de Salazar, Alzola had brought the question down to fundamentals: who had the power? The audiencia reacted by ordering him not to leave the city until directed to do so, because it was a matter that touched directly on the king's service. Alzola agreed to comply. Why he accepted an order from a body that he claimed had no jurisdiction over him is not clear, but it is possible that he wanted to stay with the bishops in their struggle. Permission for him to leave the city was not given until 12 December.[97]

On 1 December five of the bishops—Gómez de Córdoba, Medina Rincón, Montalvo, Alzola, and Ledesma—wrote to Philip II, giving him an account of the opposition the council had received and detailing the reasons for the bishops' position. The council had been for them a means of carrying out the king's will and doing God's work. Eugenio de Salazar, they said, had attempted to halt publication on the basis of certain cédulas of 1560 and 1561 that had never before been applied to provincial councils, either in New Spain or in Peru. The audiencia had originally acceded to the bishops' reasons and shown this by attending the final ceremonies of the council. Salazar had kept up the fight, however, by appealing against the entire council as prejudicial to the patronato. Not content with being attorney for the king, he evidently felt that he had to fulfill the same office for all the clergy and laity of New Spain. All of this would have caused great scandal if orders (Moya's?) had not been given, prior to promulgation, to keep the entire matter secret. The bishops praised the conduct of the archbishop in the face of his divided allegiance. Somewhat inaccurately, they said that Moya had made his protests secretly because he knew that the royal jurisdiction had not been flouted. As for the cédula brought by Villamanrique, it had brought the audiencia back into the struggle, but the bishops had not been allowed to see it. The bishops

concluded by stressing their desire to serve the king but also by emphasizing that everything had been left in a state of anarchy. Hence
they begged the king to see that the decrees of the council were approved as quickly as possible.[98] The bishops had retreated to the extent
that they regarded approval by the king on the recommendation of the
Council of the Indies as inevitable. What they were resisting was suspension of the provincial council's decrees until royal approval had
been obtained.

On 9 December Salazar requested that all the documentation be
put together and sent to the Council of the Indies, and the audiencia
agreed.[99] Ten days later, Beteta petitioned, for the second time, that he
be given the original transcriptions of the council's acta so that he
might deposit them in the archdiocesan archives and have copies made
for the various appeals being sent to the king. The audiencia refused.
A note appended to the bottom of their reply said that the bishop of
Guatemala had been ordered detained and then given permission to
leave the city.[100]

With this the dispute moved to Europe, and there is no further
evidence of its having been continued in the New World. Unfortunately there is only sparse documentation about the processes that led
to both papal and royal approbation. It seems certain that Moya's presence in Spain at the time was crucial to the success of the bishops in
having the decrees of their council approved.

From a description of events given by Beteta in 1590, we know that
the Council of the Indies saw the conciliar documents and the appeals
some time in 1586, probably late in the year, for the copies of the
appeals, written out by López de Agurto, were not made until May
1586. According to Beteta, the Council of the Indies decided to forward
the documents to Rome for approbation before taking any action itself.
There is also one reference to a letter from the third council that arrived
in Spain with the flota at the end of 1586.[101]

The whole affair, then, seems to have been transferred almost immediately to Rome, after little or no consideration in Spain. On 15
March 1587 the apostolic nuncio in Spain, Bishop Spacciani of Novara,
made a reference in a letter to Cardinal Rusticucci in Rome to some
dispatches from the bishops of the provincial council.[102] In a letter to
the bishops of New Spain (21 April 1587), Pope Sixtus V mentioned
that he had not yet received any delegations from either the king or the
bishops regarding the appeals from the council.[103]

The pope's references to the appeals would indicate a hiatus between their forwarding to Rome, mentioned by Beteta and Spacciani,
and their actual arrival in the Eternal City. That the conciliar papers
did not reach there until some time in 1587 is also indicated by some

instructions given by Philip II to his ambassador to the Holy See, the conde de Olivares, concerning the council. These were included in two letters, the first of which was dated 2 December 1586. Surprisingly, in view of the regalistic obstructionism that had characterized the opposition to the council, the king worked wholeheartedly for papal approval. He informed Olivares of his own interest in the holding of provincial councils and mentioned that the distance from the New World was responsible for the lengthy delay. He concluded by ordering his ambassador to give every possible help in securing papal approbation. "I command you to attempt as far as possible to facilitate it and, for that purpose, to help and favor the persons who have been appointed by the said prelates and holy churches."[104]

To a duplicate of this letter, dated 2 April 1587, whose bearer was supposed to be Beteta himself, the king added a note that Olivares had already received the previous letter and that Beteta was bringing the original papers of the council to Rome. Again he instructed Olivares to give him every help and consideration, adding that Beteta was a person who was highly regarded.[105]

Strangely enough, the complaints and claims of nullity were not presented to the Council of the Indies for formal consideration until 14 December 1587, by which time the king had already come out in favor of approbation.[106] It may be questioned whether they were ever forwarded to Rome, for the documents in the Vatican Archives show no direct dependence on or reference to them. There is room to surmise that Moya may have thwarted the entire appeals process.

For some reason Beteta had still not left for Rome by March 1588. On 15 March of that year Spacciani wrote to Sixtus V from Spain to say that a canon (Beteta) had come from the Indies to bring the acta of the council to the pope. He referred to Beteta's fears about the outcome because of the strong pressure being exerted by clergy and religious.[107]

On 12 June 1588 Moya wrote from Madrid to Cardinal Montalto in Rome to ask for his good offices in helping Beteta to present the bishops' case. This he did in the name of all the bishops of New Spain. He spoke of the various appeals against the council as the devil's way of hindering a good work. The bearer of the letter was Beteta, "a long-time resident in that land" (*antiguo en aquella tierra*). Everything should be carried out with dispatch and haste, because New Spain was without synodal constitutions. This request would indicate that Moya did not agree with his fellow bishops that the decrees had taken effect with their promulgation. He specifically asked for Montalto's intercession before the pope.[108] The archbishop's desire for haste was understandable, for it had been over three years since the conclusion of the council.

In January 1589 Moya wrote to Montalto again to thank him for his services in securing prompt approval of the decrees of the council and the favorable outcome of the whole affair. Perhaps he was too sanguine about his success, because the papal bull of approbation was still eight months off. Cardinal Carafa, prefect of the Congregation of the Council, a body originally established to interpret the Council of Trent, wrote on 12 August 1589 that the task of comparing the Mexican Council legislation with the decrees of Trent was finished and that the other work would be completed shortly.[109]

The decrees and other written works of the Third Mexican Provincial Council were given to the Congregation of the Council, whose archives contain a copy of the conciliar decrees with the marginal notes made by the consultors who examined them. As mentioned previously, there was a tendency to side with the diocesan clergy of New Spain with regard to the rigor of many of the penalties imposed (although there were no direct citations of their appeals) and a tendency to moderate the regalism of the Spanish bishops. The puzzlement of the annotators over some Spanish ethnic and religious prejudices has also been mentioned. The catechism of the council was also submitted, but the changes made in it were for the most part insignificant.[110]

On 28 October 1589, more than four years after the closing of the third council, Pope Sixtus V issued the bull *Romanum Pontificem,* which formally approved its works as corrected by Rome. (The mysterious subsequent fate of this bull is discussed below.) Having completed this part of his mission, Beteta prepared to return to Spain. On 30 April 1590 the Council of the Indies received a letter written by him from Rome in which he described the process of approval. After his return, he submitted the papal bull, plus the acta and the ritual, which had been approved by the Congregation of Rites, and asked for a royal cédula of approbation.

Beteta had a surprise in store for the bishops of New Spain, however, that was in all probability hardly a welcome one. In return for "how hard I have worked in this cause and the many expenses I have undertaken," the pope had granted him a monopoly on printing the decrees, ritual, catechism, and *Directorio para confesores* of the council, together with a summary of the cases of conscience. All of these, by order of the council, had to be purchased by religious houses, cathedrals, and pastors. The monopoly was to last twenty years from the date of concession, 31 October 1589.[111] There is no documentation on the reaction by Moya or the surviving bishops of the council, but it was doubtless one of the factors that hindered the printing of the council's decrees, at least until Beteta's monopoly had expired.

After this there is another gap in the history of the council, for there is no evidence to explain why royal approval was so long in coming. There is some evidence that Juan de Salcedo was in Spain in 1590, perhaps to help with the process of securing approval. It was not until 18 September 1591 that the cédula of approbation was issued.[112]

THE DISPUTE OVER PRINTING

With royal approval obtained, it would seemingly have been a simple matter to proceed to the printing of the conciliar decrees, even given Beteta's monopoly. Here again, however, there is a long and significant gap in the history of the council. The first evidence of an attempt to have the decrees printed is in the year 1614, almost twenty-five years after papal approbation. Certainly Beteta's monopoly, or perhaps attempts to nullify it, played a role. Perhaps more significant, however, is the fact that in September 1591, when the crown approved the council's decrees, four of the seven conciliar bishops—Medina Rincón, Montalvo, Alzola, and perhaps Moya—either were dead or had been transferred to other sees. The long period after Moya's departure from New Spain during which the see of Mexico lacked a resident bishop was probably also responsible for the failure to actively pursue the implementation of the council. In light of events from 1614 to 1623, it is also more than likely that the continuing opposition of the religious and diocesan clergy of New Spain played a part in the delay.

On 7 February 1614 the archbishop of Mexico, Juan Pérez de la Serna, wrote to Philip III to complain that the government of New Spain, both spiritual and temporal, was "without basis" because it lacked the legislation of the third council. He made reference to a previous instruction from the king to the Council of the Indies that the printing of the conciliar decrees be expedited. This had not been done, and Pérez de la Serna asked that the order be carried out. Nothing came of this request. One explanation may be that since the archbishop hoped to convene a new provincial council, he felt that printing the decrees of the third was not especially urgent.[113]

Some time before 1621 Pérez de la Serna returned to his efforts to have the council printed. He came before the viceroy together with the procurators and commissaries general of the most important religious orders and announced that the king had commanded the printing and had entrusted the task to him. The king had also commanded that all *doctrineros* should have copies. For that reason the archbishop re-quested the viceroy to order the representatives of the religious to declare the number of doctrinas where religious were working. They were to be given a corresponding number of volumes, whose cost they were to pay out of the alms the king gave them.

The religious were negative in their response, of course, and their answers are an interesting illustration of the continuing opposition to the work of the third council. They began by referring to the use of royal alms for this purpose as "a great abuse." They claimed that there was no justification for this, because the decrees of the third council had been presented to the pope against the weightiest appeals by the religious of New Spain and even by some of the bishops (an interesting, if inaccurate, assertion). If necessary, they would interpose a new appeal before the pope. They were particularly incensed about the decrees that subjected them to the visits and examinations of the archbishop.[114]

The entire question of the council had now been reopened, and once again complaints began to pour in to the Council of the Indies from the religious and diocesan clergy. Three of these are of particular interest, because they indicate that in the years since 1589 knowledge of the papal approbation of the council had been lost or that it had never been formally promulgated in New Spain. These three documents, all undated, were submitted by Juan Márquez, provincial of the Franciscans, the crown attorney Pedro de la Vega, and a certain López de Agurto de la Mota. All three claimed that there was no evidence that the third council had ever been approved by Rome. López de Agurto de la Mota also claimed that printing was the equivalent of promulgation and that this was a prerogative of all the bishops, not just Pérez de la Serna alone. He also maintained that there was no evidence either of the promulgation of the council by the bishops in 1585 or of its subsequent approval by Rome.[115]

Why, in the three decades that had passed since the bull *Romanum Pontificem* had been issued, was it so unknown that its very existence could be plausibly challenged? It seems certain that the original bull was never known or promulgated in New Spain, or, for that matter, even brought there. One researcher, Father Rodríguez, was able to find it in only one place, the *Bullario Romano* of the Secret Vatican Archive; according to him, it was to be found neither in the printed editions of the council nor in such standard reference works as Hernáez's *Colección de bulas*. In that he was not entirely correct, for it can be found in the 1859 edition of the council's legislation edited by Galván Rivera.[116] Nevertheless, there is no doubt that the very existence of the bull was unknown in New Spain in 1621.

The council's decrees were eventually printed, mostly through Pérez de la Serna's efforts. Philip III issued a decree ordering the printing on 9 February 1622, but he died shortly thereafter (on 31 March), and a second cédula to that effect was issued by Philip IV on 2 April 1622.[117]

The struggle was not over. On 2 June 1623 the dean and cathedral chapter of Tlaxcala wrote to Spain to ask that the decrees of the council be suspended. They claimed that they were not seeking to avoid reform, but that conditions had changed in the years since the council had been held. They requested that all the acts and decrees be reviewed and revised by the bishops at the proposed new council, and they alleged that Pérez de la Serna had had the third council printed without the knowledge or consent of his suffragan bishops.[118]

Pérez de la Serna was never to have his fourth council. On 21 August 1624 he wrote to the king to ask him to suspend the cédula that called for another provincial council. The reason was financial: he did not know how the council could be paid for. The printing of the third council's decrees had cost 8,000 pesos, and he suggested that its legislation remain the law of the land until another council could be called, which ought to be within ten years.[119]

So it was to be, but the delay was far longer than the archbishop imagined. In 1771 the Fourth Mexican Provincial Council was finally held, but it was an anti-Jesuit meeting that was never approved by Rome. In 1896 a fifth council was held, but by that time the ecclesiastical province of Mexico embraced only a small part of the country. Contrary to the intentions of friend and foe alike, the Third Mexican Provincial Council governed the life of the church in New Spain and subsequently in independent Mexico, Guatemala, and the Philippines down to modern times.

In the history of the struggle over the third council some elements stand out.

For all their surrender to the patronato in the past and their hesitation to demand their rights, the majority of the bishops seemed determined to draw the line so far as the publication of the council's acts was concerned. Despite their pettifogging over the interpretation of royal cédulas, there were valid reasons for their determination. Royal approbation prior to publication had never been demanded before; this was a fresh and unaccustomed encroachment on the church's freedom. They firmly believed that they had done no more than apply the decrees of the Council of Trent to their dioceses and that royal approval was therefore superfluous. It is also likely that, in a very human way, the bishops felt that they had been pushed too far. The attitude of the viceroy and oidores was arrogant. The will of the king and the letter of his orders were clearly against the bishops. The bishops, other than Moya, simply did not want to obey.

With regard to Moya's position, the main outlines are clear. There was definitely some wavering. At the beginning, as a staunch regalist, he stood for antecedent royal approbation. Under pressure from his fellow bishops, he agreed to promulgation despite his personal misgivings. The later intrusion of civil authority in the form of an audiencia he was investigating and a viceroy he disliked seems to have aroused his fighting instincts. More than anyone else, however, Moya can be given credit for the eventual approbation by Philip II and that monarch's support of efforts to seek papal approval. In view of the obstacles, both regalistic and legal, that had been set up against the council, only a very strong personal influence, such as that which Moya enjoyed in Spain after his return, could have effected such a favorable outcome.

The determined opposition of the diocesan clergy and the religious, which carried over into the next century, was motivated both by principle and by self-interest. There was ample justification for attacking the excessive penalties and severity of the conciliar legislation, as Rome itself agreed. At the same time both religious and diocesans were intent on preserving their status and privileges with as little interference from the bishops as possible. The reaffirmation of the bishops' power, in the spirit of Trent, was not to their liking.

The long delay in printing the council's legislation will probably never be understood in full, but doubtless the Beteta monopoly and the continuing opposition of the clergy and religious played a prominent part. So also did the disappearance (or nonappearance) of the bull *Romanum Pontificem*, whose fate during the years following the council is still a mystery.

The greatest irony of all is that the legislation of the council lasted far beyond the hopes and expectations of both opponents and proponents. At first the foes of the council, whether in 1585 or 1614, hoped to nullify it for various legal reasons. When that proved futile, friend and foe hoped variously for the day when a new provincial council would revise, reinforce, or revoke the legislation of 1585. Fate, finances, and historical processes dictated otherwise. So also, in all probability, did the legislation of the third council, which, though it was historically conditioned and eventually dated, showed a remarkable staying power and permanence. Still, so many questions remain unanswered. Why, indeed, were there such long gaps before subsequent councils were held? What was the precise impact and influence of the conciliar decrees on the church in colonial and independent Mexico? Were they truly accepted and effective throughout the land? In what way did they affect the mentality and attitudes of the later Mexican church? Why the resurgence of interest in the third council and the reprinting of its decrees in the mid and late nineteenth century? Indeed, the full history of the Third Mexican Provincial Council of 1585 remains to be written.

XI. The Final Years

In the spring of 1586 Moya de Contreras made plans to return to Spain on the flota scheduled to sail on 1 May. The work of the visita was almost finished; the provincial council had ended, and its decrees had been promulgated, although the difficult questions of papal and royal approbation remained to be resolved. It was time for him to take both these important matters to the king and the Council of the Indies and to visit the homeland he had not seen for almost fifteen years. The flota was unable to depart on schedule because of the presence of Francis Drake in the Caribbean and the first of May found the archbishop still in Mexico City. He was, however, ready to leave by early June.[1] Fray Pedro de Pravia, the Dominican theologian who had been one of the consultors to the council, was appointed administrator of the archdiocese in Moya's absence. In some ways it was a strange choice, because Pravia, though capable and learned, suffered from scruples.[2]

The archbishop realized that he would never return. On the feast of Saint Barnabas (1 June), he celebrated mass for the last time in the metropolitan cathedral he had done so much to rebuild. Persons from all over the city and from every walk of life came to pay their parting respects, and the cathedral was completely filled. In his final sermon to his people, he expressed his gratitude for all they had done for him and his regret that he would never be buried among the people he held in such high esteem. He praised the clergy of his archdiocese and asked for their prayers in his behalf. He promised the criollos that he would always intercede for them with the king, a promise he kept. The sermon ended on an emotional note as both archbishop and people broke into tears.

After mass there was a daylong concourse of visitors and friends at the archiepiscopal palace. Everyone, even the poorest, brought a gift. A delegation of free blacks gave Moya preserves and other food for his journey. So many came that the palace was practically under siege. They camped in the plaza, lighted fires, and spent the night outside. There was sentiment among the crowd for preventing the archbishop's departure, a feeling that the criollos should not be deprived of their defender and the poor of their benefactor. There was a corresponding resentment against those who were considered to be the archbishop's enemies.

Fearing another disturbance of the type too often seen in the colonial capital, Moya attempted to sneak out of his residence at dawn. The strategem failed, and he found it necessary to let the throngs accompany him on the first stage of his journey. The crowd of criollos, Indians, mestizos, blacks, and mulattoes, all carrying lighted candles, marched with him northward to the chapel at Guadalupe, which by this time was the customary place of greeting and farewell for distinguished personages. Conspicuous by his absence was the viceroy. After the archbishop's departure, public processions and litanies were held for his safe journey.

After spending three days at Guadalupe, during which he conferred with the audiencia and the archdiocesan chapter, Moya and Pedro de Ortigosa went to the Jesuit country house at Jesús del Monte. Moya had often called it his house of studies.[3] After a brief visit he continued on his way to Veracruz.

For all the power he had exercised and for all the opportunities he had had to acquire wealth, Moya left Mexico City a poor man. His charities now caught up with him. It was discovered that he did not have enough money to finance his return to Spain. His majordomo, who by then should have been accustomed to such things, reckoned the cost of the trip at 20,000 pesos, a sum the archbishop could not even approximate. A hasty collection taken up among the wealthier citizens of Mexico City soon provided more than enough money. Moya kept what was absolutely necessary for his expenses and gave the rest to the hospital in Veracruz.

He left from San Juan de Ulúa on 12 July 1586. From 4 to 18 August the flota tarried at Havana, waiting to rendezvous with the silver ships from the Spanish main. These did not appear, and with rumors circulating that Francis Drake was in the western Caribbean, the flota master decided to return immediately to Spain. The journey was a long and arduous one, beset by both storms and calm, and it was not until 5 November that Sanlúcar de Barrameda was sighted. From Sanlúcar Moya wrote a report on the visita to Philip II and then set out for Seville, where he was met by the cardinal archbishop and the principal citizens of the city. He lodged with the cardinal while attempting to recover from the strain of the journey and while waiting for the winter rains and floods to end. By Christmas he was in Córdoba, his *patria chica*, and spent the holidays there.[4]

The king had expected a swifter arrival and on 12 December sent the archbishop word that if he was not coming personally, he should at least forward the visita papers that dealt with the oficiales reales and any official who had been arrested. Moya answered with multiple excuses, and because he was unwilling to trust so many and such valuable papers to a third party, he promised to leave for Madrid on 2 January. It is said than when he came to the Escorial, the entire court turned out to meet him.

Moya de Contreras now entered on the last phase of his career, one that is as obscure as his early days. In 1587 Philip appointed him an advisor on colonial matters and then asked him to undertake a visita of the Council of the Indies, the first since that of his patron Ovando. The papers of this investigation have not been located and are presumed lost. In the period 1588–1589 he was actively involved in resolving the sentences of his visita of New Spain. After that he followed his old patron into the post of president of the Council of the Indies.[5] Extant documents do not show him to have been especially active in the position, a fact that may offer a presumption of ill-health. Contemporaries stress that he did labor on behalf of the criollos and was responsible for securing rulings that they could be named archbishops, bishops, oidores, and inquisitors. If he did so, these far-sighted measures seem to have had rather small impact on long-range Spanish policy.

What was Moya's relationship to his archdicoese during those years? There appears to have been no question of his returning to Mexico City to resume active administration, or of transferring him to a peninsular see. At an unknown date Pope Sixtus V relieved him of his responsibility for the archdiocese of Mexico. Because he no longer received the salary of an archbishop, the king awarded him 6,000 ducados worth of nonresidential benefices. Philip also bestowed a knighthood in the order of Santiago on Moya's brother-in-law, Fernández de Figueroa, thus relieving the archbishop of the worry of helping to support his sister's family—or perhaps repaying an old debt. The mysterious affair of the archbishop's niece may have played a part in this.

Although Moya was no longer archbishop of Mexico, it was not until after his death that Alonso Fernández de Bonilla, visitador of Peru since 1589, was named his successor. Bonilla had served under Moya in the Mexican Inquisition and had incurred his displeasure; he would not have been Moya's first choice for the position. Bonilla waited a full year after his appointment in 1592 before being consecrated by Toribio de Mogrovejo, archbishop of Lima. He continued with his visita and was still in Lima when he died in 1600 without ever having taken possession of his see.[6] Thus the archdiocese of Mexico was without a resident archbishop for more than fourteen years.

In February 1591 Philip wrote to the pope to try to obtain the title of patriarch of the Indies for Moya de Contreras.[7] The title had a checkered history, having been used at one time by the Spanish crown as a means of augmenting its control over the church in the Indies and at another by the papacy in an attempt to restrict that same control. Whatever its origins, the title was by 1591 a totally honorary one without any jurisdiction or authority whatever.[8] Most early sources agree that the title was bestowed.

The date of Moya's death is only a little less obscure than that of his birth. From the middle of 1590 onward, his name no longer appears on the consultas of the Council of the Indies, a fact that again may offer the presumption of progressive ill-health. This would also agree with Gutiérrez de Luna's testimony that the archbishop contracted a slowly worsening fever in October of that year. He refused the services of a physician and tried to carry on his regular work as far as possible. The likeliest date for his death is either December 1591 or January 1592.[9]

His funeral was celebrated with splendor and pomp, as Philip ordered the entire court to attend. Typically, when the secretary of the Council of the Indies, together with Fernández de Figueroa, came to examine his effects, he found that the archbishop of Mexico, patriarch of the Indies, and president of the Council of the Indies, had died in almost total poverty. The king had to assume the expenses of the funeral and pay the lingering debts.

Moya's burial place is unknown. Some sources say that it was in the parish of Santo Domingo in Madrid, but the more reliable tradition, reported by Gutiérrez de Luna, places it in the parish of Santiago, located in the heart of old Madrid at a site near the present royal palace. The parish church had been built in the twelfth century but was torn down in 1811 by order of Joseph Bonaparte and rebuilt according to plans drawn up by the architect Juan Antonio Cuervo. In all probability Moya's tomb was lost in the reconstruction. This supposition is strengthened by the fact that the immediately adjacent church of San Juan Bautista was razed at the same time but not rebuilt, with the result that the tomb of the painter Velásquez was lost. The present church of Santiago seems to be of late nineteenth- or early twentieth-century construction. The fact that Gutiérrez de Luna identified his burial place as a parish rather than the church of Santiago raises the intriguing possibility that Moya, like his patron Ovando, chose to be buried in a common cemetery rather than a church.[10] It is a special tragedy that the land of Mexico, to which he contributed so much of his life, is not his final resting place.

At the time of the archbishop's death, Philip II said, "In all truth, there has died today in my kingdom one of the best vassals in my service and one who has done all things well." In the mind of His Catholic Majesty, there could have been no higher praise. In fact there had already been a greater tribute: the long lines of the poor, blacks, mestizos, and mulattoes who had marched to Guadalupe to say a last farewell to their father and shepherd.

XII. The Man and His Work

The concept of biography implies something other than the enumeration of a person's deeds or the factual narrative of a life. To know a person, in the true biographical sense, demands that an attempt be made to penetrate the exterior, to show or at least to limn the inner person. This means searching for motivations, drives, emotions. Some people are so self-contained that they frustrate their biographers, while others leave too little behind them.

All that has been written in this book has not uncovered what the inner Pedro Moya de Contreras was like. The concentration has inevitably been on what he did rather than on who he was. He left no spiritual diary as did some of the saints, nor memoirs as have other historical personages. His own approach to his life and work was such as to hide his inmost feelings and much of his personality. He was guarded as far as his inner self was concerned. What we know of his holiness and his more personal, as opposed to administrative, attitudes comes almost entirely from the pages of Gutiérrez de Luna.

Aside from Moya's own reticence, there is also the inescapable fact that he stood at such a focal point in the history of New Spain that it is easy to lose him in the welter of movements and events that swirled about him. He seems more a symbol than an actor, a preserver of systems rather than their designer. This view is misleading, but he did submerge his own personality to such an extent that the movements and currents stand out all the more.

If one word can summarize his age, it would be consolidation. Consolidation in some form or another was at work in society, in race, in government, and in the reforming church.

The society of New Spain had passed through its formative stage and was settling into the pattern that would characterize it for the next two and a half centuries. This meant the stratification of racial and social classes, not just the clear division of the levels of society but also the hardening of the attitudes that those levels would have toward one another. Moya had the foresight to see that one of these levels, that of the criollos, would have to be incorporated more closely into the Spanish colonial system. It was his belief that royal benevolence toward the sons of the land would win their loyalty to the crown. That was the source of cohesion in the far-flung Spanish empire, not patriotism directed toward a remote nation ruling from thousands of miles away. The crown preferred to counter the centrifugal force of nascent *criollismo* with a peninsular monopoly of authority. In the long run Moya's was probably the more correct view, although that is a conclusion more easily reached in the twentieth century than in the sixteenth.

The place of the Indian was becoming increasingly locked into the structure of that society. The earlier dreams of the conquistadores had been of a subject native population that would serve them, work for them, and provide them with the riches necessary to achieve leisure, status, and honor. The earlier dreams of the bishops and friars had been of innocent and virtuous natives who would form the bedrock of an ideal Christian commonwealth based on Erasmian and Aristotelian principles, reliving the life of the early Christians, and free of the corruption and complexities of the Old World. Neither dream was fulfilled. By Moya's time the earlier humanitarian legislation was beginning to run its course. All theories to the contrary notwithstanding, the situation of the Indians was settling into what it would be down to modern times: the working foundation that by its toil would bolster and support the economic order of New Spain and independent Mexico. The bishops of the Third Mexican Provincial Council tried, as they had in the past, to alleviate the worst aspects of this exploitation, but they and their land were too enmeshed in the "American reality" and they themselves too bound by regalism.

By that time also the forms of civil government had been consolidated and the finishing touches given to an administrative system that survived until the time of the Bourbons. With the arrival of Martín Enríquez came not only greater prestige for the viceregal office but also greater stability in civil society. His *virreinato* is now being seen as a crucial stage in the development of colonial society and government. With Ovando in the ascendancy in Spain the forces of consolidation and control took the lead in all aspects of colonial life. It is no accident that the three short years from 1571 to 1574 saw the arrival of Moya de Contreras, the Inquisition, the Jesuits, the alcabala, the Ordenanza del Patronazgo, and the elevation of the first diocesan priest to the archbishopric of Mexico.

Unfortunately this consolidation also included some of the ills that would afflict government in Mexico until modern times: the view of office as a sinecure and a means to private gain, the web of relationships with the local power structure (modern *personalismo*), and a persistent pattern of corruption. The crown reacted vigorously to the worst of these abuses at least on one occasion, but failed to take any reforming steps of lasting value, perhaps because the abuses were already too entrenched. Government came to be dominated by the letrado bureaucracy, and civil life came to be as closely regulated as religious life.

Consolidation is probably the best word to describe the situation of the church in both its good and bad aspects. The establishment of the Spanish Inquisition in New Spain meant that centralization, efficiency, and order were imposed on the more diffuse and uneven episcopal inquisition. The old order resisted, albeit somewhat feebly, but the new one triumphed. Inquisitorial functions were no longer spread among the various bishops but were concentrated in a structure in which the pyramidal delineation of responsibility was clearly drawn.

There were two primary sources for this ecclesiastical consolidation: the Habsburg monarchy and the Council of Trent. The crown was putting the finishing touches on the patronato, inaugurated by Philip II's great-grandparents, and completing the transformation of the colonial church into an administrative branch of the Spanish government. The bishops made a show of resistance, but the process was too far advanced, and they themselves had accepted too much of it. Most were willing to accept the support of the crown and even to demand it, but at the same time they tried to resist the inevitable control that went with it. If nothing else, Moya was more consistent in accepting the patronato as a whole: support and control. He was an active proponent of regalism, and it certainly dominated his approach to most ecclesiastical matters. Although the history of the Third Mexican Provincial Council shows the resistance offered by the bishops on one occasion, the fact is that the ultimate victory belonged to the crown.

For all their social status and prestige, the bishops of New Spain had surprisingly little power. This seems strange to anyone accustomed to the greater authority of bishops in the modern church. With Moya's arrival in 1571, the bishops lost most of their inquisitorial functions. With the Ordenanza del Patronazgo of 1574, they lost much of their authority over their clergy. They yielded to the audiencia the right to delineate the boundaries of parishes. They were only partially successful in reclaiming some of their rights from the mendicants. The cathedral chapters were strong and in some instances almost autonomous bodies. The civil courts encroached more and more on the jurisdiction of the ecclesiastical courts. Civil power was being consolidated and enhanced at the bishops' expense.

The Council of Trent, with its eighteen years of sporadic meetings (1545–1563), generated controversy in the sixteenth century and continues to do so today. For centuries it was seen as the rallying point of a reformed church, a living symbol of the church on the move. To some modern Catholics it has been something of an embarrassment, embodying as it has seemed to do all the defensive, polarizing, and reactionary tendencies of a past age. Trent accomplished many things, but perhaps the most important was the spirit that generated in Catholic Christendom the realization that despite all the gloomy predictions, genuine reform was possible. The plethora of provincial councils that sought to imitate it and apply its legislation at the local level is evidence enough of this. In its defensive and retrenching aspects, Trent provided an impetus for consolidation. It did not reach out so much as it threw up ramparts. It provided the blueprint for structural reform (especially by its reforms of the clergy and by enhancing the position of bishops), for uniformity (especially in liturgy), and for the triumph of organization over spirit.

The onslaught of consolidation is nowhere more evident than in the conflict between the bishops and the mendicants. An illustrative parallel can be drawn between what happened in civil society and what was happening in ecclesiastical society. The original conquistadores, a small band of brave and determined men, had conquered a new land against seemingly insuperable odds. Their reward, they believed, was to be in the form of *señorío:* their right to live as semi-feudal lords on the service and labor of the conquered. Their dreams ran directly counter to the centralizing and dynastic concepts of the Spanish Habsburgs. The result was a struggle over the assertion of royal authority and the limitation of the powers of the conquistadores and early settlers, seen most clearly in the struggle over the encomienda. The conquistadores aimed at particularization, the crown at centralization. The latter won with the help of law, bureaucracy, and sometimes the clergy.

The original situation of the friars was comparable to that of the conquistadores and encomenderos. They were at first a small band of brave and determined men, who began the "spiritual conquest" of New Spain although they came nowhere near to finishing it. As those who had come first, they had a proprietary attitude toward the land and the people they evangelized. They were particularistic and, from an ecclesiastical, though not necessarily civil, point of view, their tendency was centrifugal. With the arrival of the bishops, and especially the bishops of Moya's time, bolstered and inspired as they were by Trent, came also the forces of centralization and authority. The two forces came into open and grievous conflict in New Spain. The crown, which had been an early partisan of the religious, who in turn supported the Hispanizing and imperialist aims of the Habsburgs, turned gradually against the friars in favor of the bishops, who were more directly under royal control. The friars steadily lost ground, but unlike the original conquistadores they did not suffer complete defeat. By 1585 the conquistadores were no longer necessary for New Spain, but the friars were. It was this necessity that ultimately provided them with their best weapon.

The age of this "church of friars" and the years preceding Moya de Contreras were viewed by the mendicants as the golden age of the Mexican church, and some modern historians have concurred. Such nostalgia was only natural in much criollo thinking in the late sixteenth century. Just as the conquest was being romanticized in popular thought, so, too, were the early struggles of the missionaries. The sight of Cortés kneeling before "The Twelve" in their tattered habits, the thought of brave missionaries going into an uncharted wilderness, preserving the native history and lore, and passionately defending the Indians against Spanish exploitation—all of this was far more attractive and romantic than the pedestrian bureaucracy of the bishops and the secular clergy. And all of these things had a strong attraction in 1585 precisely because they belonged to the past. The missionary situation in New Spain had changed. One suspects that a basic problem of the friars was that they were still trying to live the 1520s in the 1580s. The present and future were to be more humdrum, because they belonged to the bishops and the institutional church.

Church and society had come far since the days of the conquistadores and "The Twelve." The personal, charismatic, and often apocalyptic approach of the friars was now to be replaced by the structural approach of the Catholic Reformation. The latter would not drive the older methodology from the field, but it would gain the upper hand. The new approach was perfectly exemplified by the Third Mexican Provincial Council, which incarnated Trent on the local level, with all the virtues and imperfections of that great council. Among the third council's positive accomplishments were its efforts at true reform, the improvement of religious instruction, the extirpation of abuses, the regularization of procedures, the reform of the clergy, the attempted restoration of power and teaching authority to the bishops, and the many attempts to help the Indians. Less attractive are the rigidity of doctrinal positions; the moral rigorism; the minute regulation of daily life; the surrender to regalism; the low esteem of human nature and effort, whether European or Indian; the excessive preoccupation with minutiae; and the emphasis on externals. Consolidation is never an unmixed blessing.

Unhappily the present state of research does not permit any definitive or final statements about the third council's impact in two areas.

The first of these is the question of the Indians, and of the council's success, or lack of it, on their behalf. With regard to the Chichimeca war, its uncompromising stand seems to have had a practical effect on Spanish policy. With regard to the repartimientos, such an impact is not so readily discernible. The poignant faith that the bishops put in their *Directorio para confesores* as a means of halting abuse of the Indians indicates that spiritual weapons were all they had left. And when this weapon was rendered ineffective, so, too, were their corporate efforts. The third council was magnificent in its overall conception, but it was destined to be an incomplete reformation. In part, because of their acceptance, in greater or lesser measure, of the patronato, the bishops had only themselves to blame. Perhaps, again because of the "American reality," there was no true alternative. One has a sense of courageous struggle mingled with futility. Yet whatever criticism can be leveled against the bishops, clergy, and religious assembled in the council, credit must always be given to them for one thing: they did speak out on the great questions.

The second area still in need of study is that of the general influence of the third council on the religious thinking and outlook of the Mexican church. The council's legislation was regularly reprinted and never allowed to fall into desuetude and oblivion. It was studied in the seminaries, and Father Fortino Hipólito Vera researched it in preparation for a nineteenth-century provincial council. Clearly it must have entered into the religious mentality of Mexican Catholicism, but the present state of knowledge does not reveal the extent or nature of this influence.

At the center of all this stood Pedro Moya de Contreras. In many ways he represented and summed up the movements of his age: regalism, emerging criollismo, imperial bureaucratization, the Catholic Reformation, the decline of Renaissance humanism as a force in church and society, the emergence of a new kind of dedication, centralization, and authoritarianism. He was a man of the system, with all of its virtues and defects. He embraced and reflected the contradictions of the age.

He was cast for his role from the beginning. His class had fought the battles of the Reconquista and then been transformed into the letrados and functionaries of the burgeoning Spanish empire. He grew up in an age that saw the reform of the church, the growing importance of law both for empire and for personal careers, and the increased centralization of royal power, including control of the church. He came early under the influence of a man who personified this same age and in some ways helped to create it. As inquisitor he brought to New Spain one of the most potent instruments of royal control, but he directed it with care, restraint, and regard for due process. He was a man of the law, and he served the law faithfully and impartially, even with severity.

As archbishop he embodied the diverse trends of the Catholic Reformation: a deep personal piety combined with regard for ceremonies and liturgical pomp, sincere charity toward the poor, a genius for administration and good order, a zeal for education and the reformation of the diocesan clergy as central to the reformation of the church, and a strong sense of the importance of his own office as an instrument for reform. His efforts to elevate the educational level of his clergy began with himself. Like so many of the bishops of his time, he was drawn into civil and political matters and found no inconsistency in this. His work as visitador, so long unknown, must now be seen as a crucial event in colonial history. It was unique in many ways, and probably no other visitador wielded such power. His term as viceroy is important more for its unfulfilled promise and for the support that it gave to the work of the visita and the provincial council. Of his work with the Council of the Indies after his return to Spain, one can only hope that future research and perhaps fortuitous discoveries will complete that part of his life's story.

In 1622 Archbishop Pérez de la Serna cited Fernando Cortés and Pedro Moya de Contreras as the two outstanding men in the history of New Spain up to that time. He viewed Moya as the one who had accomplished more of enduring value. Yet the name of Moya de Contreras has remained almost unknown, or known only imperfectly at best. Happily, at least part of his story has been rescued from the oblivion that has undeservedly covered it for so many centuries. He must now be seen as a major figure in Mexican history.

Appendix I

THE MEXICAN PROVINCIAL COUNCIL DOCUMENTS
IN THE BANCROFT LIBRARY

The Bancroft Library at the University of California, Berkeley, is fortunate in having the original documentation of the Third Mexican Provincial Council and some documents of the first two councils. The route by which they came there is obscure. It is certain that the papers were in the secret archive of the archdiocese of Mexico until 1746, the year in which the secretary of the cathedral chapter, Juan Roldán de Aranguiz, made a detailed inventory of them, together with other important documents.[1] After that nothing is known of them until 1869, when they were offered for sale in London by Puttick and Simpson. The entry in their catalogue for 7 June of that year contains the following somewhat misleading description.

> Highly important, not only in reference to Ecclesiastical matters but also as to the Political, Moral, and Social questions which agitated Mexico during the first century after the conquest by the Spaniards. The collection includes Treatises on the condition of the Indians, their various capacities, the question of their being made slaves, distribution, assessment of taxes, etc. Indeed, we know of no collection of original documents capable of giving such various and, at the same time, such an immense amount of authentic information as is contained in these volumes.[2]

It is possible that they may have been among the papers taken by Archbishop Lorenzana when he returned to Spain in 1772, or that they were part of the exodus of documents that followed the downfall of Maximilian (1867). The latter possibility is bolstered by the fact that they are described as forming part of the Fischer collection "collected during 20 years official residence in Mexico." A German-born Jesuit of questionable character, Father Augustine Fischer (1825–1887) was advisor to the emperor Maximilian. He seems to have played an important role in the transport of the imperial archives and other papers to Europe at the time of the empire's collapse, but there is no way of knowing for sure how the conciliar papers came into his collection.[3]

According to Joaquín García Icazbalceta, the conciliar documents were sold to the bookdealer Quaritch for sixty pounds and then resold by him to Hubert Howe Bancroft. García Icazbalceta lamented their loss to Mexico. "It is not known in Mexico how the church lost these most important documents, which I have attempted, so far without success, to recover for it."[4] In 1879 the Mexican priest-historian Fortino Hipólito Vera voiced the same sentiment. "This very rich collection, in which are found the most precious documents of our ecclesiastical history and in which are the purest sources of our Canon Law . . . is out of the country and there is no hope whatever of being able to get it back."[5] Vera was able to write a short history of the third council from the inventory of Roldán de Aranguiz, which he published as *Compendio histórico del tercer concilio provincial mexicano* (Amecameca, 1879).

Bancroft himself considered these documents to be of the greatest importance. "In my collection of manuscripts, taken as a whole, I suppose the *Concilios Provinciales Mexicanos* should be mentioned first. It is in four volumes and is a record of the first three ecclesiastical Councils held in Mexico; in comparison with which a number of more strictly religious works are hardly worth mentioning."[6] In view of this it is all the more surprising that the four volumes lay unused for so long. There is no evidence that they were ever consulted by historians prior to 1958. In that year Father Ernest J. Burrus, of the Jesuit Historical Institute in Rome, first began to utilize their contents for scholarly purposes. Since then they have been used by others, but not to the extent they merit.

The papers are bound in four large leather volumes, catalogued as Mexican Manuscripts (MM) 266, 267, 268, and 269, with the title *Concilios provinciales*. The papers in the volumes are not in any strict or logical order. As a guide to the researcher this author has drawn up a survey of the documents, which is available at the Bancroft Library.

Appendix II

ECCLESIASTICAL TERMINOLOGY OF
THE SIXTEENTH CENTURY

Holy Orders. Fundamental to an understanding of church administration and terminology of the sixteenth century is a knowledge of the various steps or orders that then constituted the hierarchy.

The first step taken by an aspirant to the priesthood was known as *tonsure,* a ceremony whereby part of his hair was cut to symbolize renunciation of the world and entrance into the status of *cleric* (*clérigo*) or of the *clergy* (*clerecía*), terms derived from the Greek *kleros,* meaning "lot"—that is, one who has cast his lot with the Lord. In its widest sense clérigo meant any person who had entered the clerical state via tonsure. In the sixteenth century it was also synonymous with the diocesan priest—that is, a priest who served as a member of a diocese under a bishop rather than in a religious order. As a sign of their state, clerics in that century wore a small shaven area on the back of the head, which in English is called a tonsure, in Spanish *corona.*

After this the aspirant passed through eight orders or stages. Four were called minor orders: porter, lector, exorcist, and acolyte. The other four were called major orders and were subdiaconate, diaconate, priesthood, and episcopacy. Each of these steps conferred more responsibility than the preceding one. The first of the major orders, the subdiaconate, carried with it the responsibility of celibacy and the daily recitation of the canonical hours, also called the divine office or the breviary. The four minor orders and subdiaconate were not considered sacraments.

The order of deacon carried with it the obligation and right to preach, perform solemn baptisms, and conduct funerals. After this came the priesthood and episcopate, the latter in the sixteenth century being considered the fullness of the priesthood because it carried with it the power to impart orders to others.

Territorial Administration. The lowest geographical division of ecclesiastical administration was the parish (*parroquia*), which was under the direction of a priest called a pastor (*párroco*). The term *cura* was also used, although it had the more generic meaning of any priest carrying out a parochial ministry. Above the parish was the large grouping called the diocese (*diócesis, obispado*) ruled by a bishop (*obispo*), who had genuine legislative, executive, and judicial power. The bishop's immediate assistant was his vicar general (*gran vicario* or *provisor*, though the latter was also a judge), who sometimes ruled the diocese in the absence of the bishop and was his delegate for all kinds of business, especially that involving ecclesiastical trials (which were more numerous in that litigious century than now). Sometimes a bishop's successor would be appointed in the lifetime of the incumbent and would be called coadjutor with the right of succession (*coadjutor cum iure successionis*). The present practice of having auxiliary or assistant bishops was unknown in New Spain during the colonial period.

The bishop was aided (and sometimes hindered) in the administration of his diocese by the cathedral chapter (*cabildo eclesiástico* or, in archdioceses, *metropolitano*).* It had a twofold function: (1) to act as a board of consultors and advisors to the bishop, and (2) to recite the canonical hours in public in the cathedral. This latter function was carried out with varying degrees of liturgical ceremony.

The chapter usually ruled the diocese in the interim between bishops (*sede vacante*), often through an elected representative called the *vicar capitular*. In some dioceses the cabildo had the right to nominate the new bishop, but under the patronato this was not done in the Spanish dependencies.

The cabildo had four ranks: five *dignidades;* ten *canónigos,* or canons; six *racioneros;* and six *medio-racioneros.* The five dignidades, who had other functions in addition to the two mentioned above, were:

DEAN (*deán*). He was the president of the cabildo and presided over its meetings in the absence of the bishop. He was usually its senior member. He was in charge of all ceremonies and divine worship and acted more or less as the pastor of the cathedral church.

ARCHDEACON (*arcediano*). He was originally the head of the deacons who participated in the cathedral ceremonies. By the sixteenth century he was the examiner of those who presented themselves for ordination. He sometimes acted as administrator of the diocese in the bishop's absence and was ordinarily expected to have at least a bachelor's degree

---

*Much of this material is based on John Frederick Schwaller, "The Cathedral Chapter of Mexico in the Sixteenth Century," *Hispanic American Historical Review* 61, 4 (November 1981): 652–55.

in canon law. In the sixteenth century this was the most powerful position on the cathedral chapter of Mexico.

SCHOOLMASTER (*maestrescuelas*). He was in charge of the cathedral school, if there was one. He was required to offer Latin classes to all clerics and aspirants who asked for them, and he was ordinarily required to have a bachelor's degree in canon law or philosophy.

CHOIRMASTER (*chantre*). He was in charge of the cathedral choir and had to do some of the singing personally.

TREASURER (*tesorero*). He was in charge of the administration of the physical plant and the revenues from the patrimony, or foundation, of the cabildo. These included the *fábrica*, or income for the upkeep and maintenance of buildings, and the *superávit*, or superfluous funds at the end of each year.

The canónigos, racioneros, and medio-racioneros had descending orders of importance and income.

Any ecclesiastical office to which a salary (*frutos*) was attached, such as pastor or administrator of a hospital, was called a benefice (*beneficio*). Consequently a *beneficiado* was any cleric who lived by an income attached to an ecclesiastical office. *Benefice* is a wider term than *prebend* (*prebenda*), which meant the right to receive a share of the income (*mesa*) from the cathedral. All prebendados were beneficiados, but not all beneficiados were prebendados. The matter of a cleric's having an income or means to live was very important in the sixteenth century, and even until recent times no one could be ordained to the subdiaconate who did not have a guaranteed means of sustenance (*título*).

Dioceses were grouped into larger territorial units called provinces (*provincias eclesiásticas*, not to be confused with the provinces of religious orders to be mentioned below), of which the chief bishop, whose diocese was called the archdiocese (*arquidiócesis*), had the title of archbishop (*arzobispo*) or metropolitan (*metropolitano*). There was only one archdiocese in a province, the others being called suffragans (*sufragáneos*). The metropolitan had no jurisdiction over the internal administration of his suffragans, though in some cases his courts could hear appeals from theirs.

The terms *patriarch* and *primate* are honorary, although ordinarily the primatial diocese or see (*sede,* meaning seat) was the oldest one in a particular country. There is no indication of the term being used in Mexico before or after independence.

A meeting of the bishop of a diocese with his priests to resolve problems and enact legislation was called a synod (*sínodo*). A meeting of all the bishops of an ecclesiastical province was called a provincial council (*concilio provincial*).

Religious Orders. A religious order (*religión* or *orden*) was one whose members took public vows and lived together in community under a rule (for which reasons they are also sometimes called *regulares*). A monastery (*monasterio*) was a religious house in which the members were monks (*monjes*) who lived all their lives in the monastery, which was an autonomous or semi-autonomous unit. The best-known of the monastic orders are the Benedictines. It should be noted that in the sixteenth century the term monastery had come to be used loosely of any religious house of men or women.

The friars (*frailes*), on the other hand, did not commit themselves to life in an individual house, but belonged to international groupings with a different form of administration. Some of these orders had originated in the Middle Ages and were called mendicants (*mendicantes*) because they had originally lived by begging. The best-known of these orders were the Franciscans, the Dominicans, the Augustinians, and the Mercedarians. It should be emphasized that despite the erroneous attribution of some modern authors, the Jesuits were neither monks nor friars.

Mendicant administration existed side by side with that of the bishops and frequently in competition with it. By a privilege called *exemption*, most male religious orders were free of the bishop's jurisdiction in regard to their internal affairs while working in a diocese. Geographically, the orders were divided into provinces (not to be confused with the ecclesiastical provinces mentioned above) ruled by a provincial superior (*provincial*), assisted by a council (whose members were sometimes called *definidores*). Individual houses of religious were ruled by superiors or priors, who among the Franciscans were called *guardians*. In the sixteenth century the term *convent* (*convento*) was applied to religious houses of both sexes.

The term *ordinary* (*ordinario*) indicated any office or officeholder with true jurisdiction exercised in his own name and not in that of another. It is the opposite of *vicar* or *vicarious*. Although in strict canonical terminology it could be applied to the provincial of a religious order, in everyday speech it more often indicated a bishop, especially in the phrase *local ordinary*. Anyone who held ordinary power, whether bishop or religious provincial, was called a *prelate* (*prelado*).

At this point the author would like to deplore the confusion rampant among historians, journalists, critics, and some recent dictionaries, regarding the terms *novice* and *novitiate*. A novice is an individual who, having applied to a religious community, has been accepted into a probationary period of intensive training and preparation called the novitiate. A novice is a person, a novitiate is an institution or place. An individual can no more be a novitiate than he can be a presidency or governorship.

It is current practice to identify membership in a religious order by placing the initials of that order after the member's name, a practice that was not in use in the sixteenth century. Among the more common abbreviations are:

O.P.   Ordo Praedicatorum, Order of Preachers. The Dominicans.

O.F.M.   Ordo Fratrum Minorum, Order of Friars Minor. The Observant Franciscans.

O.S.A.   Ordo Sancti Augustini, Order of Saint Augustine. The Augustinians.

S.J.   Societas Jesu, Society of Jesus (in Spanish-speaking countries, the Company of Jesus). The Jesuits.

Glossary

Alcabala	Sales tax. In 1572 it was a little below 2 percent.
Alcalde del corte	Judge of the civil division of the audiencia.
Alcalde del crimen	Judge of the criminal division of the audiencia.
Alcalde mayor	Chief magistrate and administrative officer of a province. Equivalent of a corregidor.
Alcalde ordinario	A judge, usually located in a city, who had original jurisdiction in both civil and criminal cases. There were usually two per municipality. Their jurisdiction sometimes overlapped that of the alcaldes del crimen. They sometimes had administrative duties also.
Alguacil	Constable or peace officer. Used of both civil and ecclesiastical officers. The civil officer in Mexico was usually called the alguacil mayor.
Almojarifazgo	Import/export duty.
Arroba	Unit of weight, about twenty-five pounds.
Audiencia	The highest royal court of appeals within a jurisdiction, serving at the same time as a council of state to the viceroy or governor. It was also a court of first instance in certain cases (*casos de corte*), usually involving higher officials. It was divided into two chambers, one for

223

	criminal cases (*sala del crimen*) and one for civil suits (*sala de corte, sala de provincia*). The judges of the audiencia (oidores) varied in number. In 1583 the audiencia of Mexico had six. The term was also applied to the area or district under the audiencia's jurisdiction.
Auto	(1) A judicial sentence in secondary matters that ordinarily did not demand a sentence. (2) A decree of the audiencia. (3) A drama of a biblical or allegorical nature.
Auto de fe	Public ceremony at which the sentences of the Inquisition were pronounced. In English-language histories it is often given in the Portuguese form *auto-da-fé.*
Bachiller	Holder of a bachelor's degree. Less common and more prestigious in the sixteenth century than at present.
Balanzario	Official weigher of gold and silver from the mines.
Bárbaramente	Nomadic, nonurban life, the opposite of políticamente.
Barrio	Subdivision of a town. Urban district.
Bartolomico	A fellow of the Colegio Mayor de San Bartolomé at the University of Salamanca.
Beata	A single woman, usually a widow, who led a form of religious life without belonging to any order, often wearing distinctive garb and engaged in charitable works.
Beneficiado	A person holding a benefice (see following entry).
Beneficio	Benefice, an ecclesiastical office with an income attached.
Bienes de difuntos	The goods left by those who died intestate or with heirs outside the colony, usually sold and the money sent to the heirs.
Breve, bula	Brief, bull. A bull (from the Medieval Latin *bulla,* referring to a lead seal) was a papal pronouncement or letter that usually carried the name of the pope without his number, followed by the words *Episcopus Servus Servorum Dei* (Bishop, Servant of the Servants of God) and the year of his pontificate. A brief was a shorter form, without the formalities mentioned, but essentially the same as a bull.
Caballero	A knight, the lowest ranking of nobility.
Cabildo	(1) Chapter of canons. See Appendix II on ecclesiastical terminology. (2) Municipal council. It was chiefly charged with the provisioning of the city and the upkeep of public works. It was also a court of appeals for lesser cases that did not go to the audiencia. (3) The building in which the council met.

Cacique	Indian chieftain. His district was called a *cacicazgo*.
Caja	The district administered by the royal treasury officials (oficiales reales).
Caja de tres llaves	Royal strongbox for holding money and revenues.
Calzada	Causeway leading to and from Mexico City.
Capellanía	Chaplaincy; a foundation whose revenues supported a cleric in return for the celebration of a specified number of masses.
Capítulo	Chapter, an official meeting of the members of a religious order, usually held every three years.
Carga	Maximum load that could legally be carried by Indian bearers, about fifty pounds.
Carnicería	Municipal slaughterhouse or butcher shop, established to regulate the supply and price of meat.
Casa de Contratación	The Board of Trade in Seville.
Casa de moneda	The mint.
Casas reales	(1) The principal buildings of a town. (2) The residence of the viceroy and audiencia.
Castas	Generic term for the various classes of mixed blood.
Catedrático del decreto	University professor who taught Gratian's *Decree*, one of the major sourcebooks of canon law.
Catedrático de prima	University chair in law that was taught at the time corresponding to the canonical hour of Prime.
Cédula	Royal decree or order.
Chirimía	Reed flute of Moorish origin.
Clérigo	(1) A diocesan priest. (2) Any person who had received tonsure.
Cocolistli	An epidemic.
Cofradía	Religious brotherhood or confraternity.
Colación	Conferral of an ecclesiastical office.
Colegial	Fellow of a colegio, or residential college.
Coloquio	Literary composition in the form of a dialogue.
Comisario	One who has been given the charge and responsibility for carrying out a certain task. A commissary.
Comisario general	Among the Franciscans an official in Spain intermediate between the superior general and the provincials. In New Spain he was the highest official in the order and had certain powers as visitador.
Communication	In canon law refers to the granting of privileges and means that the privileges granted to one religious order are shared by all orders.

Conde	Count.
Congregación	Reconcentration or settlement of scattered Indians into fixed settlements.
Consecration	(1) Ceremony whereby a priest was raised to the rank of bishop (now called episcopal ordination). (2) Solemn blessing or dedication of a church.
Consulta	Written opinion; a consultative meeting.
Contador	(1) An accountant. (2) One of the three treasury officials of New Spain.
Convento	A religious house.
Converso	A convert from Judaism to Catholicism.
Corregidor	Spanish official in charge of a province or district.
Corregimiento	Institution, office, or jurisdiction of a corregidor.
Criollo	A person of European blood born in the New World.
Cruzada	Tax or offering levied originally to finance wars against the Moslems, in return for which the offerer received indulgences and spiritual benefits. By the sixteenth century it was used to support the expenses of empire.
Culpa	Sentence of guilt given in a residencia or visita.
Cura	A parish priest.
Definidor	A councilor in a religious order.
Depositario general	Bonded official named by the municipal cabildo to have charge of sequestered goods and those under litigation.
Desagüe	The drainage of the valley of Mexico.
Diezmo	Tithe (lit. "tenth").
Diputación	Another name for the municipal cabildo or the building in which it met.
Doctrina	Parish consisting of recently converted Indians but no longer in a strictly missionary status.
Doctrinero	Priest in charge of a doctrina.
Ducado	Coin equivalent to 374 maravedíes; a ducat.
Ejido	The common lands of an Indian community.
Encomendero	Holder of an encomienda.
Encomienda	Grant of Indians as tribute payers and laborers, or the area of the Indians granted.
Entremés	Interlude, a short production of a lighter nature presented between acts of a weightier drama.
Ermita	A chapel of ease.
Escribano	Notary or secretary in legal and judicial cases.

Escribano apostólico	Ecclesiastical notary.
Escribano de provincia	Notary in the civil chamber of the audiencia.
Escribano mayor	Notary of an audiencia.
Escribano mayor de minas y registros	Audiencia notary in charge of registering documents and papers from the mines.
Escribano real	A notary who was licensed to practice.
Escribano receptor	Notary who accompanied a juez de residencia to take evidence and testimony.
Estanco	A monopoly.
Excommunication	Ecclesiastical penalty whereby a person was barred from receiving the sacraments and participating in public worship.
Fábrica	Income used for the repair and upkeep of cathedrals.
Factor	One of the three treasury officials of New Spain, a disbursing agent and royal business manager.
Familiares	Deputies or police agents of the Inquisition.
Fanega	Unit of dry measure, about one and a half bushels.
Farsa	A short comedy skit.
Fiador	Bondsman; one who put up a bond, usually for the good conduct of an officeholder.
Fiscal	Crown attorney. In civil cases he represented the royal interests and in criminal cases was prosecutor.
Fisco	Royal treasury; also called *cámara del rey*.
Flota	Convoy, specifically those that sailed between Seville and the New World.
Fraile	Friar, a member of a mendicant order.
Fray	Title used before the first name of a friar, from the Medieval Latin for "brother."
Fuero	(1) Charter of privileges or law code. (2) Privileges, such as tax exemption, enjoyed by those in special situations, e.g., religious.
Fuerza	(1) Setback administered to a person by a judge who found against a particular party or refused to admit an appeal. (2) *Alzar fuerza*, process whereby a superior judge took a case on appeal. (3) *Por via de fuerza, recurso de fuerza*, legal process whereby a case was appealed from an ecclesiastical to a civil court, often in violation of the *privilegium fori*.
Gachupín	Opprobrious name for a peninsular Spaniard.

Grano	The smallest denomination of Spanish currency. There were ninety-six to a gold peso.
Hacienda	Overall term for the royal treasury or financial area of government.
Hacienda	A large landed estate.
Hechura	A client or protégé.
Hidalgo	A member of the lower nobility.
Iglesia de visita	Church of ease, one visited at intervals by nonresident clergy.
Imposición	Overall name for the tax and financial administration of the port of Veracruz and San Juan de Ulúa.
Interdict	*Entredicho,* ecclesiastical penalty whereby church services were forbidden in a certain church or district.
Judaizante	A Jewish convert to Catholicism who continued or was suspected of continuing the covert practice of Judaism.
Juez	Judge.
Juez de bienes de difuntos	An oidor who by rotation was in charge of the goods of those who died intestate or with heirs outside the colony. Roughly equivalent to a probate judge.
Juez de residencia	Official in charge of a residencia, or review of an official's term of office.
Juez repartidor	Official in charge of allotting conscripted native labor to public works.
Juez de visita	Official in charge of a visita; a visitador.
Justicia	Justice or judge. Local administrative officer.
Juzgado de indios	General court with jurisdiction over Indians.
Ladino	Spanish-speaking or acculturated Indian.
Legua	League, about 2.6 miles.
Letrado	Holder of a law degree, who was a professional civil servant.
Libranza	An order for payment.
Licenciado	Holder of the degree of licentiate, commonly in law.
Limpieza de sangre	Certification that one had no Jewish or Moorish blood, a presupposition for doctrinal orthodoxy.
Maestrescuelas	Member of the ecclesiastical cabildo in charge of the cathedral school.
Maravedí	A fictitious unit of Spanish currency that was used as the standard of value for the coinage.
Marqués	Marquess, marquis, margrave.
Matlazáhuatl	The epidemic of 1576.

Mayordomo	Majordomo, steward.
Mendicant	Member of a religious order that originally supported itself by begging.
Mestizo	Person of mixed Spanish and Indian parentage.
Milpa	Plot of agricultural land or cornfield; often used of those belonging to Indians.
Monastery	In the sixteenth century used generically of any house of religious.
Motu Proprio	Letter or pronouncement of the pope issued on his own initiative rather than in response to a request.
Mulato	Person of mixed white and black parentage; a mulatto.
Navío de aviso	Ship in a flota that carried correspondence.
Obraje	Workshop, usually of textiles. Sweatshop.
Obrero mayor	Superintendent in charge of some sort of public work, such as a cathedral or aqueduct.
Oficiales reales	Royal treasury officials.
Oidor	A judge of the audiencia.
Oposición	Public competition for an office.
Ordinary	An ecclesiastical official who exercised jurisdiction in his own name, not that of another. The opposite of vicar.
Pallium	Woolen religious insignia worn only by archbishops.
Párroco	Pastor or parish priest.
Parroquia	A parish.
Parroquia mayor	A cathedral parish.
Pase regio	Royal permission for the publication of papal documents in Spanish dominions.
Patronato real	Congeries of rights and privileges that regulated the relations between church and state in Spain.
Peso	The most widely used denomination of Spanish coinage. There were different kinds of peso, each with its own value in terms of the maravedí.
Políticamente	Civilized and settled form of life, usually in a city and with municipal organization. Opposite of bárbaramente.
Prebendado	Cleric whose income came from the income of the cathedral.
Prelado	Prelate; any ecclesiastical officeholder who exercised ordinary power.
Pregonero	Town crier and auctioneer.
Principal	Indian noble.

Privilegium Canonis	Ecclesiastical privilege excommunicating all who used violence against the clergy.
Privilegium Fori	Ecclesiastical privilege exempting clerics from civil tribunals.
Procurador	One who had the legal right by delegation to act in the name of another. Representatives who defended the rights and privileges of cabildos (both municipal and ecclesiastical), cities, and religious orders.
Propietario	An officeholder who held his position for life.
Propios	Lands, property, and goods that belonged to a city or town.
Provisión	(1) Order given by a tribunal that accompanied a royal decree and directed that it be implemented. (2) Act of conferring an office, such as a benefice.
Provisor	Chief ecclesiastical judge of a diocese, sometimes also the vicar general.
Pueblo	(1) A small town. (2) An Indian town.
Quinto	Royal share of the gold and silver mined in the colonies, theoretically 20 percent, but often varying.
Real	One-eighth of a peso. Also called a tomín.
Real hacienda	See *Hacienda*.
Receptor	Treasurer, receiving agent.
Regidor	City councilman, whose most important duties in the sixteenth century dealt with supervising foodstuffs and the distribution of public lands.
Regimiento	Office or institution of city councilmen. Synonymous with municipal cabildo.
Relator	Clerk responsible for drawing up accounts (*relaciones*) of cases for forwarding to judges.
Relección	University lecture.
Religión	(1) Religion in general. (2) A religious order.
Religioso	Member of a religious community, i.e., one who lived in community according to rule and under vows.
Repartidor	Same as a juez repartidor.
Repartimiento	Temporary assignment or allotment of paid Indian labor on a conscription basis for work on projects involving the common good.
Residencia	Judicial review of an official's conduct in office at the conclusion of his term.

Sala	Meeting room and court chamber of the audiencia.
Sala de provincia	Chamber of the audiencia for civil suits from outside Mexico City.
Sambenito	Distinctive garb worn by those reconciled or condemned by the Inquisition.
Sisa	Municipal tax on wine.
Suspensión	Ecclesiastical penalty whereby a cleric was forbidden the exercise of his ministry.
Tameme	An Indian porter or carrier.
Teniente	Deputy.
Tesorero	(1) Ecclesiastical official in charge of the revenues and physical goods of a cathedral or church. (2) One of the three treasury officials of New Spain.
Tiento de cargo	Preliminary accounting.
Tomín	One-eighth of a peso. Also called a real.
Traza	Boundaries of the various divisions of Mexico City, especially those separating Spaniards from the castas and Indians.
Tuna	Edible fruit of the prickly pear cactus (*nopal*), *Opuntia tuna*.
Vara	(1) Badge or staff of office. (2) Measure of length, about thirty-three inches; eight thousand to a league.
Veedor	Inspector or supervisor, overseer of royal financial interests.
Vicar	One exercising power in the name of another rather than in his own right. His authority is called *vicarious*.
Villa	Municipal corporation, one step below a pueblo.
Virreinato	Term of office of a viceroy.
Visita	(1) General or specific investigation of governmental operation and abuses. (2) Tour of inspection made by a bishop or his delegate of the parishes in the diocese. (3) Tour of inspection by an oidor in some area of the audiencia's jurisdiction. (4) Church of ease, visited at times by nonresident priests.
Visitador	A judge conducting a civil visita.

Notes

ABBREVIATIONS

AGI   Archivo General de Indias, Seville, Spain.

AHN   Archivo Histórico Nacional, Madrid, Spain.

ASV   Archivio Segreto Vaticano, Vatican City.

ASCC   Archivio della Sacra Congregazione del Concilio, Vatican City.

BV   Bibliotheca Vallicelliana, Rome, Italy.

HPK   Hans P. Kraus Collection of Latin American Manuscripts, Library of Congress, Washington, D.C.

MM   Mexican Manuscripts, Bancroft Library, University of California, Berkeley, California.

CHAPTER I

1. Information on Pedroche can be found in Pascual Madoz, *Diccionario geográfico-estadístico-histórico de España y sus posesiones de Ultramar* (Madrid, 1849), 12:746.

2. Cristóbal Gutiérrez de Luna, *Vida y heroicas virtudes del doctor don Pedro*

Moya de Contreras, arzobispo mexicano (Mexico City, 1619), reprinted in *Cinco cartas del illmo. y exmo. señor d. Pedro Moya de Contreras, arzobispo-virrey y primer inquisidor de la Nueva España, precedida de la historia de su vida según Cristóbal Gutiérrez de Luna y Francisco Sosa* (Madrid, 1962), 14. References to the letters in this volume and to the biographies by Sosa and Luna are cited hereafter as *Cinco cartas*. Note that *"heroicas virtudes"* (heroic virtues) is a term used in the process for the canonization of saints. See also Francisco Sosa, "El excelentísimo e ilustrísimo señor don Pedro Moya de Contreras, 1573–1586," in *Cinco cartas*, 64. It was originally published as a biographical sketch in Sosa's *El episcopado mexicano* (Mexico City, 1877).

Archbishop Lorenzana gives Córdoba as Moya's birthplace (*Concilium Mexicanum Provinciale III, celebratum Mexici anno MDLXXXV, praeside D. D. Petro Moya et Contreras, Archiepiscopo eiusdem Urbis, confirmatum Romae die XXVII Octobris anno MDLXXXIX, postea iussu regio editum Mexici anno MDCXXII sumptibus D. D. Ioannis Perez de la Serna Archiepiscopi demum typis mandatum cura et expensis D. D. Francisci Antonii a Lorenzana Archipraesulis* [Mexico City, 1770], 214). Father Cuevas gives the birthplace as Pedrosa, an obvious error (Mariano Cuevas, *Historia de la iglesia en México* [Tlálpam, 1922], 2:73). See also Julio Jiménez Rueda, *Don Pedro Moya de Contreras, primer inquisidor de México* (Mexico City, 1944), 23. On the Moscoso family, which was also of Galician origin, see Julio de Atienza, *Nobiliario español: Diccionario heráldico de apellidos españoles y de títulos nobiliarios* (Madrid, 1948), 974–76. For a brief, standard biography of Moya de Contreras, see Manuel Rivera Gambas, *Arzobispo don Pedro Moya de Contreras, un gobernante de México* (1962).

3. The Moya arms are a divided shield: (1) on a field of blue, a golden staircase or ladder; (2) blue and silver *veros* (small inverted bells). The arms of the Moscoso are on a field argent a wolf's head erased sable, extended tongues gules. The Contreras arms are found in a number of forms, which usually include three rods azure, a wall with battlements, and a border of windmill wheels. See Atienza, *Nobiliario español*, 222, 974–76.

4. Gutiérrez de Luna says that Moya's parents were wealthy (*Cinco cartas*, 14), but his information on the archbishop's early life is not always reliable. There is no evidence that Moya or his sister inherited any land or money from their parents.

5. A summary of his life can be found in Ruiz de Vergara y Alava, *Vida del ilustrisimo senor don Diego de Anaya Maldonado, arzobispo de Sevilla, fundador del colegio viejo de S. Bartolome y noticia de sus varones excelentes, dedicala a la Mag.d del Rey D. Felipe IV* (Madrid, n.d.), 2:210–11.

6. See Venancio Carro, *La teología y los teólogos-juristas españoles ante la conquista de América* (Madrid, 1944); Richard Kagan, *Students and Society in Early Modern Spain* (Baltimore, 1974).

7. Kagan, *Students and Society*, 82–87.

8. Some biographical data, always tantalizingly incomplete, on Ovando can be found in Vergara y Alava, *Vida*, 2:233; Marcos Jiménez de la Espada, *Relaciones geográficas de Indias* (Madrid, 1881), 1:lxviii–lxxviii; Juan Martínez Quesada, "Documentación de la capellanía y enterramiento del presidente don

Juan de Ovando," *Revista de Estudios Extremeños* 14 (1958): 145–58; and A. W. Lovett, "Juan de Ovando and the Council of Finance (1573–1575)," *Historical Journal* 15, 1 (1972): 1–21.

9. The story is recounted by Marcelino Menéndez Pelayo, *Historia de los heterodoxos españoles* (Madrid, 1956), 2:75–84, where he mistakenly gives Ovando's first name as Francisco.

10. Diego de Espinosa (1502–1572) was a native of Old Castile. He studied both canon and civil law at Salamanca and on entering the service of Philip II rose very quickly in the royal favor, to the extent that he was considered the second most powerful man in the kingdom. He was grand inquisitor, president of the Council of Castile, and a member of the king's privy council. He was made a cardinal in 1568. According to legend he died a few days after having been rebuked by the king for exceeding his powers.

11. Jiménez Rueda, *Moya de Contreras*, 23. He adds that Moya was very young at the time. Gutiérrez de Luna says that Moya's parents sent him to serve as Ovando's page when the latter was president of the Council of the Indies (*Cinco cartas*, 14). This is repeated by Sosa (*Cinco cartas*, 65).

12. The complete history is given by Vergara y Alava, *Vida*, 2:233. See also Kagan, *Students and Society*, 66.

13. See B. Rekers, *Benito Arias Montano (1527–1598)* (London, 1972).

14. It is most frustrating that Vergara y Alava does not list Moya among the colegiales of San Bartolomé. He refers to him briefly in his biography of Moya's uncle. Since he gives biographies of other colegiales who migrated to New Spain, such as Pedro Farfán, his silence is explicable only if he did not find any records for Moya, if his *vidas* are not complete, or if the archbishop was not a bartolomico. This author feels that the weight of Moya's connections makes the latter hypothesis implausible.

15. Sosa, *Cinco cartas*, 66. Lorenzana says that Moya's degree was in canon law only (*Concilium Mexicanum*, 214).

16. See his letters to Ovando of 24 March and 1 September 1574 and to Philip II, 28 March 1576, in Francisco del Paso y Troncoso, *Epistolario de Nueva España* (Mexico City, 1939–1942), 11:138, 195; and 12:10. Unless otherwise noted, all of Moya's letters were written from Mexico City.

17. Gutiérrez de Luna states quite emphatically that Moya was not ordained to the priesthood until 1571 (*Cinco cartas*, 15).

18. Francisco Javier Alegre, *Historia de la provincia de la Compañía de Jesús en Nueva España* (Rome, 1956), 1:64–65; Félix Zubillaga, ed., *Monumenta Mexicana I (1570–1580)* (Rome, 1954–1959), 1:60, n. 48; Juan Sánchez Baquero, *Fundación de la Compañía de Jesús en Nueva España, 1571–1582* (Mexico City, 1945), 37. This work has been reprinted in *Crónicas de la Compañía de Jesús en la Nueva España* (Mexico City, 1979), 53–117.

19. Ernst Schäfer, *El real y supremo consejo de las Indias* (Seville, 1947), 1:129–30; José de la Peña Cámara, "Nuevos datos sobre la visita de Juan de Ovando al Consejo de Indias," *Anuario de Historia del Derecho Español* 12 (1935): 425–38. Documentation can be found in Victor Maurtúa, *Antecedentes de la Recopilación de Indias* (Madrid, 1906), 3–18.

20. Most of this is drawn from Juan Manzano Manzano, *Historia de las recopilaciones de Indias* (Madrid, 1950), 65–90.

21. José de la Peña Cámara, "Las redacciones del Libro de la Gobernación Espiritual: Ovando y la junta de Indias de 1568," *Revista de Indias* 2 (March 1941): 93–115; "El manuscrito llamado 'Gobernación Espiritual y Temporal de las Indias' y su verdadero lugar en la historia de la recopilación," *Revista de Historia de América* 12 (August 1941): 5–72; "La copulata de leyes de Indias y las ordenanzas ovandinas," *Revista de Indias* 12 (October–December 1941): 121–46. Schäfer gives the date of Ovando's death as 8 September (*Consejo*, 1:352). Elsewhere he gives it as 6 September (*Consejo*, 1:51). Manzano Manzano gives it as 8 September (*Historia*, 104). Lovett gives 2 September ("Juan de Ovando," 18). Ovando died poor and left instructions in his will that he be buried in the parish of Santa María in Madrid, to which he belonged. This meant that he chose to be buried in the parish cemetery rather than in the church, the customary burial site for people of quality. Perhaps, too, because of his father's illegitimacy he was reluctant to be buried in the traditional Ovando church in Cáceres. The executors of his will considered this to be praiseworthy for its humility, but not something to be taken seriously. The Council of the Indies voted 1,000 ducados for a tomb and headstone in the Ovando family church of San Mateo in Cáceres. Apparently one of the executors was unfaithful to his task, or at least to his financial stewardship, so that it was not until much later that the present tombstone was erected. See *Colección de documentos inéditos relativos al descubrimiento, conquista, y organización de las antiguas posesiones españolas de ultramar* (Madrid, 1885–1932), 2d ser., 14:162; there is also a reference to a brother named Antonio as Ovando's chief heir (192). There is some reason for believing that this may have been an illegitimate son, the result of a youthful indiscretion. In a letter of 24 March 1575, Moya wrote that he had heard from some private citizens in Guatemala that Ovando had been made bishop of Santiago and president of the Council of Castile, but there is no verification of this from other sources (Paso y Troncoso, *Epistolario*, 11:253).

22. Manzano Manzano, *Historia*, 74–75.

23. Moya to Ovando, 24 January 1575, in *Cinco cartas*, 110.

24. Manzano Manzano, *Historia*, 71–72.

25. AHN, Inquisición de Murcia, leg. 2797. José Toribio Medina says erroneously that Moya served in Murcia from 1566 to 1569 (*Historia del tribunal del santo oficio de la inquisición en México* [Mexico City, n.d.], 27). Henry C. Lea is also mistaken when he identifies Moya as having been inquisitor of Zaragoza in 1541 (*The Inquisition in the Spanish Dependencies* [New York, 1922], 201, n. 1). The Inquisition of Murcia wanted to replace its familiares, but found it difficult to recruit new ones because no one in the province wanted to be associated with it.

26. *Cinco cartas*, 19–20.

27. Moya reported to Philip II that he had been in bad health ever since his arrival in the New World (Moya to Philip II, 26 October 1583, *Cinco cartas*, 158).

CHAPTER II

1. *Relacion breve y verdadera de algunas cosas de las muchas que sucedieron al padre Fray Alonso Ponce en las provincias de la Nueva Espana, siendo comisario general de aquellas partes* (Madrid, 1873), 1:174. A description of Mexico City in 1580, based on the Ponce *Relacion,* can be found in Fernando Benítez, *The Century After Cortés* (Chicago, 1965), 16–20.

2. *Relacion . . . Ponce,* 1:117.

3. Ibid., 1:178–79; Juan de Torquemada, *Monarquia indiana* (Madrid, 1723), bk. 3, chap. 26, 300.

4. Torquemada, *Monarquia indiana,* bk. 3, chap. 26, 299.

5. Ibid.

6. Edmundo O'Gorman, *Reflexiones sobre la distribución urbana colonial de la ciudad de México* (Mexico City, 1938), 16–22.

7. The origin of the term is uncertain, as is the time when it first began to be used. It is not included by Peter Boyd-Bowman (*Léxico hispanoamericano del siglo XVI* [London, 1971]), a fact that proves only that it had not been used in writing up to that time. For a detailed study of the etymological questions involved and the possibility that the word was already in use in the sixteenth century, see Cecilio A. Robeló, *Diccionario de aztequismos* (Mexico City, n.d.), 401–6.

8. On the early origins of criollo-peninsular antagonisms, see Jacques Lafaye, *Quetzalcóatl et Guadalupe: La Formation de la conscience nationale au Mexique* (Paris, 1974), chaps. 1 and 2. Cuevas claims that criollo identity began to show itself about 1570 or 1580 (*Historia de la iglesia,* 1:38) but it seems that indications can be found much earlier. For a good general treatment of the subject of the development of Mexican nationality, see Peggy K. Liss, *Mexico Under Spain, 1521–1556: Society and the Origins of Nationality* (Chicago, 1975). The question of criollo self-image and inferiority feelings has been studied by Marvyn Helen Bacigalupo, *A Changing Perspective: Attitudes Toward Creole Society in New Spain (1521–1610)* (London, 1981).

9. See Magnus Mörner, *Race Mixture in the History of Latin America* (Boston, 1967); and Norman Martin, *Los vagabundos en la Nueva España* (Mexico City, 1957).

10. These are listed in John L. Phelan, *The Kingdom of Quito in the Seventeenth Century* (Madison, 1967), 197, and are to be found in the *Recopilación de las leyes de los reynos de las Indias* (Madrid, 1681), 4: chap. 3, 8.

11. In addition to the audiencia of Mexico there was also an audiencia district in Nueva Galicia that had been independent of that of Mexico since 1572. See J. H. Parry, *The Audiencia of New Galicia in the Sixteenth Century* (Cambridge, 1948). For a good summary of the Spanish peninsular background of the audiencias, see Alfonso García-Gallo, "Las audiencias de Indias: Su origen y caracteres," in *Memoria del Segundo Congreso Venezolano de Historia* (Caracas, 1975), 1:359–432.

12. The subject of the conflicting pressures that affected the crown in

regard to Indian legislation is treated throughout Phelan's excellent study, *Kingdom of Quito*, especially 77–85. See also Margaret E. Crahan, "Spanish and American Counterpoint: Problems and Possibilities in Spanish Colonial Administrative History," in *New Approaches to Latin American History*, ed. Richard Graham and Peter H. Smith (Austin, 1974), 43–44, 50–51. Brief but excellent summaries of the Spanish concept of kingship can be found in Colin M. MacLachlan and Jaime E. Rodríguez O., *The Forging of the Cosmic Race: A Reinterpretation of Colonial Mexico* (Berkeley and Los Angeles, 1980), 96–97; and Peggy K. Liss, "Jesuit Contributions to the Ideology of Spanish Empire in Mexico: Part I," *The Americas* 29 (April 1973): 318.

    13. There is much confusion as to which Central American dioceses were suffragan to Mexico in the sixteenth century. Father Fortino Hipólito Vera says that most historians of the Mexican church err in saying that there were only eight suffragan dioceses in the sixteenth century and adds that the one usually omitted is that of Comayagua in modern Honduras, which had been created in 1539 (*Compendio histórico del tercer concilio provincial mexicano* [Amecameca, 1879], 2: n.136). See also W. Eugene Shiels, *King and Church: The Rise and Fall of the Patronato Real* (Chicago, 1961), 181. It seems, however, that Fathers Vera and Shiels also omit one. Part of the confusion arises from the fact that the letters of convocation of the third council did not include any letters to the bishop of Comayagua, but did include one to the bishop of the diocese of Vera Paz. A diocese of Vera Paz had been erected in 1554 in Guatemala, in the areas of Las Casas's famous missionary experiment. Shiels is incorrect when he locates it in Costa Rica (ibid.). The bishops of the third council, in their letter to Philip II, 16 October 1585, specifically said that Antonio de Hervías, the bishop of Vera Paz, ought to have been at the council. Hervías, a Dominican, took possession of his see in 1581 and left it in 1585 because of difficulties with his clergy and the local civil government. Enrique Dussel gives the year of Hervías's departure as 1588, but that is contradicted by the conciliar papers (*Les Évêques hispanoaméricains, défenseurs et évangélisateurs de l'indien, 1504–1620* [Wiesbaden, 1970], 234–35). Domingo de Salazar, the first bishop of Manila, in his letter to the third council, spoke of ten bishops meeting with their archbishop, though in point of fact only six bishops besides Moya were able to attend. See Ernest J. Burrus, "The Salazar Report to the Third Mexican Council," *The Americas* 17 (July 1960): 74. A total of ten suffragan bishops is possible only if both Comayagua and Vera Paz are included. Torquemada includes both as suffragans (*Monarquia indiana*, bk. 19, chap. 31, 385). Dussel gives Alonso de la Cerda, a Dominican, as bishop of Comayagua (1580?–1588). Why he was not invited to the council is not known. It is just possible that the archbishop of Mexico himself was not sure who his suffragans were. Such things have been known to happen in the history of ecclesiastical administration.

    14. On baroque Catholicism's preoccupation with religion as external practice, see Phelan, *Kingdom of Quito*, chap. 8.

    15. Antonio Joaquín de Ribadeneyra y Barrientos, *Manual compendio de el regio patronato indiano para su mas facil uso en las materias conducentes a la practica* (Madrid, 1755), 2; Shiels, *King and Church*, 1.

    16. Spanish text in Alberto María Carreño, ed., *Un desconocido cedulario del siglo XVI perteneciente a la catedral metropolitana de México* (Mexico City, 1944),

314–22; English translation in Shiels, *King and Church*, 193. A summary can be found in León Lopetegui and Félix Zubillaga, *Historia de la iglesia en la América española* (Madrid, 1965), 193–94. On the church's opposition to the Ordenanza, see Robert Padden, "The *Ordenanza del Patronazgo:* An Interpretive Essay," *The Americas* 12 (April 1956), 333–54.

17. See Shiels, *King and Church*, 123, n. 9; J. Lloyd Mecham, *Church and State in Latin America* (Chapel Hill, 1966), 29.

18. Alonso de Montúfar, *Descripción del arzobispado de México hecha en 1570 y otros documentos* (Mexico City, 1897), 385–87.

19. Torquemada speaks of only two parishes in addition to the cathedral (*Monarquía indiana*, bk. 3, chap. 26, 301). Roberto Moreno de los Arcos places the parish of San Pablo on the outskirts of the city, among the Indians ("Los territorios parroquiales de la ciudad arzobispal, 1525–1981," *Gaceta oficial del Arzobispado de México* 22, nos. 9–10 [September–October 1982]: 152–73).

20. In canonical language these were semipublic oratories rather than churches. There were some restrictions on their use. For example, they could not be used to satisfy the obligation of hearing mass on Easter Sunday nor could they be used for baptisms, marriages, or funerals.

21. Most of the following is taken from Montúfar, *Descripción*, 267–91.

22. See Francisco Cervantes de Salazar, *Life in the Imperial and Loyal City of Mexico in New Spain and the Royal and Pontifical University of Mexico* (Austin, 1953); Alberto María Carreño, *La real y pontificia universidad de México, 1536–1865* (Mexico City, 1961); Sergio Méndez Arceo, *La real y pontificia universidad de México* (Mexico City, 1952).

23. See Robert Ricard, *The Spiritual Conquest of Mexico* (Berkeley and Los Angeles, 1966), 308.

24. See Alegre, *Historia de la Compañía*, 1:582–83; Lopetegui and Zubillaga, *Historia de la iglesia*, 542–43; Cuevas, *Historia de la iglesia*, 2:331–35.

25. Montúfar, *Descripción*, 288; Cuevas, *Historia de la iglesia*, 1: chap. 19.

26. Charles Cumberland, *Mexico: The Struggle for Modernity* (New York, 1968), 48. The Ponce *Relacion* sets the 1570 European population of the city at 3,000; Torquemada says that in his day it had 7,000 Spaniards and 8,000 Indians (*Monarquía indiana*, bk. 3, chap. 26, 299).

27. See Cumberland, *Mexico*, 50; Charles Gibson, *The Aztecs Under Spanish Rule* (Stanford, Calif., 1964), 136–43; Sherburne F. Cook and Lesley Byrd Simpson, *The Population of Central Mexico in the Sixteenth Century*, Ibero-Americana, no. 31 (Berkeley, 1948); Sherburne F. Cook and Woodrow Borah, *Essays in Population History: Mexico and the Caribbean* (Berkeley and Los Angeles, 1974).

28. Moya to Ovando, 20 December 1574, in Paso y Troncoso, *Epistolario*, 11:223.

CHAPTER III

1. See Richard Greenleaf, *Zumárraga and the Mexican Inquisition* (Washington, D.C., 1961) and *The Mexican Inquisition of the Sixteenth Century* (Albuquerque, 1966), 158. Most of this chapter is based on Greenleaf's excellent works.

2. It is quoted in full in Toribio Medina, *Historia del tribunal*, 33–34. See also Greenleaf, *Mexican Inquisition*, 158–59.

3. The royal appointment is in *Un cedulario mexicano del siglo XVI* (Mexico, 1973), 180–81. The titles of appointment by Espinosa can be found in Carreño, *Un desconocido cedulario*, 430–32. The latter refer to Moya as still being the maestrescuelas of the Canary Islands. On 16 August the king also sent a cédula to the archbishop of Mexico informing him of the establishment of the Inquisition (*Un cedulario mexicano*, 182–83).

4. Greenleaf, *Mexican Inquisition*, 158–59; Toribio Medina, *Historia del tribunal*, 37. Philip II's notification of the appointment to Martín Enríquez, dated 16 August 1570, can be found in Carreño, *Un desconocido cedulario*, 426–30. It gives Cervantes's first name as Cristóbal, whereas Jiménez Rueda gives it as Juan (*Moya de Contreras*, 32).

5. The 500 ducados were worth 187,000 maravedíes. See Carreño, *Un desconocido cedulario*, 432.

6. Jiménez Rueda, *Moya de Contreras*, 36. See also the description given by Irving Leonard, *Books of the Brave* (New York, 1964), 158–61. He quotes at length an amusing poetic description of the journey by Eugenio de Salazar, who was the fiscal of the audiencia when Moya was archbishop.

7. Jiménez Rueda, *Moya de Contreras*, 18, 35–36; Toribio Medina, *Historia del tribunal*, 37.

8. Greenleaf, *Mexican Inquisition*, 159; Jiménez Rueda, *Moya de Contreras*, 37; Toribio Medina says that they arrived at Puebla on 31 August (*Historia del tribunal*, 36).

9. For biographical information on Martín Enríquez, see Torquemada, *Monarquía indiana*, bk. 5, chap. 24, 647–48; H. H. Bancroft, *History of Mexico* (San Francisco, 1883), 2: chap. 30; Antonio F. García-Abásolo, *Martín Enríquez y la reforma de 1568 en Nueva España* (Seville, 1983); Philip Wayne Powell, "Portrait of an American Viceroy: Martín Enríquez, 1567–1583," *The Americas* 14 (July 1957): 1–35; Martin Fermin Larrey, "A Viceroy and His Challengers: Supremacy Struggles During the Viceregency of Martín Enríquez, 1568–1580" (Ph.D. diss., University of California, Santa Barbara, 1963). Larrey tends to be favorable to Enríquez and somewhat critical of Moya.

10. Jiménez Rueda, *Moya de Contreras*, 39; Toribio Medina, *Historia del tribunal*, 38; Moya to the Real Consejo de la Inquisición in Seville, 31 October 1571, in *Publicaciones del Archivo General de la Nación*, no. 7: *La vida colonial* (Mexico City, 1923), 105–6.

11. Greenleaf (*Mexican Inquisition*, 176–78) gives some examples of these rivalries and also of some of the petty means used by civil authorities to vex the inquisitors, such as denying them repartimientos of Indians. The conflict with the audiencia was over power. Some oidores accused the Inquisition of being too lenient in punishing transgressors. See Larrey, "A Viceroy and His Challengers," 167–69, where the author cites a letter of the audiencia to Philip II, 29 October 1572, AGI, Méjico, leg. 19. For some interesting comments on the importance of protocol in those days, see Thomas Wright, "The Investiture of Bishops and Archbishops in Spanish America," *Journal of Church and State* 25 (Spring 1983): 281–82.

12. Jiménez Rueda, *Moya de Contreras*, 40–41; *La vida colonial*, 107–9; Larrey, "A Viceroy and His Challengers," 163–64, 168. In 1571 Moya complained to Cardinal Espinosa that Enríquez had read some of the Inquisition's mail (see Larrey, "A Viceroy and His Challengers," 167, where the author cites a letter of Moya to Espinosa, 29 October 1571, AHN, Inquisición de Méjico, bk. 1047).

13. Philip II to the archbishop of Mexico, from Madrid, 13 March 1572, in *Un cedulario mexicano*, 189–90.

14. Jiménez Rueda, *Moya de Contreras*, 41; *La vida colonial*, 109. For an amusing incident at that time, see *Documentos inéditos o muy raros para la historia de México: 5, La inquisición de México*, ed. Genaro García and Carlos Pereyra (Mexico City, 1906), 176–79.

15. Jiménez Rueda, *Moya de Contreras*, 45–46; García and Pereyra, *Documentos*, 5:248–49.

16. A description of these proceedings and the text of the cédula can be found in García and Pereyra, *Documentos*, 5:249–58. The text of the oath can be found on pp. 263–64.

17. Jiménez Rueda, *Moya de Contreras*, 46–49; Toribio Medina, *Historia del tribunal*, 39–40, 47; García and Pereyra, *Documentos*, 5:273–76. The text of the edict can be found on pp. 277–83.

18. Jiménez Rueda, *Moya de Contreras*, 51–52. On pp. 57–61, the author gives details about all the officers of the Inquisition appointed by Moya at this time. The familiares presented a problem because they enjoyed so many exemptions. These exemptions had come to constitute an abuse, as Moya had learned in Murcia, where the familiares had been a source of corruption. The familiares in New Spain had far fewer privileges than those of the peninsula. See Greenleaf, *Mexican Inquisition*, 181.

19. Greenleaf, *Mexican Inquisition*, 184–85; Jiménez Rueda, *Moya de Contreras*, 57. The papers of the Ocharte case can be found in Francisco Fernández del Castillo, *Libros y libreros en el siglo XVI: Publicaciones del Archivo General de la Nación*, no. 16 (Mexico City, 1914), 85–151. The papers on Juan Ortiz can be found on pp. 142–245.

20. Jiménez Rueda, *Moya de Contreras*, 66.

21. Ibid., chap. 7; Toribio Medina, *Historia del tribunal*, 60–67. Miles Philips's account can be found in Richard Hakluyt, *Voyages* (New York, 1968), 6:320–23. For some reason no historian seems to have questioned the veracity of all the details given by Philips, who mentions Moya only once.

22. Toribio Medina, *Historia del tribunal*, 61–64.

23. Moya had difficulty in collecting his salary for his last year as inquisitor and found it necessary to appeal to the king, who ordered the treasury officials to pay it in 1577 (Philip II to the treasury officials of New Spain, from Méntrida, 21 May 1577, in *Un cedulario mexicano*, 214).

CHAPTER IV

1. *Cinco cartas*, 15. Jesús García Gutiérrez, in his unpublished notes on the archbishops of Mexico (*Episcopologio mexicano*), says that Moya was a deacon at

the time of his arrival, but he gives no source for this information. Regarding the intervals between orders, Trent had renewed the law that at least a full year should intervene between the reception of subdiaconate and diaconate unless the bishop decided otherwise (session 13, chap. 13, in H. J. Schroeder, *Canons and Decrees of the Council of Trent* [Saint Louis, 1960], 172). There are no indications which bishop ordained Moya.

2. Cuevas, *Historia de la iglesia*, 2:71–73. Agustín Dávila Padilla says that Ledesma governed the diocese for twelve out of the seventeen years of Montúfar's term (*Historia de la fundación y discurso de la Provincia de Santiago de México de la Orden de Predicadores por las vidas de sus varones insignes y casas notables de Nueva España*, 3d ed. [Mexico City, 1955], 511).

3. The exact date of Montúfar's death is uncertain. Dávila Padilla gives it as 7 March 1569 (*Historia*, 512), as do Cuevas (*Historia de la iglesia*, 2:73) and Lopetegui and Zubillaga (*Historia de la iglesia*, 438). Jiménez Rueda gives it as 7 May 1572 (*Moya de Contreras*, 93). Sosa says March 1572 (*Cinco cartas*, 67). Bancroft gives 7 March 1572 (*History of Mexico*, 2:674). In this account 1572 is accepted as the year of his death because it better explains the delay between Moya's appointment, his actual assumption of office, and the sending to Rome for the bulls. The cédula to Enríquez can be found in Carreño, *Un desconocido cedulario*, 312–13. The viceroy received it some time around 19 October. As late as 1579 Moya still had not been paid his back salary as inquisitor. On 21 May of that year Philip II had to order the audiencia to pay the money (Philip II to audiencia of Mexico, from Toledo, HPK, no. 87).

4. Moya to Ovando, 1 September 1574, in Paso y Troncoso, *Epistolario*, 11:180. According to Dussel, the Roman consistory that approved Moya's presentation was held on 16 May 1573 (*Les Évêques*, 236–39).

5. Jiménez Rueda, *Moya de Contreras*, 94–95; Moya to Ovando, 20 October 1574, in Paso y Troncoso, *Epistolario*, 11:209. The pallium was a circular insignia, made of wool and worn over the shoulders outside the liturgical vestments, that was proper only for popes and archbishops. For an archbishop it signified his participation in the overall teaching authority of the church.

6. Jiménez Rueda states that the date of consecration was 8 December, but Moya clearly declared that it was the 5th, with the reception of the pallium on the 8th (Jiménez Rueda, *Moya de Contreras*, 94; Moya to Ovando, 20 December 1574, in Paso y Troncoso, *Epistolario*, 11:224). Sosa says that the reason for the delay was that Moya was clearing up the cases left on the Inquisition docket (*Cinco cartas*, 67).

7. Jiménez Rueda, *Moya de Contreras*, 95–100. The full text can be found in José Rojas Garcidueñas, *Autos y coloquios del siglo XVI* (Mexico City, 1939), 41–77.

8. Moya to Ovando, 12 December 1574, in Paso y Troncoso, *Epistolario*, 11:227.

9. The complete text can be found in Fernán González de Eslava, "A la consagración del dr. d. Pedro Moya de Contreras," in *Coloquios espirituales y sacramentales*, ed. José Rojas Garcidueñas (Mexico City, 1958), 1:71–127. Despite the title it was presented on 8 December for the bestowal of the pallium. See also Alfonso Méndez Plancarte, "Piezas teatrales en la Nueva España del siglo XVI—siete adiciones y una supresión," *Abside* 6 (1942): 218–24.

10. The following account is derived in part from Jiménez Rueda, *Moya de Contreras*, 107–14; and Leonard, *Books of the Brave*, 194–97. See also José Rojas Garcidueñas, *El teatro de Nueva España en el siglo XVI* (Mexico City, 1935), 80.

11. "No me hizo buen estomago (Enríquez to Ovando, 9 December 1574, in Mariano Cuevas, *Documentos inéditos del siglo XVI para la historia de México* [Mexico City, 1914], 308–9); Leonard, *Books of the Brave*, 196; Rojas Garcidueñas, *El teatro*, 80.

12. Jiménez Rueda, *Moya de Contreras*, 109. This order referred very specifically to the presentation of theatricals in churches. It can be found in full in Carreño, *Un desconocido cedulario*, 433–34. It was dated 10 December 1574.

13. Moya to Ovando, 12 December 1574, in Paso y Troncoso, *Epistolario*, 11:228–29; Jiménez Rueda, *Moya de Contreras*, 110.

14. Eslava to Moya in Rojas Garcidueñas, *El teatro*, 85–87; Jiménez Rueda, *Moya de Contreras*, 112–14.

15. Philip II to Moya, from Segovia, 27 April 1575, HPK, no. 78; *Un cedulario mexicano*, 203; Larrey, "A Viceroy and His Challengers," 199–200; Powell, "Portrait," 20. Larrey believes that the words of the council's reprimand were written by Ovando. He and Powell state that they were written in late 1575, however, and Ovando would have been dead by that time.

16. Gutiérrez de Luna, *Cinco cartas*, 18–21.

17. Ibid., 20–21.

18. Ibid., 22–23, 70–71; Alegre, *Historia de la Compañía*, 1:195–96; Cuevas, *Historia de la iglesia*, 2:75; Sánchez Baquero, *Fundación*, 108. The *Relación breve* says that in addition to his courses in theology with Ortigosa, Moya took classes in philosophy with the Jesuit scholastics (*Relación breve de la venida de la Compañía de Jesús a la Nueva España, año de 1602* [Mexico City, 1945], 29). This latter work has also been reprinted in *Crónicas de la Compañía de Jesús*, 3–50.

19. Alegre, *Historia de la Compañía*, 1:196; Sosa, *Cinco cartas*, 70–71, quoting Francisco de Florencia, *Historia de la provincia de la Compañía de Jesús de la Nueva España*, bk. 2, chap. 20, 188; Cuevas, *Historia de la iglesia*, 2:75; Sánchez Baquero, *Fundación*, 108.

20. See the complaints submitted to the third council by the representatives of the ecclesiastical chapters of New Spain, MM 268, folio 100. For a good survey of the administrative aspects of Moya's term as archbishop, see Victoria Hennessy Cummins, "After the Spiritual Conquest: Patrimonialism and Politics in the Mexican Church, 1572–1586" (Ph.D. diss., Tulane University, 1979).

21. See chapter IX.

22. Lopetegui and Zubillaga, *Historia de la iglesia*, 565–66.

23. Bartolomé de Ledesma to Philip II, from Mexico City, 7 September 1571, in Cuevas, *Documentos inéditos*, 292.

24. Moya to Ovando, 1 September 1574, in Paso y Troncoso, *Epistolario*, 11:193–95.

25. Ibid. This letter is especially strong on this point.

26. *Cinco cartas*, 69; Moya to Ovando, 25 September 1574, in Paso y Troncoso, *Epistolario*, 11:264.

27. Paso y Troncoso, *Epistolario*, 11:197.

28. *Cinco cartas*, 122–51.

29. See Diego de Encinas, *Provisiones, cédulas, capítulos de ordenanzas, instrucciones, y cartas tocantes al buen gobierno de las Indias* (1596; reprint, Madrid, 1943), 84–86.

30. Lopetegui and Zubillaga, *Historia de la iglesia*, 196; Padden, "Ordenanza del Patronazgo."

31. Moya to Ovando, 20 October 1574, in Paso y Troncoso, *Epistolario*, 11:204.

32. Moya to Ovando, 24 January 1574, in *Cinco cartas*, 115.

33. Moya to Ovando, 20 December 1574, in Paso y Troncoso, *Epistolario*, 11:221. For a detailed study of Moya's procedures, see John Frederick Schwaller, "The *Ordenanza del Patronazgo* in New Spain, 1574–1600," *The Americas* 42 (January 1986): 253–74.

34. Paso y Troncoso, *Epistolario*, 11:237–39.

35. Moya to Ovando, 24 January 1575, in *Cinco cartas*, 117–18; 24 March 1575, in Paso y Troncoso, *Epistolario*, 11:249.

36. Moya to Ovando, 24 March 1575, in Paso y Troncoso, *Epistolario*, 11:249–50; 22 April 1575, in ibid., 11:258.

37. Moya to Philip II, 28 March 1576, in Paso y Troncoso, *Epistolario*, 12:12; Philip II to Moya, from the Escorial, 17 June 1576, in HPK, no. 81; Schwaller, "The *Ordenanza del Patronazgo*," 265.

38. The Council of Trent, in session 24, chap. 2, had decreed that whenever possible the bishops should make an annual visitation of their dioceses (Schroeder, *Canons and Decrees*, 193–95).

39. "And therefore content with a modest train of horses and servants, let them strive to complete the visitation as speedily as possible, yet with due attention. Meanwhile they shall exercise care that they do not become troublesome or a burden to anyone by useless expense," Trent had decreed (session 24, chap. 13, in Schroeder, *Canons and Decrees*, 194).

40. Gutiérrez de Luna, *Cinco cartas*, 23–24.

41. Moya to Philip II, 6 November 1576, in Paso y Troncoso, *Epistolario*, 12:18–19.

42. Typhus or influenza, according to Cumberland (*Mexico*, 50); smallpox, according to Lafaye (*Quetzalcóatl et Guadalupe*, 29); pulmonary plague, according to Murdo MacLeod (*Spanish Central America: A Socioeconomic History* [Berkeley and Los Angeles, 1973], 19).

43. Torquemada, *Monarquia indiana*, bk. 5, chap. 22, 642, and chap. 23, 643; Alegre, *Historia de la Compañía*, 1:184–85.

44. Torquemada, *Monarquia indiana*, bk. 5, chap. 23, 643; Woodrow Borah, *Silk Raising in Colonial Mexico* (Berkeley, 1943), 94; Alegre, *Historia de la Compañía*, 1:184.

45. Moya to Philip II, 6 November and 10 December 1576, in Paso y Troncoso, *Epistolario*, 12:19, 25.

46. Moya to Philip II, from Texcatitlán, 15 March 1577, in Paso y Troncoso, *Epistolario*, 12:28; Sosa, *Cinco cartas*, 75. In January 1577 Moya was in the area around Tlachco. In the spring he was in Texcatitlán and Zacualpa.

47. Moya to Philip II, 24 April 1579, in *Cinco cartas*, 151–52; Philip II to

Moya, from Badajoz, 17 June 1580, in HPK, no. 98; Jerome V. Jacobsen, *Educational Foundations of the Jesuits in Sixteenth-Century New Spain* (Berkeley, 1938), 46.

48. Philip II to Moya, from Lisbon, 27 May 1582, in HPK, no. 101.

49. The story of the Tovar catechism is given in the *Relación breve . . . de la Compañía de Jesús,* 22–23. No copy of the catechism is known to exist.

50. *Cinco cartas,* 154.

51. Philip II to Moya, from the Pardo, 2 December 1578, in HPK, no. 95.

52. Carlos de Sigüenza y Góngora, *Parayso occidental plantado y cultivado por la liberal benefica mano de los muy Catholicos y Poderosos Reyes de Espana Nuestros Senores en su magnifico Real Convento de Jesus Maria de Mexico* (Mexico City, 1684), 5–18; memorial of Pedro Tomás de Denia to the third council, undated, MM 269, folio 117. The cédula reproduced by Sigüenza y Góngora can be found in MM 268, folios 118–19. The New Laws were an attempt by the crown to phase out the hereditary encomienda. In the process many of the encomiendas reverted to the crown.

53. Sigüenza y Góngora, *Parayso,* 18. This tale has been repeated in popular literature such as the anonymous *Historia y leyendas de las calles de México* (Mexico City, n.d.), 210.

54. Moya to Ovando, 24 March 1574, in Paso y Troncoso, *Epistolario,* 11:145–46.

55. Moya to Philip II, 25 October 1581, in Paso y Troncoso, *Epistolario,* 12:64–65; nuns of Jesús María to Moya, undated, in ibid., 12:66–67. The papers of the foundation and lawsuit can be found in the same volume, pp. 68–79.

56. Torquemada, *Monarquia indiana,* bk. 5, chap. 24, 647–48.

57. Consulta of 8 February 1575, AGI, Patronato, leg. 171.

58. Consultas of 2 February, 8 February, 14 March, and 14 April 1575, AGI, Patronato, leg. 171.

59. Moya to Ovando, 24 March and 20 December 1574, in Paso y Troncoso, *Epistolario,* 11:138–39, 226; Moya to Ovando, 24 January 1574, in *Cinco cartas,* 109. In 1575 Diego Romano, bishop of Puebla, suggested that Ovando intervene to put an end to the "trifles and childishness" of the disputes (Romano to Ovando, 14 March 1575, AGI, Méjico, leg. 343, cited in Schwaller, "The *Ordenanza del Patronazgo,*" 260, n. 16).

60. Moya to Ovando, 24 March 1574, in Paso y Troncoso, *Epistolario,* 11:140–41; Georges Baudot, "The Last Years of Sahagún," in *Sixteenth-Century Mexico: The Work of Sahagún,* ed. Munro S. Edmundson (Albuquerque, 1964), 171.

61. Moya to Ovando, 24 March 1575, in *Cinco cartas,* 114–15; Moya to Ovando, 22 April 1575, in Paso y Troncoso, *Epistolario,* 11:258.

62. Powell ("Portrait," 20) citing a letter from Enríquez to Ovando, 1 December 1574, AGI, Méjico, leg. 19; Moya to Antonio de Padilla y Meneses, president of the Council of the Indies, 30 October 1580, AGI, Méjico, leg. 336.

63. *Instruccion que por mandado de S. M. hizo el virrey don Martin Henriquez para el conde de Coruna, la cual el conde envio a pedir desde el camino y contiene todo lo*

mas que los vireies tienen en esta tierra a que acudir, in *Colección de documentos inéditos,* 1st ser., 3:481–82.

64. Torquemada, *Monarquia indiana,* bk. 5, chap. 24, 648.

65. Most of this is taken from Villamanrique's highly self-serving letter to Philip II of 20 May 1586, in AHN, Documentos de Indias, no. 265.

CHAPTER V

1. It should be noted that in this chapter the term *monastery* is sometimes used indiscriminately to refer to the houses of mendicants. Technically this is inaccurate, but at times the terminology has been retained because it was used by those involved in the dispute. It should also be noted that contrary to the terminology sometimes used in histories of this period, the Jesuits were neither mendicants nor monks.

2. Exemption still exists in the Catholic church for male clerical religious communities and can still be a source of discord. Technically, religious working in a diocese are subject to the bishop only insofar as the exercise of their ministry is concerned, but not in matters of rule or internal discipline. In practice, however, the two often did and still do overlap, creating a confusion of jurisdictions and also antagonisms.

3. Juan de Grijalva, *Cronica de la Orden de N. P. S. Agustin en las provincias de la Nueva Espana: en quatro edades desde el ano de 1553 hasta el de 1592* (Mexico City, 1624), 15; Padden, "Ordenanza del Patronazgo," 340–41. See also Diego Basalenque, *Historia de la provincia de San Nicolás de Tolentino de Michoacán del orden de Nuestro Padre San Agustín* (Mexico City, 1673), 322; Agustín de Vetancurt, *Teatro mexicano* (Mexico City, 1698), 1, no. 26. A complete translation of the Omnímoda into English can be found in Shiels, *King and Church,* 212–14. See also *Colección de bulas, breves, y otros documentos relativos a la iglesia de América y Filipinas,* ed. Francisco Javier Hernáez (Brussels, 1879), 1:382. On Motolinía's use of the faculty to confirm, see Ricard, *Spiritual Conquest,* 126. The *fora* referred to in the bull embrace the areas of internal conscience and external discipline.

4. By 1579 the Augustinians alone had sixty houses in New Spain. See Arthur Ennis, *Fray Alonso de la Vera Cruz, O.S.A. (1507–1584): A Study of His Life and Contribution to the Religious and Intellectual Affairs of Early Mexico* (Louvain, 1957), 30.

5. Ricard, *Spiritual Conquest,* 307.

6. Henriquez, *Instruccion,* in *Colección de documentos inéditos,* 1st ser., 3:481.

7. For example, see the comments made by Lesley Byrd Simpson in the introduction to his translation of Francisco López de Gómara's *Cortés* to the effect that one of the sources of difference between Bernal Díaz del Castillo and López de Gómara was that the latter was a *clérigo:* "In Bernal's mind nothing good can be expected of a . . . secular priest." He then quotes at length Bernal's disparaging remarks about the quality of secular priests who worked among the Indians (*Cortés: The Life of the Conqueror by His Secretary Francisco*

López de Gómara, trans. and ed. Lesley Byrd Simpson [Berkeley and Los Angeles, 1966], xxi). Since medieval times the members of the mendicant orders had usually had better reputations than had the secular clergy, and they were regarded as being the preachers par excellence. To a certain extent the Jesuits enjoy a similar reputation today. The Council of Trent sought to reverse this by emphasizing the traditional role of the bishop as preacher and by curtailing the privileges of the mendicants.

8. Ennis describes how large and pretentious these monasteries were. He also says that every writer of the sixteenth century referred to the church of San Agustín as "curiously and expensively constructed" and "very sumptuous." It had cost 162,000 pesos and most of the money had come from the encomienda of Texcoco and from royal gifts (*Vera Cruz,* 111–12).

9. Ricard, *Spiritual Conquest,* 152–53.

10. Ibid., 244; Ennis, *Vera Cruz,* 133.

11. Petition of the provisor Bartolomé de Pisa to the Third Mexican Provincial Council, MM 268, folio 131.

12. Ricard, *Spiritual Conquest,* 113.

13. Ennis, *Vera Cruz,* 151–53; Alonso de la Vera Cruz, *Speculum Coniugiorum* (Alcalá de Henares, 1572).

14. Ennis, *Vera Cruz,* 153–55.

15. Ibid., 153. For a description of the system of redonation, see Shiels, *King and Church,* 123, n. 9; and Mecham, *Church and State,* 29.

16. Regarding the doctrinas, Ricard writes: "The Council of Trent upset this simple and flexible organization by putting the parish priests under the control of the bishops. The regulars, therefore, had either to give up their doctrinas or submit to the jurisdiction of the bishops. They rejected the latter solution as contrary to the privileges of the religious orders while the former was inadmissible because of the insufficiency of the secular clergy in numbers as well as in competence" (*Spiritual Conquest,* 109). This judgment is rather harsh, as the doctrina was atypical, especially in areas where the hierarchy had been established.

17. On the role of the viceroys and civil officials as partisans of the religious, see Ricard, *Spiritual Conquest,* 254.

18. Greenleaf, *Mexican Inquisition,* 116–18, 121–22.

19. Ricard mentions that Charles V supported the bishops by a cédula of 18 December 1552 in which he reminded the religious that authority over marriage cases belonged exclusively to the bishops (*Spiritual Conquest,* 115); see also Ennis, *Vera Cruz,* 124–25. The cédula mentioned by Ricard was actually issued by Philip II as prince-regent for his father. See Vasco de Puga, *Cedulario: Provisiones, cedulas, instrucciones de Su Magestad, ordenanzas de difuntos, y audiencia para la buena expedicion de los negocios y administracion de justicia y govierno de esta Nueva Espana y para el buen tratamiento y conservacion de los indios desde el ano de 1525 hasta este presente de 63* (Mexico City, 1563), 204–7.

20. Vetancurt, *Teatro mexicano,* 1, no. 27; Basalenque, *Historia,* 324. The one to the bishops is quoted in full in Grijalva, *Cronica,* 338–39. See also Puga, *Cedulario,* 287–90; and Ennis, *Vera Cruz,* 126, n. 36. Both cédulas are quoted in

full in Carreño, *Un desconocido cedulario,* 240–42. They revoked a previous cédula of 18 December 1552 that supported the bishops' stand.

21. Puga, *Cedulario,* 291–92; Carreño, *Un desconocido cedulario,* 245–46; Fray Pablo Beaumont, *Crónica de Michoacán* (Mexico City, 1932), 3:332–78.

22. Basalenque, *Historia,* 159.

23. Bancroft calls it a "display of authority without effect," an assertion that is not entirely true (*History of Mexico,* 2:674).

24. Carreño, *Un desconocido cedulario,* 320–21. It reaffirmed the cédula of 18 December 1552, which had been revoked by the cédula of 30 March 1557 (see note 20 above). Another cédula of 17 October 1574 reconfirmed the part of the 30 March 1557 cédula ordering that religious and diocesan priests were not to be stationed together (Carreño, *Un desconocido cedulario,* 240–41). For a remarkable statement of the position of the religious at this time, see the letter of Gerónimo de Mendieta to Philip II, 8 October 1575, in Joaquín García Icazbalceta, *Cartas de religiosos, 1539–1594* (Mexico City, 1886), 39.

25. Moya to Philip II, 25 September 1575, in Paso y Troncoso, *Epistolario,* 11:262; Moya to Ovando, 1 September 1574, in ibid., 11:197.

26. Moya to Ovando, 1 September 1574, in Paso y Troncoso, *Epistolario,* 11:180–83.

27. Moya to Philip II, 25 September 1575, in Paso y Troncoso, *Epistolario,* 11:265; Moya to Philip II, 11 February 1576, in ibid., 12:2. Another difficulty was that the preachers ran out of copies of the bulls of the cruzada. Moya wanted to substitute badges and insignia, as was done in Spain. These were papers bearing testimony to the fact of the donation and the gaining of the privileges, together with a small holy picture. The viceroy and the audiencia demanded that the letter of the law be observed and copies of the bulls be secured from Spain. At a later date the viceroy and the audiencia finally yielded and Moya was allowed to use the simpler and easier form of the badges (Moya to Ovando, 20 October 1574, in Paso y Troncoso, *Epistolario,* 11:208; also 20 December 1574, in ibid., 11:221–22).

28. Moya to Philip II, 10 December 1526, in Paso y Troncoso, *Epistolario,* 11:25; Grijalva, *Cronica,* edad 3, chap. 32; Philip II to Enríquez, 23 May 1574, in HPK, no. 76; Moya to Philip II, 25 September 1575, in Paso y Troncoso, *Epistolario,* 11:266; Philip II to the audiencia of Mexico, 17 June 1576, in HPK, no. 82; Moya to Philip II, 11 February, 6 November, and 10 December 1576, in Paso y Troncoso, *Epistolario,* 12:5, 24, and 25. Moya never once mentioned Vera Cruz by name.

29. Paso y Troncoso, *Epistolario,* 12:81; Moya to Philip II, 20 December 1576, in ibid., 12:25; Basalenque, *Historia,* 94.

30. Grijalva, *Cronica,* 157; Ennis, *Vera Cruz,* 176.

31. Report by the provisor of the Indians, in Paso y Troncoso, *Epistolario,* 11:147–49; Moya to Ovando, 1 September 1574, in ibid., 11:185–89.

32. Moya had scant respect for Navarro. See his letter to Ovando, 24 March 1574, in Paso y Troncoso, *Epistolario,* 11:143. For other documents by Moya against Navarro, see García Icazbalceta, *Nueva colección,* 1:35–51.

33. Philip II to unnamed archbishop of Mexico, 26 May 1573, in HPK, no.

73; Moya to Ovando, 1 September 1574, in Paso y Troncoso, *Epistolario*, 11:189–90. In the law of the church, exemption was a privilege that applied only to male clerical communities—that is, communities the majority of whose members were intended for the priesthood. Nuns were and are not exempt from the jurisdiction of the bishops but are subject to them even in matters of internal discipline.

34. Moya to Ovando, 24 March and 1 September 1574, in Paso y Troncoso, *Epistolario*, 11:137–41, 186–88.

35. Moya to Ovando, 1 September 1574, in Paso y Troncoso, *Epistolario*, 11:187–88.

36. The law of the church required at least one full year of preparation (novitiate) before a novice could be allowed to take vows and thus be permanently incorporated into an order. Until rather recent times, especially in Europe, applicants to orders of nuns were required to turn their dowries over to the order to defray the cost of training and sustenance.

37. Moya to Philip II, 11 February and 10 December 1576, in Paso y Troncoso, *Epistolario*, 12:3, 126.

38. Moya to Philip II, 28 March 1576, in Paso y Troncoso, *Epistolario*, 12:15.

39. Moya to Philip II, 15 March 1577, in Paso y Troncoso, *Epistolario*, 12:29.

40. Moya to Ovando, 24 March 1574, in Paso y Troncoso, *Epistolario*, 11:138. Unfortunately, limitations of space do not permit consideration of Moya's involvement with the affairs of three well-known individual religious. He was tangentially concerned with the dispute involving the Franciscan commissary general Alonso Ponce. Material on this can be found in *Relacion . . . Ponce* throughout; *The Oroz Codex*, trans. and ed. Angélico Chávez (Washington, D.C., 1972), throughout, but especially 20–33; AGI, Méjico, leg. 287. Moya also championed Bernardino de Sahagún and his *Historia general de las cosas de Nueva España*. See Moya to Philip II, 28 March 1576, in Paso y Troncoso, *Epistolario*, 12:13; Moya to Philip II, 30 March 1578, in ibid., 12:50; Carreño, *Un desconocido cedulario*, 335–37; Philip II to Moya, from the Escorial, 1 July 1578, in HPK, no. 90. He was also involved in some obscure way with the difficulties surrounding the Tarascan dictionary of Fray Maturino Gilberti. See Philip II to Moya, from the Escorial, 15 May 1575, in HPK, no. 80.

41. Antonio de Remesal writes that six out of the twenty died (*Historia de la provincia de S. Vicente de Chyapa y Guatemala de la orden de Nro. Glorioso Padre Sancto Domingo* [Madrid, 1619], 673).

42. Moya to Philip II, 16 December 1577, in Paso y Troncoso, *Epistolario*, 12:50–52; 30 October 1580, in ibid., 12:59; 7 November 1584, in ibid., 12:99.

43. Sánchez Baquero, *Fundación*, 37; *Relación breve . . . de la Compañía de Jesús*, 3.

44. Alegre, *Historia de la Compañía*, 1:496–99; Moya to Philip II, 6 November 1576, in Paso y Troncoso, *Epistolario*, 12:17; Moya to Philip II, 30 March 1578, in ibid., 12:50–51; Moya to Philip II, 4 April 1579, in *Cinco cartas*, 157; Liss, "Jesuit Contributions," 324. On 1 June 1578 Philip II wrote to Moya from the Escorial that he had written to the Jesuit superior general to request more Jesuits for New Spain (HPK, no. 89).

45. Carreño, *Universidad de México*, 347–49.

46. Alegre, *Historia de la Compañía*, 1:398–99.

47. Moya to Philip II, 30 March 1578, in Paso y Troncoso, *Epistolario*, 12:50–52; Lopetegui and Zubillaga, *Historia de la iglesia*, 417; Méndez Arceo, *Universidad de México*, 50–56; Liss, "Jesuit Contributions," 325. Moya acknowledged this cédula in a letter to Philip II from Huejutla, 16 December 1578, in Zubillaga, *Monumenta Mexicana* I, 380. The cédula can be found on p. 377 and in the HPK, no. 91. See also Alegre, *Historia de la Compañía*, 1:280–81. The opposition of the viceroy is mentioned, but without a source, in Juan Bautista Olaechea Labayen, "El colegio de San Juan Letrán de México," *Anuario de estudios americanos* 29 (1972): 592–93.

48. Juan Sánchez Baquero, quoted in Liss, "Jesuit Contributions," 327.

49. Encinas, *Provisiones*, 83–86.

50. Basalenque, *Historia*, 160–61.

51. Moya to Ovando, 20 October 1574, in Paso y Troncoso, *Epistolario*, 11:204–5.

52. Torquemada, *Monarquia indiana*, bk. 5, chap. 22, 645–46.

53. Moya to Philip II, 20 December 1574, in AGI, Méjico, leg. 336, and Paso y Troncoso, *Epistolario*, 11:214–23. On 3 May 1575 Philip II wrote to Enríquez from Toledo and directed that all cédulas, past and future, concerning the religious be observed exactly (HPK, no. 79). This cédula was in response to Moya's indictment of the religious.

54. Moya to Ovando, 24 January, 24 March, and 21 December 1574, in Paso y Troncoso, *Epistolario*, 11:119, 252, and 235–36. The Dominicans sent Domingo de Salazar. Salazar was a native of Rioja and had been admitted to the Dominican order in Salamanca. He went to Spain as the representative of his order to fight both the cruzada and the Ordenanza del Patronazgo, but achieved little. After defending his position in public debate at Atocha, he went to Salamanca where in 1579 he was appointed the first bishop of the Philippines (Remesal, *Historia*, bk. 5, chap. 7, 672–73).

55. Grijalva, *Cronica*, 160–61; Torquemada, *Monarquia indiana*, bk. 5, chap. 22, 646. In a letter to the king, Moya recalled how often he had warned him about how the religious abused the *"omnímoda potestad"* granted them when New Spain was first discovered. The reason for this grant of power had been the lack of bishops, but Moya believed that this reason was no longer valid. He mentioned that he had had some conflicts with the religious because they wanted to dispense from the first and second degrees of affinity (these were nullifying impediments to marriage), and he had refused to give them approval. He asked the king to apply to the pope to have these powers returned to the bishops, to whom they rightfully belonged (Moya to Philip II, 24 October 1581, in AGI, Méjico, leg. 336).

56. Grijalva, *Cronica*, 161–62; Basalenque, *Historia*, 363; Vetancurt, *Teatro mexicano*, 1, no. 30.

57. Remesal reproduces this cédula in *Historia*, bk. 11, chap. 5, 668–69. He says that he knew of no bishop in that area who tried to implement it and blamed it entirely on one unnamed bishop, probably Romano. It is tempting to

speculate that there may have been some prearranged plan between Romano and the council to secure the cédula.

58. AGI, Méjico, leg. 336. Both Basalenque (*Historia*, 545) and Grijalva (*Cronica*, 162) claim that Moya privately sympathized with the religious because he felt that the work they did was superior to that of the diocesan clergy; because he did not have enough priests to fill the doctrinas, as the clerics were few in number and did not know the native languages; because the Indians were poor and could not support a cleric according to the demands of his state; and because the religious would have no place to go if deprived of their monasteries. There is no support for such an interpretation in any of Moya's own letters. The chroniclers seem merely to have put the arguments of the religious into his mouth.

59. Moya to Philip II, 7 November 1584 and 22 January 1585, in AGI, Méjico, leg. 336. According to the *Relacion . . . Ponce*, 72, the audiencia suspended the cédula of 1583.

60. Basalenque, *Historia*, 33; Vetancurt, *Teatro mexicano*, 1, no. 34; *Relacion . . . Ponce*, 141–46.

61. Philip II to Villamanrique, 16 March 1586; Philip II to Dominican provincial, 5 May 1585; Philip II to *consejo, justicia*, and *regimiento* of Mexico City, 1 June 1585; Philip II to the bishops of the provincial council, undated; all in AGI, Méjico, leg. 287. The cédula is summarized in Vetancurt, *Teatro mexicano*, 1, no. 34; and Basalenque, *Historia*, 335. It is reproduced in Grijalva, *Cronica*, 555–57.

62. Bishops of the provincial council to Philip II, 5 December 1585, in AGI, Méjico, leg. 287.

63. García Icazbalceta, *Cartas de religiosos*, 115; Jerónimo López to Philip II, 2 March 1587, in AGI, Méjico, leg. 287; mendicant provincials to Philip II, 7 September 1588, in AGI, Méjico, leg. 288.

64. Phelan, *Kingdom of Quito*, 315.

CHAPTER VI

1. Schäfer, *El real y supremo consejo*, 2:128.

2. Ibid., 2:129.

3. For an account of the visita of Tello de Sandoval, see Arthur Aiton, *Antonio de Mendoza: First Viceroy of New Spain* (Durham, N.C., 1927), 158–71; and Constance Carter, "The Visita General of Tello de Sandoval in New Spain" (Ph.D. diss., Columbia University, 1971). On Valderrama, see France Scholes and Eleanor B. Adams, eds., *Cartas del Licenciado Jerónimo de Valderrama y otros documentos sobre su visita al gobierno de Nueva España, 1563–1565* (Mexico City, 1961). Another visita, that of Diego Ramírez (1551), has been studied in detail by Walter Scholes, *The Diego Ramírez Visita* (Columbia, Mo., 1964), but it was provincial in character and was concerned primarily with the Indians and the encomiendas, not with the functioning of the central government of New Spain.

4. Carlos Molina Argüello, "Visita y residencia en Indias," *III Congreso del*

Instituto Internacional de Historia del Derecho Indiano, Madrid, 17–23 de enero de 1972: Actas y estudios (Madrid, 1973), 424. It should be noted that there was also a third type of investigation, called the *pesquisa*, conducted by an investigative judge, the *juez pesquisidor*. It was sporadic, however, and concerned primarily with criminal activity. For a discussion of the distinctions, see Ismael Sánchez Bella, "Visitas a Indias (siglos XVI–XVII)," in *Memoria del Segundo Congreso Venezolano de Historia*, 3:172.

5. Other authors who hold for this lack of distinction, at least by the beginning of the seventeenth century, are José M. Mariluz Urquijo, *Ensayo sobre los juicios de residencias indianos* (Seville, 1952); Guillermo Céspedes del Castillo, "La visita como institución indiana," *Anuario de Estudios Americanos* 3 (1946): 985–1025; Luis G. de Valdeavellano, "Las partidas y las orígenes medievales del juicio de residencia," *Boletín de la Real Academia de la Historia* 153 (1963): 205–46. A pioneering article on the subject was that of Leopoldo Zumalacárregui, "Visitas y residencias en el siglo XVI: Unos textos para su distinción," *Revista de Indias* 26 (October–December 1946): 917–21. For this and related questions, see Ismael Sánchez Bella, "Los visitadores generales de Indias y el gobierno de los virreyes," *Anuario de Estudios Americanos* 29 (1972): 71–101; Sánchez Bella, "Visitas a Indias"; Milagros Contreras, "Aportación al estudio de las visitas de audiencias," in *Memoria del Segundo Congreso Venezolano de Historia*, 1:181–221; Carlos Molina Argüello, "Las visitas-residencias y residencias-visitas de la Recopilación de Indias," in *Memoria del Segundo Congreso Venezolano de Historia*, 2:187–323.

6. As mentioned in chapter IV, this request was granted.

7. Juan Suárez de Peralta, *Tratado del descubrimiento de las Indias* (Mexico City, 1949), 169–70; Sosa, *Cinco cartas*, 76–79; Gutiérrez de Luna, *Cinco cartas*, 36; Torquemada, *Monarquia indiana*, bk. 5, chap. 25, 649; Bancroft, *History of Mexico*, 2:180.

8. Suárez de Peralta, *Descubrimiento de las Indias*, 169. On the general corruption of government, see Charles Gibson, *Spain in America* (New York, 1966), 107–8; Schäfer, *El real y supremo consejo*, 2:180; Bancroft, *History of Mexico*, 2:739. Juan Salmerón, a Franciscan, wrote to the king in 1583 to suggest a visita of New Spain and that the visitador be a Franciscan (Salmerón to Philip II, from Mexico, 10 January 1583, in Cuevas, *Documentos inéditos*, 317–85).

9. These commissions can be found in AGI, Indiferente general, leg. 524.

10. Philip II to Moya, from Aranjuez, 22 May 1579, and from Badajoz, 17 June 1580, in HPK, nos. 97, 98.

11. AGI, Indiferente general, leg. 524; Carreño, *Un desconocido cedulario*, 440–43. The cédulas worked on the assumption that Coruña was still alive. A cédula of notification of the visita was sent to him, dated 3 May 1583, together with instructions to cooperate with it (AGI, Indiferente general, leg. 524). Moya was happy with the instructions to bring the visita back to Spain personally, because he felt that New Spain was bad for his health (Moya de Contreras to Philip II, 26 October 1583, in *Cinco cartas*, 158).

12. Carreño, *Un desconocido cedulario*, 444.

13. AGI, Indiferente general, leg. 524.

14. Secrecy was considered an essential part of a visita. See Schäfer, *El real y supremo consejo*, 2:128.

15. Carreño, *Un desconocido cedulario*, 443; Moya to Philip II, 26 October 1583, in AGI, Méjico, leg. 336, reprinted in *Cartas de Indias* (Madrid, 1877), 225–29. There was a clear inconsistency in some of the orders sent to Moya. This was due in part to the change of visitadores and the accumulation of cédulas over the course of a year. It was also because the council wanted to provide a legal basis for different eventualities.

16. Moya to Philip II, 26 October 1583, in AGI, Méjico, leg. 336.

17. Philip II to Moya, from Madrid, 14 November 1584, in AGI, Indiferente general, leg. 524.

18. Moya to Philip II, 26 October 1583, in AGI, Méjico, leg. 336.

19. Torquemada says that it lasted five or six years, but he must have been counting the time of its conclusion in Spain (*Monarquia indiana*, bk. 5, chap. 25, 649). Ismael Sánchez Bella is similarly mistaken when he dates it from 1573 to 1590, roughly the dates of Moya's term as archbishop (*La organización financiera de las Indias* [Seville, 1968], 288, n. 123). Scholes says that the general term of a visita was three to four years (*Diego Ramírez Visita*, 13).

20. This is mentioned in Moya's letter to Philip II, 7 November 1584, in AGI, Méjico, leg. 336.

21. Moya to Philip II, 1 April 1584, in AGI, Méjico, leg. 336.

22. Moya to Philip II, 7 November 1584, in AGI, Méjico, leg. 336. H. I. Priestly is mistaken when he says that Moya was removed from office because of his severity (*José de Gálvez: Visitor-General of New Spain [1765–1771]* [Berkeley, 1916], 102). The evidence is indisputable that he considered himself a transitional figure.

23. Moya to Philip II, 7 November 1584, in AGI, Méjico, leg. 336. Priests were forbidden to act as judges in cases that involved the shedding of blood; such cases were to be turned over to lay judges. The prohibition can be found in the *Decretum Gratiani*, cause 23, question 8, canon 30, and was drawn from the Council of Toledo, 11, canon 6. On 19 February 1584, Philip II sent Moya a cédula that permitted him to delegate such judgments to whomever he wished (AGI, Indiferente general, leg. 524).

24. Santiago del Riego had had a few problems of his own, having been accused of some unspecified crime in a visita of Santo Domingo in 1571. See Schäfer, *El real y supremo consejo*, 2:124, n. 190. In the demands for another visita that were made to the king in 1596, Riego's name was mentioned again, especially for his high-handed treatment of parties involved in lawsuits (ibid., 2:134).

25. Moya to Philip II, 1 December 1585, in AGI, Méjico, leg. 336.

26. Alegre, *Historia de la Compañía*, 298. On the function of the audiencia as interim ruler, see Charles Cunningham, *The Audiencia in the Spanish Colonies* (Berkeley, 1919), 308–11. Cunningham is mistaken when he says that no audiencia exercised interim rule between 1566 and 1612.

27. Moya sent Philip II a full list of officers of Mexico on 1 May 1585 (AGI, Méjico, leg. 336). There are inconsistencies between the archival documents

and the listings by Schäfer. The latter says that Luis de Villanueva Zapata served as oidor of Mexico from 1582 to 1591 and then was named fiscal of the audiencia of Lima, where he served until 1597 (*El real y supremo consejo,* 2:490, 492). Yet Moya wrote to Philip II on 26 October 1583, "Anoche fallecio el doctor Luis de Villanueva, oydor mas antiguo desta chancilleria. Queda la sala con cinco oidores" (AGI, Méjico, leg. 336; *Cartas de Indias,* 229). Even allowing for confusion of father and son, who bore the same name, the figures do not tally. Schäfer also says that on 1 June 1585 Hernando Saavedra de Valderama was appointed oidor and died in office, but there is no mention of him in any of Moya's letters or any of the visita or provincial council documents. Schäfer also says that Lope de Miranda was oidor from 1572 until 1582 and then received license to return to Spain for three years. He was definitely absent from New Spain throughout the visita and well into 1586. Schäfer does not include García de Palacio among the oidores of the audiencia of Mexico, although he clearly was one (Schäfer, *El real y supremo consejo,* 2:453).

28. Moya to Philip II, 1 November 1583, in AGI, Méjico, leg. 336; Philip II to Moya, from Madrid, 19 February 1584, in AGI, Indiferente general, leg. 524; Moya to Philip II, 7 November 1584, in AGI, Méjico, leg. 336. For the laws of a visita, see the *Recopilación de leyes de las Indias* (1791), bk. 2, tit. 34, and specifically laws 8–12, 15–16, 19, 21, 26, 36, 41; Juan de Solórzano y Pereyra, *Politica indiana* (Antwerp, 1703), bk. 4, chap. 8, and bk. 5, chap. 10.

29. Moya to Philip II, 7 November 1584, in AGI, Méjico, leg. 336.

30. Moya to Philip II, 8 May 1584, in AGI, Méjico, leg. 336.

31. AGI, Escribanías de cámara, Méjico, leg. 271a and leg. 1180, contain all this material.

32. AGI, Escribanías de cámara, Méjico, leg. 1180.

33. Ibid.

34. Cunningham, *The Audiencia,* 137. For Sande's biography, see Alberto Miramón, *El doctor Sangre* (Bogotá, 1954). Sande had studied law at Salamanca.

35. On 30 October 1584, Sande wrote to the Council of the Indies that he had wanted to return to Spain, but that Moya would not let him because of the shortage of oidores. He explained the business dealings in the Philippines for which he was under investigation and sent along his power of attorney (AGI, Escribanías de cámara, Méjico, leg. 271a and leg. 1180).

36. Moya to Philip II, 7 November and 1 December 1584, in AGI, Méjico, leg. 336; Sande to the Council of the Indies, 30 October 1584, in AGI, Escribanías de cámara, Méjico, leg. 271a.

37. Diego López, Francisco Palao, and Domingo López de Cabrera were all imprisoned at the same time. It is not clear what role Cabrera played in the matter. A certain Juan López de Cabrera, however, acted as attorney for Francisco Palao in protesting against the auctioning of the cochineal in Seville. The questions to be asked of the witnesses can be found with the rest of the papers in AGI, Escribanías de cámara, Méjico, leg. 271a.

38. Moya to Philip II, 24 January 1586, in AGI, Méjico, leg. 336. The official account of the torture can be found in AGI, Escribanías de cámara, Méjico, leg. 271a.

39. All this material can be found in AGI, Escribanías de cámara, Méjico, leg. 271a and leg. 1180.

40. The papers on his case can be found in AGI, Escribanías de cámara, Méjico, leg. 271a and leg. 1180. Farfán was from Seville, a graduate in law from Salamanca (1564), and a fellow of San Bartolomé. He may have been related to the conquistador Pedro Sánchez Farfán, who left descendants in Mexico City (see *Memorial de los hijos de conquistadores de esta Nueva Espana, 1590*, MM 158). For two differing opinions of Farfán, see Agueda María Rodríguez, "Pedro Farfán," *Revista de Indias* 21 (July–December 1971): 221–309; and Stafford Poole, "Institutionalized Corruption in the Letrado Bureaucracy: The Case of Pedro Farfán (1568–1586)," *The Americas* 38 (October 1981): 149–71.

41. AGI, Escribanías de cámara, Méjico, leg. 1180.

42. Farfán's marital activities are a small history in themselves and present a fascinating picture of the intrigues and extralegal plottings of oidores. The documentation can be found in AGI, Escribanías de cámara, Méjico, leg. 163 and leg. 271; Villamanrique to Philip II, 1 October 1587, AGI, Indiferente general, leg. 741 (this letter is very self-serving, and the viceroy claims falsely that Farfán's marital adventures were the reason for the oidor's suspension by Moya); Sancho Sánchez de Muñón to Philip II, 20 June 1588, in AGI, Méjico, leg. 110, quoted in Schäfer, *El real y supremo consejo*, 2:57–58. Farfán's self-defense can be found in AGI, Escribanías de cámara, Méjico, leg. 271. For a summary, see Poole, "Institutionalized Corruption."

43. AGI, Escribanías de cámara, Méjico, leg. 1180.

44. The Franciscan letter carried the signatures of Pedro de San Sebastián, Rodrigo de Olivos, Francisco Vásquez, Pedro Oroz, Pedro de Regueñas, and Bernardino de Sahagún (AGI, Méjico, leg. 287); Villamanrique to Philip II, 10 May 1586, in AGI, Méjico, leg. 20; Moya to Philip II, from Sanlúcar de Barrameda, 5 November 1586, in AGI, Méjico, leg. 336. Eugenio de Salazar was an enemy of Moya because of the dispute over the publication of the provincial council. According to Schäfer, Riego was appointed on 28 September 1589, but this must refer to a permanent appointment (*El real y supremo consejo*, 2:453). The audiencia was shorthanded as late as 1588. See the consulta of 3 March 1588, in AGI, Méjico, leg. 741; and Salazar to the Council of the Indies, 20 May 1586, in AGI, Méjico, leg. 70.

45. Villamanrique to Philip II, 10 May 1586, in AGI, Méjico, leg. 20. Moya had also received a denunciation against Cristóbal de la Cerda, the relator of the audiencia. It seems that in order to get his office (as he was not a letrado) he had sold his office as lifetime notary (*escribano propietario*) for 4,000 pesos and put the money in the royal treasury. The office had been sold to a certain Antonio Ruiz Beltrán. Cerda had notified the king of this and then sought the appointment as relator. Moya asked the king to send all the documents on this case to him (Moya to Philip II, 7 November 1584, in AGI, Méjico, leg. 336). Such sales were legal, provided one-third of the money went to the crown. See the royal cédula of 13 November 1581, in *Colección de documentos inéditos*, 1st ser., 17:368–74.

46. It was called the *caja de tres llaves* because all three officials were sup-

posed to have keys and all three were supposed to be present whenever it was opened.

47. The two offices were often combined in the sixteenth century as an economy move. See Sánchez Bella, *La organización financiera*, 28.

48. A description of their functions can be found in Sánchez Bella, *La organización financiera*, 108–12. On 28 October 1584, when the visita was in full progress, the Mexican treasury officials sent the Council of the Indies a description of their schedule and functions. On Mondays and Thursdays, they took care of the quinto. On Tuesdays and Fridays, they handled the auctioning of the materials given as tribute. On Wednesdays they dealt with commissions and accounts. On Saturdays they received and collected the tributes and made all the entries in their ledger (*libro común*) as well as paid out the various libranzas (AGI, Méjico, leg. 324).

49. To save money Philip II abolished this post in New Spain in 1584, a move Moya opposed and suspended (Sánchez Bella, *La organización financiera*, 219).

50. See ibid., 124, 269–72. There was no *tribunal de Cuentas*, or supervisory body, for these accounts prior to 1605 (ibid., 219).

51. Ibid., 149, 269–82, 298, 301; Schäfer, *El real y supremo consejo*, 2:32, 180, 182; C. H. Haring, *Trade and Navigation Between Spain and the Indies in the Time of the Hapsburgs* (Gloucester, Mass., 1964), 94.

52. Quoted in Sánchez Bella, *La organización financiera*, 63.

53. Schäfer, *El real y supremo consejo*, 2:182. The laws on the bonds can be found in the *Recopilación*, bk. 8, title 4, laws 1–7.

54. Irigoyen had originally been sent out in 1570 to reform the procedures of the treasury in Mexico, and he spent the next sixteen years handling and auditing the various accounts. According to Sánchez Bella, his accounts for those years filled some 1,530 bundles or packets (*pliegos*). He reorganized the accounting system and brought in some 475,000 pesos in uncollected debts (Sánchez Bella, *La organización financiera*, 168, 276–78).

55. Moya to Philip II, 26 October 1583, in AGI, Méjico, leg. 336; *Cartas de Indias*, 17:227; Escalada to Philip II, 1 December 1750, in Paso y Troncoso, *Epistolario*, 11:96–99; Arévalo y Sedeño to Philip II, 16 October 1573, and the audiencia to Philip II, 6 November 1573, in AGI, Méjico, leg. 69.

56. This figure was later adjusted to 92,121 pesos, 3 tomines, 10 granos. A list of all the audits can be found in AGI, Contaduría, leg. 692; Moya to Philip II, 22 January 1585, AGI, Méjico, leg. 336.

57. Moya to Philip II, 7 November 1584; 8 May 1585; 1 December 1585, all in AGI, Méjico, leg. 336. The time sequence here is rather confusing. Moya speaks of three audits: 12 November 1576 to 30 March 1581; 31 March 1581 to 13 April 1585; 13 April to 27 September 1585. Santotis speaks of only one, from 22 April to 27 September 1585.

58. Moya to Philip II, 8 May 1585; Moya to Philip II, 1 December 1585; Santotis to Philip II, 1 December 1585; all in AGI, Méjico, leg. 336. A copy of the suspension can be found in *Actas del cabildo de la ciudad de México* (Mexico City, 1889–1916), 9:33.

59. Moya to Philip II, 1 December 1585; Santotis to Philip II, 1 December 1585, both in AGI, Méjico, leg. 336.

60. AGI, Méjico, leg. 2555. There is also an accounting that includes all the errors and frauds in AGI, Contaduría, leg. 692.

61. Moya to Philip II, 24 February 1586, in AGI, Méjico, leg. 336.

62. Moya to Philip II, 8 May 1585, in Paso y Troncoso, *Epistolario*, 12:142; Moya to Philip II, 1 December 1585, in AGI, Méjico, leg. 336. On 17 March 1586 Santotis wrote a report to Moya in which he said that 12,000 pesos had been paid to Irigoyen for the purchase of foodstuffs and other supplies for the Manila fleet on 26 March 1572. More than 11,000 of those pesos were unaccounted for (AGI, Contaduría, leg. 692; Moya to Philip II, 8 May 1585 and 1 December 1585; Santotis to Philip II, 1 December 1585 and 18 February 1586, all in AGI, Méjico, leg. 336).

63. The cases were those of Medina, Bavia (see below in text), Galdós, Arando, Ramírez, and Ortiz de Velasco (Moya to Philip II, 1 December 1583; Moya to Philip II, from Sanlúcar de Barrameda, 5 November 1586, both in AGI, Méjico, leg. 336; Eugenio de Salazar to Philip II, 20 May 1586, in AGI, Méjico, leg. 70).

64. Salazar appealed these sentences on the grounds that they had not followed the formalities of the law (Salazar to Philip II, 20 May 1586, in AGI, Méjico, leg. 70; Moya to Philip II, from Sanlúcar de Barrameda, 5 November 1586, in AGI, Méjico, leg. 336).

65. Moya to Philip II, 7 November 1584 and 22 January 1585, both in AGI, Méjico, leg. 336. Though technically 20 percent, the actual amount of the quinto varied from period to period. In 1585 it seems to have been about 10 percent (Haring, *Trade and Navigation*, 157).

66. Moya to Philip II, 22 January 1585 and 8 May 1585, in AGI, Méjico, leg. 336.

67. A description of the execution, unsigned and undated, can be found in AGI, Méjico, leg. 70.

68. Sánchez Bella, *La organización financiera*, 73, n. 5, and 103, 105, 266. He also says that the officials received no salary (301, n.1).

69. Cédulas of 8 May 1584 and 23 April 1585; Moya to Philip II, 7 November 1584 and 1 December 1585, in AGI, Méjico, leg. 336; Schäfer, *El real y supremo consejo*, 2:181. The indictment and other documentation can be found in AGI, Escribanías de cámara, Méjico, leg. 695 and leg. 1180. On 26 December 1570 Félix de Arrellano wrote to the king to complain about the general carelessness of the treasury officials of Veracruz (Paso y Troncoso, *Epistolario*, 11:104–8).

70. AGI, Escribanías de cámara, Méjico, leg. 1180; and AGI, Contaduría, leg. 692.

71. Moya to Philip II, 7 November 1584 and 22 January 1585, in AGI, Méjico, leg. 336; AGI, Contaduría, leg. 692. On the tribunal of the bienes de difuntos, see the *Recopilación*, bk. 4, tit. 32. As of 4 June 1586 there were still outstanding 62,127 pesos, 1 tomín, 9 granos.

72. Moya to Philip II, 8 May and 1 December 1585, in AGI, Méjico, leg. 336.

73. Moya to Philip II, 7 November 1584, 8 May and 1 December 1585, in AGI, Méjico, leg. 336. Like so many of the reports (except those of Santotis), this is not in the visita documents. The auditing of the alcabala accounts continued from 1586 until 1590, at which time they were turned over to Diego Romano, the bishop of Tlaxcala, who was taking the residencia of Viceroy Villamanrique. This may account for the statement sometimes made that Moya's visita was finished by Romano (AGI, Contaduría, leg. 692).

74. Moya to Philip II, 22 January 1585, in AGI, Méjico, leg. 336; AGI, Contaduría, leg. 692.

75. AGI, Contaduría, leg. 692. He was allowed to settle the debt at 2,278 pesos, 4 tomines, 9 granos (9 April 1587).

76. AGI, Escribanías de cámara, Méjico, leg. 1180; *Actas del cabildo*, 9:73–79.

77. AGI, Contaduría, leg. 692; AGI, Escribanías de cámara, Méjico, leg. 1180; *Actas del cabildo*, 9:131. The notice was given to the cabildo on 23 May 1586.

78. Moya to Philip II, 22 January and 8 May 1585, in AGI, Méjico, leg. 336; AGI, Contaduría, leg. 692.

79. Moya to Philip II, 8 May and 7 November 1585, in AGI, Méjico, leg. 336; AGI, Escribanías de cámara, Méjico, leg. 1180.

80. AGI, Escribanías de cámara, Méjico, leg. 1180.

81. Summary of the meeting, AGI, Méjico, leg. 20; Villamanrique to Philip II, 20 May 1586, in AHN, Documentos de Indias, no. 265.

82. Villamanrique to Philip II, 20 May 1586, in AHN, Documentos de Indias, no. 265. Apparently Philip II had given some special order with regard to the bienes de difuntos that is not to be found in the visita documents.

83. Villamanrique to Philip II, 10 May 1586, in AGI, Méjico, leg. 20; AGI, Contaduría, leg. 692.

84. Villamanrique to Philip II, 20 May 1586, in AHN, Documentos de Indias, no. 265.

85. Moya to Philip II, 24 February 1586; Moya to Philip II, from Sanlúcar de Barrameda, 5 November 1586, both in AGI, Méjico, leg. 336.

86. Moya to Philip II, from Sanlúcar de Barrameda, 5 November 1586, in AGI, Méjico, leg. 336; Suárez de Peralta, *Descubrimiento de las Indias*, 171.

87. All the following is from AGI, Escribanías de cámara, Méjico, leg. 1180.

88. Schäfer, *El real y supremo consejo*, 2:122; Ruiz de Vergara also mentions a trip to Peru (*Vida*, 239–40). The consulta of 3 March 1588 said that Farfán, Robles, and Palacio should never again be used in the Indies in any capacity (AGI, Méjico, leg. 741).

89. AGI, Méjico, leg. 1; and AGI, Escribanías de cámara, Méjico, leg. 1180.

90. On 2 March 1588, the Council of the Indies advised Philip II that the charges against Sande looked bad (AGI, Indiferente general, leg. 741).

91. The cabildo asked that Brondat not be reinstated (cabildo to Philip II, 27 April 1587, in AGI, Méjico, leg. 317).

92. Laws 9–12, 15–16, 19, 21, 26, 36, 42.

93. Molina Argüello, "Las visitas-residencias," 210.

94. Schäfer, *El real y supremo consejo*, 2:180; Gibson, *Spain in America*, 452; Phelan, *Kingdom of Quito*, chap. 7.

95. Sánchez Bella, *La organización financiera*, 51, and "Visitas a Indias," 172; Talavera to Philip II, 14 April 1587, in AGI, Méjico, leg. 287.

96. AGI, Charcas, leg. 1.

97. Carreño, *Universidad de México*, 68–73.

98. Ibid., 80–95.

99. Carreño says 17 April (ibid., 130).

CHAPTER VII

1. Moya to Ovando, 20 December 1574, in Paso y Troncoso, *Epistolario*, 11:237.

2. The alcabala went into effect on 1 January 1575 at an initial rate of 2 percent. See Borah, *Silk Raising*, 79.

3. Moya to Ovando, 20 December 1574, in Paso y Troncoso, *Epistolario*, 11:223.

4. A good description of this process and the work of the *azoguero* (amalgamator) can be found in Cumberland, *Mexico*, 89–91.

5. Moya to Ovando, 31 August 1574, in Paso y Troncoso, *Epistolario*, 11:172–73.

6. Ibid., 172–78.

7. The price was not appreciably lowered until 1750. See Cumberland, *Mexico*, 91. Two studies that highlight the shortsightedness of the royal policy are Antonia Heredia Herrera, *La renta de azogue en Nueva España, 1709–1751* (Seville, 1978); and M. F. Lang, *El monopolio estatal del mercurio en el México colonial, 1550–1710*, trans. Roberto Gómez Ciriza (Mexico City, 1977).

8. Moya to Philip II, 30 October 1580, in Paso y Troncoso, *Epistolario*, 12:61–62; and Moya to Philip II, 26 October 1583, in *Cinco cartas*, 163–64.

9. Moya to Philip II, 7 November 1584, in AGI, Méjico, leg. 336; Carreño, *Un desconocido cedulario*, 445–48. Recognition by the audiencia can be found in AGI, Méjico, leg. 286.

10. Moya to Philip II, 7 November 1584, in AGI, Méjico, leg. 336. On the abolition of the post, see Sánchez Bella, *La organización financiera*, 219. The receptor whose post was abolished was Gordián Casasano.

11. Moya to Philip II, 7 November 1584, in AGI, Méjico, leg. 336; also Moya to Philip II, 22 January 1585, in Paso y Troncoso, *Epistolario*, 12:98–104; Martin, *Los vagabundos*, 163.

12. Moya to Philip II, 7 November 1584, in AGI, Méjico, leg. 336; and Moya to Philip II, 22 January 1585, in Paso y Troncoso, *Epistolario*, 12:101–35.

13. Moya to Philip II, 22 January 1585, in Paso y Troncoso, *Epistolario*, 12:124.

14. Ibid., 124, 131–32.

15. Ibid., 134; Cumberland, *Mexico*, 91. Haring disagrees with this (*Trade and Navigation*, 161).

16. Moya to Philip II, 22 January 1585, in Paso y Troncoso, *Epistolario*, 12:131. These instructions, dated 12 June 1585, can be found in ibid., 148–57.

17. Ibid., 130–31. Moya may have become interested in this project even before he became viceroy. A certain Fray Andrés de Aguirre wrote to him after hearing about it to encourage him, telling the story of undiscovered rich lands that some Portuguese had found during a storm. Aguirre also believed that the coast of North America connected with China and the hypothetical strait of Anián (*Colección de documentos inéditos*, 1st ser., 13:545–49). The editors date the letter to 1583/1584, but it may well have been written later.

18. Villamanrique to Philip II, from Spain, 20 May 1585, in AGI, Méjico, leg. 20. The new viceroy did not approve of Moya's actions and said that when he arrived in New Spain he would give the king a full report. He also disagreed with Moya's analysis of the dangers to ships en route from the Philippines and suggested that they merely needed to touch land at a later point in their journeys. He cited Cortés's report on his voyage to Baja California as proof that there was little danger to ships on the California coast. In view of the fact that Villamanrique had never been to the New World, his views seem a little presumptuous.

19. On 5 August 1585, Moya granted a license to Hernando de Santotis and two associates, giving them exclusive rights to pearl fishing along the coast from Navidad to California. Pearls had long been one of the inducements to explore the California coast. Santotis was never able to use his license because of setbacks, including the death of one of his partners and an attack by the English corsair Thomas Cavendish. See W. Michael Mathes, "Sebastián Vizcaíno y los principios de la explotación comercial de California," *Homenaje a Don José María de la Peña y Cámara* (Madrid, 1969), 221–23.

CHAPTER VIII

1. Moya to Ovando, 21 December 1574, in Paso y Troncoso, *Epistolario*, 11:235. On 21 June 1570, Philip II wrote to the bishops of New Spain that they should obey the dictates of Trent about holding provincial councils regularly, but only every five years instead of the three stipulated by Trent (Carreño, *Un desconocido cedulario*, 301–2).

2. MM 268, folio 2. The letters to the religious, dated 30 March, were longer and more formal.

3. A thorough description of the first cathedral can be found in Manuel Toussaint, *Paseos coloniales* (Mexico City, 1939), 13–21. See also Diego Angulo Iñiguez, *Historia del arte hispanoamericano* (Barcelona and Buenos Aires, 1945), 1:409–12.

4. Most of the information about the juntas can be found in José Llaguno, *La personalidad jurídica del indio y el III Concilio Provincial Mexicano, 1585* (Mexico City, 1963), 8–13. Although this work is oriented more toward canon law than toward history, Bishop Llaguno has gathered together in one place most of the pertinent information, much of it from the conciliar papers at the Bancroft

Library at the University of California. Information on the junta of 1524 can also be found in Lopetegui and Zubillaga, *Historia de la iglesia*, 292–93; and Cuevas, *Historia de la iglesia*, 1:166–67.

5. Fortino Hipólito Vera, *Apuntamientos históricos de los concilios provinciales mexicanos y privilegios de América: Estudios previos al primer concilio provincial de Antequera* (Mexico City, 1893), 2–11; Llaguno, *La personalidad jurídica*, 29–36; Lopetegui and Zubillaga, *Historia de la iglesia*, 381–90.

6. Vera, *Apuntamientos históricos*, 11.

7. Llaguno, *La personalidad jurídica*, 35.

8. Ibid., 36–39; Vera, *Apuntamientos históricos*, 14–16.

9. Llaguno, *La personalidad jurídica*, 37.

10. Cuevas, *Documentos inéditos*, 279–85.

11. Burrus, "Salazar Report," 74; *Concilios provinciales primero y segundo, celebrados en la muy noble y muy leal ciudad de Mexico, presidiendo el Illmo. y Rmo. Senor D. Fr. Alonso de Montufar, en los anos de 1555 y 1565* (Mexico City, 1769). The acta of the first two councils were never translated into Latin.

12. Most of this material and what follows has been taken from Félix Zubillaga, "Tercer concilio mexicano, 1585: Los memoriales del P. Juan de la Plaza, S.I.," *Archivum Historicum Societatis Iesu* 30 (1961): 180–214.

13. Cardinal Sforza Pallavicino, *Storia del concilio di Trento* (Milan, 1844), 5:469.

14. The Tridentine form of seminary never became general in the church, precisely for the reasons cited by Plaza. The present seminary system in the Catholic Church originated in France in the early seventeenth century. The first seminary in Mexico City, called "conciliar" even though it did not conform exactly to the Tridentine model, was founded in the 1690s. See Pedro J. Sánchez, *Historia del seminario conciliar de México* (Mexico City, 1931), 1:56–59. A brief summary of its origins can be found in James H. Lee, "Clerical Education in Nineteenth-Century Mexico: The Conciliar Seminaries of Mexico City and Guadalajara, 1821–1910," *The Americas* 36 (April 1980): 466.

15. Francisco de Vitoria, *Prima Relectio de Indias*, ed. Ernest Nys (Washington, D.C., 1917), 250.

16. About the year 1582, Fray Pedro Juárez de Escobar had written to Philip II to complain about the practice of choosing canon lawyers as bishops. He said that "theologians rather than canonists or legists" were needed, "for the business of souls is advanced not by the Decretum and the Decretals, the Sextus and Clementines, the Codex and . . . Institutes and Pandects but by knowledge of scripture and divine letters" (*Colección de documentos inéditos*, 1st ser., 2:203).

17. Zubillaga, "Tercer concilio mexicano," 219.

18. Until very recently in the law and practice of the Catholic church a priest could not hear confessions in a diocese until he had been granted permission, called faculties, by the local bishop.

19. There is a seventh memorial by Plaza, which was either written or submitted after the close of the council, some time in 1586. It was not a series of recommendations for legislation, but rather a straightforward account of the

situation of the Indians in Peru. It was based on his own experience there and was intended to show how some of the Peruvian experience in dealing with the problems of the Indians could be helpful in New Spain. It touched principally on the policy and methods of congregación, the situation of the clergy in the reconcentrated Indian settlements, the repartimientos, and the obrajes. In view of this, it seems all the more strange that there is no memorial from Plaza on the repartimientos as such. It is quite possible that some of his memorials have not survived in the conciliar documents. Those in MM 268 end abruptly at folio 169, and someone, perhaps Roldán de Aranguiz, has added the note, "Aqui acaba esta consulta o le falta algo porque lo que sigue es a otro assumpto."

20. Llaguno, *La personalidad jurídica*, 53–54; Remesal, *Historia*, bk. 11, chap. 1, 652.

21. They are reprinted in Llaguno, *La personalidad jurídica*, 183–89.

22. This was a distinction that Mendieta, in his advice to the council, condemned as a "pernicious abuse" and wanted abolished under pain of excommunication.

23. MM 268, folios 184–201.

24. MM 268, folios 188–92.

25. The letter is reprinted in full in Burrus, "Salazar Report," 69–84.

26. The bull *In Coena Domini* (often referred to by Spanish writers simply as the *Bula de Cena*) contained many excommunications for such intrusions into ecclesiastical authority. See Cyriacus Morelli, *Fasti Novi Orbis* (Venice, 1776), 160, 180, 320–45; Francisco Suárez, *Tractatus de Religione Societatis Iesu* (Paris, 1585), 466–67.

27. Cédula of Philip II, from Toledo, 31 August 1560, in *Recopilación*, bk. 1, tit. 8, law 7.

28. These were presented to the council on 30 January, 9 February, and 8 May 1585 and can be found in MM 268, folios 220–32. See also Llaguno, *La personalidad jurídica*, 57–64.

29. Llaguno, *La personalidad jurídica*, 200.

30. Llaguno gives a summary of his attitude (ibid., 57–64).

31. See John L. Phelan, *The Millennial Kingdom of the Franciscans in the New World* (Berkeley and Los Angeles, 1956).

32. MM 268, folio 255. This was sent from Huejotzingo, 1 February 1585.

33. MM 268, folio 255.

34. MM 268, folios 65–66.

35. The petition on the clergy and their benefices can be found in *Actas del cabildo*, 9:27–28 and 29 (the latter concerning San Juan Letrán, 8 April 1585). See also MM 268, folios 111–12. They also made a request that the feast of Saint Thomas Aquinas be made a holyday of obligation. It was (*Actas del cabildo*, 9:30).

36. MM 268, folios 234–38.

37. All these memorials are in MM 268: the Denia memorial, folio 117; Francisco de Olivares, folio 120; Diego Jiménez de San Román, folio 123; Diego de Muñón, folio 124; Pedro Rodríguez, folio 127; Pedro Velázquez, folio 126; Dr. Urbina Zárate, folio 241.

38. MM 268, folio 59.

39. Moya to Philip II, 24 March 1575, in *Cartas de Indias,* 201; Moya to Philip II, 6 November 1576, in Paso y Troncoso, *Epistolario,* 12:22; bishops of the third council to Philip II, in MM 268, folio 420; Archbishop Pérez de la Serna to Philip III, 7 February 1614, in AGI, Méjico, leg. 337 (in which he mistakenly gives Salcedo's age as sixty); Pérez de la Serna to Philip III, 1618, in AGI, Méjico, leg. 337.

40. Llaguno, *La personalidad jurídica,* 41; MM 268, folios 424–25.

41. On 31 March 1584 Hervías wrote to Moya to explain his absence from the council. Although he was deeply interested in it and desired its success, he found himself "with spurs on" for his departure. One reason for his trip was that for three years he had been exiled from his diocese and the king needed to hear his explanation of how this had happened. He did not go into detail about the problems, though he did say that the religious had conspired with the alcalde mayor to see to it that there were no diocesan priests in his diocese (MM 268, folio 37). A letter to the council from the president of the audiencia of Guatemala said that Hervías had left for Spain immediately after writing the letter. He also said that there was not a single Spanish or diocesan priest left in Vera Paz, something that would indicate not only diocesan-religious but also peninsular-criollo conflict (3 May 1584, MM 268, folio 45).

42. The first working meeting of the council took place on 26 January and was marred by an altercation involving the municipal cabildo and the Inquisition. To celebrate the occasion the cabildo had ordered festivities and parades and entrusted their preparation to Guillén Brondat, who erected bleachers for the benefit of older governmental officials. Some outsiders reached the seats first and Brondat, from street level and on horseback, tried to order them off. At that moment the cuadrilla of the Inquisition marched by, and with it Pedro de Villegas, the alguacil mayor of the Holy Office. He tried to interfere on behalf of the gate-crashers, an argument ensued, and both men reached for their swords. Santiago del Riego intervened and arrested Brondat, but the Inquisition tried to claim him as its prisoner because its personnel had been involved. The regidores, who under other circumstances had little affection for Brondat, resisted strongly, because they felt that the Inquisition was overstepping its jurisdiction. Brondat was saved from the Inquisition only to be removed from office by Moya's visita (cabildo of Mexico to Philip II, 28 January 1585, in AGI, Méjico, leg. 2557; *Actas del cabildo,* 9:6, 25).

CHAPTER IX

1. The following is a general outline of the conciliar chronology.

20 January   Solemn opening.

February   First consulta: case of conscience concerning a canon.
             Consideration of a request for a uniform ritual.
             Directives by Moya that religious were to bring to the council all papal documents dealing with their privileges.

March   Second consulta: the use of certain foods on abstinence days.

April–July   Consulta on the Chichimeca war.
Consideration of the Juan Ramírez sermon on the repartimientos.

May   Fourth consulta: on repartimientos to farms, mines, and buildings.
Fifth consulta: various cases of conscience.
Sixth consulta: on seven doubts arising from the decrees of the First Council (that part dealing with the privileges of religious lasting until June).
Report by the committee on religious privileges. Decision by the bishops. Discussion on matters outside the decrees. Points to be submitted to the king and pope.
Vote on clerical involvement in business activities.

June   Vote on allowing clerics to play cards.

July   Seventh consulta: repartimientos to forage, and other tasks.

August   Eighth consulta: on frauds in sales, flota cargoes, and other business matters.
Second vote on clerical involvement in business.
Vote on public decree on religious administration of the sacraments.

September   Beginning of the dispute on publication and approval by the Council of the Indies.

October   Vote on excommunication of secular judges violating ecclesiastical immunity.
Letter to the king.

2. MM 269, folios 59–79.

3. The cases and responses can be found in MM 269, folios 162–78, 191–209.

4. By a bull of Urban VIII (11 March 1626) the legislation was extended to the Philippines. This bull is usually included in most of the later editions of the council acta, such as those of Arrillaga and Tejada y Ramiro. See Alegre, *Historia de la Compañía*, 1:304; Cuevas, *Historia de la iglesia*, 2:105. Vera mentions that the legislation remained in force in Guatemala and its suffragan dioceses even after Guatemala became an independent archdiocese (*Apuntamientos históricos*, 28).

5. The working papers on this can be found in MM 268, folios 298–306, and folio 307.

6. These can be found in MM 268, folios 325–56.

7. Alegre, *Historia de la Compañía*, 1:303. Alegre admits that Salcedo probably deserves more of the credit than his fellow Jesuit Ortigosa.

8. The annotated copy can be found in ASCC, *Concilium Provinciale Mexicanum, A.D. 1585*.

9. Bernabé Navarro, "La iglesia y los indios en el IIIer concilio mexicano," *Abside* 8 (1944): 391–446.

10. This decree is similar to one enacted by the third council of Lima. See Llaguno, *La personalidad jurídica,* 119. The original Spanish of the Mexican council's decree deserves to be quoted.

Ninguna cosa debian pensar los prelados y gobernadores destas partes que les tiene Dios mas encomendada y encargada que el defender y amparar estos pobres indios como tan recien plantados en la fe e yglesia cristiana, mirando con affecto y entrana de padres por sus necesidades corporales y espirituales, pues su natural mansedumbre y subjeccion y el perpetuo trabajo con que sustentan a los espanoles habran de mover a cualquiera gente barbara, antes ha de tenderlos y compadecerse de ellos que no perseguirlos y maltratarlos y tenerlos expuestos a la violencia, injurias y vexaciones que cada dia se les hacen por todo genero de personas, lo qual considerando este sancto concilio y doliendose como es razon de que entre gente cristiana haya tanta falta de piedad y humanidad exhorta encarecidamente a todos los gobernadores e justicias de su magestad que se muestren pios y benignos con estos miserables y refrenen la insolencia de sus ministros y de todos aquellos de quien reciben malos tratamientos y agravios, haciendo que los tengan y traten como a gente libre y no como a esclavos y porque a este santo concilio ha sido hecha relacion de diversos generos de agravios que se les hacen asi en sus haciendas como en sus personas se declaren y ponen en el directorio de confesores aprobado por este santo concilio y se da aviso de ellos asi a las justicias para que los remedien como aquellos que los hacen para que se enmienden en lo porvenir y se informen de hombres doctos de la satisfacion y restitucion que son obligados a hacer por lo pasado y a los confesores para que a los hallaren que no se quieren enmendar ni satisfacer no los absuelvan.

The following is added in a different hand:

guardando en todo lo que cerca de agravios y vexaciones destos naturales se ensena en la dicha direction [*sic* for *directorio*] y examen de penitentes y confesores, en cuyo cumplimiento esta santo concilio encarga la conciencia y amenaza el divino juicio de Dios nuestro senor a los trangresores y maltratadores.

11. Stafford Poole, "Church Law on the Ordination of Indians and *Castas* in New Spain," *Hispanic American Historical Review* 61 (November 1981): 637–50.
12. Bk. 1, tit. 4.
13. This aspect of the bishops' thinking has been summarized by John Eliot in the following words:

We can trace more closely the decline of sympathy and the narrowing of vision by comparing the opinions expressed at the meetings of the clergy of Mexico at different moments during the sixteenth century. While a meeting held in 1532 emphasizes the spiritual capacity of the Indians, the First Mexican Provincial Council of 1555 depicts them as feeble and inconstant creatures with a natural inclination to vice, and the picture that emerges from the Third Mexican Provincial Council of 1585 is almost uniformly dismal ("Renaissance Europe and America: A Blunted Impact?" in *First Images of America: The Impact of the New World on the Old*, ed. Fredi Chiappelli, Michael J. B. Allen, and Robert Benson [Berkeley and Los Angeles, 1976], 1:15).

These words should be taken with some caution.

14. On the Third Council's attempted reform of the clergy, see Stafford Poole, "The Third Mexican Provincial Council of 1585 and the Reform of the Diocesan Clergy," in *The Church and Society in Latin America*, ed. Jeffrey A. Cole (New Orleans, 1984), 21–37.

15. At the time of the fifth provincial council of 1896 the province of Mexico consisted of the archdiocese of Mexico City and the dioceses of Chilapa, Tulancingo, Cuernavaca, and Veracruz. See *Acta y Decreta Concilii Provincialis Mexicani Quinto celebrati An. Dom. MDCCCXCVI Metropolita Illustrissimo ac Reverendissimo D. D. Prospero Maria Alarcon y Sanchez de la Borquera* (Rome, 1898).

16. There are two copies of this letter in MM 269, folios 24–41 and folios 43–50. A transcription can be found in Llaguno, *La personalidad jurídica*, 287–324. Some matters that were discussed and decided by the bishops in the preparation of this letter were not included in the final copy. They had planned to ask the king to seek from the pope a prorogation and concession without any time limit for the privileges conceded to the Indians. In the section in which they complained about beneficiados coming from Spain with an appointment by the Council of the Indies, they omitted a complimentary reference to criollo priests who knew the native languages. They did not include a complaint about the mendicants not following proper canonical procedure in preparing Indians for marriage and in giving dispensations from impediments. They omitted the intended request to the king not to have to hold provincial councils every five years because of the difficulties of travel in the New World. They had originally intended to ask the king to let the bishops decide parish boundaries, but their final request in this regard was much milder.

17. MM 269, folio 42.

18. MM 269, folios 51–61.

19. *Directorio del Sancto Concilio Prov[inci]al Mexicano celebrado este ano de 1585* in the Archivo Capitular de la Catedral Metropolitana de México. A second, more complete copy is to be found in the cathedral archive of Burgo de Osma, Spain, probably brought there by Bishop Juan de Palafox y Mendoza of Puebla when he returned to Spain. Both copies are subsequent to the council. The one in Mexico is dated 16 October 1585, but the hand is of the seventeenth century and the signatures are copies. It also contains an appendix citing civil laws from the "new *recopilación*," which would put it after 1681. Just recently J. F. Schwaller has discovered a third copy in the AHN, copied from an origi-

nal brought to Spain by Juan de Salcedo in 1590. This would indicate the possibility that Salcedo was in Spain to help in obtaining approbation of the council from the Council of the Indies.

20. Ernest J. Burrus, "The Author of the Mexican Council Catechisms," *The Americas* 15 (October 1958): 171–82.

21. Burrus, "Author of the Catechisms," 174; Vera, *Apuntamientos históricos*, 5.

22. Vera, *Apuntamientos históricos*, 31.

CHAPTER X

1. Schroeder, *Canons and Decrees*, 226.

2. MM 269, folios 19–20.

3. MM 269, folios 21–23.

4. MM 269, folios 180–91.

5. This was incorporated into their letter to the king and can be found transcribed in Llaguno, *La personalidad jurídica*, 290–96.

6. Nigel Davies, *The Toltecs Until the Fall of Tula* (Norman, Okla., 1977), 160; Philip Wayne Powell, *Soldiers, Indians, and Silver: The Northward Advance of New Spain, 1550–1600* (Berkeley and Los Angeles, 1952), 33. This is by far the most thorough treatment in English of Chichimeca life and mores, as well as of the wars waged by and against them. The same author deals with the question from a different perspective in *Mexico's Miguel Caldera: The Taming of America's First Frontier, 1548–1597* (Tucson, Ariz., 1977). See also Juan Focher, *Itinerarium Catholicum ad infideles convertendos* (Seville, 1574), pars 3a, prima veritas. A Latin-Spanish edition of this work was published in Madrid in 1960 by Antonio Eguiluz, under the title *Itinerario del misionero en América*. A useful technical work is Pedro Carrasco Pizana, *Los Otomíes: Cultura e historia prehispánica de los pueblos mesoamericanos de habla otomiana* (Mexico City, 1950). On the general question of the lawfulness of warring against the natives of the New World, see Lewis Hanke, *The Spanish Struggle for Justice in the Conquest of America* (Boston, 1965); Honorio Muñoz, *Vitoria and the Conquest of America: A Study on the First Reading on the Indians "De Indis Prior"* (Manila, 1935); Bartolomé de las Casas, *In Defense of the Indians: The Defense of the Most Reverend Lord, Don Fray Bartolomé de las Casas, of the Order of Preachers, Late Bishop of Chiapa, Against the Persecutors and Slanderers of the People of the New World Discovered Across the Seas*, trans. Stafford Poole (DeKalb, Ill., 1974); Pedro Leturia, "Maior y Vitoria ante la conquista de América," *Estudios eclesiásticos* 2 (1932): 44–82. Though some works have made passing reference to the fact that the question of the morality of the war against the Chichimecas came before the Third Mexican Council, the only treatment of the subject has been Stafford Poole, "War by Fire and Blood: The Church and the Chichimecas in 1585," *The Americas* 22 (October 1965): 115–37.

7. Powell, *Soldiers, Indians, and Silver*, chap. 3.

8. See Alegre, *Historia de la Compañía*, 1:313.

9. Quoted in Vera, *Compendio histórico,* 259, n. 8.

10. See Powell, *Soldiers, Indians, and Silver,* 39; "enteramente desnudos" as Alegre put it (*Historia de la Compañía,* 1:413).

11. Powell, *Soldiers, Indians, and Silver,* 39.

12. Quoted in Vera, *Compendio histórico,* 249.

13. Ibid.

14. Powell, *Soldiers, Indians, and Silver,* 11.

15. Ibid., chap. 5.

16. Ibid., 181.

17. Ibid., 141, 204.

18. Moya to Ovando, 31 August 1574, in Paso y Troncoso, *Epistolario,* 11:171.

19. Cited in Powell, *Soldiers, Indians, and Silver,* 181–82.

20. *Relacion que Su Majestad manda se envie a su real consejo del obispo de Michoacan, Valladolid de Michoacan, 4 de marzo, 1582,* in AGI, Méjico, leg. 374.

21. In 1561 Vasco de Quiroga, bishop of Michoacán, wrote to Philip II to complain about the way the Spaniards were treating the Chichimecas. For more than twenty years, according to Quiroga, the Indians had been coming to Michoacán for the purpose of receiving baptism. Of late, however, Spaniards, blacks, and Hispanized Indians (*ladinos*) had been lying in wait to capture and enslave them. Also, in defiance of all royal orders, all available Chichimecas were being captured and enslaved in retaliation for the crimes of a few. The bishop demanded that this be stopped and that those enslaved be freed (Quiroga to the Council of the Indies, 17 February 1571, in AGI, Méjico, leg. 374, published in Cuevas, *Historia de la iglesia,* 1:314–15).

22. The raid is mentioned in Powell, *Soldiers, Indians, and Silver,* 183, and in the official request of the cabildo (to be mentioned later). Powell says that the raid impelled the request for a discussion on the morality of the war. This may be partly true, but the question was already on the agenda prior to the raid.

23. Data on Robles in connection with the Chichimeca war can be found in Powell, *Soldiers, Indians, and Silver,* 116–17; and in the Medina Rincón *Relacion* (cited in n. 20 above), folio 10. It seems certain that the bishops were aware that the Chichimeca war would be one of their most pressing problems. The Robles report was first shown to the audiencia on 4 March 1585 and given to the bishops on 26 March. The formal request for consideration of the Chichimeca war was not made by the cabildo until 6 April.

24. Robles report, MM 269, folio 86. I have not found this accusation mentioned in other sources, and it may well have been an invention of Spanish prejudice.

25. In 1570 Philip II had requested an opinion on this very subject from a group of Spanish theologians, of whom Ortiz de Hinojosa was one. The group decided not only that such a war was lawful but also that under the circumstances it was a positive obligation. See Focher, *Itinerarium,* pars 3a, prima veritas, 83. This decision does not seem to have influenced governmental pol-

icy. Apparently some of the bishops entered the council already convinced that war by fire and blood was both immoral and senseless.

26. MM 269, folio 85. The request can also be found in the *Actas del cabildo,* 9:33–34.

27. MM 269, folio 85.

28. Ibid.

29. *Parecer de la orden de Sancto Domingo desta Nueva Espana sobre este caso y relacion,* MM 269, folio 89. The only response that carries a date (9 May) was signed by Fray Juan Ramírez (Pedro de Feria's delegate), Fray Domingo de Aguiñaga (the provincial), Fray Cristóbal de Ortega, Fray Pedro de Pravia, and two others whose signatures are illegible.

30. MM 269, folio 98. The report was signed by Fray Melchor de los Reyes, Fray Juan Adriano, Fray Pedro de Agurto, Fray Juan de Contreras, and other members of the faculty of the Colegio de San Pablo. Much of the document is illegible and part of it is lost in the binding of the volume.

31. MM 269, folio 93. The report was signed by Fray Alonso Ponce (the commissary), Fray Pedro de San Sebastián, Fray Diego Vengel, Fray Antonio de Salazar, Fray Pedro de Torres, Fray Antonio de Quijada, Fray Juan de Casteñeda, Fray Juan de los Olivos, Fray Pedro Oroz, and Fray Juan de León. In addition there are two illegible signatures, one of which was probably that of Bernardino de Sahagún. The Franciscans at the third council consistently displayed a more pro-Indian attitude than any other single group, with the exception of the bishops themselves.

32. MM 269, folio 99. It was signed by Fathers Pedro de Ortigosa, Juan de la Plaza, Pedro Díaz, Pedro de Morales, and Antonio Rubio.

33. The memorial of Ortiz de Hinojosa can be found in MM 269, folios 101–4, and is dated 8 May 1585. That of Fulgencio de Vich can be found in the same volume, folios 105–9.

34. MM 269, folio 133.

35. MM 269, folio 48.

36. Ibid. Emphasis in the original.

37. Vera, *Apuntamientos históricos,* 102. This section has been adapted from my article, "The Church and the Repartimientos in the Light of the Third Mexican Council, 1585," *The Americas* 20 (July 1963): 3–36.

38. Navarro, "La iglesia," 443.

39. See Robert S. Chamberlain, "The Castilian Backgrounds of the Repartimiento-Encomienda System," in *Contributions to American Anthropology and History* 5 (Washington, D.C., 1939).

40. It was also known as the repartimiento or the repartimiento-encomienda. For the sake of clarity it is here referred to only as the encomienda. According to Las Casas, it was introduced into the New World by Columbus (*Historia de las Indias,* ed. Agustín Millares Carlo, intro. Lewis Hanke [Mexico City, 1951], bk. 1, chap. 60, 2 and 71).

41. *The Laws of Burgos of 1512–1513: Royal Ordinances for the Good Government and Treatment of the Indians,* trans. Lesley Byrd Simpson (San Francisco,

1960). Other materials on the encomienda can be found in Hanke, *Spanish Struggle*; Silvio Zavala, *New Viewpoints on the Spanish Colonization of America* (Philadelphia, 1943), and *La encomienda indiana* (Mexico City, 1973); Silvio Zavala and María Casteló, eds., *Fuentes para la historia del trabajo en Nueva España* (Mexico City, 1939–1945).

42. Gibson, *Aztecs Under Spanish Rule*, 224.

43. For a good description of the functioning of the repartimiento, see ibid.

44. Zubillaga, *Tercer concilio provincial*, 244. For a good survey of the obrajes, see Richard Greenleaf, "The Obraje in the Late Mexican Colony," *The Americas* 23 (January 1967): 227–50.

45. *Breve y sumaria relación* in García Icazbalceta, *Nueva colección*, 3:166.

46. Gibson lists ecclesiastical institutions that depended on repartimiento labor (*Aztecs Under Spanish Rule*, 119). The whole question needs further study. It is clear, both from the existing records and from the complaints of churchmen who inveighed against abuses, that many ecclesiastics and church organizations profited handsomely by the repartimiento. "The Church, like all the other institutions brought in by the Spaniards, rested in its physical part, upon the labor of the Indians, and the clergy's use of repartimientos and forced labor generally differed in no essential respect from that of other agencies" (Lesley Byrd Simpson, *The Repartimiento System of Native Labor in New Spain and Guatemala*, Ibero-Americana, no. 13 [Berkeley, 1938], 82). Yet there was no lack of critics, whether "mendicant moderates," such as Motolinía, or "root and branch," such as Mendieta, who sought to protect the Indian laborer in one way or another. See Phelan, *Millennial Kingdom*. About 1580, for example, the Jesuits Antonio Rubio and Pedro de Ortigosa (Moya's theology teacher), both of whom attended the third council, sent an opinion to Philip II condemning the repartimientos (Cuevas, *Historia de la iglesia*, 2:245–47). Likewise, Moya himself, in a letter to the king dated 22 January 1585, denounced the system as "the principal ruin and destruction of the Indians" and enumerated the chief abuses (in Paso y Troncoso, *Epistolario*, 12:128–29).

47. *Recopilación*, bk. 6, tit. 12, law 1.

48. Phelan, *Kingdom of Quito*, 63.

49. See Cuevas, *Historia de la iglesia*, 2:225–26.

50. The documentation on this incident can be found in MM 269, folios 1–5.

51. MM 268, folios 227–28 and folio 233.

52. MM 269, folio 114.

53. This third memorial can be found in MM 269, folios 124–34. It is undated and was signed by Fray Pedro de San Sebastián (the provincial), Fray Juan Ramírez (not to be confused with the Dominican of the same name), Fray Diego Vengel, Fray Pedro Oroz, and Fray Gaspar de Recarte. The original Recarte memorial can be found in Cuevas, *Documentos inéditos*, 354–85. Recarte was a long-time opponent of the repartimiento. All that is known of him is taken from the correspondence of Mendieta. About the year 1584 he was a preacher at the convent of San Francisco in Mexico City, but in 1585 he re-

turned to Spain for the purpose of opposing the repartimiento and discussing the Indian situation with the king. There exists a request for an audience with Philip II, sent from Salamanca on 10 April 1587, and Recarte seems to have been responsible for the dispatch of several cédulas favorable to the natives. In 1587 Mendieta recommended him to Philip II as "a chosen servant of Jesus Christ" (Cuevas, *Documentos inéditos,* 24; Mendieta to Philip II, from Puebla, 15 April 1587, in AGI, Méjico, leg. 287).

54. MM 269, folio 127.

55. MM 269, folio 128.

56. It is interesting that the version of the Recarte report given to the bishops here omits a line from the original: "but believe me, just as there was a Red Sea to drown Pharaoh and his vassals in their pursuit of the Children of Israel, so shall there be a sea of hell for your unfortunate Spaniards who unjustly offend and oppress these poor Indians" (MM 269, folio 132; Cuevas, *Documentos inéditos,* 378). For a similar comparison by Mendieta, see Phelan, *Millennial Kingdom,* 95. The implied comparison between Pharaoh and the Spanish crown may have been considered too provocative.

57. MM 269, folio 124.

58. MM 269, folio 136–37. Those present included Pedro de Pravia, Melchor de los Reyes, Juan de la Plaza, Ortiz de Hinojosa, Alonso Ponce, Pedro de San Sebastián, Juan Zurnero, Fulgencio de Vich, Pedro Morales, Juan de Salcedo, and the entire Franciscan house of San Francisco. The latter also signed and approved the document as theologians.

59. MM 269, folio 161; and Llaguno, *La personalidad jurídica,* 101. On 8 May, ten days prior to this meeting, Moya had written to Philip II with some suggestions about Indian labor. In so doing he made a suggestion that for centuries brought obloquy on the head of Bartolomé de las Casas, who had once said something similar. It was that the king should import more black slaves at moderate prices in order to relieve the Indians of some of their burdens. In support of this he sent along a memorial from Antonio Díaz de Cáceres, "a Portuguese but honored and of experience and credit" (Moya to Philip II, 8 May 1585, in AGI, Méjico, leg. 336). As mentioned on page 187, above, this suggestion found its way into the *Directorio para confesores.*

60. MM 269, folio 50.

61. Ibid.

62. *Directorio para confesores,* folios 127–28.

63. Ibid. See note 59 above.

64. This section is based on my article, "Opposition to the Third Mexican Council," *The Americas* 25 (October 1968): 111–59.

65. MM 269, folio 6. The 1560 cédula can be found in the *Recopilación,* bk. 1, tit. 7, law 6. This was the first instance of the legal predicament in which Moya found himself. It should be remembered, however, that he had specifically promised the king that the council would have royal approval prior to publication.

66. MM 269, folios 6–7.

67. MM 269, folio 7.

68. The cédula was dispatched from Toledo on 31 August and contained the same instructions as that of 1560, but was addressed to all the bishops of New Spain (MM 269, folio 7).

69. MM 269, folio 264; AGI, Indiferente general, leg. 2986.

70. MM 269, folio 267; AGI, Indiferente general, leg. 2986.

71. MM 269, folio 269; AGI, Indiferente general, leg. 2986.

72. AGI, Indiferente general, leg. 2986. This is one of the few documents not duplicated in the Bancroft collection.

73. MM 269, folio 258.

74. MM 269, folio 169.

75. MM 269, folio 172.

76. MM 269, folios 173–75. Canon law recognized two kinds of appeals. One (in suspensivo) suspended a decision or law until the appeal had been heard, the other (in devolutivo) did not.

77. MM 269, folio 170. Some of the passages in this document are very obscure and it is impossible to date it exactly.

78. MM 269, folio 242. The appeal is dated 24 October and carries the signature of Salamanca alone.

79. Ibid.

80. MM 269, folio 272. Emphasis in the original. Another copy of the letter, addressed only to the audiencia, can be found in AGI, Indiferente general, leg. 858 and leg. 2986. The deprivation of income was a common threat to bring recalcitrant churchmen into line.

81. A copy of this cédula is in MM 269, folio 273; and in AGI, Indiferente general, leg. 2986.

82. AGI, Indiferente general, leg. 858. The bishops had a belated revenge when Diego Romano was put in charge of Villamanrique's residencia. See Bancroft, History of Mexico, 2:755–56, where he is incorrectly identified as Pedro Romano.

83. MM 269, folio 274, contains the audiencia's order, and folio 296 Moya's notification to the bishops. See also AGI, Indiferente general, leg. 2986.

84. MM 269, folio 181. There are also two undated appeals in folios 181–89, submitted by Juan Hernández, Hernán Vela, and Ortiz de Hinojosa. They covered much the same territory as the others, but the first one adds a new note—that is, an effort to prevent the bishops from making any copies of the conciliar documents, either for their own use or for forwarding to Spain. The physicians' appeal is in MM 269, folio 191, the bishops' answer on folio 192.

85. MM 266, folio 248.

86. MM 266, folio 275. See also folio 189.

87. MM 266, folio 276; AGI, Indiferente general, leg. 2986.

88. MM 266, folio 185.

89. MM 266, folio 277; AGI, Indiferente general, leg. 2986.

90. MM 266, folio 299; AGI, Indiferente general, leg. 2986.

91. MM 266, folio 278; AGI, Indiferente general, leg. 2986.

92. This was on 22 November. See MM 266, folios 255, 300, 304; AGI, Indiferente general, leg. 2986.

93. MM 266, folios 278–79, 304–6; AGI, Indiferente general, leg. 2986.

94. According to a dossier on Beteta (1563), he originally belonged to the diocese of Michoacán. He understood and spoke Tarascan and was considered a man of good character, "muy amigo de los indios" (AGI, Méjico, leg. 207).

95. Beteta was appointed the bishops' delegate on 27 November and 5 December. See MM 266, folio 283; and AGI, Indiferente general, leg. 2986. His petition to the audiencia is in MM 266, folio 282; and in AGI, Indiferente general, leg. 2986.

96. MM 266, folio 279; AGI, Indiferente general, leg. 2986.

97. MM 266, folio 261. This or the case of the bishop of Guatemala (mentioned on page 197, above) may be the incident referred to by Fray Francisco Jiménez, rector of the college of San Luis de la Puebla de los Angeles, when writing to Villamanrique on 9 February 1588: "From the moment Your Excellency entered this city, you have been entangled and bound by many very serious censures and excommunications because of the many injuries and violence that you have committed against the church and its ministers. For as soon as you entered Mexico you clashed with the prelates of the council and by an order that you issued you held one of them prisoner in the city, or, to speak more courteously, you detained him, but all the same it was force and violence" (García Icazbalceta, *Cartas de religiosos*, 157).

98. AGI, Méjico, leg. 2547.

99. MM 266, folio 287; AGI, Indiferente general, leg. 2986. All the copies of appeals now in the AGI are those of Salazar alone—that is, those involving the patronato. They were made by Sancho López de Agurto on 20 May 1586 for forwarding to Spain.

100. MM 266, folio 259.

101. AGI, Méjico, leg. 287, and Indiferente general, 1237.

102. ASV, vol. 19, folios 150–51; Ernest J. Burrus, "The Third Mexican Council (1585) in the Light of the Vatican Archives," *The Americas* 23 (April 1967): 405.

103. Juan Manuel Rodríguez, *La iglesia en Nueva España a la luz del III concilio mexicano (1585–1596)* (Isola dei Liri, Italy, 1937), 149–51; Burrus, "Third Mexican Council," 405.

104. Rodríguez, *La iglesia*, 143. He located the document in the Archivo de la Embajada de España (archives of the Spanish Embassy), Vatican City, leg. 7, folio 192.

105. Rodríguez, *La iglesia*, 143–44; Archivo de la Embajada, leg. 7, folio 193.

106. AGI, Méjico, leg. 339.

107. ASV, vol. 34 (no foliation).

108. Rodríguez, *La iglesia*, 151; ASV, vol. 37, folio 231. Rodríguez refers to the recipient as an unidentified person, but Burrus identifies him as Montalto ("Third Mexican Council," 405).

109. ASV, vol. 38, folio 515.

110. ASCC. The volume has no catalogue number, only the title *Concilium Provinciale Mexicanum, A.D., 1585*. More details on this can be found in Burrus,

"Third Mexican Council." The extent of the differences between the Spanish original and the Latin translation, and the influence of Rome on these, has yet to be studied in full. There is need for a good critical edition of the decrees of the third council. For a more detailed consideration of Rome's impact on the decrees, see Poole, "Opposition to the Third Mexican Council," and "Church Law." The catechism is also in the same archive. A note at the end of the consultor's comments says that it was the *Catechismus maior et minor* and that it was signed and sealed by the bishops on 16 October 1585. The date of the catechism itself is 11 May 1586, which, as Burrus has indicated, was either the date on which the Latin translation was made or else the date when it was received by the Congregation of the Council ("Third Mexican Council," 406). Following the catechism are some pages of corrections and annotations titled *In Doctrinam Mexicanam* (folio 278). On folio 280 is a page titled *Dubia in Ecclesia Mexicana occurrentia quoru[m] desideratur resolutio.* These are all doubts and questions about ceremonies.

111. AGI, Méjico, leg. 287.

112. *Recopilación,* bk. 1, tit. 8, law 7.

113. AGI, Méjico, leg. 337.

114. Ibid.

115. Ibid. The Franciscan provincial Juan Márquez held the office from 1620 to 1623. See Agustín Vetancurt, *Menologio franciscano de los varones más señalados que con sus vidas ejemplares, perfección religiosa, ciencia, predicación evangélica, en su vida y muerte ilustraron la provincia del Santo Evangelio* (Mexico City, 1871), 4:478.

116. *Concilio III provincial mexicano, ilustrado con muchas notas del R. P. Basilio Arrillaga* (Barcelona, 1870).

117. The first cédula can be found in Rodríguez, *La iglesia,* 145–46, and the second on 146–47.

118. AGI, Méjico, leg. 337.

119. Ibid.

CHAPTER XI

1. Most of the material in this chapter has been taken from Gutiérrez de Luna, 37–43, and Sosa, 89–96, both in *Cinco cartas;* and Jiménez Rueda, *Moya de Contreras,* 164–66.

2. On Pravia, see Dávila Padilla, *Historia,* 584–99. In 1583 he had declined the archbishopric of Panama. The papers on this can be found in AGI, Méjico, leg. 286. While governing the archdiocese of Mexico, he wrote to Philip II to complain about the repartimiento and to suggest that the Indians should have a protector at court as they had had in the days of Las Casas (8 December 1588, AGI, Méjico, leg. 288).

3. Alegre, *Historia de la Compañía,* 1: 318.

4. Moya to Philip II, from Córdoba, 21 December 1586, in AGI, Méjico, leg. 336.

5. Schäfer writes that he was president of the Council of the Indies from 7 January 1591 until his death on 14 December 1592, thus further complicating the question of the date of his death (*El real y supremo consejo*, 1:112–13).

6. Moya to Ovando, 26 March 1574, in AGI, Méjico, leg. 278; Lewis Hanke, "El visitador lic. Alonso Fernández de Bonilla y el virrey del Perú, el conde del Villar (1590–1593)," in *Memoria del Segundo Congreso Venezolano de Historia*, 2:28.

7. Philip II to Sixtus V, and to the conde de Olivares (Spanish ambassador), 8 February 1591, in AGI, Patronato, leg. 183.

8. Shiels, *King and Church*, 131–33.

9. Jiménez Rueda gives the date as 14 December (*Moya de Contreras*, 165). Schäfer gives it as 14 December 1592 (see note 5 above).

10. For information on the church, see Ramón Mesoneros Romanos, *El antiguo Madrid* (Madrid, 1925), 1:243; and Elías Tormo y Monzó, *Las iglesias del antiguo Madrid* (Madrid, 1927), 112–13. There is a cenotaph for Moya de Contreras in the present cathedral of Mexico.

APPENDIX I

1. Joaquín García Icazbalceta, *Fray don Juan de Zumárraga, primer obispo y arzobispo de México*, ed. Rafael Aguayo and Antonio Castro Real (Mexico City, 1947), 4:65.

2. *Biblioteca Mejicana: A Catalogue of an Extraordinary Collection of Books and Manuscripts Wholly Relating to the History and Literature of North and South America, Particularly Mexico. To Be Sold at Auction by Mssrs. Puttick and Simpson* (London, 1869), entry no. 1856.

3. John Walton Caughey, *Hubert Howe Bancroft: Historian of the West* (Berkeley, 1946), 76.

4. García Icazbalceta, *Zumárraga*, 4:67, n. 2.

5. Vera, *Compendio histórico*, 135.

6. Hubert Howe Bancroft, *Literary Industries* (San Francisco, 1890), 209.

Bibliography

Actas del cabildo de la ciudad de México. [Title varies.] 54 vols. Mexico City: El Correo Español, 1889–1916.

Aguirre Beltrán, Gonzalo. *La población negra de México, 1519–1810, estudio etnocéntrico.* Mexico City: Ediciones Fuente Cultural, 1946.

Aiton, Arthur. *Antonio de Mendoza: First Viceroy of New Spain.* Durham, N.C.: Duke University Press, 1927.

Alegre, Francisco Javier. *Historia de la provincia de la Compañía de Jesús en Nueva España.* Edited by Ernest J. Burrus and Félix Zubillaga. 2 vols. Rome: Institutum Historicum Societatis Iesu, 1956.

Alonso, Amado. "Biografía de Fernán González de Eslava." *Revista de Filología Hispánica* 2 (1940): 213–319.

Altamira y Crevea, Rafael. *Diccionario castellano de palabras jurídicas y técnicas tomadas de la legislación indiana.* Comisión de Historia, no. 25. Estudios de Historia, no. 3. Mexico City: Instituto Panamericano de Geografía e Historia, 1951.

Alvarez Mejía, Juan. "La cuestión del clero indígena en la época colonial." *Revista Javeriana* [Facultad de Ciencias Económicas y Jurídicas, Universidad Javeriana] 45, 222 (March 1956): 57–67; 45, 225 (June 1956): 209–19.

Angulo Iñiguez, Diego. *Historia del arte hispanoamericano.* 2 vols. Barcelona and Buenos Aires: Salvat, 1945–1950.

Archivo Mexicano: Documentos para la historia de México. Mexico City, 1852–1853.

277

Arrom, José. *El teatro de Hispano-América en la época colonial.* Havana: Anuario Bibliográfico Cubano, 1956.

Atienza, Julio de. *Nobiliario español: Diccionario heráldico de apellidos españoles y de títulos nobiliarios.* Madrid: M. Aguilar, 1948.

Bacigalupo, Marvyn Helen. *A Changing Perspective: Attitudes Toward Creole Society in New Spain (1521–1610).* London: Tamesis Books, 1981.

Bancroft, Hubert Howe. *History of Mexico.* Vol. 2. San Francisco: The History Company, 1883. (Appears as vol. 10 of Bancroft's *Works.*)

―――. *Literary Industries.* San Francisco: The History Company, 1890. (Appears as vol. 39 of Bancroft's *Works.*)

Basalenque, Diego. *Historia de la provincia de San Nicolás de Tolentino de Michoacán del orden de Nuestro Padre San Agustín.* Mexico City, 1673.

Baudot, Georges. "The Last Years of Sahagún." In *Sixteenth-Century Mexico: The Work of Sahagún,* edited by Munro S. Edmonson. Albuquerque: University of New Mexico Press, 1964.

Bayle, Constantino. "España y el clero indígena en América." *Razón y Fe* 84 (1931): 213–25.

Beaumont, Pablo. *Crónica de Michoacán.* 3 vols. Publicaciones del Archivo General de la Nación, nos. 17–19. Mexico City, 1932.

Benítez, Fernando. *The Century After Cortés.* Translated by Joan MacLean. Chicago: University of Chicago Press, 1965.

Beristáin de Sousa, José Mariano. *Biblioteca Hispano-americana Sententrional.* 2d ed., revised by Fortino Hipólito Vera. 2 vols. Amecameca: Tipo del Colegio Católico, 1883.

Biblioteca Mejicana: A Catalogue of an Extraordinary Collection of Books and Manuscripts Wholly Relating to the History and Literature of North and South America, Particularly Mexico. To Be Sold at Auction by Mssrs. Puttick and Simpson. London, 1869.

Borah, Woodrow. *New Spain's Century of Depression.* Ibero-Americana, no. 35. Berkeley and Los Angeles: University of California Press, 1951.

―――. *Silk Raising in Colonial Mexico.* Ibero-Americana, no. 20. Berkeley: University of California Press, 1943.

Boyd-Bowman, Peter. *Léxico hispanoamericano del siglo XVI.* London: Tamesis Books, 1971.

Bravo Ugarte, José. *Historia de México.* 3 vols. Mexico City, 1944–1947.

Brown, John Scott. *The Spanish Origin of International Law.* London, 1934.

Burrus, Ernest J. "The Author of the Mexican Council Catechisms." *The Americas* 15 (October 1958): 171–82.

―――. "The Salazar Report to the Third Mexican Council." *The Americas* 17 (July 1960): 65–84.

―――. "The Third Mexican Council (1585) in the Light of the Vatican Archives." *The Americas* 23 (April 1967): 390–405.

Carrasco Pizana, Pedro. *Los Otomíes: Cultura e historia prehispánica de los pueblos mesoamericanos de habla otomiana.* Publicaciones del Instituto de Historia, no. 5. Mexico City, 1950.

Carreño, Alberto María. "El colegio de Tlaltelolco y la educación indígena en el siglo XVI." *Divulgación histórica* 1 (1940): 196–202.

———. *La real y pontificia universidad de México, 1536–1865.* Mexico City: Universidad Nacional Autónoma de México, 1961.

———, ed. *Un desconocido cedulario del siglo XVI perteneciente a la catedral metropolitana de México.* Mexico City: Ediciones Victoria, 1944.

Carro, Venancio. *La teología y los teólogos-juristas españoles ante la conquista de América.* 2 vols. Madrid: Talleres Gráficos Marsiega, 1944.

Cartas de Indias. Madrid: Manuel G. Hernández, 1877.

Carter, Constance. "The Visita General of Tello de Sandoval in New Spain." Ph.D. diss., Columbia University, 1971.

Caughey, John Walton. *Hubert Howe Bancroft: Historian of the West.* Berkeley: University of California Press, 1946.

Cavo, Andrés. *Historia de México.* Annotated by Ernest J. Burrus, with a prologue by Mariano Cuevas. Mexico City: Editorial Patria, 1949.

Cedulario indiano, recopilado por Diego de Encinas. Facsimile of the 1596 edition, edited by Alfonso García-Gallo. 4 vols. Madrid: Ediciones Cultura Hispánica, 1945.

Un cedulario mexicano del siglo XVI. With prologue and notes by Francisco González de Cosío. Mexico City: Ediciones del Frente de Afirmación Hispanista, 1973.

Cervantes de Salazar, Francisco. *Life in the Imperial and Loyal City of Mexico in New Spain and the Royal and Pontifical University of Mexico.* Translated by Minnie Lee Barrett Shepard and edited by Carlos Eduardo Castañeda. Austin: University of Texas Press, 1953.

Céspedes del Castillo, Guillermo. "La visita como institución indiana." Escuela de Estudios Hispano-americanos de la Universidad de Sevilla, *Anuario de Estudios Americanos* 3 (1946): 985–1025.

Chamberlain, Robert. "The Castilian Backgrounds of the Repartimiento-Encomienda System." In *Contributions to American Anthropology and History*, 5: 23–66. Washington, D.C.: Carnegie Institution of Washington, 1939.

Cinco cartas del illmo. y exmo. señor d. Pedro Moya de Contreras, arzobispo-virrey y primer inquisidor de la Nueva España, precedida de la historia de su vida según Cristóbal Gutiérrez de Luna y Francisco Sosa. Madrid: Porrúa Turanzas, 1962.

Colección de bulas, breves y otros documentos relativos a la iglesia de América y Filipinas, dispuesta, anotada e ilustrada por el p. Francisco Javier Hernáez. 2 vols. Brussels, 1879.

Colección de cánones y de todos los concilios de la iglesia de España y de América. Annotated and illustrated by Juan Tejada y Ramiro. 5 vols. Madrid, 1859.

Colección de documentos inéditos relativos al descubrimiento, conquista y organización de las antiguas posesiones españolas de América y Oceania, sacados de los archivos del reino y muy especialmente del de Indias. 1st series. 42 vols. Madrid, 1864–1884.

Colección de documentos inéditos relativos al descubrimiento, conquista, y organización de las antiguas posesiones españolas de ultramar. 2d series. 25 vols. Madrid: Real Academia de Historia, 1885–1932.

Colección de documentos inéditos para la historia de Ibero-América. 14 vols. Madrid: Compañía ibero-americana de publicaciones, 1927–1932.

Collectio Maxima Conciliorum Omnium Hispaniae et Novi Orbis. Edited by José Saenz de Aguirre. Rome, 1694.

Concilio III Provincial Mexicano, ilustrado con muchas notas del r. p. Basilio Arrillaga de la Compañía de Jesús. Barcelona: Mariano Galván Rivera, 1870.

Concilios provinciales primero y segundo celebrados en la muy noble y muy leal ciudad de Mexico, presidiendo el Illmo. y Rmo. Senor D. Fr. Alonso de Montufar, en los anos de 1555 y 1565. Published by Archbishop Francisco Antonio Lorenzana. Mexico City, 1769.

Concilium Mexicanum Provinciale III, celebratum Mexici anno MDLXXXV, praeside D. D. Petro Moya et Contreras, Archiepiscopo eiusdem Urbis, confirmatum Romae die XXVII Octobris anno MDLXXXIX, postea iussu regio editum Mexici anno MDCXXII sumptibus D. D. Ioannis Perez de la Serna Archiepiscopi demum typis mandatum cura et expensis D. D. Francisci Antonii a Lorenzana Archipraesulis. Mexico City, 1770.

Contreras, Milagros. "Aportación al estudio de las visitas de audiencias." *Memoria del Segundo Congreso Venezolano de Historia*, 1:179–221. Caracas, 1975.

Cook, Sherburne F., and Woodrow Borah. *Essays in Population History: Mexico and the Caribbean.* Berkeley and Los Angeles: University of California Press, 1974.

———. *The Indian Population of Central Mexico, 1531–1610.* Ibero-Americana, no. 44. Berkeley and Los Angeles: University of California Press, 1960.

Cook, Sherburne F., and Lesley Byrd Simpson. *The Population of Central Mexico in the Sixteenth Century.* Ibero-Americana, no. 31. Berkeley: University of California Press, 1948.

Costa, H. de la. "Church and State in the Philippines During the Administration of Bishop Salazar, 1581–1594." *Hispanic American Historical Review* 30 (August 1950): 314–35.

Crahan, Margaret E. "Spanish and American Counterpoint: Problems and Possibilities in Spanish Colonial Administrative History." In *New Approaches to Latin American History*, edited by Richard Graham and Peter H. Smith. Austin: University of Texas Press, 1974.

Crónicas de la Compañía de Jesús en la Nueva España. Prologue and selection by Francisco González de Cossío. Mexico City: Biblioteca del Estudiante Universitario, Universidad Nacional Autónoma de México, 1979.

Cuevas, Mariano. *Documentos inéditos del siglo XVI para la historia de México.* Mexico City: Museo Nacional de Arqueología, Historia y Etnología, 1914.

———. *Historia de la iglesia en México.* 5 vols. Tlálpam–El Paso: Asil Patricio Sanz, 1921–1928.

Cumberland, Charles. *Mexico: The Struggle for Modernity.* New York: Oxford University Press, 1968.

Cummins, Victoria Hennessy. "After the Spiritual Conquest: Patrimonialism and Politics in the Mexican Church, 1572–1586." Ph.D. diss., Tulane University, 1979.

Cunningham, Charles. *The Audiencia in the Spanish Colonies.* Berkeley: University of California Press, 1919.

Davies, Nigel. *The Toltecs Until the Fall of Tula*. Norman, Okla.: University of Oklahoma Press, 1977.

Dávila Padilla, Agustín. *Historia de la fundación y discurso de la Provincia de Santiago de México de la Orden de Predicadores por las vidas de sus varones insignes y casas notables de Nueva España*. 3d ed. Prologue by Agustín Millares Carlo. Mexico City, 1955.

Documentos históricos de México. Edited by Luis García Pimentel. 4 vols. Mexico City, 1903–1906.

Documentos inéditos o muy raros para la historia de México. Vol. 5, *La inquisición de México*. Edited by Genaro García and Carlos Pereyra. Mexico City: Viuda de C. Bouret, 1906.

d'Olwer, Luis Nicolás. *Fray Bernardino de Sahagún, 1499–1590*. Mexico City, 1952.

Dussel, Enrique. *Les Évêques hispanoaméricains, défenseurs et évangélisateurs de l'indien, 1504–1620*. Wiesbaden: F. Steiner, 1970.

Eguiara y Eguren, Juan J. de. *Biblioteca Mexicana*. Mexico City, 1755.

Eliot, John. "Renaissance Europe and America: A Blunted Impact?" In *First Images of America: The Impact of the New World on the Old*, edited by Fredi Chiappelli, Michael J. B. Allen, and Robert L. Benson, 1:11–23. Berkeley and Los Angeles: University of California Press, 1976.

Encinas, Diego de. *Provisiones, cédulas, capítulos de ordenanzas, instrucciones, y cartas tocantes al buen gobierno de las Indias*. Facsimile of 1596 edition. Edited by Alfonso García-Gallo. 4 vols. Madrid: Ediciones Cultura Hispánica, 1943.

Ennis, Arthur. *Fray Alonso de la Vera Cruz, O.S.A. (1507–1584): A Study of His Life and Contribution to the Religious and Intellectual Affairs of Early Mexico*. Louvain: E. Warny, 1957.

Fernández del Castillo, Francisco. *Libros y libreros del siglo XVI. Publicaciones del Archivo General de la Nación*, no. 16. Mexico City: Tipografía Guerrero Hermanos, 1914.

Focher, Juan. *Itinerarium Catholicum ad infideles convertendos*. Seville, 1574.

———. *Itinerario del misionero en América*. Edited by Antonio Eguiluz. Madrid, 1960.

Fonseca, Fabián de, and Carlos de Urrutia. *Historia general de real hacienda*. 6 vols. Mexico City, 1845–1853.

García, Genaro. *El clero de México durante la dominación española según el Archivo Archiepiscopal Metropolitano*. Mexico City: Viuda de C. Bouret, 1907.

García-Abásolo, Antonio F. *Martín Enríquez y la reforma de 1568 en Nueva España*. Publicaciones del la Excma. Diputación Provincial de Sevilla, bajo la dirección de Antonia Heredia Herrera. Serie: V centenario del descubrimiento de América, no. 2. Seville, 1983.

García-Gallo, Alfonso. "Las audiencias de Indias: Su origen y caracteres." *Memoria del Segundo Congreso Venezolano de Historia*, 1:359–432. Caracas, 1975.

García Icazbalceta, Joaquín. *Bibliografía mexicana del siglo XVI*. Mexico City: Andrade y Morales, 1886.

———. *Cartas de religiosos, 1539–1594*. Mexico City: Andrade y Morales, 1886.

———. *Fray don Juan de Zumárraga, primer obispo y arzobispo de México*. Edited by Rafael Aguayo and Antonio Castro Real. 4 vols. Mexico City: Porrúa, 1947.

————, ed. *Nueva colección de documentos para la historia de México.* 5 vols. Mexico City: Andrade y Morales, 1886–1892.

Gay, José Antonio. *Historia de Oaxaca.* 2 vols. Mexico City: Dublan, 1950.

Gerhard, Peter. *A Guide to the Historical Geography of New Spain.* Cambridge: Cambridge University Press, 1972.

Gibson, Charles. *The Aztecs Under Spanish Rule.* Stanford, Calif.: Stanford University Press, 1964.

————. *Spain in America.* New York: Harper and Row, 1966.

————. *Tlaxcala in the Sixteenth Century.* Stanford, Calif.: Stanford University Press, 1952.

Gómez de Cervantes, Gonzalo. *La vida económica y social de Nueva España al finalizar el siglo XVI.* Edited by Alberto María Carreño. Biblioteca histórica mexicana de obras inéditas, 1st ser., no. 19. Mexico City, 1944.

González de Eslava, Fernán. *Coloquios espirituales y sacramentales.* Edited by José Rojas Garcidueñas. 2 vols. Mexico City, 1958.

Greenleaf, Richard. *The Mexican Inquisition of the Sixteenth Century.* Albuquerque: University of New Mexico Press, 1966.

————. "The Obraje in the Late Mexican Colony." *The Americas* 23 (January 1967): 227–50.

————. *Zumárraga and the Mexican Inquisition.* Washington, D.C.: Academy of American Franciscan History, 1961.

Grijalva, Juan de. *Cronica de la orden de N. P. S. Agustin en las provincias de la Nueva Espana: en quatro edades desde el ano de 1533 hasta el de 1592.* Mexico City, 1624.

Gutiérrez de Luna, Cristóbal. *Vida y heroicas virtudes del doctor don Pedro Moya de Contreras, arzobispo mexicano.* Mexico City, 1619.

Hanke, Lewis. *The Spanish Struggle for Justice in the Conquest of America.* Boston: Little, Brown, 1965.

————. "El visitador lic. Alonso Fernández de Bonilla y el virrey del Perú, el conde del Villar (1590–1593)." In *Memoria del Segundo Congreso Venezolano de Historia,* 2:11–128. Caracas, 1975.

Haring, C. H. *Trade and Navigation Between Spain and the Indies in the Time of the Hapsburgs.* Gloucester, Mass.: Peter Smith, 1964.

Heredia Herrera, Antonia. *Catálogo de las consultas del Consejo de Indias (1529–1591).* Madrid: Dirección General de Archivos y Bibliotecas, 1972.

————. *La renta de azogue en Nueva España, 1709–1751.* Seville: Escuela de Estudios Hispano-Americanos, 1978.

Instrucciones que los virreyes de Nueva Espana dejaron a sus sucesores. 2 vols. Mexico City: Imprenta Imperial, 1867.

Jacobsen, Jerome V. *Educational Foundations of the Jesuits in Sixteenth-Century New Spain.* Berkeley: University of California Press, 1938.

Jiménez de la Espada, Marcos. *El código ovandino.* Madrid, 1891.

————. *Relaciones geográficas de Indias.* 4 vols. Madrid, 1881.

Jiménez Rueda, Julio. *Don Pedro Moya de Contreras, primer inquisidor de México.* Mexico City: Ediciones Xochitl, 1944.

Kagan, Richard. *Students and Society in Early Modern Spain.* Baltimore: Johns Hopkins University Press, 1974.

Kubler, George. *Mexican Architecture of the Sixteenth Century.* 2 vols. New Haven: Yale University Press, 1948.

Lafaye, Jacques. *Quetzalcóatl et Guadalupe: La Formation de la conscience nationale au Mexique.* Paris: Gallimard, 1974.

Lambertini, Prospero [Pope Benedict XIV]. *De Synodo Diocesano.* Rome, 1783.

Lang, M. F. *El monopolio estatal del mercurio en el México colonial, 1550–1710.* Translated by Robert Gómez Ciriza. Mexico City: Fondo de Cultura Económica, 1977.

Larrey, Martin Fermin. "A Viceroy and His Challengers: Supremacy Struggles During the Viceregency of Martín Enríquez, 1568–1580." Ph.D. diss., University of California, Santa Barbara, 1965.

Las Casas, Bartolomé de. *In Defense of the Indians: The Defense of the Most Reverend Lord, Don Fray Bartolomé de Las Casas, of the Order of Preachers, Late Bishop of Chiapa, Against the Persecutors and Slanderers of the Peoples of the New World Discovered Across the Seas.* Translated with notes by Stafford Poole. DeKalb, Ill.: Northern Illinois University Press, 1974.

———. *Historia de las Indias.* Edited by Agustín Millares Carlo, with an introductory essay by Lewis Hanke. 3 vols. Mexico City: Fondo de Cultura Económica, 1951.

The Laws of Burgos of 1512–1513: Royal Ordinances for the Good Government and Treatment of the Indians. Translated with an introduction and notes by Lesley Byrd Simpson. San Francisco: J. Howell, 1960.

Lea, Henry C. *The Inquisition in the Spanish Dependencies.* New York, 1922.

Lee, James H. "Clerical Education in Nineteenth-Century Mexico: The Conciliar Seminaries of Mexico City and Guadalajara, 1821–1910." *The Americas* 36 (April 1980): 465–67.

Lee, Raymond. "The Viceregal Instructions of Martín Enríquez de Almanza." *Revista de Historia de América* 21 (1951): 97–119.

Leonard, Irving. *Books of the Brave.* New York: Gordian Press, 1964.

Leturia, Pedro. "Maior y Vitoria ante la conquista de América." *Estudios Eclesiásticos* 2 (1932): 44–82.

Leza, Jesús de. "Fray Juan Ramírez, O.P., un riojano defensor de los indios." *Berleo* 7, 22 (January–March 1952): 41–60; 7, 23 (April–June 1952): 309–19; 7, 24 (July–September 1952): 457.

Liebman, Seymour. *The Jews of New Spain: Faith, Flame, and the Inquisition.* Coral Gables, Fla.: University of Miami Press, 1970.

Liss, Peggy K. "Jesuit Contributions to the Ideology of Spanish Empire in Mexico: Part I." *The Americas* 29 (January 1973): 314–33.

———. *Mexico Under Spain, 1521–1556: Society and the Origins of Nationality.* Chicago: University of Chicago Press, 1975.

Llaguno, José. *La personalidad jurídica del indio y el III Concilio Provincial Mexicano, 1585.* Mexico City: Porrúa, 1963.

Lopetegui, León, and Félix Zubillaga. *Historia de la iglesia en la América española desde el descubrimiento hasta los comienzos del siglo XIX.* Madrid: Biblioteca de Autores Cristianos, 1965.

López de Gómara, Francisco. *Cortés: The Life of the Conqueror by His Secretary.*

Translated and edited by Lesley Byrd Simpson. Berkeley and Los Angeles: University of California Press, 1964.

Lovett, A. W. "Juan de Ovando and the Council of Finance (1573–1575)." *Historical Journal* 15, 1 (1972): 1–21.

MacLachlan, Colin M., and Jaime E. Rodríguez O. *The Forging of the Cosmic Race: A Reinterpretation of Colonial Mexico.* Berkeley and Los Angeles: University of California Press, 1980.

McLeod, Murdo. *Spanish Central America: A Socioeconomic History.* Berkeley and Los Angeles: University of California Press, 1973.

Madoz, Pascual. *Diccionario geográfico-estadístico-histórico de España y sus posesiones de Ultramar.* 15 vols. Madrid: D. Madoz, 1849.

Manzano Manzano, Juan. *Historia de las recopilaciones de Indias.* 2 vols. Madrid: Ediciones Cultura Hispánica, 1950.

Mariluz Urquijo, José M. *Ensayo sobre los juicios de residencias indianas.* Seville: Escuela de Estudios Hispano-americanos, 1952.

Martin, Norman. *Los vagabundos en la Nueva España.* Mexico City: Editorial Jus, 1957.

Martínez Quesada, Juan. "Documentación de la capellanía y enterramiento del presidente don Juan de Ovando." *Revista de Estudios Extremeños* 14 (1958): 145–58.

Mathes, W. Michael, "Sebastián Vizcaíno y los principios de la explotación comercial de California." *Homenaje a Don José María de la Peña y Cámara.* Madrid, 1969.

Maurtúa, Victor. *Antecedentes de la Recopilación de Indias.* Madrid: B. Rodríguez, 1906.

Mecham, J. Lloyd. *Church and State in Latin America.* Chapel Hill: University of North Carolina Press, 1966.

Memoria del Segundo Congreso Venezolano de Historia. 3 vols. Caracas, 1975.

Méndez Arceo, Sergio. *La real y pontificia universidad de México.* Mexico City: Consejo de Humanidades, 1952.

Méndez Plancarte, Alfonso. "Piezas teatrales en la Nueva España del siglo XVI—siete adiciones y una supresión." *Abside* 6 (1942): 218–24.

Mendieta, Gerónimo de. *Vidas franciscanas.* Prologue by Juan B. Iguíniz. Mexico City: Universidad Nacional Autónoma de México, 1945.

Menéndez Pelayo, Marcelino. *Historia de los heretodoxos españoles.* 2 vols. Madrid: Biblioteca de Autores Cristianos, 1956.

Mesoneros Romanos, Ramón. *El antiguo Madrid.* 2 vols. Madrid: Renacimiento, 1925.

Millares Carlo, Agustín, and José Ignacio Montecón. *Album de paleografía hispanoamericana de los siglos XVI y XVII.* Vol. 1, *Introducción.* Mexico City: Instituto Panamericano de Geografía e Historia, Comisión de Historia, 1955.

Miramón, Alberto. *El doctor Sangre.* Academia Columbiana de Historia, Biblioteca Eduardo Santos, no. 8. Bogotá, 1954.

Molina Argüello, Carlos. "Visita y residencia en Indias." In *III Congreso del Instituto Internacional de Historia del Derecho Indiano: Madrid, 17–23 de enero de 1972: Actas y estudios.* Madrid, 1973.

————. "Las visitas-residencias y residencias-visitas de la Recopilación de Indias." *Memoria del Segundo Congreso Venezolano de Historia,* 2:187–323. Caracas, 1975.

Montúfar, Alonso de. *Descripción del Arzobispado de México hecha en 1570 y otros documentos.* Edited by Luis García Pimentel. Mexico City, 1897.

Monumenta Mexicana I (1570–1575). Edited by Félix Zubillaga. Vol. 8 of *Monumenta Missionum Societatis Iesu.* Vol. 77 of *Monumenta Historica Societatis Iesu a patribus eiusdem Societatis edita.* Rome: Monumenta Historica Societatis Iesu, 1956.

Morelli, Cyriacus. *Fasti Novi Orbis et Ordinationum Apostolicarum ad Indias Pertinentium Breviarium, cum adnotationibus.* Venice, 1776.

Moreno de los Arcos, Roberto. "Los territorios parroquiales de la ciudad arzobispal, 1525–1981." *Gaceta Oficial del Arzobispado de México* 22, 9–10 (September–October 1982): 152–73.

Mörner, Magnus. *Race Mixture in the History of Latin America.* Boston: Little, Brown, 1967.

Muñoz, Honorio. *Vitoria and the Conquest of America: A Study on the First Reading on the Indians "De Indis Prior."* Manila, 1935.

Navarro, Bernabé. "La iglesia y los indios en el IIIer Concilio Mexicano (1585)." *Abside* 8 (1944): 391–446.

O'Gorman, Edmundo. *Reflexiones sobre la distribución urbana colonial de la ciudad de México.* XVI Congreso Internacional de Planificación y de la Habitación. Mexico City: Editorial Cultura, 1938.

Olaechea Labayen, Juan Bautista. "El colegio de San Juan Letrán de México." *Anuario de estudios americanos* 29 (1972): 585–96.

The Oroz Codex. Translated and edited by Angélico Chávez. Washington, D.C.: Academy of American Franciscan History, 1972.

Padden, Robert. "The *Ordenanza del Patronazgo:* An Interpretive Essay." *The Americas* 12 (April 1956): 333–54.

Parry, J. H. *The Audiencia of New Galicia in the Sixteenth Century.* Cambridge: Cambridge University Press, 1948.

Paso y Troncoso, Francisco del, ed. *Epistolario de Neuva España, 1505–1818.* 16 vols. Mexico City: Porrúa, 1939–1942.

Peña Cámara, José de la. "La copulata de leyes de Indias y las ordenanzas ovandinas." *Revista de Indias* 2 (October–December 1941): 121–46.

————. "El manuscrito llamado 'Gobernación Espiritual y Temporal de las Indias' y su verdadero lugar en la historia de la Recopilación." *Revista de Historia de América* 12 (August 1941): 5–72.

————. "Nuevos datos sobre la visita de Juan de Ovando al consejo de Indias." *Anuario de historia del derecho español* 12 (1935): 425–38.

————. "Las redacciones del Libro de la Gobernación Espiritual: Ovando y la junta de Indias de 1568." *Revista de Indias* 2 (March 1941): 93–105.

Phelan, John L. *The Kingdom of Quito in the Seventeenth Century: Bureaucratic Politics in the Spanish Empire.* Madison: University of Wisconsin Press, 1967.

————. *The Millennial Kingdom of the Franciscans in the New World.* Berkeley and Los Angeles: University of California Press, 1956.

Philips, Miles. "The Voyage of Miles Philips." In Richard Hakluyt, *Voyages*, 6:320–23. New York: Dutton, 1968.

Poole, Stafford. "The Church and the Repartimientos in the Light of the Third Mexican Council, 1585." *The Americas* 20 (July 1963): 3–36.

———. "Church Law on the Ordination of Indians and *Castas* in New Spain." *Hispanic American Historical Review* 61 (November 1981): 637–50.

———. "Institutionalized Corruption in the Letrado Bureaucracy: The Case of Pedro Farfán (1568–1586)." *The Americas* 38 (October 1981): 149–71.

———. "Opposition to the Third Mexican Council." *The Americas* 25 (October 1968): 111–59.

———. "Research Possibilities of the Third Mexican Council." *Manuscripta* 5 (1961): 151–63.

———. "Successors to Las Casas." *Revista de Historia de América* 61–62 (January–December 1966): 89–114.

———. "The Third Mexican Provincial Council of 1585 and the Reform of the Diocesan Clergy." In *The Church and Society in Latin America*, edited by Jeffrey A. Cole. New Orleans: Tulane University Press, 1984.

———. "La visita de Moya de Contreras." In *Memoria del Segundo Congreso Venezolano de Historia*, 2:417–41. Caracas, 1975.

———. "War by Fire and Blood: The Church and the Chichimecas in 1585." *The Americas* 22 (October 1965): 115–37.

Powell, Philip Wayne. *Mexico's Miguel Caldera: The Taming of America's First Frontier, 1548–1597.* Tucson: University of Arizona Press, 1977.

———. "Portrait of an American Viceroy: Martín Enríquez, 1567–1583." *The Americas* 14 (July 1957): 1–35.

———. *Soldiers, Indians, and Silver: The Northward Advance of New Spain, 1550–1600.* Berkeley and Los Angeles: University of California Press, 1952.

Priestly, Herbert I. *José de Gálvez: Visitor-General of New Spain (1765–1771).* Berkeley: University of California Press, 1916.

Publicaciones del Archivo General de la Nación, no. 7: *La vida colonial*. Mexico City: Imprenta de H. L. Sánchez, 1923.

Puga, Vasco de. *Cedulario: Provisiones, cedulas, instrucciones de Su Magestad, ordenanzas de difuntos, y audiencia para la buena expedicion de los negocios y administracion de justicia y govierno de esta Nueva Espana y para el buen tratamiento y conservacion de los indios desde el ano de 1525 hasta este presente de 63.* Mexico City, 1563.

Recopilación de las leyes de los reynos de las Indias. 4th ed. 4 vols. Madrid, 1681.

Rekers, B. *Benito Arias Montano (1527–1598).* London: Warburg Institute, University of London, 1972.

Relación breve de la venida de la Compañía de Jesús a la Nueva España, año de 1602. Anonymous manuscript from the Archivo Histórico de la Secretaría de Hacienda. Prologue and notes by Francisco González de Cossío. Mexico City: Imprenta Universitaria, 1945. [Cited as *Relación breve . . . de la Compañía de Jesús*]

Relacion breve y verdadera de algunas cosas de las muchas que sucedieron al padre Fray Alonso Ponce en las provincias de la Nueva Espana, siendo comisario general de aquellas partes. 2 vols. Madrid, 1873. [Cited as *Relacion . . . Ponce*]

Remesal, Antonio de. *Historia de la provincia de S. Vicente de Chyapa y Guatemala de la Orden de Nro. Glorioso Padre Sancto Domingo.* Madrid, 1619.

Ribadeneyra y Barrientos, Antonio Joaquín de. *Manual compendio de el regio patronato indiano para su mas facil uso en las materias conducentes a la practica.* Madrid, 1755.

Ricard, Robert. *The Spiritual Conquest of Mexico.* Translated by Lesley Byrd Simpson. Berkeley and Los Angeles: University of California Press, 1966.

Riva Palacio, Vicente. *México a través de los siglos.* 5 vols. Barcelona, 1888–1889.

Rivera Gambas, Manuel. *Arzobispo Don Pedro Moya de Contreras, un gobernante de México.* N.p.: Suma Veracruzana, 1962.

Robeló, Cecilio. *Diccionario de aztequismos o sea jardín de raíces aztecas.* Mexico City: Ediciones Fuente Cultural, n.d.

Rodríguez, Agueda María. "Pedro Farfán." *Revista de Indias* 21 (July–December 1971): 221–309.

Rodríguez, Juan Manuel. *La iglesia en Nueva España a la luz del III concilio mexicano (1585–1596).* Isola dei Liri, Italy, 1937.

Rojas Garcidueñas, José. *Autos y coloquios del siglo XVI.* Mexico City: Luis Alvarez, 1935.

Ruiz de Vergara y Alava. *Vida del ilustrisimo senor don Diego de Anaya Maldonado, arzobispo de Sevilla, fundador del colegio viejo de S. Bartolome y noticias de sus varones excelentes, dedicala a la Mag.d del Rey D. Felipe IV.* Madrid, n.d.

Sáenz de Aguirre, José. *Collectio Maxima Conciliorum Omnium Hispaniae et Novi Orbis.* Vol. 4. Rome, 1693.

Sahagún, Bernardino de. *Historia general de las cosas de Nueva España, 1547–1585.* 4 vols. Mexico City: P. Robredo, 1936.

———. *Historia general de las cosas de Nueva España.* Edited by Angel María Garibay K. 4 vols. Mexico City: Porrúa, 1956.

Sánchez, Pedro J. *Historia del seminario conciliar de México.* Vol. 1. Mexico City, 1931.

Sánchez Baquero, Juan. *Fundación de la Compañía de Jesús en Nueva España, 1571–1582.* Mexico City: Porrúa, 1945.

Sánchez Bella, Ismael. *La organización financiera de las Indias.* Seville, 1968.

———. "Los visitadores generales de Indias y el gobierno de los virreyes." *Anuario de Estudios Americanos* 29 (1972): 71–101.

———. "Visitas a Indias (siglos XVI–XVIII)." In *Memoria del Segundo Congreso Venezolano de Historia,* 3:165–208. Caracas, 1975.

Schäfer, Ernst. *El real y supremo consejo de las Indias: Su historia, organización y labor administrativa hasta la terminación de la casa de Austria.* 2 vols. Seville: M. Carmona, 1935–1947.

Scholes, France, and Eleanor B. Adams, eds. *Cartas del licenciado Jerónimo de Valderrama y otros documentos sobre su visita al gobierno de Nueva España, 1563–1565.* Mexico City, 1961.

Scholes, Walter. *The Diego Ramírez Visita.* Columbia: University of Missouri Press, 1964.

Schroeder, H. J. *Canons and Decrees of the Council of Trent: Original Text with English Translation.* St. Louis: B. Herder, 1960.

Schwaller, John Frederick. "The Cathedral Chapter of Mexico in the Sixteenth Century." *Hispanic American Historical Review* 61, 4 (November 1981): 651–674.

―――. "The *Ordenanza del Patronazgo* in New Spain, 1574–1600." *The Americas* 42 (January 1986): 253–74.

Shiels, W. Eugene. *King and Church: The Rise and Fall of the Patronato Real.* Chicago: Loyola University Press, 1961.

Sigüenza y Góngora, Carlos de. *Parayso occidental plantado y cultivado por la liberal benefica mano de los muy Catholicos y Poderosos Reyes de Espana Nuestros Senores en su magnifico real convento de Jesus Maria de Mexico.* Mexico City, 1684.

Simpson, Lesley Byrd. *The Encomienda in New Spain.* Berkeley and Los Angeles: University of California Press, 1966.

―――. *The Repartimiento System of Native Labor in New Spain and Guatemala.* Ibero-Americana, no. 13. Berkeley: University of California Press, 1938.

Solórzano y Pereyra, Juan de. *Politica indiana.* Antwerp, 1703.

Suárez, Francisco. *Tractatus de Religione Societatis Iesu.* Paris, 1585.

Suárez de Peralta, Juan. *Tratado del descubrimiento de las Indias.* Mexico City: Secretaría de Educación Pública, 1949.

Toribio Medina, José. *Historia del tribunal del santo oficio de la inquisición en México.* Mexico City, n.d.

Tormo y Monzó, Elías. *Las iglesias del antiguo Madrid.* Madrid: A. Marzo, 1927.

Torquemada, Juan de. *Monarquia indiana.* Madrid, 1723.

Toussaint, Manuel. *Paseos coloniales.* Mexico City: Imprenta Universitaria, 1939.

Ulloa, Modesto. *La hacienda real de Castilla en el reinado de Felipe II.* Madrid: Fundación Universitaria Española, 1977.

Valdeavellano, Luis G. de. "Las partidas y las orígenes medievales del juicio de residencia." *Boletín de la Real Academia de la Historia* 153 (1963): 205–46.

Valle-Arizpe, Artemio de. *Historia de la ciudad de México según los relatos de sus cronistas.* 4th ed. Mexico City: P. Robredo, 1946.

Vera, Fortino Hipólito. *Apuntamientos históricos de los concilios provinciales mexicanos y privilegios de América: Estudios previos al primer concilio provincial de Antequera.* Mexico City, 1893.

―――. *Compendio histórico del tercer concilio provincial mexicano.* Amecameca, Mexico: Colegio el Católico, 1879.

Vera Cruz, Alonso de la. *Speculum Coniugiorum.* Alcalá de Henares, Spain, 1572.

Vetancurt, Agustín de. *Menologio franciscano de los varones más señalados que con sus vidas ejemplares, perfección religiosa, ciencia, predicación evangélica, en su vida y muerte ilustraron la provincia del Santo Evangelio.* In vol. 4 of reprint of *Teatro mexicano.* Mexico City, 1871.

―――. *Teatro mexicano: Descripcion breve de los sucesos exemplares, historicos, politicos, militares y religiosos del nuevo mundo occidental de las Indias.* 2 vols. Mexico City, 1698.

Vitoria, Francisco de. *Prima Relectio de Indis.* Edited by Ernest Nys. Washington, D.C.: Carnegie Institution of Washington, 1917.

Wright, Thomas. "The Investiture of Bishops and Archbishops in Spanish America." *Journal of Church and State* 25 (Spring 1983): 281–97.

Zabálburu, F., and J. Sancho Rayón, eds. *Nueva colección de documentos inéditos para la historia de España y de sus Indias.* Madrid: M. Ginés Hernández, 1896.

Zavala, Silvio. *La encomienda indiana.* Mexico City: Porrúa, 1973.

———. *New Viewpoints on the Spanish Colonization of America.* Philadelphia: University of Pennsylvania Press, 1943.

———, and María Casteló, eds. *Fuentes para la historia del trabajo en Nueva España.* 8 vols. Mexico City: Fondo de Cultura Económica, 1939–1945.

Zorita, Alonso de. *Life and Labor in Ancient Mexico: The Brief and Summary Relation of the Lords of New Spain.* Translated and with an introduction by Benjamin Keen. New Brunswick, N.J.: Rutgers University Press, 1963.

Zubillaga, Félix. "Tercer concilio mexicano, 1585: Los memoriales del P. Juan de la Plaza, S.I." *Archivum Historicum Societatis Iesu* 30 (1961): 180–244.

———, ed. *Monumenta Mexicana I (1570–1575).* Vol. 8 of *Monumenta Missionum Societatis Iesu.* Vol. 77 of *Monumenta Historica Societatis Iesu a patribus eiusdem Societatis edita.* Rome: Monumenta Historica Iesu, 1956.

Zumalacárregui, Leopoldo. "Visitas y residencias en siglo XVI: Unos textos para su distinción." *Revista de Indias* 26 (October–December 1946): 917–21.

Index

291

Designer:	Janet Wood
Compositor:	Huron Valley Graphics
Text:	10/12 Palatino
Display:	Palatino
Printer:	Braun-Brumfield, Inc.
Binder:	Braun-Brumfield, Inc.